Freedom and Ground

SUNY series in Contemporary Continental Philosophy

Dennis J. Schmidt, editor

Freedom and Ground
A Study of Schelling's Treatise on Freedom

MARK J. THOMAS

Published by State University of New York Press, Albany

© 2023 State University of New York

All rights reserved

Printed in the United States of America

No part of this book may be used or reproduced in any manner whatsoever without written permission. No part of this book may be stored in a retrieval system or transmitted in any form or by any means including electronic, electrostatic, magnetic tape, mechanical, photocopying, recording, or otherwise without the prior permission in writing of the publisher.

For information, contact State University of New York Press, Albany, NY
www.sunypress.edu

Library of Congress Cataloging-in-Publication Data

Name: Thomas, Mark J., author.
Title: Freedom and ground : a study of Schelling's Treatise on freedom / Mark J. Thomas.
Description: Albany : State University of New York Press, [2023] | Series: SUNY series in contemporary continental philosophy | Includes bibliographical references and index.
Identifiers: LCCN 2022037693 | ISBN 9781438493008 (hardcover : alk. paper) | ISBN 9781438493015 (ebook) | ISBN 9781438492995 (pbk. : alk. paper)
Subjects: LCSH: Schelling, Friedrich Wilhelm Joseph von, 1775–1854 Philosophische Untersuchungen über das Wesen der menschlichen Freiheit. | Liberty. | Grounding (Philosophy)
Classification: LCC B2898 .T37 2023 | DDC 123/.5—dc23/eng/20230206
LC record available at https://lccn.loc.gov/2022037693

10 9 8 7 6 5 4 3 2 1

for my parents, Ann and Fred

Wenn man einmal philosophiren zu wollen vorgibt,
so kann man die Frage warum nicht mehr abweisen.

Once one purports to philosophize,
the question *why?* can no longer be dismissed.

—SW II, 35

Von einer Handlung der absoluten Freiheit läßt sich
kein weiterer Grund angeben; sie ist so, weil sie so ist,
d. h. sie ist schlechthin und insofern nothwendig.

No further ground can be provided for an act of
absolute freedom; it is so, because it is so—
that is, it simply is, and to that extent it is necessary.

—SW VII, 429

Contents

ACKNOWLEDGMENTS xiii

ABBREVIATIONS xv

INTRODUCTION 1

CHAPTER 1
Ground and the Question of a System of Freedom 19

1. The Concept of System 20
2. The Principle of Ground and the Concept of System 28
3. Jacobi and the Conflict between System and Freedom 32
4. Two Predominant Metaphors for System 38
5. Conclusion: Heidegger and the Alleged Failure of a System of Freedom 41

CHAPTER 2
Identity, Ground, and the Meaning of the Copula in Judgments 47

1. Pantheism and the Nature of Identity 50
2. Explication of Schelling's Four Accounts of the Copula 54
3. Conclusion: The Unity of Schelling's Account of the Copula? 69

Chapter 3
The Creative Unity of the Law of Identity — 75

1. The Unity Expressed by the Law of Identity — 77
2. The Co-originality of the Laws of Identity and Ground — 79
3. The Transformation of the Law of Ground — 88
4. Divine Grounding and the Possibility of Freedom — 96

Chapter 4
Schelling's Fundamental Distinction between Ground and What Exists — 109

1. General Characterization of the Distinction — 111
2. The Distinction in Relation to the Doctrine of Potencies — 119
3. The Distinction within the Distinction — 126
4. The Grounding Character of the Ground of Existence — 132
5. Grounding Relations in a System of Freedom — 139

Chapter 5
Evil and the Irrational — 145

1. The Ground of Evil — 148
2. Evil as a Ground of Revelation? — 157
3. The Irrational and the Irreducible Remainder — 166
4. The Living Character of Schelling's Rationalism — 175

Chapter 6
The *Ungrund* as the Ultimate Origin — 183

1. The Context of Schelling's Treatment of the *Ungrund* — 187
2. The *Ungrund* as the *Wesen* of the Two Principles in God — 190
3. Characteristics of the *Ungrund* and Its Relation to Schelling's Previous Descriptions of the Absolute — 197
4. Indifference and the Grounding Character of the *Ungrund* — 203
5. The *Ungrund* and the Relationship between Essence and Form — 211

Chapter 7
Freedom, Necessity, and Self-Grounding — 217
1. The Formal vs. the Real Concept of Freedom — 219
2. The Unity of Freedom and Necessity beyond Appearance — 222
3. The Intelligible Deed — 230
4. Self-Grounding and the Concept of *Causa Sui* — 237

Conclusion
Ground in a System of Freedom — 245

Notes — 261

Bibliography — 315

Index — 325

Acknowledgments

This book would not be possible without the contributions of so many teachers, colleagues, and friends over the last several years. In particular, I owe much to John Sallis in my approach to reading the history of philosophy. His lectures, which I attended as a doctoral student at Boston College, demonstrate how to open up the most challenging texts through clear, patient exegesis. I am deeply grateful for his encouragement and support of my project from the beginning.

Much of the initial research for this book was conducted at the Albert-Ludwigs-Universität Freiburg in 2012–13, funded by a grant from the Deutscher Akademischer Austauschdienst. While in Freiburg, I had the good fortune to participate in seminars and hear lectures by Lore Hühn, Günter Figal, and Philipp Schwab. I thank them for their hospitality and their generous feedback on my initial ideas.

While in Boston and Germany, I got to know a number of younger scholars of German philosophy who have shaped my thinking in countless conversations. In particular, I am grateful for my friendship with Alexander Bilda and Philipp Höfele, with whom I have met for weekly Schelling readings for almost a decade. I also thank Jon Burmeister, Nikola Mirković, Sylvaine Gourdain Castaing, Georg Spoo, Tobias Keiling, Ole Meinefeld, Marcela García-Romero, Anthony Bruno, and Ian Moore.

I presented portions of this book at the last four meetings of the North American Schelling Society, including material on the irrational, non-being, contingency, and "the mystery of love." My thanks to Jason Wirth and Sean McGrath for their leadership of the society—and to the conference organizers and participants for a lively exchange of ideas in a very friendly environment.

I owe a debt of gratitude to Vanessa Rumble at Boston College for her generous feedback on an early version of the manuscript—and for her advice and encouragement throughout the process of revision. Jumping back in time, I would also like to express my appreciation to Cyril O'Regan, who first inspired me to study German Idealism when I was an undergraduate at Notre Dame.

The editors at SUNY Press have been extraordinarily helpful throughout the process. In particular, I thank Dennis Schmidt for his incisive questions about evil in the *Freiheitsschrift* and for his support of my project. I am also grateful for the thoughtful suggestions from anonymous reviewers.

Finally, a special thanks to my department colleagues at Central College: David Timmer, Chad Ray, Elena Vishnevskaya, Terry Kleven, Anna Christensen, Lori Witt, Cynthia Mahmood, Chia Ning, Timothy Olin, and Mark Barloon. It is an honor—and a pleasure—to teach philosophy at a liberal arts college, surrounded by so many dedicated teachers and friends. I also thank President Mark Putnam and Vice President Mary Strey for their generous support of my scholarship while at Central.

A small part of chapter 2 draws on material in my article "The Mediation of the Copula as a Fundamental Structure in Schelling's Philosophy," *Schelling-Studien* 2 (2014): 21–40. Also, in chapter 7 I have reused small portions of my essay "Freedom and Self-Grounding: A Fundamental Difference between Schelling and Schopenhauer," published in *Freedom and Creation in Schelling*, ed. Henning Tegtmeyer and Dennis Vanden Auweele (Stuttgart-Bad Cannstatt: Frommann-Holzboog, 2022). I thank both publishers for granting permission to reuse this material.

Abbreviations

Schelling's Works

HKA *Historisch-kritische Ausgabe*, I. Werke; II. Nachlaß; III. Briefe. Edited by the Schelling-Kommission der Bayerischen Akademie der Wissenschaften. Stuttgart-Bad Cannstatt: Frommann-Holzboog, 1976–.

SW *Sämmtliche Werke*, Division I: 10 vols. (= I–X); Division II: 4 vols. (= XI–XIV). Edited by Karl Friedrich August Schelling. Stuttgart: Cotta, 1856-61.

WA *Die Weltalter: Fragmente*, in the original versions of 1811 and 1813. Edited by Manfred Schröter. Munich: Beck, 1946.

GPP *Grundlegung der positiven Philosophie: Münchener Vorlesung WS 1832/33*. Edited by Horst Fuhrmans. Turin: Bottega d'Erasmo, 1972.

Plitt *Aus Schellings Leben: In Briefen*. Edited by Gustav L. Plitt. 3 vols. Leipzig: Hirzel, 1869–70.

T *"Timaeus." (1794)*. Edited by Hartmut Buchner. Stuttgart-Bad Cannstatt: Frommann-Holzboog, 1994.

TB *Philosophische Entwürfe und Tagebücher 1809–1813: Philosophie der Freiheit und der Weltalter*. Edited by Lothar Knatz, Hans Jörg Sandkühler, and Martin Schraven. Hamburg: Meiner, 1994.

Kant's Works

AA *Gesammelte Schriften.* Edited by the Preußische Akademie der Wissenschaften. Berlin: De Gruyter, 1900–.

KrV *Kritik der reinen Vernunft* (1781/87). Translation: *Critique of Pure Reason.* Translated by Werner S. Pluhar. Indianapolis: Hackett, 1996.

KpV *Kritik der praktischen Vernunft* (1788). Translation: *Critique of Practical Reason.* Translated by Werner S. Pluhar. Indianapolis: Hackett, 2002.

KU *Kritik der Urteilskraft* (1790). Translation: *Critique of Judgment.* Translated by Werner S. Pluhar. Indianapolis: Hackett, 1987.

Other Abbreviations

AT Descartes, René. *Oeuvres de Descartes.* Edited by Charles Adam and Paul Tannery. Revised edition. 11 vols. Paris: Vrin/C.N.R.S., 1964–76. Translation: *The Philosophical Writings of Descartes.* Translated by John Cottingham, Robert Stoothoff, and Dugald Murdoch. 3 vols. Cambridge: Cambridge University Press, 1984–91.

JW Jacobi, Friedrich Heinrich. *Werke.* Edited by Friedrich Roth and Friedrich Köppen. 6 vols. Leipzig: Gerhard Fleischer, 1812–25.

FW Fichte, Johann Gottlieb. *Sämmtliche Werke.* Edited by Immanuel Hermann Fichte. 8 vols. Berlin: Veit, 1845–46.

HW Hegel, Georg Wilhelm Friedrich. *Werke in zwanzig Bänden: Theorie-Werkausgabe.* Edited by Eva Moldenhauer and Karl Markus Michel. Frankfurt: Suhrkamp, 1969–71.

PhG Hegel, Georg Wilhelm Friedrich. *Phänomenologie des Geistes* (HW 3).

ASW Schopenhauer, Arthur. *Sämtliche Werke.* Edited by Wolfgang Frhr. von Löhneysen. 5 vols. Frankfurt: Suhrkamp, 1960–65.

GA Heidegger, Martin. *Gesamtausgabe.* Frankfurt: Klostermann, 1975–.

Introduction

"Ground" is one of the distinctive terms in German philosophy. Its most common meaning is roughly "reason why," which accounts for its appearance in the German name for the principle of sufficient reason: *Satz vom Grund*, "principle of ground." Thus, the word can stand in for other terms associated with explaining or providing reasons, such as "cause," "condition," and "principle." But it also has a meaning connected to its metaphorical roots: the ground is the foundation on which something rests. What lacks a ground is an *Abgrund*—abyss.

Long before its association with modern philosophy, "ground" was one of the key words of German mysticism, going back to Meister Eckhart. In fact, the tradition of mystical thought developed by Eckhart and his followers has been termed "the mysticism of the ground."[1] In Eckhart, the word refers above all to the mysterious union of God and the soul's innermost being.[2] "Ground" is therefore the key term for two very different currents in German thought: (1) a rationalist current concerned with providing reasons and (2) a mystical current concerned with revealing what is hidden from our everyday ways of thinking.

The two currents come together in Schelling's *Philosophical Investigations into the Essence of Human Freedom* (1809), the last major work published during his lifetime and one of the classic texts of German Idealism. It is therefore no coincidence that "ground" is one of the central terms in the work. But my claim in this book is stronger: Schelling's treatise as a whole is an answer to what I call "the problem of ground," that is, the problem of sorting out the different kinds of grounds and the structure of the grounding relations within the system. Though largely implicit, Schelling's distinction between senses of ground is the key to his project of constructing a system that can satisfy reason while accommodating objects that seem to defy rational explanation—including evil, the origins of nature, and absolute freedom. It thus allows him to unite reason and mystery, providing a rich model for philosophizing about freedom and evil today.

This book is a new interpretation of Schelling's path-breaking treatise, focusing on the problem of ground. Commonly known in German as the *Freiheitsschrift*, the treatise has been extremely influential within the Continental tradition. Indeed, Heidegger refers to it as "one of the most profound works of German, thus of Western, philosophy."[3] It is also one of the most demanding and complex texts in German Idealism. Despite its enormous influence, many passages remain puzzling, and the work as a whole demands a focused interpretation. By tracing the problem of ground through the *Freiheitsschrift*, this book aims to provide a unified reading of the text, while unlocking the meaning of some of its most challenging passages.

To explain my motivation for this approach, let me begin with a curious fact about the *Freiheitsschrift*: though "human freedom" is in the title, the bulk of the work is concerned with other topics. Schopenhauer already observed this, sardonically: "Only a small part of that treatise deals with freedom; instead, its principal topic is a detailed report about a God with whom the author betrays an intimate acquaintance, since he even describes for us his coming to be" (ASW III, 609). The genesis of God (his becoming fully actual in the world) is indeed one of the main themes—but there are many others, including the meaning of pantheism, the nature of identity and the copula, the problem of evil, the formation of nature, and the varieties of necessity. Why does Schelling treat all of these topics in a treatise ostensibly devoted to human freedom?

The full title of the work provides a first clue. The investigations are to concern both the essence of human freedom and "the matters connected therewith" (*die damit zusammenhängenden Gegenstände*). In other words, Schelling does not treat freedom as an isolated topic but in the context of everything connected to it. And if freedom is one of the "ruling center points of the system," as Schelling observes in the opening lines (SW VII, 336),[4] then it is connected to all the major points in his system. This accounts for the text's comprehensiveness, despite Hegel's comment that it "pertains to just this one point."[5] Indeed, what we might call Schelling's contextualization of human freedom is one of the most attractive features of his approach, setting it apart from most other treatments of the question. The central task is to construct a "system of freedom," not only in the negative sense of showing how system and freedom are not mutually exclusive, but in the genuinely positive sense of showing how freedom is connected to everything else.

Even if this systematicity explains in general terms the lack of focus on human freedom, it leaves unexplained why so much of the text places the accent elsewhere, exploring topics where the connection to freedom is distant and not explicitly stated. The lack of focus has also tempted interpreters to define with more specificity what Schelling is doing in the treatise—to say what the text is *really about*. Thus, a number of commentators have claimed that the heart of the text is something other than freedom. Heidegger famously declares that "Schelling's treatise . . . is at the core a metaphysics of evil."[6] Friedrich Hermanni, on the other hand, contends that the "leading intention" of the text is to carry out a theodicy.[7] Markus Gabriel has even proposed that the heart of the work is a theory of predication, thus applying the framework of Wolfram Hogrebe's influential interpretation of the *Ages of the World* to the *Freiheitsschrift*.[8] Other commentators maintain the focus on freedom, but prioritize a specific aspect of the problem. Thus, Michelle Kosch suggests that Schelling's main concern is explaining how a fully free choice of moral evil is possible.[9] And in a classic essay, Michael Theunissen notes that the "main problem" of the *Freiheitsschrift* is the question of how the absoluteness of human freedom can also be *not* absolute.[10]

These interpretations all identify essential aspects of the treatise. The problem is that they privilege one aspect at the expense of others, and so the reading they offer is necessarily partial. My contention is that it is possible to read the *Freiheitsschrift* as a whole if we interpret it as an answer to the problem of ground. This is because the problem, as I define it, is not an isolated question but brings together the major problems in the text: pantheism and identity, evil, the origin and nature of God, the conflict between freedom and necessity. Each of these problems requires for its resolution the consideration of the kinds of grounds and the structure of the grounding relations within the system. Implicit in the architecture of the *Freiheitsschrift*, therefore, is Schelling's insight that these "problems of ground"[11] are interconnected and must be treated together. In particular, the problem of freedom has to be understood as part of the larger problem of ground.

Of course, the centrality of "ground" is already obvious if one simply notes where the word occurs in the text. At the heart of the treatise is the distinction between that-which-exists and the ground of existence

(SW VII, 357). Schelling notes that his investigation is "founded on" this distinction, and it provides the ontological framework for most of the work. Much later, Schelling discusses the ultimate origin, which he calls "the primordial ground [*Urgrund*] or rather the *non-ground* [*Ungrund*]" (SW VII, 406). This enigmatic way of designating the absolute, using a term (*Ungrund*) from the mystic Jacob Boehme, already suggests that its role in grounding is problematic. Moreover, in the famous passage where Schelling declares that willing is primordial being, he lists "groundlessness" as one of its predicates (SW VII, 350). Finally, in a remarkable statement in the discussion of pantheism, he claims that the law of ground is "just as original" as the law of identity (SW VII, 346). Previously the law of identity was *the* principle of his system. Now the law of ground is said to be just as original.

These striking references to ground are all on the surface. If one digs a little deeper, one can see its essential connection to Schelling's project of constructing a system of freedom and the three main problems associated with it: determinism, pantheism, and evil. To understand the connection, it is helpful to briefly introduce the background of a "system of freedom," which we will discuss in greater detail in chapter 1. The phrase brings together two desiderata of German Idealism, both with origins in Kant: (1) to know reality as an interconnected whole (system); and (2) to provide a central place for autonomy, particularly the autonomy of the human subject (freedom). Indeed, early in his career Schelling had declared himself a champion of the latter: "The beginning and the end of all philosophy is—freedom!" (SW I, 177; cf. III, 376).

But the very possibility of a system of freedom had been called into question some twenty-four years before the *Freiheitsschrift*—thus, before post-Kantian German Idealism had even begun. In his *Spinoza Letters* (1785), Jacobi had declared that any attempt to construct a consistent system of reason would lead to Spinoza's philosophy and the denial of freedom. In fact, Schelling alludes to Jacobi's "old" charge in the opening pages of his treatise (SW VII, 337–38). But why is a system of freedom problematic? The answer has to do with grounding. System requires everything to be connected to form a whole, and this connection is accomplished by grounding—both the grounding of the system's parts by other parts, and their ultimate grounding in the principle of the system (God).[12] But if this universal grounding is deterministic, then the freedom of the parts is compromised. Thus, the first problem associated with a system of freedom is determinism. A second problem arises if the system is a form of pantheism, which is true for Schelling's system, as it was for Spinoza's. Pantheism affirms some form of identity between God and creatures, but this identity would seem to compromise the independence that human beings need for freedom. Schelling also regards this as a problem of ground, though the connection is less obvious. In pantheism, God is identified with creatures, but he is also their ground: the God-creature relation is one of grounding identity. By defining more precisely the nature of divine grounding, Schelling intends to show how pantheism does not compromise independence.

Both determinism and pantheism are connected to Jacobi's original allegations. The third problem associated with a system of freedom arises out of something Schelling emphasizes for the first time in the *Freiheitsschrift*: the "real and living concept" of human freedom as "a capacity of good and evil" (SW VII, 352). The evil in the world is also a problem of ground, because it appears to be inexplicable and thus "groundless." Where does evil come from, if an all-good Creator is the ground of all things? Resolving the problem of evil therefore requires clarifying how God grounds the world and the ways in which evil is grounded. It also requires articulating evil's ontological structure—the "metaphysics of evil," to borrow Heidegger's phrase—and this essentially involves the ground of God's existence and the aspect of human beings that corresponds to it.

Thus, the three main problems associated with a system of freedom all require distinguishing senses of ground and understanding the network of grounding structures. The problem of a system of freedom is really the problem of ground.[13] Reframing it in this way gives Schelling's intention greater specificity: the goal of the treatise is not just to investigate freedom and whatever is connected to it, but to uncover the complex web of grounding relations in which freedom is embedded. This framing also helps clarify why Schelling devotes so much space to discussing parts of the web not obviously connected to freedom, but which shed light on fundamental grounding structures. And framing the treatise in terms of the problem of ground reveals strikingly original features of Schelling's solution to the problem, which anticipate—and challenge—developments in contemporary philosophy.

In anticipation of the analysis in the book itself, let me sketch some of the aspects of that solution; this will allow me to introduce some of the innovative features of Schelling's approach and place them in historical context. The key to his solution is his insight into the variety of grounds and the implications for combining dependence and independence.

Although "ground" has a number of meanings depending on the context, three senses are most prominent: (1) ground as condition of the possibility, (2) ground as what determines, and (3) ground as what begets (brings forth without determining). Each sense of ground thus corresponds to a different verb: to condition (*bedingen*), to determine (*bestimmen*), and to beget (*zeugen*). By distinguishing these senses, Schelling is able to claim that something is grounded in one sense, but not another. This allows him to formulate grounding relations that combine dependence and radical independence—an innovation that is essential for addressing the various problems of ground in the text.

Of course, distinguishing senses of ground is nothing new in philosophy. In fact, if one thinks of ground as a rough equivalent of ἀρχή and αἴτιον, one can cite Aristotle's account of the four causes as a precedent.[14] A couple generations before Schelling, both Christian Wolff and Crusius had emphasized the distinction between the ground of being (*ratio essendi*) and the ground of knowing (*ratio cognoscendi*)—a distinction that Kant uses to explain the relationship between freedom and the moral law.[15] And Jacobi had made the distinction between ground and cause an essential part of his critique of Spinoza, as we will discuss in chapter 3. Notwithstanding these distinctions and variations, the dominant tendency—both in German philosophy and the wider metaphysical tradition—is to regard the deterministic sense of ground as primary. To ground something is to provide a sufficient reason for its existence and thereby determine it.

In the *Freiheitsschrift*, Schelling breaks decisively with this tendency. The first and third senses of ground mentioned above are non-deterministic. And one of my central claims in this book is that the primary meaning of ground in the *Freiheitsschrift* is condition of the possibility. In a letter to Georgii the following year (1810), Schelling makes clear that the word "ground" in the phrase "ground of God's existence" does not mean "cause" but conditio sine qua non—that without which God cannot exist.[16] This same sense of ground plays an essential role in Schelling's solution to the problem of evil and his characterization of the "non-ground" as primordial ground. Moreover, the third sense (to beget), which defines God's relation to free beings, incorporates this primary sense and builds on it.

One might say that the emphasis on this sense of ground has its roots in Kant, since determining the conditions of the possibility of knowledge is what defines his transcendental method—the same method that underlies Schelling's *System of Transcendental Idealism* (1800). In the *Freiheitsschrift*, however, this sense of ground plays a role that is primarily metaphysical, not methodological: it defines the grounding relations of reality. This allows Schelling to offer a highly original alternative to what I call the "all-from-one model" of grounding relations, the model to which rationalist philosophies are naturally drawn. What is this model? We begin with a single, absolute starting point, usually called God. This starting point contains the sufficient reason for everything that follows from it. For any single thing that exists, someone with enough knowledge could trace its every feature back to the absolute beginning. Thus, a single ultimate ground inaugurates a deterministic progression reaching into every corner of the universe.[17] Leibniz's philosophy is perhaps the clearest example of this model, but many other philosophers with rationalist tendencies have been drawn to it in one form or another. Indeed, Schelling's earlier *Identitätsphilosophie* seems to follow this model, at least at first glance: absolute identity is the principle of the system, and all else follows with necessity. Even if there are good reasons for distinguishing the *Identitätsphilosophie* from the all-from-one model, both sympathetic interpreters and critics have often assumed that it is operative—for example, when objecting that Schelling does not adequately explain how finite reality is "derived" from the absolute.[18] Along these lines, Wilhelm Traugott Krug challenged Schelling to deduce his quill pen from the principle of his system.[19]

By making "condition of the possibility" the primary sense of ground, Schelling is able to move decisively away from the all-from-one model. Everything is grounded by God, but this does not mean that everything is derived deterministically from the divine essence. Instead, God is the ground of all things primarily in the sense of making them possible. This rejection of the all-from-one model has decisive consequences for the system's structure—and sheds light on features of the text we might otherwise view as flaws. First, since Schelling is no longer obliged to derive every feature of reality from a single beginning, he is free to multiply the beginning points for his system. Indeed, through the ultimate act of freedom, each human being becomes a new starting point, a "free and eternal beginning" (SW VII, 386). This plurality of starting points has a "decentering" effect that is reflected in the structure of the *Freiheitsschrift* itself. Unlike other presentations of the system, the discussion of "the unconditionally absolute" (SW VII, 408) occurs toward the end of the text rather than at the beginning, thus avoiding the impression that everything is derived from a single absolute. And at various points in the treatise, the transitions between topics are abrupt, as if Schelling is making a new beginning.[20] Dieter Sturma has even referred to Schelling's philosophy as a *System von Brüchen* on account of such structural breaks throughout his mature philosophy.[21] Indeed, commentators sometimes imply that this is a shortcoming, a failure to explain how we get from point A to point B—for example, from negative philosophy to positive philosophy in Schelling's late lectures. But this presupposes the all-from-one model of deriving each point from what came before. If we reject this model of grounding, each point can still be grounded by the conditions of its possibility, while beginning something radically new.[22]

The multiplication of beginnings is connected to another aspect of Schelling's break with traditional ontology: his movement toward equiprimordiality (*Gleichursprünglichkeit*), Heidegger's notion that multiple beings can be "equally original."[23] In *Being and Time*, Heidegger notes the failure of traditional metaphysics to acknowledge this concept and links this failure to the all-from-one model of grounding: "The phenomenon of the *equiprimordiality* of constitutive factors has often been disregarded in ontology on account of a methodologically unrestrained tendency to derive everything and anything from a simple 'primordial ground.' "[24] By rejecting this tendency, Schelling is able to introduce grounding structures that allow for co-originality—in particular, the "circle from which everything comes to be," where there is "no first and no last because all things mutually presuppose each other" (SW VII, 358). Remarkably, this movement toward equiprimordiality leads Schelling to grant free beings a quasi-divine status, summed up in the astonishing (and seemingly paradoxical) phrase "derived absoluteness or divinity" (SW VII, 347). At the same time, Schelling challenges the anti-systematic tendencies within contemporary philosophy, showing how equiprimordiality can be incorporated within a system: while multiple points are equally original, they are nonetheless grounded non-deterministically and thereby integrated into the larger whole.

Having sketched aspects of Schelling's approach to the problem of ground, I would like to highlight two topics of special importance for setting up this problem and appreciating Schelling's solution. The first is the role of the *Satz vom Grund*—known in English as the "principle of sufficient reason." In its simplest form, the principle states *there is nothing without reason*, or *there is nothing without a ground*. In other words, it affirms the universality of being grounded. Though one can find versions of this principle already in ancient philosophy, it did not receive a name—and the recognition that comes with a name—until Leibniz.[25] Between Leibniz and Kant there was a lively debate among German philosophers about the principle's status and possible derivation, and some years later Schopenhauer would devote his dissertation to it. Schelling, on the other hand, does not seem particularly interested in the principle, at least at first glance: he rarely mentions it in his writings, and there is only one explicit reference to it in the *Freiheitsschrift*. It is therefore unsurprising that the principle has received very little attention from Schelling scholars. And yet the single reference in the *Freiheitsschrift* is decisive: Schelling declares that the law of ground is *just as original* as the law of identity (SW VII, 346), which he had previously regarded as the highest principle of his system. Moreover, he affirms the principle of ground indirectly in other passages—for example, when discussing the formal concept of freedom (SW VII, 383).

We are therefore confronted with an interesting puzzle: on the one hand, Schelling acknowledges the central place of the principle; on the other hand, he hardly ever writes about it explicitly. As I argue in chapter 3, part of the solution is that for Schelling the principles of identity and ground have merged into one—discussions of the former are therefore implicitly discussions of the latter. But more generally, I wish to demonstrate that the principle of ground plays a decisive role behind the scenes in the *Freiheitsschrift*, even when Schelling's references to it are indirect or implicit. As we will see, Jacobi himself identifies a version of the principle as the source of the problem of a system of freedom. This is no accident: the principle is essential for articulating and understanding the problem of ground as I have defined it. This is because the principle makes a claim about the total structure of grounding relations in the system, thus defining its large-scale architecture. Of course, the precise form this architecture takes depends on the meaning of ground in the claim "nothing is without a ground." Indeed, we will see that the three main senses of ground in the *Freiheitsschrift* correspond to three different versions of the principle, only the first of which is explicitly labeled "the law of ground." I will therefore refer to the principle of "ground" rather than "sufficient reason" when it is important to leave open what meaning of ground is intended.

Examining the role of the principle in the *Freiheitsschrift* is also essential for understanding Schelling's relationship to rationalism, another puzzling aspect of the text and a place where my approach is quite different from other interpreters. By "rationalism," I mean a commitment to the fundamental intelligibility of the world as expressed in the "principle of sufficient reason" in its traditional Leibnizian form. The acceptance or rejection of this principle is an excellent gauge of a philosopher's level of commitment to rational order: is it true that *nothing* is "without reason"? But here we encounter a problem, because Schelling seems to affirm *and* deny the traditional principle. On the one hand, he implicitly affirms it when ruling out chance and contingency (SW VII, 383) and endorsing "absolute necessity" (SW VII, 397). On the other hand, he seems to deny it by introducing "irrational" phenomena such as evil and the "irreducible remainder" (SW VII, 359–60). The dominant tendency among commentators has been to emphasize these irrational, "dark" elements, implying that Schelling rejects the principle of sufficient reason and thus any form of rationalism.[26] I will argue that such an interpretation is mistaken. This requires showing how Schelling's distinctive way of circumventing the all-from-one model allows him to affirm the principle while leaving room for "irrational" phenomena and a qualified form of contingency. Instead of rejecting rationalism, Schelling transforms it into what I call a "living rationalism."

Closely related to Schelling's relationship to rationalism is his stance on absolute contingency and determinism—both at large and with respect to his account of freedom. Indeed, those who approach the *Freiheitsschrift* with an interest in the freewill debate may wonder if Schelling ultimately endorses a form of libertarianism (and thus contingency) or compatibilism (and thus determinism). The answer is neither—at least as those terms are usually understood. Like Kant, with whom he shares key premises, Schelling develops an account of freedom that defies easy classification. The usual (libertarian) way of rejecting the all-from-one model would be to deny the principle of ground and thus accept that certain phenomena are absolutely contingent: not everything has a *determining* ground. By contrast, in my reading, Schelling's solution to the problem of ground is distinctive in both (1) affirming that everything has a determining ground *and* (2) rejecting the all-from-one model. He accomplishes this by conceiving ultimate freedom as an act of radical self-grounding outside of time. Each free being is determined in its essence, but not by another: it is *causa sui*. Though this account contains mysterious elements, its aim is to meet the demands of ultimate moral responsibility—demands that are impossible to satisfy with a non-mysterious account of freedom, as both Galen Strawson and Peter Van Inwagen have shown.[27]

Unlike the principle of ground, the importance of the second topic I wish to highlight is immediately evident when reading the text. This is the fundamental distinction between that-which-exists and the ground of existence. According to Schelling, "the present investigation is founded" on the distinction (SW VII, 357), which provides the ontological framework for his account of God, nature, and evil. Indeed, the distinction is the focal point of Heidegger's various Schelling interpretations, especially his 1941 lecture course (GA 49). Despite its unparalleled importance for understanding Schelling's philosophical development, the distinction is widely misunderstood, even by careful interpreters. Accordingly, one of the contributions of this book is to help clarify this distinction at the heart of the *Freiheitsschrift*. Let me briefly sketch two widespread interpretative tendencies that I hope to correct. This will also help to define some of the distinctive features of my approach.

The first mistaken tendency is the conflation of existence and that-which-exists. Thus, the distinction would no longer be between *that-which-exists* and the ground of existence but between *existence* and the ground of existence. Heidegger makes this mistake throughout his interpretation of Schelling's treatise—and, because of Heidegger's immense influence, the conflation is widespread in the secondary literature, especially in English. However, Schelling himself points out this error in his published reply to Eschenmayer, who had made the same mistake as Heidegger. According to Schelling, existence and that-which-exists are "two concepts that are worlds apart" (SW VIII, 172; cf. SW VIII, 164). I call this *the distinction within the distinction*.

But what difference does this make? If something is the ground of existence, would it not also be the ground of that-which-exists? This would only be true if by "existence" Schelling simply meant "being" in the usual sense of the term: the ground of a thing's being is also a ground of that thing. However, we will see that "existence" for Schelling does not mean "being" in the usual sense: its core meaning is *revelation*, or the external manifestation of what was previously enclosed inside itself. And if existence means revelation, then that-which-exists means that-which-is-revealed. This shows the consequence of conflating existence and that-which-exists: in effect, one would be collapsing the difference between revelation and what is revealed. But Schelling clearly wishes to distinguish the two. It is possible to be without being revealed—to use Schelling's language, it is possible to be without existing. Indeed, all revelation presupposes a prior state of hiddenness, a state of being before existence. Moreover, Schelling's identification of existence and revelation allows us to reformulate his fundamental distinction using the language of revelation. The distinction between (1) that-which-exists and (2) the ground of existence amounts to a distinction between (1) what is revealed and (2) the condition of its revelation.

The second mistaken interpretative tendency has wider implications for the problem of ground in Schelling. When discussing the ground of existence, commentators often treat the word "ground" as if it were a proper name rather than a concept that has applicability beyond what it designates. What I mean can be illustrated through an example. One can use the phrase "the queen of England in 2021" to refer to the person Elizabeth II: it is a description that uniquely designates her. However, Elizabeth as a person has attributes—the details of her private life, for example—that go beyond her role as queen. How does this apply to the ground of existence? Schelling uses this phrase to designate one of the principles in God (the real principle) and provides a rich description of this principle in its relationship to that-which-exists (the ideal principle). However, one cannot assume that every aspect of this description pertains to the real principle's function as ground of existence, just as one cannot assume that every aspect of Elizabeth pertains to her function as queen. Instead, one has to investigate what is true of the ground of existence qua ground, and this reveals a meaning of ground that applies more broadly. Indeed, in the letter to Georgii mentioned above, Schelling explains that the core meaning of "ground" in his distinction is conditio sine qua non—the same sense of ground that appears in other contexts in the treatise. Thus, by recognizing that "ground" is a concept with wider applicability, one can connect the ground of God's existence to the larger problem of ground.

These considerations also allow me to distinguish my project from that of Miklos Vetö, whose book on *le fondement* in Schelling is a landmark of French scholarship. At first glance, our projects look very similar, because we share a focus on "ground." And indeed, Vetö's treatment of the ground of existence in the *Freiheitsschrift* is especially rich and insightful. However, he is not primarily interested in placing it in the context of the larger problem of ground and thus showing the connection to other grounding structures in the *Freiheitsschrift*. Instead, his focus is on the structural role of the ground of existence within Schelling's system and the various elements of Schelling's earlier and later philosophy that occupy the same structural role—including "reason" in the negative philosophy. Tracing the "avatars and metamorphoses"[28] of the ground throughout Schelling's philosophical development is no doubt important, but there remains the task of exploring the diverse grounding structures *within* the *Freiheitsschrift*, especially since this reveals an inner unity among the text's central questions and Schelling's response to them.

Up to this point, I have emphasized the distinctiveness of approaching the *Freiheitsschrift* as an answer to the problem of ground. But my interpretation also differs from other approaches in methodological respects. First, I engage with the significant body of German scholarship on Schelling, which tends to be neglected in anglophone commentary. On certain interpretative questions, the German scholarly discussion is more advanced. Moreover, much of the commentary on Schelling is as challenging to read as the philosopher himself. In part, this is a consequence of his style of philosophizing, which places great demands on the reader. Indeed, the pages of the *Freiheitsschrift* are filled with bold claims formulated in enigmatic language, often with little supporting argumentation. At times, the text can seem more a record of mystical insight than a philosophical treatise—an impression memorably captured by the great Swiss theologian Hans Urs von Balthasar. After referring to the *Freiheitsschrift* as "the most titanic work of German Idealism," he adds: "Schelling no longer deduces anything; he *views* the inner history of God with the stony and incontrovertible gaze of a sibyl."[29]

To be sure, Schelling is a philosopher of profound insight with an appreciation for mystery that is rare in modern philosophy. However, he is also a philosopher who values reason and systematicity, as he himself attests in the *Freiheitsschrift*. I hope to demonstrate that his claims can be formulated and explained with greater clarity, making explicit the implied argumentation and logical connections while remaining faithful to his intentions. The goal is to attain the same combination of depth and transparency that Schelling earlier had attributed to the imagination: "Klarheit mit Tiefe" (SW VII, 146).

Key to accomplishing this goal is to read the treatise as much as possible in light of texts Schelling wrote in the years leading up to its publication as well as texts immediately following it. I do not mean to suggest that other commentators ignore these writings. But too often passages of the *Freiheitsschrift* are read on their own terms without reference to works that shed light on the same issues—and even ignoring later texts that explicitly address the passages in question. I mentioned already a salient example of the latter tendency: the widespread mistaken interpretation of the fundamental distinction, which Schelling himself corrects in statements to Georgii and Eschenmayer. More generally, many of Schelling's bold but unexplained assertions are based in previous texts in his philosophical development; evidently, he does not always see fit to retrace the ground he had already covered. For example, the famous line that "willing is primordial being" (SW VII, 350) is based in Schelling's early, Fichte-inspired writings and represents for him the fundamental insight of idealism. Moreover, many of the ideas that are inchoately expressed in 1809 appear in more developed form in the *Stuttgart Private Lectures* (1810) and *Ages of the World* drafts (1811–15).

In the preface to the *Freiheitsschrift*, Schelling refers to his writings as "fragments of a whole," whose connection is not easy to see (SW VII, 334). We can infer from this that one has to bring the pieces together to understand the whole. Schelling himself signals the continuity of the treatise with what came before by first publishing it side by side with republished earlier works in the first volume of his *Philosophische Schriften*, and by referencing texts in his *Identitätsphilosophie* in footnotes throughout the work.[30] Unfortunately, comparatively little attention has been paid to texts in the "philosophy of identity," which has the reputation for being "the most sterile moment" in Schelling's development.[31] This reputation is certainly unfair, and I attempt in this book to demonstrate the ongoing relevance of the *Identitätsphilosophie* for understanding the nature of identity, the *Ungrund*, the principles within God, and other key themes of the *Freiheitsschrift*.

Of course, one can object that Schelling's citation of his previous writings is a self-stylization on his part—an attempt to disguise significant changes in his thinking by insisting on continuity. Along these lines, it has been debated among commentators whether the *Freiheitsschrift* really is continuous with his previous philosophy or instead marks a radical break, inaugurating a more dynamic period of philosophizing with a greater appreciation for historicity and the irrational.[32] No doubt Schelling at times overstates the consistency of his oeuvre, but I think debates about the continuity and periodization of his philosophy are largely misguided. His development is best regarded as a path. At any point on the path Schelling draws on what came before even as he adds something new: continuity and disruption exist side by side. In any case, we cannot assume we will understand what is said about a topic in the *Freiheitsschrift* simply by reading about the same theme in another work. The proof of the usefulness of other texts is the resulting interpretation: do they help us to understanding what Schelling says in the *Freiheitsschrift* on its own terms? This is important to remember when considering themes that are central to Schelling's later philosophy, like the relationship between divine freedom and creation. One should be careful not to read into the *Frei-*

heitsschrift positions he will only adopt later—for example, the view that God has the freedom to create or *not* to create. The connection between divine freedom and alternative possibilities is notably absent in 1809.[33]

Finally, there is one other respect in which my approach differs from much of the other commentary on Schelling's treatise. There is a common—often tacit—assumption that his project to construct a system of freedom ultimately fails (*es scheitert*).[34] The task of understanding the treatise thereby becomes a matter of discerning where and why it fails—and perhaps must do so. Whether Schelling's project ultimately succeeds is, of course, an essential question to ask. But it is dangerous to pose the question too soon, given the enormous challenges in interpreting the treatise. Indeed, it is relatively easy to point to difficulties in the text and declare the project a failure. Instead, I have attempted to interpret the treatise so as to make it as coherent as possible, resolving apparent difficulties whenever feasible. Of course, so long as difficulties remain, one cannot declare the project an unqualified success. Despite the open questions, however, I hope to show how Schelling offers a compelling answer to the problem of ground and a system of freedom.

Before giving a brief overview of the contents, I want to note one limitation of my treatment of ground in the *Freiheitsschrift*. Although I occasionally refer to the writings of Meister Eckhart and Jacob Boehme, from whom Schelling borrows the term *Ungrund*, the connections between mysticism and Schelling's understanding of ground are not a focus of my study. In part, this is because significant work on the Boehme-connection has already been done.[35] But more importantly, I believe that the nature of Schelling's relationship to Boehme—and mysticism in general—limits the usefulness of the latter's writings, and even makes their extensive consideration misleading, if one's primary interest is understanding Schelling's philosophical thought. It is certainly true that Schelling borrows language from Boehme (1575–1624) and the theosophist Friedrich Oetinger (1702–82), especially in the passages describing the ground of God's existence and the *Ungrund*. But we should not be too quick to infer from this that he is appropriating their ideas or that his reading of Boehme fundamentally transformed his thinking on ground. In fact, we will see that Schelling had already developed key aspects of his account of the ground and *Ungrund* years earlier.

In my view, Boehme's significance for Schelling lies above all in his gift for language and vivid metaphors. Throughout his philosophical development, Schelling never settles on a fixed set of terms but is constantly experimenting with new language. (I suspect this is due to his appreciation for the limits of language in articulating the phenomena he describes.) So when he read Boehme, Schelling recognized a powerful vocabulary for expressing positions resembling his own; he then freely borrowed from this vocabulary when writing the *Freiheitsschrift* without feeling bound to the precise meaning the language had in Boehme.[36] If this account is correct, the best means of understanding the mystical language in Schelling is not to focus on Boehme's texts but to follow the thread of philosophical ideas within the *Freiheitsschrift* itself.[37] Nonetheless, Schelling's willingness to borrow mystical language reveals something important about his conception of ground: though rational in certain respects, grounding also involves mysterious elements that go beyond our ordinary ways of speaking. The *Freiheitsschrift*, in addressing the problem of ground, unites reason and mystery.

I begin by introducing the problem of a system of freedom, which involves discussing its historical context and showing its essential connection to the problem of ground. I also argue against Heidegger's interpretation of Schelling's famous line that God is not a system but a life (chapter 1). The next two chapters treat the relationship between identity and ground as a means of addressing the nature of identity and the problem of pantheism. This first involves a careful examination of Schelling's accounts of the copula in judgments, showing in what way the subject and predicate exhibit a grounding relation (chapter 2). The discussion of the copula sets the stage for my interpretation of the claim that "the law of ground is just as original as the law of identity" and the resulting transformation of the principle of ground. Through a close reading of Schelling's account of the "creative unity" of the law of identity, I then examine key features of divine grounding and its relationship to freedom, including the concept of "begetting" and its correlate, "derived absoluteness" (chapter 3).

The book's central chapter is devoted to the fundamental distinction between that-which-exists and the ground of existence. After characterizing the distinction in relation to the doctrine of potencies, I develop the implications of the above-mentioned "distinction within the distinction," which allows us to understand the meaning of "existence" and the precise relation between ground and that-which-exists. Examining the grounding character of the ground of existence reveals a rich set of meanings, one of which Schelling extends to grounding relations throughout the system (chapter 4). The fundamental distinction then provides the basis for Schelling's account of evil and theodicy, treated in the next chapter. I discuss the ways in which evil is grounded in his account and weigh in on the debate about whether evil is a necessary condition (or "ground") of revelation. I also examine the nature of other "irrational" phenomena, including the "irreducible remainder," and draw the consequences for Schelling's relationship to rationalism (chapter 5).

Next, I turn to Schelling's most striking challenge to the all-from-one model of grounding: his account of the enigmatic *Ungrund*. I attempt to shed light on this account by showing the connection of the *Ungrund* to the copula and Schelling's previous descriptions of the absolute. On the basis of a close reading of the passage on "indifference," I argue that the *Ungrund* is a ground in one sense but not in another—and this explains its unique place within the system (chapter 6). The topic of the final chapter is Schelling's formal account of freedom, which is a creative extension of Kant's solution to the third antinomy in the *Critique of Pure Reason*. Here Schelling unites freedom and necessity in an act of self-grounding outside of time. I compare this radical self-determination to the traditional concept of *causa sui* and show its connection to Schelling's rejection of the all-from-one model; this allows for multiple "eternal beginnings" and ultimate moral responsibility (chapter 7). I conclude by summing up and critically evaluating Schelling's solution to the problem of ground.

1

Ground and the Question of a System of Freedom

Unlike several of Schelling's other works, the *Freiheitsschrift* does not have a systematic form.[1] He names the work "Philosophical *Investigations* into the Essence of Human Freedom," a title that suggests the treatise is more of an inquiry than the presentation of a completed system. And the sequence of subjects treated in the text does not follow a systematic order;[2] instead, as he notes in a footnote toward the end, "everything arises as a sort of dialogue" (SW VII, 410). Yet, despite its lack of a systematic form, Schelling intends the *Freiheitsschrift* to be systematic in another, more essential sense. This sense is spelled out in the two tasks he aims to accomplish in the treatise: (1) to determine the concept of freedom, and (2) to treat the connection of this concept with the whole (SW VII, 336). It is the second task that defines the systematic nature of the inquiry: the treatise must show how freedom is connected within the larger system. This means that the treatise is systematic insofar as it investigates freedom not as an isolated topic, but as connected with everything else. But this presupposes that freedom *can* be connected with everything else in a system, and that freedom and system are not essentially incompatible. Thus, for Schelling to accomplish the two primary tasks of the treatise, he must accomplish a third: to establish the possibility of a system of freedom.

Though Schelling devotes a significant portion of the introduction to discussing the claim that freedom is incompatible with system (SW VII, 336-38), as well as the related claim that system entails pantheism and thus fatalism (SW VII, 338-47), it is not clear from this discussion why the difficulty of a system of freedom even arises—and must arise.

Indeed, Schelling writes much of this section in a polemical mode that can leave the reader with the impression that the entire issue is a false problem: it arises only for those who make questionable assumptions about the concepts, and these assumptions crumble on examination. And yet Schelling underscores the importance of this question in giving it a prominent place at the beginning of the treatise and returning to it at the end (cf. SW VII, 413). Moreover, he indicates the source and the magnitude of the difficulty when describing the task of connecting freedom to the system as a whole: "This great task alone is the unconscious and invisible driving force of all striving for knowledge, from the lowest to the highest; without the contradiction of necessity and freedom not only philosophy but each higher willing of the spirit would sink into the death that is proper to those sciences in which this contradiction has no application" (SW VII, 338). Here Schelling juxtaposes the task of connecting freedom to the system with the contradiction of necessity and freedom, implying that they are essentially linked.[3] But how? What is the connection between system and necessity, a connection that seems to be the source of the tension between system and freedom? Schelling never explicitly answers this question.

In this chapter, I attempt to show that the problem of a system of freedom is rooted in the tension between freedom and grounding—and more specifically, the relationship between freedom and the principle of ground. The conflict between system and freedom arises because the principle is essentially connected to the concept of system. And this connection accounts for the fact that Schelling links the question of a system of freedom with the contradiction between freedom and necessity. Before determining the role of the principle of ground in this question, however, we first need to identify the characteristics of system and distinguish between possible meanings of the term. With this characterization in mind, we will be in the position to see how the concept of system relates to the principle, and how this relation in turn poses difficulties for freedom. Finally, we can address what possible avenues are open to Schelling with respect to resolving these difficulties.

1. The Concept of System

Like all philosophical terms, "system" can mean different things in different contexts, and what Schelling means by the word may not be what other philosophers mean. He notes this himself when first responding to the claim that freedom is incompatible with system: "For who knows which limiting notions have already been linked to the word system, so that the claim asserts something which is of course very true, but also very trivial" (SW VII, 336). The challenge for us will be to characterize system in such a way that "limiting notions" are left out and what is essential remains. This is the only way to ensure that the difficulty of a system of freedom involves the things themselves and is not just a matter of definition.[4]

But how do we determine what is essential in the concept of system? One approach would be to examine historical examples of systems and extract from them what they have in common. Leibniz was one of the first philosophers to use the term system in referring to his own philosophy.[5] As we will see in more detail below, Jacobi considered Spinoza to be the paradigmatic example of a systematic philosopher in the so-called Pantheism Controversy, to which Schelling alludes indirectly. Even if Kant never completed a system, he had ambitions to do so, and he provides a detailed description of system in the *Critique of Pure Reason*. Finally, the works of Fichte, Schelling, and Hegel are attempts to carry out the requirements of system—in varying degrees of completeness. However, the problem with a purely historical approach is that it does not allow us to distinguish between accidental and essential features of historical systems. It is conceivable that all the historical examples have a certain characteristic that a system need not have. More importantly, a purely historical method does not give the reasons why a system must have the characteristics it does—only *that* it has those characteristics.

In the *Freiheitsschrift*, Schelling notes that the evidence used by others (such as Jacobi and Friedrich Schlegel) to argue for the incompatibility of system and freedom has been merely historical, and that he has not encountered "arguments that were drawn from the essence of reason and knowledge [*Erkenntnis*] themselves" (SW VII, 338).[6] Something about the nature of reason requires system; thus, the essential characteristics of system are to be found in the demands of reason rather than in historical examples. Accordingly, our treatment of the characteristics of system will have to show how these characteristics arise out of the nature of reason itself.

Although Schelling does not elaborate on the precise connection between reason and system, he provides hints about their connection in the treatise itself, particularly in his discussion of Fichte. He characterizes Fichte's philosophy as a kind of denial of system: each individual *I* is an absolute substance that determines its own center. But, he adds, Fichte finally had to recognize the unity among these individual I's: "Reason, which strives for unity . . . is, however, always dismissed only by a fiat that lasts for a while and finally comes to ruin" (SW VII, 337). Reason strives for unity; Fichte's philosophy is non-systematic insofar as it lacks unity among the individual I's.[7] *Unity*, therefore, is an essential characteristic of system—a characteristic that arises out of the nature of reason, which demands unity.

This reference to reason's demand for systematic unity points back unmistakably to Kant. In the Transcendental Dialectic of the first *Critique*, Kant begins his characterization of reason in this way: "All our cognition starts from the senses, proceeds from there to understanding, and ends with reason, beyond which there is found in us nothing higher to work on the material of intuition and bring it under the highest unity of thought" (A 298–99/B 355). This sentence outlines a progression by which knowledge becomes increasingly unified. First, the understanding provides unity to appearances by gathering intuition into concepts and rules. Although the unity provided by the understanding constitutes knowledge (*Erkenntnis*), it does not yet reach the level of science (*Wissenschaft*). For knowledge to become science, reason adds higher levels of unity by unifying the rules of the understanding under principles (A 302/B 359), and ultimately a highest idea. Indeed, Kant defines science and system in terms of the unity provided by this highest idea: "Systematic unity is what first turns common cognition into science. . . . By a system I mean the unity of the manifold cognitions under an idea" (A 832/B 860).

Thus, the nature of reason is defined for Kant by a movement toward unity, a movement that begins with intuition and ends with system.[8] This is true for reason in the broad sense that includes the understanding, but especially true in the narrower sense of reason as the power of principles and ideas.[9] As a consequence of this striving for unity, reason is by nature *architectonic*, that is, "it regards all cognitions as belonging to a possible system" (A 474/B 502). Accordingly, reason's demand for the highest unity of thought is at the same time a demand for system.[10]

So far, we have identified the first of the essential characteristics of system, *unity*. But the demand for unity already suggests a second characteristic. Reason's unifying movement would not be necessary unless there were *multiple parts* in need of unification. In the later work "On the Nature of Philosophy as Science" (part of the 1821 *Erlangen Lectures*), Schelling connects the initial fragmentation of the parts with the Greek etymology of "system." Originally, the elements of knowledge are ἀσύστατον—they do not "exist together" (*zusammenbestehen*) (SW IX, 209; HKA II/10, 613, 681). The Greek participle Schelling cites, as well as the word "system" itself (σύστημα), comes from the verb συνίστημι, which means "to put together, combine."[11] To form a system, the parts are combined in such a way that they form a whole; as a result, they are σύστατον—standing together in unity.

But how are the many parts combined to form one whole? At the very least, they must be compatible with one another, but compatibility alone does not unite them. Nor can they merely be added together like apples in a barrel or books on a shelf: these form accidental unities that require no effort to dissolve. Instead, the parts must be *essentially connected* if they are to form a real unity. Schelling alludes to the connectedness of system when first addressing the charge that freedom and system are incompatible: "Since individual freedom is surely connected [*zusammenhängt*] in some way with the world as a whole, some kind of system must be present, at least in the divine understanding, with which freedom coexists [*zusammenbesteht*]" (SW VII, 336–37).[12] The connectedness of freedom is what brings it into the system and allows it to stand together with the other parts to form a whole. Anything that is unconnected or isolated cannot be part of the system. Here Schelling presupposes the connectedness of freedom without argument: reason itself demands this connectedness as the condition of the unity of science. A few lines earlier, Schelling had linked science with connectedness: "No concept can be defined in isolation, and only proof of its connection with the whole also confers on it final scientific completeness" (SW VII, 336).

From the characteristics of system described so far, it is clear that the question of system is essentially linked to the question of the one and the many, going back to Parmenides. The variety or multiplicity of the world seems obvious to us from appearances, yet reason demands that this multiplicity be a single whole. Schelling alludes to this one-many structure of system in the *Erlangen Lectures* cited above: "This continual being one and yet always another is what is characteristic of knowledge [*Wissen*]. Knowledge is neither in what always remains one and never emerges from itself, nor in what simply falls apart, in what lacks unity and connection. Knowledge is coherence, one and yet many, constantly another and yet always one" (SW IX, 244; HKA II/10, 641). At one extreme is complete fragmentation and the dissolution of unity; at the other, complete monotony and the disappearance of difference. System thus requires a connectedness that maintains the balance between (a) the "synthetic" unification of parts into a whole and (b) the "analytic" division of the whole into distinct parts.

So far, we have identified two essential characteristics of system that arise from the nature of reason: (1) unity and (2) the connectedness of parts. There are two other essential characteristics, which are more difficult to describe because they apply in two different ways, depending on the nature of the system. The first of these is *totality*. All of the parts of a system combine to form a whole (*ein Ganzes*); a system is all-encompassing and has no remainder. If there were something *outside* the system, to that extent there would not be unity: instead, there would be the system *plus* that other thing. In other words, the unity of system must be comprehensive. According to Jacobi's account in the *Spinoza Letters*, Lessing adopted as his motto ἓν καὶ πᾶν, "one and all"—a reference to the unity and totality of system in general and Spinoza's system in particular. In fact, years later Jacobi labeled Schelling's own philosophy the *Alleinheitslehre* ("the all-one doctrine") in distinction from Fichte's *Wissenschaftslehre*.[13]

I mentioned that totality can be applied to system in two different senses corresponding to two different kinds of systems. The first sense can be called "absolute totality," and it is relatively easy to understand. In this sense, absolutely nothing is outside the system—it embraces everything that is (τὸ ὄν). The second sense can be called "relative totality," and it is more difficult to define. It applies to systems (plural) that are not *the* system but are found within it. For example, Schelling titles his famous 1800 work *System of Transcendental Idealism*. The "system" contained in this work is not the whole of philosophy but is complemented by the philosophy of nature, which also forms a system.[14] Together they constitute two "basic sciences" (*Grundwissenschaften*)—two systems that comprise the total system of philosophy (cf. SW III, 340).[15] At an even smaller level, living organisms are also systems within the larger system of nature. Kant in the third *Critique* describes organized nature in the same terms as he had described system in the first,[16] and he elsewhere refers to natural forms as "so many particular systems" (AA 20, 217).

If these systems are not all-encompassing, in what sense can we attribute totality to them? Their totality can only be relative, not absolute.[17] Each system is quite literally a microcosm, a miniature world whose structure reflects that of the larger world, of which it is a part.[18] To understand the structure of each system, one can regard each *as if* it were the whole of reality: everything outside it is bracketed. Of course, one can also consider each relative system in a larger context in which it relates to things outside itself—but in that case, one is not regarding it qua system but qua part of a larger whole. We can therefore distinguish (a) these *relative* systems, which possess relative totality, from (b) the (one and only) *absolute* system, which possesses absolute totality. The latter is system in the strictest sense—system par excellence. But we should keep in mind that *the* system is really a "system of systems," a whole composed of smaller and smaller wholes.

Like totality, the fourth essential characteristic of system also applies in different senses to (a) relative systems and (b) the absolute system. And in this last characteristic we can begin to see the connection between system and the principle of ground. In the *Stuttgart Private Lectures* (1810), delivered a year following the publication of the *Freiheitsschrift*, Schelling identifies this requirement of system: "It must have a principle that supports itself [*sich selbst trägt*], that subsists in and through itself" (SW VII, 421). This self-supporting principle lies at the ground and supports the entire system. Because it is grounded by a principle that is contained within it, the system *grounds itself* by virtue of this principle.[19] But why is this self-grounding an essential characteristic of a system? If it did not ground itself, it would have to be grounded by something outside itself. However, because of the system's essential unity and totality, there is nothing outside itself that could ground it.[20] Therefore, if the system is to be grounded at all, it must be grounded by itself. Of course, this line of reasoning presupposes that the system, like all things, must be grounded. In other words, it presupposes the principle of ground.

In the Transcendental Dialectic of the first *Critique*, Kant traces this requirement for an ultimate grounding to the nature of reason—although he articulates it in terms of an unconditional foundation of the system of knowledge.[21] It is the nature of reason constantly to be seeking the grounds or conditions for anything that is conditional;[22] once these conditions are found, reason again seeks the conditions for these conditions, and so on. However, to bring completion to the series, reason demands the unconditional—something that grounds the entire series of conditions but is not grounded by anything outside itself. Kant calls this demand the *principle of pure reason*: "If the conditioned is given, then the entire series of conditions subordinated to one another—a series that is hence itself unconditioned—is also given" (A 307–8/B 364).[23] Of course, according to Kant, such a principle has a purely regulative function: it does not allow us to obtain knowledge of the unconditional. Nevertheless, he affirms that the ultimate grounding provided by the unconditional is necessary to bring completeness to our knowledge.[24] It is reason's demand for such completion that prompts Schelling to regard self-grounding as an essential characteristic of system.

Like the requirement for totality, the requirement for self-grounding poses a difficulty in its application to relative systems. The absolute system is self-grounding on account of its principle, which supports itself and the entire system. This means that this principle grounds—at least indirectly—all the relative systems, insofar as these are part of the absolute system. Yet, as systems, these also are self-grounding. Schelling makes this very claim about organisms early on in his career: "Each organic product bears the ground of its existence within *itself*, for it is cause and effect of itself" (SW II, 40).[25] But if this is true, how can the organic product also be grounded by the principle of the system of nature, and ultimately the absolute system? If it is self-grounded, it would seem to need no other grounding. We will return to this difficulty in chapters 3 and 7, when discussing the possibility of a "derived absoluteness" (cf. SW VII, 347).

We now have identified four essential characteristics of system that arise out of the nature of reason: (1) unity, (2) connectedness of parts, (3) totality, and (4) self-grounding. Before we turn to a more precise examination of the relationship of system to grounding and the principle of ground, it will be helpful to distinguish further between the various meanings of system. An important distinction is suggested by the already-cited quotation from the *Freiheitsschrift*: "Since individual freedom is surely connected in some way with the world as a whole . . . some kind of system must be present, at least in the divine understanding, with which freedom coexists" (SW VII, 337). This sentence refers to system in two senses: (a) the world as a whole is a system, and (b) a system is present in the divine understanding. These two senses correspond to the distinction between the real and the ideal, object and knower. System is not merely the form that knowledge takes—even the form of divine knowledge. Schelling here implies that the conception of reality in the divine understanding fully corresponds to reality as such: because reality is in the form of a system, one must also be present in the divine understanding. The real and the ideal system mirror each other.[26]

At the beginning of the *Stuttgart Private Lectures* (1810), Schelling defines his task in terms of the real and ideal senses of system: "To what extent is a system possible at all? Answer: long before man decided to make a system, a system already existed—the system of the world. Thus, our proper task is to find this system. The true system cannot be *invented*; it can only be found as a system already *present* [*vorhandenes*] in itself, namely in the divine understanding" (SW VII, 421). Schelling's own system of philosophy, insofar as it is the "true system," will correspond to the real system (the system of the world), which in turn corresponds to the ideal system present in the divine understanding. Schelling's philosophy is systematic only because reality itself is systematic. He arrives at his system by *finding* the system of the world—the original system of what is. His writings, in turn, are presentations of this system in concepts, and the more systematic of these presentations can also be called systems.

Schelling then adds an interesting qualification in the *Stuttgart Private Lectures*: "The true system cannot be found in its *empirical* totality, because that would require knowledge of all its parts [*Mittelglieder*], even the most particular [*einzelnsten*]" (SW VII, 421). One of the objections that Kierkegaard will raise against system is that it only includes concepts or what is universal, thus leaving out concrete individuals in their particularity—and thus excluding their freedom.[27] Here Schelling provides the basis for an answer to that objection: even if philosophical systems are necessarily restricted to the universal, the "true system"—the system of the world, reflected in the mind of God—includes all reality, even what is most particular.

Thus, we can distinguish system in the following senses: (a) the system of the world, or the original system of what is, (b) the (ideal) system in the divine understanding, (c) philosophy as a system of knowledge, and (d) the presentation of the system in writing.[28] The first two senses have clear priority; the last two are derivative and represent the philosopher's attempts to discover and articulate system in the first two senses. Among which of these senses, then, will the conflict between system and freedom play out? This question brings us back to Schelling's earlier statement that the conflict between freedom and system must not be stated merely in terms of historical systems, but in terms of the nature of reason—which refers to the highest reality, at least in the writings of the *Identitätsphilosophie* leading up to the *Freiheitsschrift*.[29] If the conflict is a genuine one, it will originate in the nature of things—in the system of the world and the divine understanding that reflects it. Any genuine conflict that arises in a particular philosophical system would be derived from that more original conflict.

2. The Principle of Ground and the Concept of System

I am arguing that the principle of ground is essentially connected to the concept of system, and that this connection accounts for the conflict between system and freedom. We have already seen one connection: the requirement that system be *self*-grounded presupposes that the system must be grounded. And because the system must be grounded, the parts must also be grounded, insofar as they make up the whole of the system: one cannot ground the whole without thereby grounding its parts qua members of the whole. Thus, the self-grounding of system entails the same universality of grounding stated in the principle of ground: *nothing is without ground*.

Beyond the relation of the whole to the parts, another relation is significant for linking system to the principle: that of the parts to one another. As stated in our discussion of the second characteristic of system, the parts are connected in such a way as to form a whole. But what is it that accomplishes this connection? In answering this question, we have to keep in mind that the connection must be essential if the system is to be *integrally* connected. Nothing can happen in one part of the system without other parts being affected. But this can only be true if the parts are connected through a relationship of dependence: one part depends on and is affected by another. And this dependence involves a kind of grounding, because what is dependent is conditioned or grounded by that on which it depends. Accordingly, the integral connection of the parts needed to form a whole is accomplished by a thoroughgoing grounding of the system's parts by other parts. The principle of ground, by requiring each thing to be grounded, ensures the connectedness needed for the system. Indeed, Schopenhauer will also acknowledge this essential function in his treatise devoted to the principle: "What else than the principle of sufficient reason connects the components [*Glieder*] of a system?" (ASW III, 14, §4).

Admittedly, the precise nature of the grounding is not determined by the system's need for integral connections; it is conceivable that the system's parts be connected through a form of grounding different from that found in the traditional principle of sufficient reason. In any case, the nature of this grounding historically has been determined by a particular conception of a system of knowledge, going back to ancient philosophy: system as *science* (ἐπιστήμη). Examining historical examples of the scientific conception of system will therefore help us to understand how system can pose a threat to freedom. However, we should bear in mind the methodological caveat mentioned above, namely, that particular historical examples of systems may have features that are not essential to a system as such.

One might say that the first treatise on system is Aristotle's *Posterior Analytics*, the work that lays out the criteria for organizing knowledge as a science. Here Aristotle makes clear that the construction of a science requires the search for the causes or the reasons why (αἴτια), and this search ultimately leads to the principles (ἀρχαί). Every truth must be linked through explanatory grounds back to ultimate truths that have no other ground. Within the Aristotelian conception of science, therefore, the grounding of truths by other truths provides the connectedness needed for system. Moreover, the grounding relation between truths is defined by the structure of demonstration (ἀπόδειξις), where the conclusion follows from the premises by logical necessity. In other words, a truth is grounded in Aristotle's science if it is a conclusion of a demonstration.[30] Any truth can be traced back through a chain of demonstrations to the principles, the ultimate premises that are not the conclusion of any demonstration.[31] The science obtains its unity, because all truths are thereby connected to the principles. And, since the conclusion of a demonstration follows from the premises by logical necessity, all truths are derived with necessity from first principles.

The structure of science that Aristotle describes bears a close resemblance to the axiomatic structure of geometry: geometrical theorems are "grounded" insofar as they can be traced by a line of proof back to axioms and definitions. Along these lines, Heidegger notes that the "predominance of the mathematical" was a precondition for the formation of system in the modern era.[32] Though the geometrical model had some influence on ancient philosophy,[33] Spinoza was the first to fully adopt its axiomatic structure in the *Ethics*, the work that Jacobi will cite as the paradigm of a philosophical system in the Pantheism Controversy. Like Euclid, Spinoza begins with a list of definitions and axioms and proceeds to deduce theorems about God or nature (*deus sive natura*) and his modes. Moreover, the geometrical structure of Spinoza's system mirrors its content: just as the conclusions follow necessarily from his principles, so do all the finite modes follow necessarily from the essence of God or substance. To use the distinction developed in the first section of this chapter: the ideal presentation of his system reflects the real system of what is.

Finally, to complete the historical survey, we can see the essential role of the scientific conception of grounding in the early attempts of Fichte and Schelling to develop systems. In the wake of Kant in the 1790s, the construction of a system became one of the central preoccupations of German philosophy. Fichte followed Reinhold in attempting to raise Kant's philosophy to the level of science by grounding it in a single principle. In the 1794 text "Concerning the Concept of the *Wissenschaftslehre*," Fichte articulates this task in terms of the form of science: "A science possesses systematic form. All the propositions of a science are joined together in a single first principle, in which they unite to form a whole" (FW I, 38).[34] Here Fichte specifies the relation between science and system: system is the *form* of science, and this requires that all its propositions are joined together or connected (*zusammenhängen*).[35]

But these connected propositions might all be false: what is it that ensures their truth? This is the question of the ultimate groundedness (*Gründlichkeit*) or groundlessness (*Grundlosigkeit*) of our knowledge (FW I, 44). Connection alone cannot provide an ultimate ground. This can only be provided by an absolutely first principle that possesses certainty that is independent of everything else. The other propositions possess certainty only insofar as they are connected to the first principle as their ultimate ground. This is because of the nature of the connection, according to Fichte: "This connection between propositions is established by showing that if proposition *A* is certain, then proposition *B* must also be certain, and that if proposition *B* is certain, then proposition *C* must also be" (FW I, 42).[36] Connection within the system is a grounding that communicates certainty from one proposition to another. Thus, all propositions within the system are grounded through a chain of connections leading back to the absolutely certain first principle.

Schelling's early writings show the marked influence of Fichte's *Wissenschaftslehre*. In fact, one of his first publications, "On the Possibility of a Form of Philosophy as Such" (1794), treats precisely the systematic character of the *Wissenschaftslehre* we have been discussing; an interest in the nature of system thus reaches back to the beginning of Schelling's career. He also identifies the grounding connectedness of system as the necessary condition of the system's unity: "*Science* as such, no matter what its content, is a whole that stands under the form of *unity*. This is only possible insofar as all its parts are subordinated to *one* condition, and each part determines another part only insofar as it is itself determined by that one condition" (SW I, 90). Here Schelling specifies the character of the grounding that connects the parts to produce a whole: it is a thoroughgoing determination (*Bestimmung*), beginning with the first principle. In other words, the first principle is a determining ground (*Bestimmungsgrund*)—a ground that necessitates what follows from it. As Fichte expresses it, "If the first principle is given, then *all* of the propositions must be given as well" (FW I, 58).[37] Thus, the first principle is the sufficient reason for the system as a whole. Everything has a sufficient reason, because everything is determined from the beginning. This is the all-from-one model of grounding relations that I introduced in the introduction.

Although Schelling does not directly address the nature of system in the *Freiheitsschrift*, and he makes only one explicit—albeit pivotal—reference to the principle of ground, his remarks on the formal essence of freedom (SW VII, 382–88) confirm the essential connection between system and the principle. Schelling raises the issue of chance and contingency, by which he means the absence of a determining ground, as in the swerve of Epicurus's atoms. Schelling writes: "But chance [*Zufall*] is impossible; it contests reason as well as the necessary unity of the whole; and, if freedom is to be saved by nothing other than the complete contingency [*Zufälligkeit*] of actions, then it is not to be saved at all" (SW VII, 383). Something about contingency is incompatible with the unity of system that reason demands. As we have seen, grounding connects the parts in such a way as to form a unity. The principle of ground, which requires the universality of this grounding, is the ultimate principle of connectedness. But contingency undermines this connectedness; it introduces gaps—things that are without reason, gratuitous, and, consequently, set apart from the unity of the whole.[38]

The question of contingency that Schelling raises leads us back to the connection of system and necessity implied in the introductory section of the *Freiheitsschrift*. By denying contingency in the passage on the formal essence of freedom, Schelling affirms necessity within the system.[39] This necessity, which involves the complete determination of the system and its parts, is required by the principle of ground in its traditional formulation, which states that nothing is without a determining ground.[40] Thus, the connection between system and the principle of ground accounts for the connection between system and necessity: system requires the connectedness and unity provided by the principle of ground; the principle in its traditional form requires the necessity of complete determination. The principle of ground is thus the mediating link between system and necessity.

As we saw above, Schelling considers the contradiction of necessity and freedom to be decisive for philosophy: without this contradiction, philosophy would sink into death (SW VII, 338). In the preface he had identified the opposition of necessity and freedom as the "innermost center point of philosophy" (SW VII, 333). We can therefore conclude that, by underlying the necessity of system, the principle of ground itself stands at the center of philosophy.[41]

3. Jacobi and the Conflict between System and Freedom

Now that we have considered (1) the essential characteristics of system and (2) the connection of system to the principle of ground, we are in a position to examine in what ways the principle of ground is the source of the conflict between system and freedom. Although I indicated above that this conflict can be traced to the things themselves and that it is not merely a historical issue, Schelling himself frames his discussion in the *Freiheitsschrift* in terms of certain historical claims about the conflict: "According to an old but in no way forgotten legend, the concept of freedom is in fact said to be completely incompatible with system" (SW VII, 336). A little later on, Schelling writes: "The same opinion has been more determinately expressed in the phrase: the only possible system of reason is pantheism, but this is inevitably fatalism" (SW VII, 338).

Although Friedrich Schlegel had made similar claims in his recently published treatise *On the Language and Wisdom of the Indians* (1808),[42] the allegations ultimately come from a controversy twenty years earlier—a controversy that profoundly shaped the history of German philosophy and made a strong impression on Schelling years before writing the *Freiheitsschrift*. In 1785 Friedrich Heinrich Jacobi published *On the Doctrine of Spinoza, in Letters to Moses Mendelssohn*. The work set off an intellectual firestorm. Mendelssohn, to whom the letters in the book were addressed, had undertaken to write a book about his departed friend Lessing, a leading figure in the German Enlightenment. In the correspondence reproduced in his *Spinoza Letters*, Jacobi informed Mendelssohn that Lessing had revealed to him he was a Spinozist. Jacobi—and perhaps Lessing, posthumously?—intended to provoke a scandal, because Spinoza's philosophy was notorious for denying freedom of the will and the orthodox concept of God. The unexpected result of the Pantheism Controversy, as it came to be known, was that Spinoza was rehabilitated and became an ongoing source of inspiration, particularly for the Romantics.[43] Schelling himself proclaims in an early letter to Hegel: "I have become a Spinozist!"[44]

In the letters to Mendelssohn and the commentary that accompanies them, Jacobi makes claims closely resembling those that Schelling cites in the *Freiheitsschrift*. He charges that any consistent philosophy leads to the denial of freedom. This is because Spinoza's system is the paradigm of philosophy, and Spinoza is a pantheist and fatalist. Though the general thrust of Jacobi's position is clear enough, his discussion is not focused, and it brings together many issues without clearly defining how they relate to each other. The reader can easily get the impression that Jacobi's argument consists in a crude series of identities: any system of philosophy is Spinozism, Spinozism is pantheism, and pantheism is fatalism. Despite the lack of focus and clarity, Jacobi has a number of remarkable insights, and his interpretation of Spinoza is at times quite nuanced. At the heart of his argument for the incompatibility of system and freedom is the principle of ground.[45] Jacobi recognizes the essential link between the principle and the concept of system, as we saw in the previous section, and he draws the consequences for freedom.

In Jacobi's retelling of his conversation with Lessing, the latter remarks that there is no other philosophy than Spinoza's. To this Jacobi replies, "This might be true. For the determinist, if he wants to be consistent, must become a fatalist: the rest then follows by itself." Jacobi's statement implies that determinism is essential to philosophy as such: there is no other philosophy than that of Spinoza, because determinism somehow leads inevitably to Spinoza's system. Lessing then asks about the "spirit of Spinozism" and the source of inspiration for Spinoza. Jacobi answers, "It is certainly nothing other than the ancient *a nihilo nihil fit* [nothing comes from nothing]."[46] Later on in the book, Jacobi repeats his claim: "What distinguishes Spinoza's philosophy from all the others, what constitutes its soul, is that it maintains and applies with the strictest rigor the well-known principle, *gigni de nihilo nihil, in nihilum nil potest reverti*."[47] This claim of Jacobi did not escape the young Schelling. In his *Philosophical Letters on Dogmatism and Criticism* (1795) he refers to Jacobi's statement concerning the spirit of Spinozism and writes, "I do not believe that the spirit of Spinozism could be better tied down" (SW I, 313).[48]

"Nothing comes from nothing" is another way of formulating the principle of ground. Each individual thing is grounded and thereby determined in all respects. If there were some respect in which a thing was not determined, something could be said to have come from nothing. This is the reason why Spinoza's philosophy is connected with determinism:

the principle of ground, which is the spirit of his philosophy, requires the determination of everything in its standard interpretation. This also explains why Lessing (in Jacobi's account) states that Leibniz was "at heart a Spinozist" and Jacobi agrees that "no doctrinal system . . . concurs with Spinozism as much as Leibniz's does."[49] Leibniz, of course, gave the principle of ground a name and made it one of the foundations of his system. Since reason itself requires this principle, any consistent system of philosophy ends up in the same determinism.

The statements of Jacobi that we have discussed so far concern the "real system," or the system of the world: nothing in this system can come from nothing. But Jacobi makes the same point in terms of the "ideal system," or the system of knowledge. I noted above that Spinoza's *Ethics* imitates the geometrical method of Euclid, and this mode of presentation reflects the content of the system: just as Spinoza's conclusions follow necessarily from his principles, so do all the finite modes follow necessarily from the essence of God or substance. For this reason, Jacobi alternates between the terms "demonstration" and "determination" when making his claims: the principle of ground requires that everything in the *system of knowledge* be demonstrated from first principles, just as it requires that everything in the *system of the world* be determined by prior causes. "Every avenue of demonstration ends up in fatalism,"[50] just as determinism leads to fatalism.

How does all this relate to pantheism? Despite the fact that the ensuing dispute is often referred to as the Pantheism Controversy (*Pantheismusstreit*), the issue of pantheism is not the central focus of the *Spinoza Letters*. In fact, when Jacobi summarizes his fundamental position in six theses, there is no mention of pantheism.[51] Insofar as it is discussed, however, Jacobi relates it to the principle of ground. All things together form One, which Spinoza calls God. Why? Couldn't God be a being that is separate from the world he creates? Jacobi argues—rather elliptically—that Spinoza's God must be an indwelling cause of the universe (a pantheistic God) and not a transcendent cause (the orthodox concept of God), because the latter requires a change in the infinite, and this change requires something to come out of nothing.[52] Though the meaning is obscure, Jacobi seems to be making the following argument. God is by nature infinite, eternal, and unchanging. This means that God cannot suddenly, at some point in time, begin to create finite things: that would involve a change in God—from not-creating to creating—and that is impossible if God is immutable. Thus, if the finite world were to come to be, it would have to come to be *from nothing*.⁵³

But if the finite world does not come to be, how does it exist? According to Jacobi's interpretation of Spinoza, it must exist *within* the infinite from all eternity. In other words, if finite things do not come to be from nothing, they must exist from the beginning within God. Jacobi also expresses this as Spinoza's rejection of "any *transition* from the infinite to the finite," because such a transition would require something to come out of nothing.⁵⁴ But if there is no transition, the infinite and the finite must be originally one. And if God (the infinite) is the cause of the finite, he cannot be a transcendent cause (a cause that produces an effect outside itself). Instead, the causal relation would have to be immanent: the effect must exist within the cause.

Jacobi's reasoning is not airtight: couldn't a transcendent God will to create an "external" finite world from all eternity? Arguably, this would not require a change within the infinite, if the will to create is itself eternal.⁵⁵ In any case, it is clear enough that Jacobi intends to trace even Spinoza's pantheism back to the principle of ground. And this role of the principle (again) did not escape the young Schelling. He summarizes Jacobi's argument linking pantheism and the principle in the *Philosophical Letters* (SW I, 313–14), and the premise that there is no transition between the infinite and the finite becomes a motif in his subsequent works as well as an impetus for the *Identitätsphilosophie*.⁵⁶ We will have occasion to return to this motif in chapter 3.

So far, we have seen how Jacobi regards the principle of ground as the heart of Spinoza's system—and indeed any consistent philosophical system—and that this principle for him requires determinism and pantheism. How does this relate to the alleged impossibility of a system of freedom? System, by way of the principle of ground, seems to require the denial of freedom in two distinct, though related, ways that are connected to two kinds of grounding relations within a system. These are (1) the relation of the part to other parts, and (2) the relation of the part to God (understood as both the whole and the ultimate ground). Both relations involve the issue of determinism; the second also involves pantheism.

It is not difficult to see the problem that both of these grounding relations pose for freedom, if the grounding involved is understood as complete determination. This means that if the human will is part of the system, it must be completely determined by forces outside itself—by other parts of the system and ultimately by God. But freedom for Jacobi is not compatible with the complete external determination of the will.[57] (The same can be said for Kant and Schelling, at least at this stage of his philosophical development.[58]) Freedom requires that the will be the absolute beginning of a series, but this absolute beginning would come from nothing. By denying that anything can come from nothing, determinism ends up in fatalism. In summary, if (a) system requires the connection of parts through grounding, (b) this grounding is a complete determination of each part by other parts, and (c) such determination of the will is incompatible with freedom, then a system of freedom is not possible.[59] Similarly, if (d) system requires the grounding of everything by God as the ultimate principle, and (e) God's grounding of all things is a complete determination (the all-from-one model of grounding), then a system of freedom is not possible.

In the *Freiheitsschrift* Schelling affirms that Spinoza's denial of freedom is a result of his determinism. After discussing pantheism at length, Schelling offers his "definite opinion" about Spinozism: "His arguments against freedom are entirely deterministic. . . . He treats the will also as a thing and then proves very naturally that it would have to be determined in all its activity through another thing that is in turn determined by another, and so on *ad infinitum*" (SW VII, 349). To resolve the difficulty that determinism poses for human freedom, Schelling will need to show how a system is possible without the kind of fatalistic determinism that he criticizes in Spinoza. He can only do this by accomplishing two tasks. We have already seen that Schelling denies all contingency in the *Freiheitsschrift*, thereby affirming the principle of ground as a principle of sufficient reason. First, he will need to show how it is possible to affirm the principle of ground—and a form of necessity—and yet avoid Spinoza's determinism. Second, if system is not connected by the determination of each part by other parts, he will need to show how the parts of the system can be connected through some other form of grounding. We will see how Schelling conceives the grounding relation of God to free beings in chapter 3 and the grounding relations among the parts of the system in chapter 4. But Schelling's final answer to the problem of determinism is found in his discussion of the "formal essence" of freedom (SW VII, 382–88), the subject of chapter 7.

Beyond the issue of determinism, the relation of the individual human being to God also poses a problem for freedom if that relation is understood pantheistically. Spinoza famously claimed that there was only a single substance, *deus sive natura*. The finite beings that are commonly conceived as substances are actually modes or affections of God—hence the label "pantheism." This means that human beings, like other finite beings, are not independent enough as individuals to deserve the name "substance."[60] But freedom requires independence and individuality: otherwise it is not the human being that acts, but only God or the system as a whole. Without a sufficient degree of independence, the individual is swallowed up in the system. Jacobi does not formulate this objection as precisely as his objection concerning determinism, and his criticism is mostly implicit. He writes an imaginary dialogue between himself and Spinoza in which his character objects that fatalism requires St. Peter's Basilica to build itself. Spinoza replies, "The Church of St. Peter in Rome did not build itself; everything that is contained in the entire universe of bodily extension has contributed to it."[61] Because everything is connected through grounding to form a single universe, any activity—either in thought or extension—can be attributed to the whole universe, insofar as the whole universe contributes to it. Accordingly, I cannot rightfully call any action *my own*: at best, I can say that God or the system acts through me. But the ownership of action is necessary for freedom; even more, the ownership of action is necessary for there to be a subject to whom one can even attribute freedom.[62]

The connection of the principle of ground to pantheism is more difficult to see than the connection to determinism. What is at stake is the relation of the part to the whole, the topic that Schelling addresses in his long discussion of pantheism in the *Freiheitsschrift* (SW VII, 338–47). This discussion and Schelling's solution to the difficulty are the subject of chapter 3. Here I will only say that Schelling defines this relation as one of grounding, and in doing so he makes his only explicit reference to the principle of ground in the *Freiheitsschrift*. In this instance, the principle of ground, instead of posing a difficulty for human freedom, plays a role in making it possible.

In any case, the two relations that pose a difficulty for human freedom—(1) the relation of the part to other parts, and (2) the relation of the part to God—both involve grounding. The possibility of a system of freedom hinges on how this grounding is conceived. Schelling, by reaching back nearly a quarter century to the Pantheism Controversy, implicitly recognizes the decisive manner in which Jacobi poses the question of ground and freedom. Though Jacobi frames his polemic in terms of a specific, historical system (Spinoza's), his insights into the fundamental role of the principle of ground in Spinoza and the difficulties this poses for freedom apply to system as such. System demands the connectedness of grounding, but grounding challenges the independence of freedom. The problem of a system of freedom is therefore a problem of ground.

4. Two Predominant Metaphors for System

Before we leave the topic, there is one further point to discuss about the nature of system—a point that has implications for how Schelling will address the question of a system of freedom. In the first two sections of this chapter, we focused on the essential characteristics of system. But beyond these characteristics, there are two different ways of conceiving system, found to a certain extent in all the philosophers discussed above. These two ways of conceiving system are represented by two metaphors—sometimes implied, often explicit.

In the first metaphor, a system is a building. Descartes famously begins his *Meditations* by invoking this metaphor:

> Some years ago I was struck by the large number of falsehoods that I had accepted as true in my childhood, and by the highly doubtful nature of the whole *edifice* that I had subsequently based on them. I realized that it was necessary, once in the course of my life, to demolish everything completely and start again right from the foundations if I wanted to establish anything at all in the sciences that was stable and likely to last.[63]

Like a building, the system is built upward from solid foundations. Without such foundations, the building would crumble. Recall that Kant's discussion of system in the *Critique of Pure Reason* is titled "The Architectonic of Pure Reason," a name that seems to suggest a link between system and architecture. And Fichte uses this metaphor in his essay "On the Concept of the *Wissenschaftslehre*": "Science may be imagined as a building whose main object is soundness. . . . Every part of the building is attached to the foundation and to the other parts, and in this way the entire building becomes sound. . . . [The foundation] itself is based not upon some additional foundation, but rather upon the solid earth" (FW I, 42–43).[64] Of course, the word "ground" (*Grund*), with which we have been concerned, quite literally invokes the image of something physically resting on something else.⁶⁵

In the second metaphor, system is a living organism. As mentioned above in the discussion of relative systems, Kant describes "organized nature" in the third *Critique* in the same terms that he had described system in the first; he even refers to organisms as systems (here the relationship is more than metaphorical, just as it will be more than metaphorical for Schelling). Surprisingly, this metaphor is even present in Jacobi's *Spinoza Letters*. According to Jacobi, Lessing "thought the whole after the analogy of an organic body" as a result of his study of Spinoza.⁶⁶ Moreover, in the "Introduction to the Outline of the Philosophy of Nature" (1799), Schelling incorporates the language of organic nature into his account of system: "There is no true system which is not at the same time an organic whole [*ein organisches Ganzes*]. For, if in every organic whole everything reciprocally bears and supports each other, this organization as a whole must have existed prior to its parts" (SW III, 279).⁶⁷ Indeed, this idea has roots in Schelling's 1794 unpublished commentary on Plato's *Timaeus*, in which he discusses Timaeus's characterization of the cosmos as a "living being" (ζῷον) (T 29–33).⁶⁸

What is the significance of the two different metaphors? They underscore a difference in the way of conceiving how the parts of the system relate to one another, as well as how they relate to the ultimate foundation of the system. In the previous sections, we already identified these relations as grounding connections. In the case of the building metaphor, the grounding connection of the parts is straightforward enough. One brick is supported by another brick, which is supported by another brick, all the way down to the foundation. The series of grounds proceeds linearly in one direction toward an ultimate ground. Thus, this metaphor fits most naturally with the all-from-one model of grounding. By contrast, the quotation from Schelling shows the difference when it comes to organisms: "everything reciprocally bears and supports each other." The grounding series is no longer linear and one-directional, but reciprocal. This way of conceiving organic nature is derived from Kant's third *Critique*. In the "Critique of Teleological Judgment," Kant characterizes one of the requirements of a natural purpose: "What is needed is that all its parts, through their own causality, produce one another as regards both their form and combination, and that in this way they produce a whole" (KU §64, AA 5, 373). Like a building, the parts of the body are connected through a grounding dependence. But in a building, one can demolish the upper floors without affecting the integrity of the whole structure. This is not the case in an organism, in which everything depends on everything else.

Though Fichte explicitly cites the building metaphor in discussing the structure of his system, elements of the organic metaphor exist side-by-side with the architectural characteristics in his account. This is further evidence that the two metaphors represent a tension that runs through the thinking about system in these philosophers.[69] Fichte, for example, states that once the principle is given, all the other propositions are given as well (FW I, 58). This, of course, conforms perfectly to the architectural, all-from-one understanding of a system built up deterministically from an absolute foundation. But then Fichte notes something else: "The very principle from which we began is at the same time our final result" (FW I, 59). This is completely incomprehensible in terms of the building metaphor. How can one return to the foundation by building from the ground up? The ultimate circularity that Fichte describes—beginning and ending with the principle—points to a more organic understanding of system. In a similar vein, Fichte notes the interdependence of the propositions within the system: if any one of them is true, they all are true; if any one is false, they all are false (FW I, 61). This interdependence fits nicely with the system of an organism, whose parts ground one another, so that their fate quite literally "hangs together."

The relationship among the parts has consequences for the relationship of the parts to the whole. In a building, the parts precede the whole: the whole is simply the sum of the parts, or what Kant calls an "aggregate" (*Aggregat*). This is why it is always possible to add additions onto already existing buildings. Since the grounding only goes in a single direction, I can add as many stories as I wish onto the top of the building. There is no idea of the whole that determines what the parts should be and when the building is finished.[70] In an organism, by contrast, the whole precedes the parts.[71] According to Kant's account of organic nature in the third *Critique*, the purpose of an organism is the idea of the whole, "which must determine a priori everything that the thing is to contain" (§65, AA 5, 373). For this reason, when speaking about system in the first *Critique*, Kant notes that nothing can be added on to it contingently and that it "can indeed grow internally but not externally; that is, it can grow like an animal body" (A 833/B 861).

There is one final distinction between the two ways of conceiving system, represented by the two metaphors. This concerns the identity of

Ground and the Question of a System of Freedom | 41

the system's original or primal being (*Urwesen*). With respect to the architectural conception of system, the original being is simply the foundation of the structure—that upon which the whole building rests. God is a *part* of the system, albeit a part not grounded by any other part. The grounding of parts by other parts is a series that ends with God. In an organic system, by contrast, if one follows the grounding series of parts by other parts, one never reaches an end. This is because all the parts ground each other reciprocally: one will go in circles, following the grounding series. The primal being must be outside this series: it is the whole itself.[72] Since this primal being is traditionally identified as God, an organic model of system is often linked to a pantheistic understanding of God. Not only is the conception of the original being different in the two kinds of system; the relation of the original being to the parts is very different. In one, God is the ultimate ground in a series of grounds; in the other, God is the whole and not a member of a series of finite grounds. To be sure, this difference will have consequences for how Schelling conceives God's relationship to human freedom.

The difference between the two ways of conceiving system also has important implications for the philosophical presentation of the system. The architectural model has an obvious affinity with the geometrical method of demonstration. One simply begins with the principles (the foundation) and deduces theorems. The order of grounding dictates the order of demonstrating *more geometrico*. In contrast, the organic model does not fit easily with a linear presentation. One can certainly begin with the principle, the idea of the whole. But where does one go from there? With which of the parts does one begin?[73] Precisely because system in this model is no longer linear, the order of presentation is not fixed. I suspect that Schelling found it increasingly difficult to present his thought in systematic form because of the organic nature of his system.[74]

5. Conclusion:
Heidegger and the Alleged Failure of a System of Freedom

We have seen how the principle of ground is connected to the problem of a system of freedom. To recapitulate the main points: A system requires the universality of grounding expressed in the principle of ground. This is because everything must be grounded in order to be connected within the system. But if this grounding is a complete determination of each part by other parts, and such a determination of the will is incompatible with freedom, then a system of freedom is not possible.

However, if the problem—in large part—concerns freedom and determinism, why frame it in terms of a system of freedom? There are two answers to this question. First, this framing allows us to see that the resolution of the problem requires rethinking the nature and structure of the grounding relations within the system as a whole. In other words, the problem of freedom has to be addressed as part of what I have called the problem of ground. Establishing freedom's possibility is not simply a matter of deciding whether determinism in general is true and whether it is compatible with freedom. Instead, one has to understand freedom's place within the larger network of grounding relations—between God and the world, and among created beings. And since the problem of evil requires sorting out these same grounding relations, framing the problem of freedom in terms of system also reveals its essential connections with the problem of evil, the other major problem in the *Freiheitsschrift*. Both are part of the larger problem of ground.

The second reason for this framing is that it provides a context for the claim of determinism and shows what is at stake in denying it. One cannot simply declare oneself in favor of indeterminism without jeopardizing the unity necessary for system. And the unity of system—indeed, system itself—is not some arbitrary formal feature of certain philosophies that can be eschewed to make room for freedom. The unity of system is a demand of reason itself. As Schelling declares in the section on the formal concept of freedom: "Chance [*Zufall*] is impossible; it contests reason as well as the necessary unity of the whole" (SW VII, 383).[75] If one denies the unity of the whole, one must deny reason.

Some thinkers are inclined to do precisely this. They would deny the claims of reason and system in order to affirm freedom. Indeed, one might even think that this is the path Schelling is forced to take at the end of the *Freiheitsschrift*, because the project of a system of freedom fails. However, in the first pages of the *Freiheitsschrift* he rules out the renunciation of reason as a solution: "Reason, which strives for unity, like feeling, which insists on freedom and personality, is, however, always dismissed only by a fiat [*Machtspruch*] that lasts for a while and finally comes to ruin" (SW VII, 337). Both reason and feeling are essential to human nature, and any attempt to renounce one or the other will ultimately fail. One cannot resolve the tension by dismissing one of the sides: "To pull oneself out of the conflict by renouncing reason seems closer to flight than to victory.

With the same justification, another could turn his back on freedom in order to throw himself into the arms of reason and necessity without there being cause for triumph on either the one or the other side" (SW VII, 338). Fleeing from the conflict also has consequences for the vitality of philosophy. Schelling declares that the task of connecting freedom with the whole is the "unconscious and invisible driving force of all striving for knowledge, from the lowest to the highest." A flight from the conflict leaves philosophy to "sink into death" (SW VII, 338).

We have to keep these statements about the indispensability of reason and system in mind when we read the much-cited line toward the end of the *Freiheitsschrift*: "In the divine understanding there is a system; yet God himself is not a system, but a life" (SW VII, 399). Here Schelling seems to be restricting the domain of system. There is a system in the divine understanding, but this is not the whole of God. Rather, God is a life, which means he is the living unity of the understanding (that-which-exists) and the ground of existence (cf. SW VII, 394–95). Accordingly, it seems as if the ground of existence falls outside the system. Indeed, this is Heidegger's interpretation: "When the system is only in the understanding, the ground and the whole opposition of ground and understanding are excluded from system as its other and system is no longer system with regard to beings as a whole."[76] But this would have devastating consequences for the possibility of system. As we saw in the first section, one of the essential characteristics of system is totality.[77] But if there is something *outside* the system, then the system is no longer the whole. And because system, by its nature, must be the whole, there is no longer a system.[78]

However, it is not obvious how to interpret the line that identifies God as a life and not a system.[79] To begin with, it is curious that Schelling opposes system to life, especially in light of Schelling's understanding of system. In fact, he often compares system to a living organism: a true system is "an organic whole" (*ein organisches Ganzes*).[80] Why then is God a life but not a system? Why not a system *and* a life—a living system? This opposition between system and life suggests that Schelling has a particular (narrower) sense of system in mind when making that statement.

In the first section of this chapter, we saw how Schelling implicitly distinguishes two senses of system at the beginning of the *Freiheitsschrift*: "Since individual freedom is surely connected in some way with the world as a whole . . . some kind of system must be present, at least in the divine understanding, with which freedom coexists" (SW VII, 337). In these lines Schelling refers to two senses of system: the world as a whole (*das Weltganze*) is a system, and there is a system in the divine understanding. The latter is system in an ideal sense—the system of (divine) knowledge. It is true that system in this sense, insofar as it is only *within* the divine understanding, is not all that is. Nevertheless, this system of divine knowledge reflects the world as a whole, or system in the real sense. This is implied in the cited passage: if freedom is connected to the world as a whole, freedom must be included in the system within the divine understanding, since this "mirrors" the world as a whole.[81]

Schelling articulates the same twofold sense of system at the beginning of the *Stuttgart Private Lectures* (1810) in a passage we discussed in the first section of this chapter: "To what extent is a system possible at all? Answer: long before man decided to make a system, a system already existed—the system of the world. Thus, our proper task is to find this system. The true system cannot be *invented*; it can only be found as a system already *present* [*vorhandenes*] in itself, namely in the divine understanding" (SW VII, 421). Schelling defines his task as finding "the system of the world." But in the very next line he says that the system to be found is already present in the divine understanding. Since the divine understanding as such does not exhaust all there is in the world, this can only mean that the system in the divine understanding is an ideal reflection of all that is—that is, the system of the world. Two points about this passage are helpful for interpreting the famous line about God as a life and not a system: (1) Schelling here—as well as at the beginning of the *Freiheitsschrift*—refers to a system in the divine understanding. But this clearly is not intended to be a restriction of the concept of system to a "part" of the whole. Instead, the system in the divine understanding is an ideal reflection of the system of the world—which is comprehensive and thus includes what is beyond God's understanding. (2) Even after the *Freiheitsschrift*, Schelling has no intention of giving up his systematic ambitions. The proper task (*eigentliche Aufgabe*) is to find the system of the world. And Schelling also emphasizes in the *Stuttgart Private Lectures* the need for a ground of God's existence so that God is a life.[82] We must therefore conclude that this ground, though outside the divine understanding, is included within the system that Schelling seeks to find.

With these points in mind, we can return to the famous line "In the divine understanding there is a system; yet God himself is not a system, but a life." The passage continues: "And the answer to the question as to the possibility of evil in regard to God . . . also lies in this fact alone. All existence demands a condition so that it may become real, namely personal existence" (SW VII, 399). When Schelling says that God is a life and not a system, he is expressing in rhetorical fashion his fundamental criticism of idealism, which he had voiced much earlier in the *Freiheitsschrift* (cf. SW VII, 356).[83] By "system" Schelling here means the ideal system within the divine understanding—just as we have seen him connect system and the divine understanding in other contexts. God is not merely his understanding (the ideal principle), because he also has within himself the ground of his existence (the real principle): it is the combination of the real and the ideal principles that makes God a life. Idealism, on the other hand, is one-sided and ignores the real principle: it reduces God to the divine understanding, and therefore it is unable to account for the origin of evil (SW VII, 356). Thus, Schelling follows his statement that God is a life and not a system by connecting it to the possibility of evil and the need for a "condition" or ground of God's existence.

Accordingly, Schelling does not intend in the passage to exclude the ground from the system, thereby undermining the very idea of system as the totality of what is. Instead, his intention is to affirm a more comprehensive conception of God than that found in a one-sided idealism. One therefore cannot conclude that Schelling, in saying that God is a life but not a system, concedes that a system of freedom is impossible. The sincere attempt to find and articulate such a system stretches to the end of the *Freiheitsschrift* and beyond.

Whether Schelling succeeds in finding and articulating a system of freedom is something that we must investigate in the chapters that follow. But from what we have seen, it is clear that Schelling regards both system and freedom as indispensable. To bring the two together, he must resolve the apparent conflict between them. And since the principle of ground is the source of this apparent conflict, its resolution requires a reconsideration of the principle of ground and the meaning of ground operative within it.

2

Identity, Ground, and the Meaning of the Copula in Judgments

I begin this chapter with a mystery. Up to this point I have attempted to show how the concept of ground and the principle of ground underlie the difficulties connected with a system of freedom. Indeed, insofar as Schelling's *Freiheitsschrift* is an attempt to overcome these difficulties and to construct a system of freedom, I am claiming that the principle of ground is at the very heart of what he is doing in the text. And yet there are hardly any explicit references to the principle in Schelling's writings. He briefly discusses it in the 1794 *Formschrift* (SW I, 102–4), and he makes only a single reference to it in the *Freiheitsschrift*. Between these two texts, nothing. What can be the reason for this silence, if the principle of ground has the importance I am claiming?

One possibility is that Schelling simply fails to recognize the importance of this principle for his own thought. Though he makes constant reference to grounds, and he pursues the question *why?* throughout his works, he neglects to reflect on the principle that underlies so much of his questioning. In this respect, he would be no different from other philosophers throughout history who presuppose the principle but do not recognize it as a presupposition and examine it explicitly. After all, the principle only received a name—and the recognition that comes with a name—from Leibniz, long after Aristotle had discovered the principle of non-contradiction.[1]

Such an oversight on Schelling's part might account for his silence, if the *Freiheitsschrift* contained only a casual reference to the principle. In fact, the immense weight he assigns to it only serves to deepen the mystery. Schelling notes that the relation of subject and predicate in statements of identity is the relation of ground and consequence. He then adds: "The law of ground [*Gesetz des Grundes*] is for that reason just as original as the law of identity" (SW VII, 346).

Anyone acquainted with Schelling's philosophical development in the preceding decade will recognize how powerful a statement this is. In the *Darstellung meines Systems* (1801), the text cited at a pivotal moment in the *Freiheitsschrift*,[2] Schelling makes clear the unparalleled position that the law of identity has in his philosophy: "The highest law for the being of reason, and since there is nothing outside of reason, for all being . . . is the law of identity" (§4, SW IV, 116). Schelling goes still further, noting that this is the *only* law that applies to what is *in itself* (§4, SW IV, 117). Moreover, the law is not merely a logical principle, as it had been in Kant: through it, the being of absolute identity, or God, is also posited (§6, SW IV, 117). And the law retains its unparalleled position in the texts leading up to the *Freiheitsschrift*.[3] This is, after all, why commentators refer to this period of Schelling's development as his *Identitätsphilosophie*.

In light of the singular importance of this law in Schelling's previous philosophy, one can only marvel at the statement in the *Freiheitsschrift*: "The law of ground is just as original as the law of identity." In previous texts, Schelling had claimed that the law of identity is *the* principle of his philosophy, but now the law of ground is said to be *just as original*. What does Schelling mean by this puzzling statement, which elevates the principle of ground to the highest place in his philosophy? Why does he hardly ever mention the principle, either before or after the *Freiheitsschrift*, if it is just as original as the foremost principle of his system? Strangely, Schelling commentators have not been troubled by these questions.[4]

In this chapter and the following, I offer the following solution: the reason Schelling does not mention the principle of ground in his previous writings is that the principles of identity and ground have merged into one. Schelling does not need to discuss a principle of ground that is separate from the principle of identity, because the latter principle includes the former within itself. In other words, the law of identity is itself a law of ground, and this is the meaning of Schelling's statement in the *Freiheitsschrift*.

Of course, Schelling is not the first philosopher to link the two laws. Already Leibniz had grouped them together as his "two great principles"[5]—though he often exchanges the principle of identity for that of contradiction.[6] Between Leibniz and Kant, there was a debate among German metaphysicians regarding the meaning of the principle of ground and its subordination to a higher principle: Christian Wolff and his followers had attempted to derive it a priori from the principle of contradiction, an effort attacked by Crusius, who wished to exempt freedom from the principle.[7] And after Kant, Fichte had presented the principles of identity, contradiction, and ground as logical abstractions from the first three principles of the *Wissenschaftslehre* (FW I, 79). Thus, by making the principle of ground "just as original" as the principle of identity, Schelling is weighing in on a long-standing dispute about its origin and relation to other metaphysical principles. Indeed, we will see that he follows Leibniz in linking the principle of ground to the nature of truth as identity. But, unlike Leibniz, the principle in Schelling is not regressive but *progressive.*

As the last line indicates, the merging of the two principles in Schelling involves a transformation of both from the way they were traditionally understood. Though the roots of this transformation are in the *Identitätsphilosophie,* Schelling lays a new foundation for it in the *Freiheitsschrift* through his treatment of the copula in judgments, which is the focus of this chapter. The full meaning and implications of the transformation are then revealed in the passage on the "creative unity" of the law of identity (the subject of the next chapter).

At first glance, the copula seems to have little relevance to the principle of ground—or the wider problem of ground and freedom. The term refers to the word "is" when used to connect the subject and predicate in judgments (for example, "the sky is blue"), a topic usually confined to logic or the philosophy of language. And yet, immediately before claiming that the principles of identity and ground are equally original, Schelling cites the copula's meaning as justification: the relation of subject and predicate—as defined by the copula—is the relation of ground and consequence. In what follows, we will have to investigate what this means and how it justifies the co-originality of principles. We will see that, despite its apparently narrow focus, the explication of the copula has far-reaching ontological implications: it reveals structures that apply at all levels of Schelling's system. And because these structures involve grounding, the meaning of the copula has implications for understanding the network of grounding relations in which freedom is embedded.

Indeed, the context of Schelling's treatment of the copula provides a first clue about these wider implications. This context is a discussion of pantheism—a topic that raises profound ontological questions about the relationship of God to things. Schelling's approach, however, is largely polemical: he considers four false conceptions of pantheism, showing how each is inadequate for rejecting a system of freedom—either because it is not necessary to system as such, or because it does not rule out freedom. Schelling gives his own position mostly by way of contrast, and at times it is difficult to draw the line between his view and his defense or explication of Spinoza. Rather than adhere strictly to the structure of the text, I take a thematic approach. After addressing the relationship between pantheism and identity, I focus on the meaning of the copula in judgments and the implications for the nature of identity and the relationship of God to things. This sets the stage for considering in the next chapter Schelling's remarkable statement that "the law of ground is just as original as the law of identity" (SW VII, 346). In the process, we will begin to recognize new senses of ground and grounding.

1. Pantheism and the Nature of Identity

We have already noted that the context of Schelling's discussion of identity in the *Freiheitsschrift* is his treatment of pantheism,[8] which arises out of his discussion of the claim that freedom is incompatible with system. After an introductory discussion, he cites a "more definite" (*bestimmter*) expression of this opinion: "The only possible system of reason is pantheism, but this is inevitably fatalism" (SW VII, 338), that is, a denial of freedom. Ultimately, Jacobi is the "troublemaker" behind this claim, though Schelling also has in mind a more proximate source. In his recently published treatise *On the Language and Wisdom of the Indians* (1808), Friedrich Schlegel had claimed that pantheism is "the system of pure reason," and this involves an annihilation of difference and individual existence.[9] In any case, the claim about pantheism is "more definite," because it gives the reason why freedom and system are incompatible: whatever other features it may have, it is a system's pantheistic character that excludes freedom. This "more definite" expression, therefore, actually makes two claims: (1) Pantheism is essential to system as such. (2) Pantheism, in the sense that is essential to system, rules out freedom.

Of course, to evaluate these claims, one must first define the sense of pantheism common to them. As Schelling remarks, "All depends on the closer determination of the concept" (SW VII, 339). Thus, he proceeds in the sequel (SW VII, 339–47) to consider four definitions of pantheism:

1. the immanence of things in God (SW VII, 339)
2. the complete identification of God with things, or a blending (*Vermischung*) of creator and creature (SW VII, 340)
3. the denial of all individuality, or the claim that things are nothing (SW VII, 343)
4. the denial of freedom (SW VII, 345)

There is more at stake in this discussion of pantheism than the refutation of a particular claim made years earlier—though we noted in the last chapter that this claim and the events surrounding it (the so-called Pantheism Controversy) had enormous influence on the development of German philosophy. As mentioned above, the question of pantheism concerns the relationship between God and the world. The word "pantheism" itself names the two elements in the relationship: θεός (God) and πᾶν (all that is). Their juxtaposition implies an identity: God is all things. Thus, the discussion of identity arises in this context because of the need to understand the meaning of the identity of God and things affirmed by pantheism. Or, stated in slightly different terms, the topic arises because of the need to understand the meaning of "is" in the statement "God is everything."[10]

One of the remarkable features of Schelling's discussion is that he never calls into question the claim that every system of reason is pantheism. Jacobi intended his argument that all systems of reason must be pantheistic to be a *reductio ad impietatem*: the word "pantheism" is itself objectionable because of its association with heresy and the denial of the orthodox conception of God. But for Schelling the question is not whether pantheism is true or not, but what pantheism means as a true description of the relationship between God and all that is.[11] Thus, he actually affirms that every system of reason is pantheism, if the term is understood in a certain way: "If pantheism denotes nothing more than the doctrine of the immanence of things in God, every rational viewpoint in some sense must be drawn to this doctrine. But precisely the sense here makes the difference" (SW VII, 339). Hence Schelling himself, insofar as his viewpoint is rational, affirms pantheism in the sense of the immanence of things in God.[12] If we interpret the sentence "God is all things" accordingly, it means "All things are *in* God." Schelling's version of pantheism could therefore be designated "panentheism" (πᾶν ἐν θεῷ), a term coined by Karl Christian

Friedrich Krause (1781–1832), who studied with Fichte and Schelling in Jena.[13] Indeed, Schelling and Hegel have been called the "godfathers of modern panentheism."[14]

We can connect this treatment of pantheism to our discussion in chapter 1 of the whole-part relationship within a system. If all things are in God, according to the doctrine of immanence, there can be nothing outside of God. God is totality—the whole that embraces all that is. And because individual things are within the whole but not the whole itself, they must be parts of the whole. Thus, the relationship of God to things, according to the doctrine of immanence, is the relationship of the whole to its parts. This is one of the two relationships we identified as problematic for human freedom within a system. It is problematic insofar as the parts seem to lose their independence and become "lost in the whole." To establish that pantheism does not compromise human freedom, Schelling must clarify the relationship between the whole and the parts in a system. And since this relationship turns out to be one of identity, Schelling must clarify the nature of this identity and show the possibility of freedom within identity.

This clarification begins in his discussion of the copula, which arises in the course of his treatment of the second false conception of pantheism. Pantheism is supposed to be "a complete identification of God with things; a blending [*Vermischung*] of creature with the creator" (SW VII, 340). The relationship of God to things would thus be an identity that excludes difference—the kind of inferior identity that Schelling had associated with the understanding and reflection in his earlier writings (cf. SW IV, 236; VII, 52). Schelling first responds to this interpretation of pantheism by discussing the relationship between God and things in Spinoza, showing that *even* in Spinoza there is not a complete identification. Jacobi had regarded Spinoza's philosophy as both pantheistic and the paradigm of a philosophical system—"the system of reason κατ' ἐξοχήν," as Schelling later puts it (SW VII, 347). If this second conception of pantheism does not apply to Spinoza, widely regarded as the most pantheistic of modern philosophers, then a fortiori it cannot apply to all possible systems of reason. Schelling shows that there is not a "complete identification of God and things" in Spinoza by giving an account of Spinoza's "differentiation" (*Unterscheidung*) of God from things. This differentiation takes place on two levels. On the one hand, God is different from the individual thing or "mode." On the other hand, God is different from the sum total or aggregate (*Zusammenfassung*) of things (SW VII, 340–41). We will have occasion to return to this discussion of Spinoza in more detail later, since much of what Schelling says about the relationship of God to things in Spinoza applies to his own philosophy.

After discussing Spinoza, Schelling takes a step back and identifies the source of the mistaken view that pantheism involves a lack of distinction between God and things: "The reason for such misinterpretations . . . lies in the general misunderstanding of the law of identity or the meaning of the copula in judgment" (SW VII, 341). Here Schelling associates the principle of identity with the meaning of the copula, though he does not define their precise relationship. Indeed, in what follows he focuses on the copula and the relationship between the subject and predicate without directly addressing the principle of identity. We will revisit the connection to the principle below.

"Copula" is a Latin word meaning "link" or "bond." In a logical context, it refers to the word "is" in statements where "is" has the function of connecting the subject to the predicate.[15] How does the meaning of "is" relate to a misunderstanding of pantheism? As mentioned above, the juxtaposition of the words θεός (God) and πᾶν (all that is) in "pantheism" indicates an identity, which can be expressed in the statement "God is all things." The meaning of "is" in this statement determines the relationship between God and things. Those who think that pantheism consists in a complete identification mistakenly believe that the "is" expresses a total identification of subject and predicate. "x is y" would mean "There is no difference between x and y." Against such a view, Schelling writes: "It can at once be made comprehensible to a child that in no possible proposition (which according to the assumed explanation states the identity of the subject with the predicate) is stated a total sameness [*Einerleiheit*]" (SW VII, 341). If no proposition expresses a total sameness between subject and predicate, then in all propositions there must be some difference between them.[16] The copula not only allows for but requires difference between the terms it connects. Nevertheless, Schelling still affirms that the relationship between the subject and the predicate is a relationship of identity, as Leibniz had done before.[17] The copula must therefore express an identity that includes difference—the kind of higher identity Schelling had associated with reason in earlier writings (cf. SW VII, 52).

So far Schelling has given a negative account of the identity expressed by the copula: it does not exclude difference. What then is his positive theory? We can actually distinguish four accounts he offers—without explicitly stating how they fit together. These four accounts are:

1. The subject has a mediated connection with the predicate. There is a *tertium quid* to which both subject and predicate relate.

2. The subject relates to the predicate as *antecedens* to *consequens*. The subject is what precedes, and the predicate is what follows.

3. The subject relates to the predicate as *implicitum* to *explicitum*. The predicate is what is developed or unfolded from what is enveloped or enfolded in the subject.

4. The subject relates to the predicate as ground to consequence.

These accounts are not developed by Schelling. In fact, the first is mostly implicit in the *Freiheitsschrift*, and the fourth is only stated retrospectively in a later discussion (SW VII, 346). Schelling's method of proceeding is to give a series of example sentences and to interpret each in turn—along the way, giving hints about the copula's meaning. I will therefore develop each of the four accounts in turn, drawing on the examples.[18] In the process, I will attempt to show how the accounts fit together and pave the way for Schelling's connection of identity to ground.

2. Explication of Schelling's Four Accounts of the Copula

ACCOUNT 1: THE SUBJECT HAS A MEDIATED CONNECTION WITH THE PREDICATE.[19]

Although Schelling does not directly spell out this account in the *Freiheitsschrift*, he makes an indirect reference to it immediately after introducing the topic of identity: "In no possible proposition . . . is stated a sameness or even an unmediated connection of [the subject and predicate]" (SW VII, 341).[20] If no proposition expresses "an unmediated connection," then the connection between subject and predicate must be *mediated*. But what kind of mediation is involved? Schelling's interpretation of the first example sentence provides a clue: "The proposition 'This body is blue,' does not have the meaning that the body is, in and through that in and through which it is a body, also blue, but rather the meaning that the same thing which is this body is also blue, although not in the same respect" (SW VII, 341). In the example, the subject ("this body") does not have an immediate connection with the predicate ("blue"). Instead, the two are connected by virtue of their belonging to "the same thing" (*dasselbe*). In other words, the same thing—unnamed in the original sentence—is both (a) this body and (b) blue. Finally, Schelling adds that the same thing is not this body and blue "in the same respect [*Betracht*]." The same thing is in one respect this body and in another respect blue. In other words, being this body and being blue are different aspects of the same (underlying) thing.

This mediated account of the copula comes from Leibniz. Schelling acknowledges this explicitly in the *Ages of the World* (1811), where he gives a full explanation of what is only implied in 1809.[21] Leibniz had developed the logic of the copula in an early text defending the doctrine of the Trinity—a text cited in the *Freiheitsschrift* (SW VII, 342n; 346).[22] In fact, Schelling refers to this theological context in the *Ages of the World*: "Already the scholastics found that for explaining the concept of the Trinity it is necessary to determine the true meaning of the copula [*Band*] in every judgment more clearly than is the case in the logic of our times" (WA I, 28).[23] One might be tempted to write off the scholastic debates about the Trinity as subtle reasoning about a theological topic with little philosophical relevance. But Schelling early on in his *Identitätsphilosophie* recognized the significance of the Trinity for understanding the three-in-one structures within his philosophy: "If one were to look among well-known symbols for one that would express that unity of the finite with the infinite in and with the eternal, one could find none more suitable than that of the Trinity" (SW IV, 390). Since this same three-in-one structure is repeated throughout Schelling's philosophy, the nature of the copula vis-à-vis the Trinity has far-reaching systematic implications. In particular, it will be essential for understanding the three-in-one structure of the fundamental distinction within God at the heart of the *Freiheitsschrift*.[24]

After noting this context, Schelling summarizes this account of the copula in a rule: "The true meaning of every judgment, for example, the simplest, 'A is B,' is this: 'That which is A *is* that which is also B'" (WA I, 28). In Leibniz's terminology, there is a *commune tertium*, a third thing besides the subject and the predicate that serves as a "single substratum" for both the subject and the predicate.[25] Schelling calls it simply X. In the previous example, X would be the "same thing" (*dasselbe*) that is both this body and blue. How can X unite the subject and the predicate if they are two different things? Schelling cites an example from Leibniz:

the same thing that is *in one respect* body is *in another respect* soul. (The example sentence "The soul is one with the body" is cited a little later in the passage in the *Freiheitsschrift*.[26]) In the same way, the subject and predicate are each a different respect (*Betracht*) of a single substratum (X).[27] Thus, it is the ability of the same X to be considered in different respects that allows it to join subject and predicate together in identity despite the difference between them.[28]

Moreover, Schelling affirms that the mediation of X is a kind of grounding. After giving the general formula for translating the copula, Schelling adds: "It is thus shown how the copula [*das Band*] underlies [*zu Grunde liegt*] both the subject and predicate" (WA I, 28). But how can the word "is" underlie anything? Here we can see Schelling's ontologizing of the copula—assigning it a role beyond that of a grammatical connecter or an indicator of logical form. On a grammatical level, the word "is" serves as the copula, because it links the subject to the predicate. But on an ontological level, this linking is accomplished by X—the "same thing" that is in one respect the subject and in another respect the predicate. Thus, the term "copula" can also refer to this single substratum, which underlies the two. The copula is not just a word, but a thing—the unnamed X.[29]

How does Schelling characterize X? In the *Ages of the World*, he refers to it as "that not always named *same thing* [*dasselbe*] of which subject and predicate are both predicates" (WA I, 28). That X is not always named is one of its most interesting features. Heidegger notes in his lectures on the *Freiheitsschrift* that we typically do not pay attention to the "is" in sentences but take it for granted.[30] Despite its importance, it remains hidden in plain sight. The unnamed X is also ignored, but unlike the "is," there is no direct reference to it in most sentences. Though silently present, the X has a fundamental—indeed, the most fundamental—role: it makes possible the connection of the subject and predicate, and thus the sentence could not be true without it.

In the cited line, Schelling also says that the subject ("A") and predicate ("B") are both *predicates* of X. This means that X is a ground in two senses: (1) It grounds the subject and predicate in the same way that a substance underlies its predicates. They are thus dependent on X for their existence. (2) It grounds the identity of subject and predicate. As their common substrate, X allows them to be connected, and thus is the condition of their being united—both in reality and in the sentence. A is B, only because of X.

Moreover, there are two peculiar features of the relation of A and B to X—features that will prove consequential for relating this account to the other accounts of the copula in the *Freiheitsschrift*. First, it is peculiar that the relation of A and B to X is one of predication, because there is *already* the relation of predication between A and B as subject and predicate. This would mean that B is a predicate of A *as well as* of X. Indeed, we will see other places where X shares some of the same features as A, especially when the logic of the copula is applied to the sentence "God is all things" (since God can function as both X and A). The second peculiarity is related. If A and B are both predicates of X, they have the same status vis-à-vis X. If this were an exhaustive account of the copula, we would have to say that there is a structural or formal symmetry, and thus the sentence "A is B" has the exact same meaning as "B is A": both affirm that A and B are predicates of a common substrate (X) without giving priority to either one.[31] However, we will see in Schelling's other accounts that statements of identity are not structurally symmetrical, and that "A is B" says something very different from "B is A."

Schelling gives one further description of X in the *Ages of the World*, which will later prove decisive for relating the copula to the *Ungrund*. Dismissing the view that the copula is just a logical connector, he writes: "The copula in a judgment is never a mere part of the judgment—even if we suppose it to be the most preeminent part—but its entire essence [*Wesen*], and the judgment is actually just the unfolded copula itself" (WA I, 28). The copula is the entire essence or being (*Wesen*) of the judgment. The judgment is the unfolded copula: this means that the judgment must somehow be enfolded within it. How so? We have seen that the subject and the predicate are aspects of X, which is the real copula. All the elements of the judgment—subject, predicate, and the "is" that signals their relation—are present already in that copula. The judgment merely expresses or unfolds what the copula already contains within itself.[32]

But what does Schelling mean by essence (*Wesen*) in this context? The word is often ambiguous in German philosophy. Like the Greek word οὐσία, *Wesen* can mean (1) essence or nature, or (2) a being (for example, *Lebewesen* means "living being"). Both senses have at their core the meaning "what it really is."[33] In my view, Schelling often exploits the word's ambiguity in such a way as to move beyond the distinction between the two meanings. In the context of the copula, both apply. On the one hand, the copula is a being—a substratum underlying subject and predicate. On the other hand, the copula is the essence of the judgment: its true nature—what it is essentially—is the copula. Later on we will see the importance of the word *Wesen* for applying the logic of the copula to the distinction between principles in God—and relating them to the *Ungrund*. In fact, Schelling hints at this deeper ontological connection in interpreting the fourth example sentence in the *Freiheitsschrift*: "What is necessary and what is free are explained as one, the meaning of which is that the same thing [*dasselbe*] (in the last analysis) which is the essence [*Wesen*] of the moral world is also the essence of nature" (SW VII, 342). Without giving it a name, Schelling refers to a mysterious X, the "same thing" that is the essence of both nature and the moral world.

ACCOUNT 2: THE SUBJECT RELATES TO THE PREDICATE AS *ANTECEDENS* TO *CONSEQUENS*.

Schelling formulates this account in a single sentence: "The ancient [*alte*] profoundly meaningful logic differentiated subject and predicate as what precedes and what follows (*antecedens et consequens*) and thereby expressed the real [*reelen*] meaning of the law of identity" (SW VII, 342). Despite the reference to the ancient provenance of this account, its proximate source again seems to be Leibniz. Though the terms *antecedens* and *consequens* can be traced to the logic of the Stoics, they were almost always applied to the clauses of conditional statements (if x, then y), not the subject and predicate in statements of the form A is B.[34]

Leibniz extends the application of the *antecedens* and *consequens* so that they can refer to the subject and the predicate *as well as* the parts of conditional statements.[35] In one of his papers, he writes: "A proposition is true when its predicate is contained in the subject, or *more generally*, when its consequent is contained in its antecedent."[36] Here Leibniz introduces the terms "antecedent" and "consequent" after mentioning that the subject contains the predicate in itself.[37] This suggests that the terminology is linked to the inclusion of the predicate in the subject—the equivalent of what I have labeled the third account of the copula. We will see that this link between the accounts is confirmed by Schelling's language when introducing that third account.

Even if the second account cannot ultimately be separated from the third, it is instructive to consider it on its own terms. Above all, it introduces a key concept not only for understanding the copula, but also for understanding the problem of ground: priority. The subject is

Identity, Ground, and the Meaning of the Copula in Judgments | 59

the *antecedens*, "that which precedes" (*Vorangehendes*). The predicate is the *consequens*, "that which follows" (*Folgendes*). That is, the subject is prior to the predicate. But in what sense? In the *Freiheitsschrift* Schelling proceeds as if the meaning of priority were clear. Of course, it is obvious that the subject is prior with respect to the (usual) order of the sentence, but this hardly adds to our understanding of the meaning of the copula or the subject-predicate relationship.

The concept of precedence plays a decisive role at key moments in the *Freiheitsschrift*. In these passages it is clear that Schelling has an appreciation for different senses of priority, even as he resists defining the precise sense he intends. When treating the "formal essence of freedom," for example, he speaks of an intelligible deed that "precedes consciousness, just as it precedes the essence [*Wesen*], indeed, first *makes* it" (SW VII, 386). A little later he associates this deed with a "life before this life" and then adds: "except that it is not to be thought as preceding with respect to time, since that which is intelligible is altogether outside of time" (SW VII, 387). Here Schelling defines the sense of priority only negatively: it is not temporal. Moreover, the intelligible act precedes the essence in such a way that it is able to make the latter.

The question of priority also arises in the discussion of gravity and light—the natural forces analogous to the two principles in God. Schelling writes: "Gravity precedes [*vorgeht*] light as its ever-dark ground, which itself is not *actu*, and flees into the night as the light (that which exists) dawns" (SW VII, 358). A few lines later he adds, "Incidentally, as far as this precedence [*Vorhergehen*] is concerned, it is to be thought neither as precedence according to time nor as priority of essence" (SW VII, 358). Here again Schelling defines the sense of priority negatively, and he does not explain what a priority of essence would mean.[38] Nonetheless, the first sentence hints at a link between ground and priority: gravity precedes light *as* its ground.[39]

To understand how Schelling conceives priority, we need to have in mind the different ways something can be prior—to be tested against the other things he says in the text. For help in formulating these possibilities, we can turn to another philosopher who emphasizes the concept of priority: Aristotle. In Book Δ of the *Metaphysics*, Aristotle enumerates the possible meanings of prior (πρότερον) and posterior (ὕστερον).[40] First, something can be prior because it is "nearer some beginning [ἀρχή] determined either absolutely and by nature, or by reference to something" (1018^b 10–11). In this sense, something can be prior with respect to place, time, power, and order. In Schelling's philosophy, this would apply to priority with respect to potency: lower potencies are "prior" insofar as they are nearer the beginning of the process of development and provide the foundation for what comes "after."[41] In another sense, something can be prior for knowledge: what we know first (our immediate perceptions) are not what is first by nature (first principles).

Of particular significance is Aristotle's final sense, what he calls priority "according to nature and substance" (κατὰ φύσιν καὶ οὐσίαν). He notes that, in a way, all things that are called prior are called prior with respect to this final sense (1019ᵃ 11–12). The things that are prior according to nature and substance are "those which can be without other things, while the others cannot be without *them*—a distinction which Plato used" (1019ᵃ 3–4). Here Aristotle defines priority in terms of grounding—but grounding of a particular kind. What is prior is a ground insofar as it is the conditio sine qua non or the condition of the possibility of what is posterior. As an example, Aristotle points to the priority of substance with respect to what is predicated of it. Substance, as substratum or subject (τὸ ὑποκείμενον), underlies its predicates, and thus it is their necessary condition. Without the underlying substance, the predicates would not exist. This, of course, has an obvious application to Schelling's antecedent-consequent account of the copula. The subject of the sentence is the logical equivalent of substance in reality. Just as a substance is the condition of the possibility of its predicates, so too is the subject of the sentence the condition of the possibility of *its* predicates.

That Schelling is aware of this sense of priority is evident from what he later says in the *Freiheitsschrift* about the relationship between God and the ground of his existence: "God is again the *prius* of the ground insofar as the ground, even as such could not exist if God did not exist *actu*" (SW VII, 358). The ground *could not exist* without God existing—and thus God is prior. (Incidentally, the word *prius* and the designation "the absolute *prius*" appear with some frequency in Schelling's later philosophy—thus showing his ongoing interest in priority.[42])

We should note something else about "priority according to nature and substance," since it will prove consequential for the problem of ground in Schelling. Though what is prior is the condition of what is posterior, this does not necessarily mean it is the *cause*. To use one of Aristotle's examples: one is prior to two, because if two (of something) exist, it follows that one exists.[43] But the existence of one hardly causes the existence of two. And yet Aristotle in the *Categories* does mention an additional sense of priority that involves causality: "For in those things which reciprocate as to implication of existence, that which is in some way the cause [αἴτιον] of the other's existence might reasonably be called prior by nature."[44] Here Aristotle acknowledges that there are cases that involve a reciprocal conditioning: x requires y, but y also requires x. In such cases, what is prior is the cause—that which determines the other to exist.

We can conclude, therefore, that the concept of priority in Aristotle is connected to grounding in two distinct senses. On the one hand, what is prior can be a ground in the sense of a condition of the possibility of what is posterior. On the other hand, what is prior can be a ground in the sense of cause or determining ground (*Bestimmungsgrund*). In fact, the latter sense of priority is reflected in our language. We refer to the effects of an event as its "consequences" (in German, *Folgen*), or the things that "follow from it." The effects *follow* the cause, not only in a temporal sense, but ontologically: the being of what comes after is derived from what comes before.[45]

With the possible senses of priority in mind, we can turn to the example Schelling discusses to illustrate the *antecedens-consequens* account. He notes that the sentence "the body is body" seems tautological, just repeating the subject in the predicate. If the sentence is meaningful, however, we think different things for each.[46] For the subject, we think of the unity of the concept of body, which is *antecedent*. For the predicate, we think of the various properties contained within the concept (like extension and mass), which are *consequent* (SW VII, 342).

How is the unity of the concept of body prior (or antecedent) to the multiple properties contained within that concept? Certainly, the reference to containment suggests that the properties are first enfolded within the concept (which is prior) and then come to be unfolded in the predicate (which is posterior)—an interpretation that aligns with the next account of the copula. But the concept is also prior to the properties in the sense of being the condition of their possibility: without the concept of the body there would be no bodily properties. The relationship between concept and properties is therefore analogous to the relationship between a substance and its predicates, which Aristotle cites as an example of priority "according to nature and substance." Moreover, Schelling elsewhere confirms the general notion that the subject is prior because the predicate would not be possible without it. In the 1806 *Aphorisms on the Philosophy of Nature*, he writes: "The relation of the predicate . . . to the subject . . . is a relation of something that could *not* exist in and for itself but exists [only] through conjunction with the subject" (SW VII, 219). We will see that this sense of priority has far-reaching systematic implications for Schelling. Indeed, one of my central claims is that "condition of the possibility" is the primary sense of ground in the *Freiheitsschrift*.

ACCOUNT 3: THE SUBJECT RELATES TO THE PREDICATE AS *IMPLICITUM* TO *EXPLICITUM*.

Schelling introduces this account immediately following his interpretation of the sentence "the body is body." He adds: "Just this is the meaning of another ancient explanation according to which subject and predicate are set against each other as what is enfolded to what is unfolded (*implicitum et explicitum*)" (SW VII, 342). The phrase "just this is the meaning" connects this account to the interpretation he had just given (associated with the second account). This provides us with the key to an initial understanding of this third account. The subject is what is enveloped (*das Eingewickelte*) or enfolded, insofar as many properties are contained within the unity of its concept (in the example sentence, the concept of the body). On the other hand, the predicate is what is unfolded (*das Entfaltete*) or developed, insofar as it expresses one or more of those contained properties. The subject-predicate relationship is a matter of *containment*.

Once again, this account draws from Leibniz, though it has deeper roots in Aristotle. According to Leibniz's inclusion theory of truth, "A proposition is true when its predicate is contained [*continetur*] in the subject, or more generally, when its consequent is contained in its antecedent."[47] As mentioned already, Leibniz uses the antecedent-consequent terminology at the same time that he discusses containment, thus confirming the link between Schelling's second and third accounts. The predicate *follows* the subject, the subject is prior to the predicate insofar as the predicate is already contained within the subject. But what does "containment" mean precisely? Is it the same as "being-enfolded" and "being-enveloped"—the other terms Schelling uses?

In the text titled "Primary Truths," Leibniz connects his containment theory to Aristotle: "The predicate or consequent is always in the subject or antecedent, and the nature of truth in general or the connection between the terms of a statement consists in this very thing, as Aristotle also observed."[48] According to Aristotle, a predicate is ἐν ὑποκειμένῳ, in an underlying subject. He defines substance (οὐσία) in the *Categories* as what is *not in* anything else, but has other things (predicates) in it.[49]

Accordingly, Leibniz applies what Aristotle says about the relationship between a substance and its predicates to the relationship between the subject and predicate in a sentence or proposition. To be sure, this relationship applies to the subject and predicate as concepts: the concept of the predicate is included in the concept of the subject. But the "ideal" realm of logic and concepts is closely connected to the "real" realm of metaphysics for Leibniz—just as it had been for Schelling in the texts leading up to the *Freiheitsschrift*. What Leibniz says about the relationship between the subject and predicate in a sentence reflects the relationship between the substance (monad) and its predicates in reality. Similarly, when applied to the sentence "God is all things," what Schelling says about the relationship between the subject and predicate bears directly on the nature of God and the relationship of God to finite things.

In any case, we have seen that Aristotle himself gives the relationship of substance to predicate as an example of priority "according to nature and substance."[50] In fact, our previous discussion of the priority of the unity of the concept to the multiplicity of its properties is merely another way of articulating this same relationship. The predicates depend on a substance that underlies them and is thereby the condition of the possibility of their existence. We will return to the substance-predicate relationship below when discussing Spinoza. The precise manner in which this relationship is defined has consequences for the doctrine of the immanence of all things in God—a doctrine that Schelling also conceives as "containment."[51]

And yet there is an important respect in which the relationship between subject (as enfolded) and predicate (as unfolded) is different from the relationship between a substance and its predicates. The opposition is not between (1) a subject abstracted from all predicates and (2) one or more of its predicates. Rather, the opposition is between (1) the subject with all of its predicates enfolded within it and (2) one or more of these predicates unfolded. That is, the same predicate or properties that appear as the predicate of the sentence are *already* present in the subject of the sentence—albeit implicitly. There is therefore a repetition or a doubling of the predicates in the subject and predicate of the sentence. This has consequences for the sense in which the subject is prior. The subject is not only the necessary condition of the predicate; it also determines the predicate's content insofar as this content is merely the repetition of what is already contained in the subject. It is not the case that *any* property can appear as the predicate of a sentence—if the sentence is to be true. Rather, a property can only appear as the predicate if the subject already contains it implicitly. The subject thus determines what the predicate of the sentence can be.

In fact, this determination of the predicate by the subject provides the basis for the connection of Leibniz's containment theory of truth to the principle of ground. If every true sentence involves a repetition of *the same* predicate, it also involves an *identity* of the predicate in the subject with the predicate in the predicate. In tautologies this identity is explicit—for example, "The marble sculpture is marble." For most sentences, however, it is only implicit. According to Leibniz, even when the identity is not explicit, it is possible to show that the predicate is contained in the subject by means of an a priori proof. This provides the ground or the sufficient reason why the sentence is true by showing the grounding of the predicate in the subject. The principle of ground, therefore, claims that all truths that are not explicit identities—which require no grounding—can be led back to identity by means of an a priori proof.[52] In Heidegger's formulation, "The *principium rationis* is the principle for unfolding the identity that is to be revealed."[53]

Thus, the repetition or doubling of the predicate—both in the subject and the predicate of the sentence—provides the basis for the principle of ground in Leibniz. The subject is a ground of the predicate of the sentence, not only as its necessary condition, but as its *determining* ground (*Bestimmungsgrund*), and the principle of ground in Leibniz states that this determining connection between subject and predicate can always be revealed (at least by an infinite mind). But there is a questionable assumption in Leibniz's connection of the principle of ground to the containment of the predicate in the subject. Saying that a true sentence is always an explicit or implicit identity is different from saying that a true sentence can always be *revealed* to be an identity, that is, resolved into an identity through an a priori proof. It is at least conceivable that the predicate be contained in the subject, but this containment cannot be shown.

These remarks on the need to reveal an underlying identity point to a feature that is implied in Schelling's account but not discussed explicitly in the text: there must be a mediating process between the subject (as enfolded) and the predicate (as unfolded). We have seen that the subject and predicate correspond to two *states* of the predicate: the state of being enfolded (subject), and the state of being unfolded (predicate). But how is there a transition from one state to the other? This can only happen through a process of unfolding (*Entfaltung*) by which the predicate enfolded in the subject comes to be revealed in the predicate of the sentence. The logic

Identity, Ground, and the Meaning of the Copula in Judgments | 65

of the copula provides the framework for *revelation*, one of the central themes of the *Freiheitsschrift* and Schelling's later work.

This connection to the process of revelation has consequences for the nature of the grounding relationship between subject and predicate in the sentence. We have seen the sense in which the subject determines the predicate. What is not determined, however, is that there should be an unfolding of what is implicitly contained in the subject. The subject, considered in itself, need not be developed. It could remain forever enfolded. As a consequence, the subject (considered as what is enfolded) does not completely determine the predicate (considered as what unfolded). It is indeed the ground of the possibility of the predicate, and it determines the predicate's possible content (though we will see in the next chapter that Schelling qualifies this with respect to God's grounding). Nevertheless, purely as what is enfolded, the subject does not determine the process of unfolding that results in the predicate of the sentence. To anticipate later material: this status of the enfolded subject corresponds to the *Ungrund*, which on its own is closed off to revelation.

At this point, we can return to the sentence "God is all things," the basic statement of pantheism. If we apply the present account of the copula, "God" (the subject) is what is enfolded, and "all things" (the predicate) is what is unfolded. This means all things are somehow enfolded or hidden in God, and there is a consequent unfolding in which they emerge into appearance. In the polemic against Jacobi (1812), one of the few things he published after the *Freiheitsschrift*, Schelling articulates this same unfolding but in a slightly different way, distinguishing between two "states" of God: "I posit God as the first and the last, as A and Ω, but as A he is not what he is as Ω . . . [as A] he would be the *not-unfolded* [*unentfaltet*] God, *deus implicitus*, since as Ω he is *deus explicitus*" (SW VIII, 81).[54] This quotation allows us to note an ambiguity in the phrase "what is unfolded." On the one hand, it can refer to what is originally contained within the subject and subsequently comes to light. On the other hand, it can also refer to the subject, that *in which* something is originally contained—just as Schelling refers to God as "unfolded" in this quotation.[55] Thus, the subject and predicate of the sentence not only correspond to two states of the predicate; they also correspond to two states of the *subject* (enfolded vs. unfolded).

I will briefly note the connection of this theme of an unfolding God to Schelling's doctrine of potencies, which we will discuss in more detail in chapter 4. Initially, all the potencies are contained within God, but in an undifferentiated fashion. The creation of the world is the progressive unfolding of these potencies in order—from the outermost to the innermost. From the beginning, the potencies are contained "potentially" (*potentiâ*) in God, but only gradually do they enfold as existing "actually" (*actu*) as they successively come to appearance.[56]

ACCOUNT 4: THE SUBJECT RELATES TO THE PREDICATE AS GROUND TO CONSEQUENCE.

Already in the previous accounts we have seen connections to grounding. Somewhat later in the *Freiheitsschrift*, in the passage about the law of ground, Schelling makes explicit the role of grounding in understanding the copula: "In the relation of subject and predicate we have already shown [*aufgezeigt*] that of ground and consequence, and the law of the ground is for that reason just as original as the law of identity" (SW VII, 346). Though Schelling says he has "already shown" this relation, he had never used the language of ground explicitly in the previous discussion of the copula. Nevertheless, it is precisely the grounding relation between subject and predicate that provides the basis ("for that reason") for asserting the co-originality of the two laws.

Even if Schelling had not explicitly mentioned this grounding relation, there are two ways in which he could claim to have "shown" it: (1) The other accounts of the copula—and the accompanying examples—have implicit connections to grounding. (2) Schelling does use the language of ground and consequence when characterizing the relationship between God and things in Spinoza. This treatment of Spinoza (SW VII, 340–41) immediately precedes the discussion of the copula (SW VII, 341–42) and provides the context for the latter. Schelling asserts directly that the misinterpretations of Spinoza arise from a misunderstanding of identity and the meaning of the copula (SW VII, 341). To this extent, the subject-predicate relationship in statements of identity is meant to shed light on the relationship between God and things in Spinoza—and vice versa. Moreover, the discussion of Spinoza introduces a key concept for understanding the copula and its connection to grounding: affirmation.

In the passage on Spinoza, Schelling is characterizing the dependence of finite things. The aim is to demonstrate their "differentiation" (*Unterscheidung*) from God within Spinoza's pantheism: God is different from both the individual thing and the sum total of individual things. Speaking of the concept of God in Spinoza, Schelling writes: "The latter concept alone is what is independent and original, alone what affirms itself, that to which everything else can be related only as affirmed, only as consequence to ground (SW VII, 340).⁵⁷ God relates to things as ground (*Grund*) to consequence (*Folge*). If pantheism can be expressed in the sentence "God is all things," this means that the subject is ground, and the predicate is consequence—as Schelling will claim in the later passage.

In what sense is God the ground of things? Schelling states that everything besides God is "affirmed" (*Bejahtes*) and thus a consequence of God as ground. In other words, God grounds things by *affirming* them. Notably, the language of affirmation does not actually appear in Spinoza. The term comes from the traditional table of logical judgments, which Kant famously employs in the first *Critique* (A 70–72/B 95–97) in parallel to the table of the categories (A 80/B 106). (Reality is the category that corresponds to affirmative judgments.) The language of affirmation appears a few times in Schelling's early, Fichte-inspired writings. Here Schelling uses the word "affirm" more or less as a synonym for the word "posit" (*setzen*), one of the key terms in Fichte's *Wissenschaftslehre*. For example, in the essay *On the I as Principle of Philosophy*, Schelling writes: "[The ultimate principle of knowledge] has to exist . . . because it is thought: its affirming [*Bejahen*] must be contained in its thinking; it must bring forth [*hervorbringen*] itself through its thinking" (SW I, 163). This passage gives Schelling's interpretation of the self-positing character of the absolute I: its being follows from its thinking.⁵⁸

The use of the word "affirm" in this early passage goes beyond its logical meaning. It has to do with the *being* of something, not just the *truth* of a proposition. Here, the I posits itself; in the passage in the *Freiheitsschrift*, God affirms himself. Positing, affirming have to do with bringing into being, or grounding something in its being. This transferal of a logical term into a metaphysical context is in line with the unification of logic and metaphysics in Schelling's *Identitätsphilosophie*. Incidentally, the word "posit" (*setzen*), which plays such an important role in Fichte and many of Schelling's writings, also has its origins as a philosophical term in logic.⁵⁹

Schelling retains the Fichtean language of "positing" through the writings of his *Identitätsphilosophie*—for example, in the pivotal *Darstellung meines Systems* (1801).⁶⁰ In the 1804 *Würzburg System*, however, he introduces the Latin cognates *affirmieren/Affirmation* as his preferred way of designating positing and self-positing activity.⁶¹ In this same work, Schelling employs the distinction we have seen in the *Freiheitsschrift* between (1) what is self-affirming and (2) what is affirmed, and uses this distinction to define absoluteness:

> *Only the absolute or God is such that it affirms itself and thus is affirmed by itself.* For, according to the general idea, what is *absolute* exists [*ist*] of itself and through itself. But to exist from itself and through itself means *to exist through its own affirmation.* . . . On the other hand, what is not absolute in general is that which is determined to exist through another, [or that] whose affirmation lies outside of itself. . . . The cause [*Ursache*] of a thing is what affirms the thing; the thing as effect is that which is affirmed. Both are necessarily one in the absolute, but not one in that which is not absolute. (§7, SW VI, 148)

The distinction between the absolute and the non-absolute is defined in terms of the distinction between self-affirmation and affirmation by another. Later in the *Freiheitsschrift*, Schelling will list "self-affirmation" (*Selbstbejahung*) as one of the predicates of primordial being (*Ursein*), which he identifies with willing: "Wollen ist Ursein" (SW VII, 350). In light of this passage, we can say that *absoluteness* is one of the predicates of primordial being as well.

In the passage, the affirmation in question seems to be deterministic: Schelling describes what is not absolute as being *affirmed*, and thus "determined" to exist by another. If God affirms all things, this would mean that God determines all things—thus jeopardizing their freedom. We should note, however, that Schelling writes "determined to exist" (*zum Dasein bestimmt*). In other words, God determines *that* finite things exist, but this (potentially) leaves undetermined *how* they exist and what their concrete features are.

Indeed, this interpretation is supported by Schelling's discussion of Spinoza in the *Freiheitsschrift*. Spinoza's concept of finite things as mere modes of God is "admittedly a purely negative one that expresses nothing essential or positive. Initially, however, it serves merely to determine the relationship of things to God but not what they may be, considered for themselves" (SW VII, 344). In this passage Schelling distinguishes (1) the relationship of things to God from (2) what they are considered for themselves. The former involves a "purely negative" concept, the latter something "essential or positive." Without God, the finite things could not exist—but this does not determine what they are (positively) or for themselves. In any case, we will see in the next chapter how Schelling introduces a new sense of ground to describe God's non-deterministic affirmation of created things.

Finally, Schelling's other comments about affirmation in the *Würzburg System* help us to relate this discussion back to the meaning of the copula. All knowledge (*Wissen*) is an affirmation, and thus involves something that affirms (*ein Affirmierendes*) and something that is affirmed (*ein Affirmiertes*).[62] What affirms is subjective, what is affirmed is objective. In other words, knowledge involves an essential unity of thought (the subjective) and object (the objective). This same subject-object, affirming-affirmed structure of knowledge is reflected in the structure of sentences.[63] The subject of the sentence is what affirms, the predicate is what is affirmed. In the case of the principle A = A, the subject (the first "A") is absolutely identified with the predicate (the second "A"). This means that what affirms (the subject) is absolutely identified with what is affirmed (the predicate), and thus the principle A = A expresses the self-affirmation of absolute identity (§5, SW VI, 145–46).

We have already seen how Schelling, in his discussion of Spinoza in the *Freiheitsschrift*, identifies the relationship between what affirms and what is affirmed as a relationship between ground and consequence (SW VII, 340). If the relationship between the subject and predicate of a sentence is also a relationship of what affirms to what is affirmed (as Schelling states in the *Würzburg System*), we can conclude that subject and predicate *also* relate to each other as ground to consequence. And this is precisely the claim that Schelling makes later in the *Freiheitsschrift*, immediately before he mentions the law of ground (SW VII, 346). In this way, the discussion of Spinoza relates to the meaning of the copula by means of the concept of "affirmation."

3. Conclusion: The Unity of Schelling's Account of the Copula?

In this chapter, we have examined in detail Schelling's explanations of the meaning of the copula in judgments, with a view to understanding the relationship between identity and ground. We have seen that Schelling's discussion of the copula in the *Freiheitsschrift* is important for two main reasons. First, it sheds light on the relationship between God and things by defining the word "is" in the statement "God is all things" (the basic statement of pantheism). As we have seen, "is" does not exclude difference between subject and predicate but requires it: the subject (God) relates to the predicate (all things) as *antecedens* to *consequens*, as what is enfolded to what is unfolded, as ground to consequence.

Second, the discussion of the copula also prepares us to understand the meaning of Schelling's statement that the law of ground is just as original as the law of identity (SW VII, 346). He connects this statement with the claim that the relation of subject and predicate is that of ground and consequence, and we will examine the link between the two claims in the next chapter. In any case, we have seen two possible ways the subject can be the ground of the predicate: (1) as condition of its possibility and (2) as its determining ground. On the one hand, the subject makes possible the predicate, insofar as it provides the underlying substance in which the predicate inheres. On the other hand, the subject determines the predicate, insofar as it already contains the (enfolded) predicate in itself, and it posits or "affirms" its existence. In the next chapter, we will examine how Schelling attempts to resolve this tension between determining and making possible, thus showing how freedom is compatible with divine grounding.

In concluding this chapter, I would like to reflect on the *Freiheitsschrift*'s theory of the copula as a whole. In particular, I want to pose the following questions: How do the four accounts fit together—are they even compatible? And what is the precise connection between the meaning of the copula and the law of identity? Schelling clearly thinks of the two as a pair: the misinterpretations of Spinoza arise from "the general misunderstanding of the law of identity or the meaning of the copula in judgment" (SW VII, 341). But how exactly do his reflections on the copula relate to the law of identity?

With respect to the compatibility of the accounts of the copula, they do not contradict each other explicitly. Nevertheless, there is a clear divide between the first account (mediated connection through X) and the three remaining accounts. As we have seen, the first account considered by itself treats the subject and predicate in the same way: both are aspects of a single underlying X. This is in clear contrast to the other three accounts, which posit an asymmetrical relationship between subject and predicate. However, this does not mean that the first account is necessarily incompatible with the others. The first account only treats the relation of subject and predicate to X, without treating how they relate to each other. Thus, it can be true that A and B are aspects of a single underlying thing, and at the same time true that A is the ground of B—insofar as the predicate is unable to exist (as an aspect of the underlying X) unless the subject is also present as an aspect of the underlying X. For example, in the sentence "This body is blue," being this body and being blue are two aspects of the same X. And yet the subject "this body" is still a ground of the predicate "blue," insofar as "blue" could not be an aspect of X unless X is also a particular body. Colors require bodies as underlying substrates: if X were not a body, X could not be blue.

The second and fourth accounts of the copula are the most general. The fourth, as I have formulated it, states that the subject is the ground of the predicate. The second account states that the subject precedes or is prior to the predicate. As we have seen in Aristotle, one of the ways in which the subject can be prior is by being the ground or condition of the possibility of the predicate. Thus, the second and fourth accounts can fit together, and both exhibit a certain flexibility or indeterminacy, insofar as it is not specified exactly what it means to be "prior" or what it means to be a "ground"—although we were able to draw certain conclusions about this from Schelling's examples. From the perspective of the coherence of Schelling's explanations of the copula, the account that is most problematic is the third (*implicitum-explicitum*). This is not incompatible with the other accounts as such. We have seen how the subject, as enfolded, can be the ground of the predicate, as unfolded (and, as ground, the subject is prior to the predicate). And what is enfolded (the subject) and what is unfolded (the predicate) can both be aspects of an underlying X.

The problem arises when we attempt to apply this third account of the copula to some of Schelling's other examples, particularly "the perfect is the imperfect" and "good is evil." These sentences can be interpreted relatively easily according to the first, second, and fourth accounts of the copula: The same thing (X) that is perfect in one respect is imperfect in another respect (*first account*). The imperfect relies on the perfect for its being, and thus the imperfect is grounded by the perfect (*fourth account*). The perfect, as ground of the imperfect, is thereby prior to the imperfect (*second account*). But then we come to the third account. In what sense can we say that the predicate is enfolded or otherwise contained in the subject in the above examples? There is no obvious sense in which we can affirm that good, as such, contains evil—or that the latter is enfolded in the former. To do so would seem to destroy goodness as such.[64]

The problematic examples follow directly after Schelling's remark about the false assumption made in relation to the "higher application [*Anwendung*] of the law of identity" (SW VII, 341). The implication is that these examples are illustrations of the law's higher application. Indeed, these examples, as well as the two that follow them—"the necessary and the free are one" and "the soul is one with the body"—depart most radically from ordinary language or "common sense" logic. The fact is, the third account of the copula is what anchors Schelling's explanation of the copula, considered as a whole, to everyday speech. Leibniz's inclusion theory, on which the account is based, ultimately comes from Aristotle and reflects the relationship between subject and predicate in ordinary language. Without the third account of the copula, sentences are possible that are completely foreign to "common sense." "Good is evil" is one such sentence.

What, then, are we to make of the coherence of Schelling's account of the copula as a whole? One possible way to resolve the difficulties is to allow that not every one of the accounts applies to every instance of the copula. In particular, in instances of what Schelling refers to as the "higher application of the law of identity," the predicate need not be included or enfolded in the subject. Nevertheless, all of the accounts of the copula *can* apply to other instances of the copula, and indeed sentences in ordinary language can be interpreted according to all four accounts. However, this approach to the difficulty has the disadvantage of dividing Schelling's account into two, without providing a clear explanation of *why* the third account applies to some judgments but need not apply to the copula's higher application. In any case, it is clear that Schelling wishes to provide an account of the copula that can explain instances of the word "is" in ordinary language without being limited to ordinary language. Everyday speech often reflects the assumptions of "common sense" (*gesunder Menschenverstand*), which is defined by what Schelling had called "reflection" in earlier writings. Philosophy must sometimes express itself in a language that appears strange if not absurd from that perspective.

Turning now to the second question, what is the precise relationship between the copula and the law of identity? Schelling identifies the source of the misinterpretations of Spinoza as the "general misunderstanding of the law of identity or the meaning of the copula in judgment," but in the sequel he discusses only the meaning of the copula directly. To clarify this relationship, we can begin by distinguishing the law of identity (A = A) from what one could call "statements of identity." These are sentences of the form *S* is *P*, such as the examples that Schelling gives to illustrate the meaning of the copula.[65] If Schelling is correct in saying that all propositions state the identity of subject and predicate (SW VII, 341), then all truths are in fact statements of identity.[66] The copula is present in both the law of identity (A is A) and a statement of identity: both contain the word "is." To this extent, what Schelling says about the copula in general should also apply to the copula as it appears in the law of identity. But this formulation puts things in reverse. The copula in the law of identity is not one instance of the copula among many. Rather, it is the *original* copula, which is also expressed in every (lower) statement of identity. The principle of identity, as the principle of all philosophy, is at the same time the principle of all truth,[67] because all truths share its form or structure (S is P).[68]

We can therefore explain the connection that Schelling draws between misunderstanding the law of identity and the meaning of the copula. Because of the essential connection between the two, if one misunderstands the role of the copula in uniting subject and predicate, one misunderstands the nature of absolute identity, and vice versa. Thus, if one misinterprets the copula as an indicator of sameness devoid of difference, one will also misinterpret the law of identity as a law of undifferentiated sameness.

Finally, since this law of identity expresses the essence of absolute identity or God, these reflections on the copula shed light on the innermost nature of God himself. As Schelling writes in his 1806 *Aphorisms*: "Regard that law in itself, know the content that it has, and you will view God" (SW VII, 148). In the next two chapters, we will see the consequences of these reflections on the copula for understanding the divine nature.

3

The Creative Unity of the Law of Identity

The last chapter laid the groundwork for understanding the precise relationship between the principles of identity and ground in the *Freiheitsschrift*. Having noted the ways in which the identity expressed by the copula involves a grounding relation, we come now to the remarkable passage in which Schelling mentions the "law of ground"—the only explicit reference to the principle in the entire work. But the passage is significant for reasons that go beyond understanding the place of a fundamental metaphysical principle in Schelling's philosophy. As we will see, the principle expresses the relation between God and all things—one of the most important relations for the problem of ground. And in defining the way in which God grounds all things, Schelling introduces a sense of ground that allows God to create without jeopardizing our freedom as creatures. At the same time, it allows Schelling to show how a pantheistic God can be a Creator—thus going beyond Spinoza's pantheism and answering one of Jacobi's most incisive objections.

As we saw in the last chapter, the context of Schelling's account of the copula was the discussion of the meaning of pantheism and its compatibility with human freedom. At the end of this discussion, after treating the fourth and final candidate for the definition of pantheism, Schelling draws the following conclusion: "Hence, it appears that the denial or assertion of freedom in general is based on something completely other than the assumption or non-assumption of pantheism (the immanence of things in God)" (SW VII, 345). This conclusion not only comes down decisively against the claim that all systems, *insofar as* they are pantheistic, must deny freedom; it also provides Schelling's conception of the true sense of pantheism: "the immanence of things in God." As we saw in the discussion of copula in the last chapter, the sentence "God is all things" is a statement of this immanence, because—according to the third account of the copula—the predicate is contained in the subject. Thus, immanence is precisely the *being-in* or containment of all things in God.

But Schelling does not stop at his negative conclusion that freedom and pantheism are not incompatible. He also wishes to explain the *appearance* of incompatibility, and from there provide a positive account of the relationship between God and things. Earlier, immediately before his discussion of the copula, Schelling had cited the misunderstanding of the law of identity as the reason for the misinterpretations of the relationship between God and things in Spinoza (SW VII, 341). Now, after concluding the discussion of pantheism, Schelling cites this misunderstanding again—this time as the source of the appearance that freedom and identity are incompatible: "For, if, admittedly, it seems at first glance as if freedom, which was unable to maintain itself in opposition [*Gegensatz*] to God, had perished in identity here, then one can say that this appearance is only the result of an imperfect and empty notion of the law of identity" (SW VII, 345).

Of course, the discussion of the copula had shown that statements of identity not only allow for but require difference between subject and predicate in the statement "God is all things." But Schelling has not yet shown that such a difference provides enough space for freedom. Granted that things are different from God, can the freedom of these things "maintain itself in opposition to God"? To answer this question, Schelling further characterizes the principle of identity:

> This principle does not express a unity which, turning itself in the circle of sameness [*Einerleiheit*], would not be progressive and, thus, unfeeling and non-living. The unity of this law is an immediately creative one. In the relation of subject and predicate we have already shown that of ground and consequence, and the law of ground is for that reason just as original as the law of identity. Therefore, the eternal must also be a ground immediately and as it is in itself. (SW VII, 345–46)

I will devote this chapter to interpreting these sentences and the equally remarkable passages that follow. My goal is threefold: (1) to understand more precisely how the law of identity relates to the law of ground; (2)

to determine in what senses God is the ground of things; and (3) to see what consequences the grounding relation between God and things has for the possibility of freedom.

1. The Unity Expressed by the Law of Identity

Schelling begins the cited passage by contrasting two kinds of unity—one that the principle of identity does express, and one it does not. It is tempting to view the rejection of lifeless, monotonous unity as Schelling's answer to Hegel's quip about the absolute as the "night in which all cows are black" (PhG §16; HW 3, 22), and Schelling may indeed have Hegel in mind. However, Schelling had long distinguished kinds of identity in his *Identitätsphilosophie*—in particular, (1) relative identity, which is opposed to difference, and (2) absolute identity, which includes difference within itself (cf. SW IV, 235–36). The first is the understanding's conception of identity; the second is the true identity of reason (SW VII, 52). Indeed, in the *Stuttgart Private Lectures* delivered the following year, Schelling maintains, somewhat defensively, "I have always declared that absolute identity for me is not *mere* identity, but identity of unity and opposition" (SW VII, 445).

In any case, how does Schelling characterize the unity expressed by the law of identity in this passage? The first thing to note is that he uses the word "unity" (*Einheit*) and not "identity." This is nothing new: in previous works, particularly in *Bruno* (1802), Schelling had sometimes substituted the word "unity" in contexts where "identity" would normally appear. This provides us with a helpful translation of the word "identity," which avoids associations with sameness that the latter normally carries. In the *Stuttgart Private Lectures*, Schelling even defines absolute identity as "an organic unity of all things" (SW VII, 421–22).

The passage in the *Freiheitsschrift* begins with a description of the kind of unity that is *not* expressed by the law of identity. This inferior unity is characterized negatively: it is "not progressive," and thus "unfeeling" (*unempfindlich*) and "non-living" (*unlebendig*). By implication, the unity that *is* expressed by the law of identity is progressive, feeling, and living. The inferior unity is not progressive, because it merely "turns itself in a circle of sameness [*Einerleiheit*]." This characterization resembles Schelling's earlier description of the "merely formal" law of identity, in which you can only recognize the "empty repetition of your own thinking" (SW

VII, 147–48). This "merely formal" law can be formulated: "If I think A, I think A" (SW VII, 218). It merely repeats what one thinks—that is, it never leaves the circle of one's own thought. It goes without saying that such a conception of identity excludes the possibility of difference.

In contrast to an empty unity "spinning in a circle," the unity of the law of identity is *progressive*. Below we will see the full implications of this word. At this point, we can note that Schelling is not simply referring to a progression within *thought*. It is true that the traditional (logical) law of identity only deals with conceptual relations and has nothing to say about whether things actually exist. In Schelling's *Identitätsphilosophie*, however, the law had been transformed, becoming "the highest existential principle" (SW VII, 218).[1] In other words, the unity expressed in the principle brings forth (or grounds) existence—and in this sense it is progressive. Here already we have a first clue about the co-originality of the principles of identity and ground.

This unity's other attributes are "living," "feeling," and "creative." In a passage from his 1806 anti-Fichte polemic (published before Hegel's *Phenomenology*), Schelling uses remarkably similar language to contrast the (higher) identity of reason with the identity of the understanding. The only identity the understanding can know is "the negation of opposition [*Gegensatz*], that is, empty, uncreative [*unschöpferische*] unity" (SW VII, 52). Reason's unity, on the other hand, is a "living identity." What makes it living? The presence of opposition: "There must be opposition, because there must be life; for opposition itself is the life and the movement in unity" (SW VII, 52).[2] Along these lines, Schelling formulates the "basic law of opposition" in the *Stuttgart Private Lectures* (1810): "No life without opposition" (*Ohne Gegensatz kein Leben*) (SW VII, 435). The dynamic nature of life requires a tension and interplay among opposed elements within a living whole. And Schelling had already implied that the ability to "maintain itself in *opposition* to God" is a necessary condition of freedom.

Schelling concludes the passage in the anti-Fichte polemic by characterizing the unity of reason as "dynamic" (*beweglich*), "gushing forth" (*quellende*), and "creative" (*schaffende*) (SW VII, 52). In the *Freiheitsschrift*, he also says that the unity of the law of identity is "immediately creative." But how can unity be "creative"—and *what* does it create? Creation is a kind of grounding; that which is created is *grounded* in a certain sense. We will therefore find answers to these questions when we determine in what sense the creative unity is a ground.

2. The Co-originality of the Laws of Identity and Ground

If we continue with the passage on the laws of identity and ground in the *Freiheitsschrift*, we can observe that the next sentences contain a pair of inferences. After noting that the relation of subject to predicate is one of ground to consequence, Schelling concludes that it is "for this reason" (*darum*) that the law of ground is just as original as the law of identity. From this, he draws another conclusion: "therefore" (*deswegen*) the eternal must also be a ground immediately and as it is in itself. But it is not at all obvious how these three statements relate in such a way that one can infer one from the other. Interpreting the passage is also complicated by the fact that Schelling never says precisely what he means by "the law of ground." In previous writings, he had transformed the meaning of the law of identity: instead of being a purely logical principle, it comes to express the self-affirmation of the Absolute. We therefore cannot take for granted that "law of ground" here simply means "principle of sufficient reason," as traditionally understood.

To interpret this passage, we need to reconstruct the argument that Schelling does not spell out, but to which he points by using inferential language. As with so many other passages in the *Freiheitsschrift*, this requires examining other passages within the same work as well as other Schelling texts that treat the same themes in a more developed manner. Of course, we cannot simply assume that his position on a given topic remains unchanged throughout his works, and that we can understand what he is saying in the *Freiheitsschrift* simply by reading his discussion of the same theme in another work. The proof of the usefulness of other texts will be the *Freiheitsschrift* itself: do they help to make the thought within it more intelligible on its own terms? I should note that these texts come from the period of the *Identitätsphilosophie* (1801–6). It is sometimes debated among Schelling commentators whether the *Freiheitsschrift* is in continuity with this previous period or breaks with it, going in a radically new direction.[3] In my view, this is a false choice: like other works by Schelling, the *Freiheitsschrift* builds on previous texts even as it makes significant innovations. If the present passage is largely in continuity with the *Identitätsphilosophie*, we will see more discontinuity in the chapters that follow.

We have discussed in the last chapter the first claim in the series of inferences, namely, that the subject relates to the predicate as ground to consequence. From this Schelling infers that the law of ground is just as original as the law of identity. How does this follow? The missing piece in the puzzle, it seems, is the meaning of "the law of ground." If we know what Schelling means by this law, we can relate it to what we have already discussed about the law of identity and the relationship between subject and the predicate. But how do we determine what Schelling means, if this is his only explicit reference to the law of ground in the *Freiheitsschrift*, and he rarely mentions it by name in works preceding or following its publication?[4] Although we cannot take for granted that the law in the *Freiheitsschrift* has the same meaning as the traditional principle of sufficient reason, it is likely to have some resemblance to the latter. If we are able to find something in Schelling that resembles the traditional principle of ground *and* fits coherently into the series of inferences in the passage of the *Freiheitsschrift*, this will be strong evidence that we have found the meaning of the law of ground in this context.

The traditional principle of sufficient reason in its short formulation reads: "Nothing is without reason" or "Nothing is without a ground." The principle as stated has two essential elements: (1) the *universality* of (2) *being grounded*. The universality of the principle is what makes it a law: it applies to *all* things insofar as they exist. The second element, "being grounded," is what is attributed universally. Depending on how the principle is interpreted, "being grounded" can have different meanings, and we can leave its precise meaning open for the moment. Does anything in the *Freiheitsschrift* share these same elements? In other words, is there in the *Freiheitsschrift* a claim that all things are grounded? There is such a claim; in fact, it has been "under our noses" for some time. Schelling's entire discussion of the copula arose out of a need to understand the meaning of the "is" in the sentence "God is all things." According to the fourth account of the copula, the subject relates to the predicate as ground to consequence. This means that the subject ("God") is the ground of the predicate ("all things"). But if God is the ground of all things, it is also true that all things are grounded. Therefore, the sentence "God is all things" contains the two essential elements of the law of ground: it affirms the universality of being grounded.[5]

In the next section I will have more to say about the consequences of reformulating the principle of ground in this way. But first we have to be sure that this formulation fits into the context in the *Freiheitsschrift* and allows us to make sense of the inferences Schelling draws. The first inference reads: "In the relation of subject and predicate we have already shown that of ground and consequence, and the law of the ground is for that reason just as original as the law of identity" (SW VII, 345–46). As we have just seen, the first claim in this sentence (subject-predicate relate as ground-consequence) allows us to conclude that the statement "God is all things" is a formulation of the principle of ground. But what does this tell us about the relationship between the laws of ground and identity? How can we infer that the law of ground is just as original?

To answer these questions, we need to determine how the law of identity relates to the sentence "God is all things." Of course, this sentence is what I have called a "statement of identity," because it has the form A is B. But it is more than just one statement of identity among others. As we have noted already, this sentence is a formulation of pantheism, understood as the immanence of all things in God. In other contexts, Schelling refers to this same doctrine of immanence as the "identity of the infinite and the finite"—in particular, when discussing the relationship between God and things in Spinoza (SW I, 313–14). This same language is also present in Schelling's discussion of Spinoza in the *Freiheitsschrift*. He refers to things as "what is finite" (SW VII, 340) and God as "infinite substance" (SW VII, 344). Thus, we can translate the sentence "God is all things" as "the infinite is the finite."

How does this help relate this formulation of the principle of ground to the principle of identity? The phrase "identity of the infinite and the finite" is one of Schelling's expressions for absolute identity itself.[6] In the 1806 *Aphorisms* Schelling relates the principle of identity to this expression: "The sentence A = A, the principle of identity, states nothing but the eternal copula of that which exists in itself with that which cannot exist in and for itself, i.e., the *absolute identity of the infinite and the finite*" (SW VII, 219).[7] In other words, because God is the infinite and things are finite, the principle of identity expresses the absolute identity of God and things—the very same identity expressed in the sentence "God is all things." We can conclude, therefore, that the sentence "God is all things" is just as original as the law of identity, because both express the same identity of the infinite and the finite. And, because the sentence "God is all things" is a way of formulating the law of ground, we can conclude that the law of ground is just as original as the law of identity. In fact, we can go even further. The law of identity, by expressing the identity of the infinite and the finite, also expresses the universality of grounding. Thus, the law of identity is itself a law of ground.

We can therefore ask: are the laws of identity and ground *two* laws or *one*? The conclusion of the last paragraph suggests *one*, but Schelling's formulation in the *Freiheitsschrift* seems to require *two*. I believe the answer is "both." The law of identity contains within itself the law of ground as one of its aspects: according to the law of identity, God grounds all things. To this extent, there is just one law.[8] But to the extent that the law of ground is *one* aspect of the law of identity and does not exhaust it,[9] we can separate them and speak of two laws. If my interpretation is correct, it would explain why Schelling does not speak of the principle of ground in other texts: it is an aspect of the principle of identity, and this aspect is treated in his discussions of the highest principle and the nature of identity.

Before we consider the consequences of the co-originality of the two laws or principles, we still have Schelling's second inference to consider. After stating that the law of ground is just as original as the law of identity, he writes: "Therefore, the eternal must also be a ground immediately and as it is in itself" (SW VII, 346). The phrase "the eternal" (*das Ewige*) seems to come out of nowhere. Is this simply another way of referring to God? One clue is Schelling's very similar statement a couple of lines earlier: "The unity of [the law of identity] is an immediately creative one" (SW VII, 345). Both this sentence and the line about the eternal as ground use the word "immediately" (*unmittelbar*) in reference to grounding or creativity: the eternal is immediately ground; the unity of the law of identity is immediately creative. In context, therefore, we can infer that the phrase "the eternal" also refers to the unity of the law of identity. Of course, this unity is precisely *absolute identity*, which Schelling identifies in other contexts with God.

This identification is confirmed by Schelling's use of the word "eternal" in other texts that treat the "absolute bond" or copula, which is another way he refers to absolute identity in the years immediately preceding the *Freiheitsschrift*. In these texts, Schelling also calls the absolute copula the "eternal copula"[10] or simply "the eternal."[11] However, if the phrase "the eternal" refers to the unity of the law of identity or the absolute copula in the *Freiheitsschrift*, this presents a problem. It lies in the question: what exactly is the ground in the passage? So far, we have been focusing on the fact that *the subject* is the ground of the predicate, which Schelling explicitly states. But if the phrase "the eternal" refers to the copula or absolute identity, then the copula—that which connects subject and predicate—is *also* a ground. The subject is a ground, and the copula is a ground. But the ensuing discussion seems to take for granted that there is only one ground of things, namely God. We encountered the same problem when considering the first account of the copula in the last chapter: both the subject and the copula (X) ground the predicate.

These difficulties are a result of the unusual character of the sentence "God is all things." In this sentence, God is identified with all things. But God in Schelling's *Identitätsphilosophie* is precisely absolute identity, that which unites (as absolute copula) the subject and predicate. Thus, God is *both* the subject *and* the copula. In the 1806 *Aphorisms*, Schelling writes about the subject and predicate in true sentences: "Formally or analytically the two [elements] would not be one; *without God* they would not be one; but through God they are not synthetically but absolutely-one" (SW VII, 219). Thus, in the sentence "God is all things," God unites *himself* with all things.[12] Although this seems paradoxical, it follows from the fact that Schelling's first principle (absolute identity) is precisely what unites or gives unity. But what unites all things to it? If the principle is itself what gives unity, it must unite all things with itself.

We now have the first piece of the puzzle. The subject and copula are both identified as ground, because God as absolute identity is both the real copula and the subject in the sentence "God is all things." But how is God *immediately* a ground by virtue of the co-originality of this sentence with the law of identity? To answer this question, we have to examine this law's structure as expressed in the formula $A = A$. This structure reaches back to Schelling's first statement of the *Identitätsphilosophie*, the *Darstellung meines Systems* (1801), and ultimately stems from the self-positing I of Fichte's *Wissenschaftslehre*. However, his most developed treatment of this structure and its relation to God's creative activity is found in the 1804 *Würzburg System*.

As we saw in the last chapter, Schelling uses the language of "affirmation" to describe God or the absolute in the *Würzburg System*. Like the absolute I in Fichte, God posits or affirms himself (SW VI, 148). In his act of absolute self-affirmation, God is both that which affirms (the subject) and that which is affirmed (the object). This is reflected in the structure of the law of identity, $A = A$. The first A is the subject, which affirms; the second A is the object or predicate, which is affirmed. Thus, $A = A$ expresses the identity of that which affirms and that which is affirmed (i.e., self-affirmation). God or absolute identity is precisely this self-affirmation (SW VI, 148), which means that he is the *unity* of that which affirms and that which is affirmed (SW VI, 164). Thus, in the structure $A = A$, God appears in not just one, but in three places: God is A as affirming (subject), A as affirmed (predicate), and the unity or identity of himself as affirming and affirmed (copula).

There is a further structural feature of the law of identity that is directly connected to the "creative unity" expressed in it. Because the same A is the subject and predicate, $A = A$ expresses the self-affirmation of A. But A, as God or absolute identity, is precisely the self-affirmation. Thus, A as subject (affirming) is also self-affirmation, and A as object (affirmed) is also self-affirmation. In other words, the A that is subject, *in addition to* affirming, must also be affirmed; the A that is object, *in addition to* being affirmed, must also be affirming.

If we represent A as *affirming* with the letter S (subject), A as *affirmed* with the letter O (object), we can express this structural feature symbolically. $A = A$ is not merely S = O, because S is itself an S = O (self-affirmation), and O is itself an S = O (self-affirmation). Therefore, $A = A$ can be more accurately expressed as (S = O) = (S = O). But this formulation also is not sufficient. Each S and O is also A, meaning each is *again* S = O. One can see immediately how this structure must be repeated ad infinitum. Schelling summarizes this infinite reduplication in the *Würzburg System*: "Thus, in God we never encounter something that is [merely] affirming, or something that is [merely] affirmed, for in all directions he is only the infinite affirmation of himself" (SW VI, 172). We can represent the initial iterations of this structure in the following diagram.

```
                    S           =              O
          S    =    O                S    =    O
    S  =  O    S  =  O          S  =  O    S  =  O
  S=O  S=O   S=O  S=O        S=O  S=O    S=O  S=O
```

Two things should be noted about this infinite reduplication contained within the structure of the law of identity. (1) The same A is repeated again and again. No matter where one places oneself in this structure, one always encounters an A that is affirming itself. A represents the essence (*Wesen*) of absolute identity or God, and Schelling insists throughout his *Identitätsphilosophie* that there can never be any qualitative difference, or difference with respect to essence (SW IV, 123; VI, 179). But one can object: what is the point of the infinite reduplication, if it amounts to an infinite repetition of the same? Isn't this precisely the mindless repetition ("circle of sameness") that Schelling had criticized with respect to the common understanding of the law of identity? This leads to a second point: (2) Even if there is no difference with respect to *essence* in this structure (*A* is repeated again and again), there are differences with respect to *form*, depending on where a particular S = O is with respect to the whole. In previous writings, Schelling had claimed that difference with respect to form accounts for the richness and diversity of what is contained within absolute identity (cf. SW IV, 404–5). Nevertheless, one can object: it is not clear how this formal variation can account for the richness and diversity of reality, even if in principle it allows for infinite degrees of difference. In this respect, Hegel's critique of Schelling's "formalism," even if something of a caricature, does point to a problematic feature in the *Identitätsphilosophie*.[13]

In §24 of the *Würzburg System*, Schelling draws the consequences of the infinite reduplication within the law of identity for our discussion of ground. He seeks to prove the following proposition: "By virtue of the self-affirmation of his idea, God is immediately the absolute All" (SW VI, 174). In this proposition we can see the basic statement of pantheism, which I have interpreted as the law of ground: "God is all things." How does God's self-affirmation lead to his identity with all things? By affirming himself, God affirms an infinite reality in an infinite manner (*auf unendliche Weise*) (cf. SW VI, 169).[14] This is Schelling's way of expressing the infinite reduplication we observed in the structure of the law of identity, which demonstrates the infinite fecundity of God: "The infinite follows from the self-affirmation of God in an infinite manner, because there is no affirmation in God that is not as such immediately *affirmed*, and vice versa—so that the infinite gushes out [*hervorquillt*] from the infinite" (SW VI, 174). Elsewhere Schelling explains that God affirming himself "in an infinite manner" means he affirms himself "in all forms, degrees and potencies of reality" (SW II, 362).[15] In other words, if God's self-affirmation is truly *infinite* (unlimited), it includes *all* reality. In affirming himself, God affirms totality.

We now have the materials we need to return to the *Freiheitsschrift* and complete our interpretation of the series of inferences involving the creative unity of the law of identity. After concluding that "the eternal must be a ground immediately and as it is in itself" (SW VII, 346), Schelling specifies that the eternal is a ground through its essence (*durch sein Wesen*).[16] As I have argued, the conclusion that the eternal is immediately ground is another formulation of Schelling's statement a few lines earlier that the unity of the law of identity is "immediately creative" (SW VII, 345). We have seen in what way absolute identity is immediately creative: by affirming itself, this identity at the same time affirms an infinite reality—an infinite series of self-affirmations within self-affirmations. And Schelling understands affirmation as a kind of grounding, as we discussed in the last chapter. The creative unity of the law of identity, by affirming itself, affirms all things—thus, by grounding itself, it grounds all things. As Schelling writes at the end of §24 of the *Würzburg System*: "Only now is the meaning clear in which all is *one* and one all" (SW VI, 175). Through the infinite affirmation of God, ἓν καὶ πᾶν has the meaning that One *is* All and that One *grounds* All.

In the passage in the *Freiheitsschrift* (and other texts dealing with God's relationship to the All), there is a word that is easily overlooked, but has enormous significance: "immediately" (*unmittelbar*). "The unity of the law [of identity] is an *immediately* creative one" (SW VII, 345). "The eternal must be a ground *immediately* and as it is in itself" (SW VII, 346). "By virtue of the self-affirmation of his idea God is *immediately* the absolute All" (SW VI, 174). "The infinite = A is *as* this *immediately* also the finite = B" (SW VII, 204n).[17] What is the point of the word "immediately" in these sentences?

To appreciate its significance, we have to recall a theme we touched on in chapter 1 with respect to Jacobi's *Spinoza Letters*. According to Jacobi, Spinoza rejects "any transition from the infinite to the finite."[18] Such a transition (*Übergang*) would require something to come from nothing: the infinite is an unlimited unity, and there is no reason why limitation and multiplicity should suddenly emerge from it. Schelling cites approvingly this passage from Jacobi in the seventh of his *Philosophical Letters on Dogmatism and Criticism* (1795). He then adds that the transition from the infinite to the finite is "the problem of *all* philosophy, not just a single system," and that "Spinoza's solution is the only possible solution" (SW I, 313–14).[19] Spinoza's solution, according to Jacobi, is precisely the rejection of any transition. But if we reject any transition between the infinite and the finite, how can there be a finite world in addition to God? The answer to this question is the essential unity or identity of the infinite and the finite. The finite is in the infinite, just like the predicate of a sentence is in the subject.[20]

This is the reason why Schelling uses the word "immediately" in the sentences cited above. God is *immediately* the All, and the infinite is *immediately* the finite. If God were not immediately all things, there would have to be some transition between God and the All; thus, there would have to be a reason why finitude and multiplicity should emerge from God's infinite unity. But because God's infinite unity is immediately and as such finite and manifold, nothing arises ex nihilo. No transition is necessary, because there is an original unity.

Schelling is often criticized for failing to account for how the finite emerges from the infinite. In the *Identitätsphilosophie*, so it is claimed, God or absolute identity is defined in such a way as to preclude the possibility of the emergence of finitude and difference without some kind of "leap" or "fall"[21] from the infinite—an emergence that is otherwise unexplainable.[22] It is then claimed that this inability to explain the emergence of the finite prompted Schelling to break with his earlier *Identitätsphilosophie* and assert the radical freedom of God in creating the finite world.[23] It is true that Schelling comes to reconceive the role of divine freedom with respect to creation. However, this interpretation of Schelling's development identifies as the fatal flaw of the *Identitätsphilosophie* a problem that was one of the central motivations for its construction: the impossibility of a transition from the infinite to the finite.[24] The infinite and the finite must be absolutely one, according to Schelling, precisely because such a transition is impossible. Thus, any demand for an explanation of how the finite "emerges" from the absolute misunderstands the nature of absolute identity. As Schelling remarks in the 1806 *Aphorisms*, "If God could emerge from himself, he would not be God, not absolute" (SW VII, 158).[25] But then the question arises: how are we to conceive of God as a "progressive unity" (cf. SW VII, 345) if nothing can emerge from God? Doesn't the concept of a progression require transcendence and emergence? The nature of this grounding progression is the subject of the next two sections.

Before continuing, however, I would like to briefly consider two objections to God's immediate grounding of all things. First, if God (as absolute identity) is *immediately* creative, where is divine freedom? It would seem that God has no choice but to create; it is simply part of his nature, and therefore not a free act. As mentioned above, Schelling in later works will reconceive God's freedom: creation is considered a free act to the extent that God also has the freedom *not* to create.[26] In the *Freiheitsschrift*, however, Schelling develops an understanding of divine freedom that is compatible with necessity—so long as this necessity flows from God's nature as a living person and is not a blind necessity. Indeed, in his discussion of divine freedom later in the text (SW VII, 394–98) he will add personal elements to creation (like goodness and love) that are missing from his earlier discussion of creative unity.[27] In this respect, the *Freiheitsschrift* moves beyond the impersonal necessity of the *Identitätsphilosophie*, even if it retains a form of necessity.

Second, if God grounds all things, isn't Schelling falling back into the all-from-one model of grounding—the model that I claim he is rejecting? Actually, no. The all-from-one model requires that everything be *derived* from a single principle. As we will see below, God's grounding does bring forth all things, but it does not determine what they are for themselves. It thus allows for aspects of created things that are themselves underived and "absolute."

3. The Transformation of the Law of Ground

In the last section, I argued that the law of identity in the form "God is all things" expresses the same universality of grounding as the traditional law of ground. We can therefore think of the sentence "God is all things" as Schelling's version of the law of ground. Or, because the grounding relation between God and all things is an aspect of the law of identity, we can speak of the "grounding character" of the law of identity, or the law of identity *as* law of ground.

Even if this version of the law of ground shares with the traditional principle of sufficient reason the universality of being grounded, it has three significant differences: (1) The orientation or directionality of the law is reversed: it no longer goes from what is grounded to the ground, but from the ground to what is grounded. (2) The ground is not left undetermined in its reference, but is specifically identified with God. (3) The nature of grounding is different insofar as it involves a "grounding identity" and not a sufficient reason. In this section, I will develop the meaning and implications of these three transformations of the traditional principle.

(1) *Change in directionality*. In its simplest form, the traditional principle of sufficient reason reads: "Nothing is without reason," or "Nothing is without a ground." This formulation contains a double negation, and thus can be reformulated positively as "Everything that is has a ground," or "If something exists, it has a ground."[28] The movement of thought in the traditional principle is *regressive*, going from what is grounded to its ground. Likewise, when posing the question *why?* we begin with what is grounded and inquire after its ground. The ground is thus given as the

result, not the beginning of the movement of thought in the traditional principle.

This feature accounts for the principle's use in a posteriori proofs for the existence of God. Immediately after Leibniz introduces the principle of sufficient reason in his essay "Principles of Nature and Grace, Based on Reason" (1714), he poses his famous question: "why is there something rather than nothing?" He then proceeds to inquire into the ground or the sufficient reason for the existence of the universe.[29] The principle thus demands a regression from contingent existence to the ground of this existence. But only God as a necessary being can provide the sufficient reason for contingent things. Thus, the principle leads Leibniz from finite existence back to God as the ultimate ground of existence as such.

In the passage in the *Freiheitsschrift*, however, the direction of this movement is reversed. The movement is *progressive*—not from what is grounded to the ground, but from the ground to what is grounded. Thus, Schelling notes that the unity of the law of identity is "progressive" and "immediately creative." We begin with the eternal as "immediately ground," and only afterward do we speak of its consequences. In the statement "God is all things," God as ground is *antecedent* to what is grounded—both grammatically and logically. Indeed, this follows from the second (*antecedens-consequens*) account of the copula discussed in the last chapter.

This reversal of direction does not mean that Schelling's transformation of the law is incompatible with the traditional understanding. In fact, they can be viewed as offering two different perspectives: Schelling's formulation is from the perspective of the ground (God), while the traditional formulation is from the perspective of what is grounded (things). And yet the two perspectives and the corresponding formulations are not equally original: the new formulation has priority. One reason this is true is because it *grounds* the traditional formulation, insofar as it provides the underlying reason why it is true. All things are grounded *because* God is the ground of all things.[30]

We can also understand the originality of Schelling's new formulation in terms of Aristotle's famous distinction at the beginning of the *Physics* between what is more knowable for us and what is more knowable by nature.[31] According to Aristotle, the order of human knowledge is the reverse of the natural order: while nature begins with the principles, human knowledge reaches them only at the end. In the *Nicomachean Ethics*, he cites the question that Plato used to ask: "whether the path is from the principles or toward the principles."[32]

This is also the question with respect to the law of ground. The traditional formulation follows the path of finite knowledge, while Schelling's law of ground follows the more original path, beginning with the ultimate ground—what is "first by nature." This reorientation of the law fits Schelling's overall conception of philosophy, at least in the writings of his *Identitätsphilosophie*. Unlike Kant, who wished to place strict limitations on our knowledge and distinguish it from divine knowing, Schelling in his identity philosophy affirms the possibility of attaining the divine perspective through intellectual intuition. To use Spinoza's phrase, the perspective of philosophy is *sub specie aeternitatis*. This does not mean that Aristotle's distinction between the order of nature and the order of finite knowledge is no longer valid. Rather, philosophy first begins when we transcend the limits of finite knowledge and view things from their origins. One could also draw a connection here with Schelling's much later characterization of positive philosophy, which takes as its starting point the Creator as free cause of the world (see GPP 77–81).

Besides the change in perspective, there is something else implied in Schelling's reversal of the direction for the law of ground—something potentially more radical. Years later he makes this more explicit in his lectures on the philosophy of revelation. He critiques Fichte's conception of God by inverting the traditional principle ex nihilo nihil fit, which is another way of formulating the principle of ground, as we saw in chapter 1. According to Schelling, Fichte claims that nothing comes to be in God or from God. This, he insists, robs God of the highest prerogative: "To this [line of reasoning] one can apply in reverse the old principle, *ex nihilo nihil fit*: that from which nothing *comes* is itself nothing; thus if nothing comes from God, he is nothing" (SW XIV, 102). In other words, only that from which something comes is something. Anything that exists, *insofar as it exists*, is the ground of something else.

According to the traditional formulation of the law of ground, part of what it means to be is "to be grounded." According to this new formulation in the philosophy of revelation, part of what it means to be is "to ground." Anything that does not ground something by that very fact cannot be. Although the cited passage comes much later than the *Freiheitsschrift*, the same insight can be found in the section from the *Würzburg System* (1804) that we discussed earlier. Schelling notes that "in God there is no affirmation that is not immediately as such again *affirmed*, and vice versa, so that infinite gushes forth from infinite" (SW VI, 174). There is nothing that is *merely* affirmed or grounded. Anything that is affirmed or grounded is immediately also *affirming* and *grounding*, because of the structural features of the law of identity discussed above. In the 1806 *Aphorisms* Schelling cites Leibniz, who said that every drop of liquid is "a sea of living beings" (SW VII, 181). The divine plenitude (*Fülle*) is such that everything that it affirms is infinitely affirming, and—as Leibniz says about every drop of liquid—there are infinities within infinities.[33]

(2) *Identification of the ground.* In the traditional law of ground, it is left undetermined to what the word "ground" applies. Nothing is without a ground, but it may be different for different things. In contrast, what we have been regarding as Schelling's law of ground explicitly identifies what the ground is: "God is all things," that is, "*God* is the ground of all things."

At first glance this appears to be a severe restriction of the principle. Because the traditional law does not identify the ground, it seems to allow for a plurality of grounds and thus a plurality of grounding relations. In particular, Kant and others have interpreted the traditional law as a "universal causal principle," which therefore applies to the myriad instances of causality in the interactions of the physical world.[34] However, this apparent openness to a range of possible grounds misses an important aspect of the principle, at least as it was originally conceived by Leibniz. Although Leibniz sometimes formulates the principle in the simple form, "nothing is without a reason," the word reason (*ratio*) in this context does not mean just any ground or explanation, but a reason in the fullest sense (*ratio plena*), which Leibniz sometimes designates as a "sufficient reason."[35] A physical cause cannot be a full reason for something, because it itself requires a reason for its own existence. A truly sufficient reason does not itself require any other reason for its own existence and can therefore provide a complete explanation of what is grounded. Accordingly, only God can be a reason in the full sense, because only God does not require a reason outside himself.[36] This is why Leibniz is able to infer the existence of God almost immediately from the principle of sufficient reason and the existence of contingent things: anything contingent requires a sufficient reason, which only God can provide.

We can conclude, therefore, that the statement "God is/grounds all things" makes explicit two things that are already implied in Leibniz's principle: (1) It is God that is the ground of all things, because only God is ground in the fullest sense. (2) What is primarily at stake in the law of ground is not the sum of grounding relations in general (including the causal relations of physics) but the *original* grounding relation between God and things. The other grounding relations only become possible as result of this original relation. Indeed, because God grounds that which is also a ground, or affirms that which also affirms, we can say that these second-order grounding relations are already contained within God's original grounding. In other words, God grounds *through* other grounds, or God's grounding itself involves a series of grounds.

As I mentioned above, the traditional law of ground is what prompts Leibniz to pose his famous question: "Why is there something rather than nothing?" The question only arises because God is not already identified as the ultimate reason for existence. In the face of Schelling's transformation of the law of ground, this question becomes redundant: it assumes a perspective that is not God's. In fact, when Schelling treats Leibniz's famous question in the *Würzburg System* (1804),[37] he notes its redundancy in light of God's affirmation of all reality: "By virtue of this affirmation, which is the essence of our soul, we know *that non-being is eternally impossible*. . . . [Thus] the question 'why is there not nothing, why is there anything at all?'—the last question of the understanding as it teeters on the edge of infinity's abyss—is cast aside eternally through the knowledge that *being* necessarily is" (SW VI, 155). Nevertheless, it seems as if something important is lost when, from reason's perspective, we no longer need to pose the "ultimate why question."[38] This is the sense of wonder the question inevitably provokes. Wonder arises because the ground is not already identified, and we need to seek an answer to the question *why*? Philosophy begins in wonder, as Socrates says in Plato's *Theaetetus* (155d), and this surely has something to do with philosophers asking *why*? again and again.[39] But when the direction of the law of ground is reversed and the ground is identified from the beginning, this question never arises.

One can formulate this another way. The perspective of the *Identitätsphilosophie* is the perspective of God. But does God ever experience wonder? Even if the answer is no, it would be a mistake to conclude that wonder is unimportant for Schelling. Indeed, much of the language of the *Freiheitsschrift* evokes a sense of mystery, particularly the passages on the ground of existence and the eternal deed of freedom. One might even say that the *Freiheitsschrift* recovers a sense of wonder, which was largely absent in the *Identitätsphilosophie*.[40] Though the treatise continues to offer glimpses of a divine perspective, the language makes us more aware of the strangeness of reality and its distance from our ordinary view of the world, which is difficult to discard.

(3) *The nature of grounding.* Schelling's third innovation with respect to the law of ground is a change in the nature of grounding. In the traditional principle, the ground is understood as a "sufficient reason." The "sufficiency" of the ground is important: it must be enough to determine every aspect of what exists. For Leibniz, therefore, the principle expresses the thoroughgoing determination of all that is from the nature of God. In the passage in the *Freiheitsschrift*, however, Schelling offers a different conception of God's grounding relation to the world. We will examine this relation in more detail in the next section, relating it to the possibility of freedom. However, I would like to make a preliminary remark on the character of divine grounding, based on the material we have encountered so far.

We have seen the close relationship between the law of identity and the law of ground—according to Schelling, the latter is "just as original" as the former. This close relationship between the two laws reflects the close relationship between identity and ground, the "subjects" of these laws. "God is all things" means "God grounds all things." The identity of subject and predicate is a *grounding identity*. In the section on pantheism in the *Freiheitsschrift*, Schelling emphasizes the implications that this has for the nature of identity: if subject and predicate relate as ground and consequence, their identity is not a tautological sameness but must allow for difference between the terms. Identity must be identity in difference. But this linking of identity to ground *also* has implications for the nature of ground. We can clearly see this if we consider the phrases "progressive unity" and "creative unity," which summarize the character of absolute identity in this passage (SW VII, 345). Of course, the words "progressive" and "creative" fit naturally with our common conception of ground. A *creative* being creates something else, which is a kind of grounding. And we naturally think of a ground as inaugurating a *progression*, or series of consequences.

However, our ordinary way of conceiving what is "progressive" and "creative" becomes problematic when we add the word "unity." Usually a progression begins with the ground and moves *outward* in a series of consequences. But the "progressive unity" to which Schelling refers is a progression *within* unity. The unity is creative and grounds other things, but it does not ground something outside itself. Instead, its consequences are internal, its progression is an *internal progression*. God is the ground of all things, and yet at the same time God *is* all things.

Schelling notes in the passage: "That of which the eternal is a ground through its essence [*Wesen*] is in this respect dependent and, from the point of view of immanence, also something contained within the eternal" (SW VII, 346). The true meaning of pantheism is the immanence of all things in God. God grounds all things, and yet what he grounds is contained within him. We can therefore say that God is the *immanent ground* of all things. If we return to the structure of the law of identity, we can see this immanent grounding in the character of the infinite self-affirmation of God. Above I illustrated the first iterations of this self-affirmation in a diagram.

$$
\begin{array}{cccccccc}
& & S & & = & & O & \\
& S & = & O & & S & = & O \\
S = O & & S = O & & S = O & & S = O
\end{array}
$$

But this diagram is misleading insofar as it looks as if the S = O that is underneath the original S is beneath and thus outside the original S = O. But (1) the S = O that is underneath the original S and (2) the S = O that is underneath the original O are both *within* the original S = O. Thus, the original S = O is really

$$(S = O) = (S = O)$$

And when we consider that each of the S's and each of the O's in this line are again S = O, the line grows internally:

$$[(S = O) = (S = O)] = [(S = O) = (S = O)]$$

And so on, ad infinitum. Thus, the original S = O inaugurates a progression, but one that is internal to it. The line grows infinitely, but always within the overarching structure of the original S = O.

To appreciate the historical significance of this "progressive unity" for the problem of ground, we have to return—once again—to Jacobi. In Appendix VII of the *Spinoza Letters*, Jacobi accuses Spinoza of conflating "ground" and "cause" as concepts.[41] According to Jacobi, "ground" is a logical concept and involves an atemporal relation of dependence: what is grounded is dependent on its ground. By contrast, "cause" is a concept derived from experience and involves the production of one thing by another in temporal succession: what is caused is generated by its cause.[42] The problem with Spinoza's pantheism, Jacobi argues, is that it mixes these two concepts in its understanding of God's relation to things. On the one hand, God is the *ground* of all things: they are in God and depend on God, just as accidents depend on an underlying substance. On the other hand, God is also supposed to be *cause* of all things: Spinoza notes that God "produces" things, and all things "follow" from the divine nature.[43]

Why is this problematic? Even though Spinoza uses the language of causality and production with respect to God, he does not actually show how God generates things or brings them into being. In fact, there is no generation or coming-into-being of things. Instead, God's relation to things is purely logical or mathematical: things "follow" necessarily from God just as properties follow necessarily from the definition of a geometrical figure. But one could hardly say the definition of triangle causes its properties in the sense of bringing them into being. They are grounded in this definition, but their existence is just as eternal as the nature of the triangle itself. The same objection applies to Spinoza's pantheism. Things are grounded in God like predicates are grounded in a subject. But being-in God is not the same as being created or caused by God. Jacobi summarizes the consequence of treating the divine grounding of things as if it were causality: "Things come into being without coming into being; they change without changing; they are before and after each other, without being before and after each other."[44]

Expressed in terms of pantheism, Jacobi's objection is essentially this: a pantheistic God is not a Creator. If we view Schelling's remarks on creative unity in light of this objection, we can see that he is providing an implicit answer to Jacobi. The immanent, progressive grounding he describes allows a pantheistic God to be a Creator. As a creative unity, God is all things *and* generates all things. We could therefore say that Schelling combines "ground" and "cause" (in Jacobi's sense) in his conception of God's grounding activity. But combining the two is different from confusing them, as Spinoza is alleged to have done. Though all things are in God, this by itself does not make God their cause. Instead, God must also actively bring them forth within this overarching immanence. Unlike Spinoza, Schelling conceives of God's grounding as an act: as we will see, it is the "begetting" of something independent, which is also an act of self-revelation.[45]

4. Divine Grounding and the Possibility of Freedom

In the last two sections we have seen how Schelling, drawing on his *Identitätsphilosophie*, conceives of God as immediate ground of all that is. Furthermore, we have noted that God's grounding activity is an immanent but creative grounding, insofar as what is generated is not something external to God but within himself. I would now like to examine further the meaning of this grounding with a view to its implications for freedom—the subject of the remainder of the passage in the *Freiheitsschrift*.

Immediately following the series of inferences discussed above, Schelling introduces the two aspects of the grounding relation that he will examine further: "That of which the eternal is a ground through its essence [*Wesen*] is in this respect dependent and, from the point of view of immanence, also something contained within the eternal" (SW VII, 346). Being grounded by God involves (1) dependence (*Abhängigkeit*) and (2) containment (*Begriffensein*). In the next series of lines, Schelling first treats the nature of dependence, then—more briefly—the nature of containment, showing that the two concepts are not incompatible with freedom. We should note, however, that at this point in the *Freiheitsschrift* Schelling has not yet provided a positive account of freedom. He instead focuses on the compatibility of grounding with two things that are closely associated with freedom—indeed, two of its necessary conditions: (1) independence and (2) life. Of course, this means that a full account of the compatibility of freedom and ground will have to wait until we have a more complete understanding of what freedom is.

Schelling begins his discussion of dependence by emphasizing what it does *not* involve: "But dependence does not abolish independence, it does not even abolish freedom. Dependence does not determine the essence [*Wesen*] and says only that the dependent, whatever it also may be, can be only as a consequence of that of which it is a dependent; dependence does not say what the dependent is or is not" (SW VII, 346). Though dependence (*Abhängigkeit*) would seem to be the opposite of independence (*Selbständigkeit*),[46] the same thing can be both dependent and independent—though in different respects, as we will see. Even freedom is not incompatible with dependence. How is this possible? Here Schelling introduces the decisive distinction we encountered in the last chapter, the distinction between (1) determining ground and (2) ground as condition of the possibility. First, he denies that the dependence of things on God involves the first kind of ground: "Dependence does not determine the essence [*Wesen*]" (SW VII, 346). As noted before, *Wesen* is a problematic word, which can refer to either essence or an individual substance. Fortunately, the context provides us with another formulation: "Dependence does not say what the dependent is or is not" (SW VII, 346). To determine the *Wesen* is to say what the thing is.[47] Although, strictly speaking, this could apply to a thing's species (for example, human being), in context it seems to be more extensive, encompassing what is true about a thing.[48] Dependence does not determine its *Wesen*, because it does not determine what is true about it—including how it acts or does not act. As we will see in chapter 7, Schelling uses the phrase "intelligible essence" (*intelligibles Wesen*) similarly when treating the formal essence of freedom.

So far dependence is characterized negatively (as non-determination of the essence). What are its positive characteristics? Here the second sense of ground—what I have called the central sense of ground in the *Freiheitsschrift*—comes into play: "Dependence . . . says only that the dependent, whatever it also may be, can be only as a consequence of that on which it is dependent" (SW VII, 346). In other words, without that on which it is dependent, the dependent thing *cannot be*. The ground, insofar as something is dependent on it, is a condition of the thing's possibility. But as such it does not necessarily determine what the thing is. Soil is a condition of the possibility for most plants, but it does not determine their concrete features—even if it plays a role in shaping what some of these features will be. Because God as ground does not determine what a thing is but serves as the condition of its possibility, freedom and independence are preserved. I should note that it is unclear in this passage whether Schelling is ruling out *any* determination or just *complete* determination. If the former, one could object that a thing can be determined *in some respects* by something outside itself without this partial determination compromising its independence.

In any case, in light of what we have already discussed concerning God's grounding relation to the world, this characterization of God as condition of the possibility is incomplete. God is a creative unity, a unity that is progressive. However, as we saw above when discussing Jacobi's distinction between ground and cause, progression or creation demands more than a condition of the possibility: it requires the ground to *bring forth* that which it grounds, not just to ensure its possible existence. Even the word "consequence" (*Folge*) that Schelling uses in the passage implies more than mere dependence: something *follows* from something. In fact, ground as condition of the possibility is traditionally associated with a regression, not a progression. We begin with some given fact, and then "regress" to the conditions of its possibility. This transcendental movement is famously illustrated by Kant, who sought to define the conditions of the possibility of knowledge in the first *Critique*. However, as we saw in the last section, the movement in this passage is in the opposite direction, from the ground to what it grounds. Such a progressive movement is more naturally associated with a determining ground: the cause determines an effect and thereby begins a progression with further effects. But Schelling rules out this kind of determination with respect to the things that are dependent on God.

His task, therefore, is to build on the conception of ground as condition of the possibility in such a way that God as ground can bring forth what he grounds without determining its content. God as ground must (1) be a condition of the possibility of what he grounds, and (2) bring it forth in a progression, but (3) do so in a non-deterministic way. Schelling combines these three elements in his conception of grounding as "begetting" (*Zeugung*), a term with origins in both theology and biology. If we skip ahead in the passage for a moment, Schelling turns to the specific character of God's grounding: "A much higher standpoint is granted by consideration of the divine being itself, the idea of which would be fully contradicted by a consequence which is not the begetting, that is, the positing [*Setzen*] of something independent" (SW VII, 346). Begetting involves the positing or bringing forth of something that is independent. And yet what is begotten is dependent on that which begets it: without the latter, what is begotten would not be brought forth into existence. Begetting involves a combination of independence and dependence.

In fact, it allows for something more than independence: the *absoluteness* of what is begotten. Earlier in the passage Schelling had cited Leibniz on the Trinity: "It is not inconsistent, says Leibniz, that he who is God is at the same time begotten [*gezeugt*] or vice versa; just as little is it a contradiction that he who is the son of a man is also himself a man" (SW VII, 346).[49] A "begotten God" seems like an obvious contradiction: God is by nature absolute; that which is begotten is derived from something else and therefore dependent. Isn't a "dependent absolute" an absurdity? Nonetheless, at the end of the passage, Schelling affirms the concept, making his boldest claim in the entire treatise: "The concept of a derived [*derivierte*] absoluteness or divinity is so little contradictory that it is rather the middle term of philosophy as a whole" (SW VII, 347).

By calling "derived absoluteness" the "middle term" (*Mittelbegriff*) of all philosophy, Schelling is not just drawing attention to its centrality.

The word *Mittelbegriff* has its origins in syllogistic logic and refers to the middle term between two other terms, which are joined in the conclusion.[50] In the 1800 *System of Transcendental Idealism* Schelling uses the word twice, both times to refer to a concept that resolves a contradiction by reconciling two extremes (SW III, 384; 542).[51] And this is what he intends the concept of "derived absoluteness" to do as well—reconcile the extremes of being derived and being absolute.

But isn't this concept itself contradictory? An initial way to resolve the contradiction is to appeal to the distinction between dependence and determination of the essence that we discussed above. The absoluteness in question concerns the essence: it is absolute, insofar as the thing is not determined by something outside itself, but is instead self-determining. However, what is absolute with respect to its essence can nevertheless be "derived," insofar as another brings it forth into existence. In fact, this partial absoluteness is analogous to what Fichte had said about the absoluteness of his second and third principles: "Should the *Wissenschaftslehre* turn out to have other first principles in addition to this absolute first one, these others can be only partially absolute; they must, however, be partially conditioned by this first and supreme principle" (FW I, 49).[52]

This explanation of "derived absoluteness" can be expressed succinctly in terms of Schelling's later distinction between "the that" (*das Daß*) and "the what" (*das Was*), corresponding to the classical distinction between existence and essence (cf. SW XIII, 57–58). For something that is begotten but at the same time absolute, the begetting determines *that it is* without determining *what it is*. I believe this is the sense of the following line: "Every organic individual exists [*ist*], as something that has become, only through another, and in this respect is dependent according to its becoming but by no means according to its being" (SW VII, 346). The organic individual is dependent according to *becoming*: it "comes into being" when something else produces it. But this does not require a dependence according to *being* (*Sein*). Though Schelling does not make clear what he means by "being" here, the Platonic distinction between being and becoming suggests that it refers to the eternal form or essence of a thing, which is undetermined by its coming to be.[53] Indeed, much later in the treatise he writes: "There is indeed in each human being a feeling . . . as if he had been what he is already from all eternity and had by no means become so first in time" (SW VII, 386). We will return to this theme in chapter 7 when treating the formal essence of freedom.[54]

An alternative interpretation of "derived absoluteness" would draw on the structure of self-affirmation within the law of identity, which we discussed earlier. In the *Würzburg System*, Schelling defines "the absolute" as what is *self-affirming*: what affirms itself is "from itself and through itself" (SW VI, 148)—in traditional terminology: *a se*. Now, as infinite self-affirmation, God is the affirmation of infinite self-affirmations, which are the reduplications we saw above (cf. SW VII, 159, §83). These self-affirmations—the products of God's creative unity—are *absolute* insofar as they are self-affirming, but *derived* insofar as they are affirmed in the original self-affirmation of God. In other words, they have derived absoluteness. It is true that, in the *Würzburg System*, self-affirming does not seem to involve *self-determination* in a sense that would be meaningful for freedom. But we will see in chapter 7 that Schelling uses the Fichtean language of self-positing (the equivalent of self-affirming)⁵⁵ when describing the eternal act of determining one's essence (SW VII, 385). In any case, if derived self-affirmation involves freely determining one's essence, then this second interpretation of derived absoluteness can be combined with the first: each self-affirmation is generated (in its being) through God's self-affirmation, but it is nonetheless absolute (with respect to the determination of its essence).⁵⁶

How, then, does derived absoluteness relate to begetting? The two concepts have an essential correlation: begetting produces derived absoluteness. We have already seen a connection in Schelling's citation of Leibniz: it is not a contradiction for God to be begotten. This is a clear reference to the Nicene Creed, which refers to the Son of God as *genitum non factum*, "begotten not made" (γεννηθέντα οὐ ποιηθέντα). If the Son of God were made, this would compromise his divinity. Beyond the Christian theological context, Schelling had developed the connection more extensively in his lectures on the philosophy of art (1802–3) when discussing the relation of dependence among the gods.⁵⁷ This relation can only be conceived as a relation of begetting (*Zeugung*): "For begetting is the only kind of dependence in which the dependent nonetheless remains in itself absolute" (SW V, 405). Divinity requires absoluteness, which is the highest form of independence. The dependence of begetting does not jeopardize this absolute independence—although here he does not explain how this is possible.

But how, we may ask, does the question of derived divinity or absoluteness relate to the compatibility of freedom and ground, which is Schelling's principal question? One answer is that he is giving an argument a fortiori. If a certain kind of grounding dependence is compatible with divinity and absoluteness, it is *all the more* compatible with freedom. But there is something more significant in play: the references to divinity are part of Schelling's general tendency to characterize freedom in divine terms—to "divinize" free beings, as it were. Insofar as their essence is not determined by God, they are "outside the created order" (SW VII, 386), even self-creating. As we will see in chapter 7, a free being is a kind of *causa sui*—a phrase usually reserved for God. This tendency to "divinize" freedom is aligned with the treatise's general movement toward equiprimordiality (*Gleichursprünglichkeit*), which I noted in the introduction. Clearly God and free creatures are not equally original; the latter, as creatures, are derived after all. Nevertheless, insofar as they are absolute and undetermined, there is a sense in which they are as original as God himself.

The statement that derived absoluteness or divinity is the "middle term of philosophy as a whole" (SW VII, 347) points to another connection with freedom. In the preface to the *Freiheitsschrift*, Schelling had emphasized the importance of the opposition between necessity and freedom, adding that with this opposition "the innermost center point of philosophy first comes into consideration" (SW VII, 333).[58] Thus, he places both (1) derived absoluteness and (2) the opposition between freedom and necessity at the center of philosophy. Indeed, both are expressions of the same thing: the relation of freedom to ground, or the problem of a system of freedom. The phrase "derived absoluteness" encapsulates this problem: *freedom* demands the absoluteness of self-determination, but *system* demands that such absoluteness be connected within the larger system and ultimately derived from the system's principle. "Derived absoluteness" and a "system of freedom"—these are the two "square circles" that express the problem of freedom and ground.[59]

So far we have focused in this section on the possibility of combining independence and dependence by conceiving God's grounding as "begetting." But dependence is only the first challenge to independence addressed in this passage; the other is the containment (*Begriffensein*) of things in God.[60] At the end of the last section, we noted that God's grounding has this peculiar feature: the progression of its consequences is internal to God; his grounding is an immanent grounding or a grounding identity. In other words, what is grounded by God is *contained within* him. This unique grounding relation is also found in Schelling's account of begetting in his lectures on the philosophy of art. "Theogony" or the begetting of the gods is an image (*Sinnbild*) of the way in which the ideas in the *Identitätsphilosophie* (1) are in one another, and (2) proceed from one another—that is, it is an image of an immanent progression.[61] Schelling then relates begetting more directly to containment in God: "The absolute idea or God grasps [*begreift*] all ideas in himself, and they are begotten from him [*aus ihm gezeugt*], insofar as they are thought as grasped in him but also as for themselves absolute" (SW V, 405).[62] This passage indicates that Schelling gives begetting the same unique grounding character we have noted already. Begetting is associated with childbirth, especially in biblical and mythological contexts. But in childbirth the offspring is *outside* of the begetting parents. Here what is begotten remains internal to what begets it—as if it were an eternal pregnancy (though pregnancy precedes rather than follows birth).

In the passage in the *Freiheitsschrift*, Schelling's discussion of containment is brief compared to his discussion of dependence but introduces two central themes: life and the organic nature of grounding. These themes are presented in an analogy with the parts of the body: "An individual body part, like the eye, is only possible within the whole of an organism; nonetheless, it has a life for itself, indeed a kind of freedom, which it obviously proves through the disease of which it is capable" (SW VII, 346). Here again we see the sense of ground as condition of the possibility: the individual body part is *only possible* within the whole organism (cf. KU §65, AA 5, 373). The whole is ground of the part insofar as it contains the part and thereby makes possible its existence. But this dependence still allows for independence: individual body parts have their own life (*ein Leben für sich*) in independence from the whole, and thus a kind of freedom. This reflects Schelling's understanding of life as a whole composed of smaller wholes, a system of systems—each level of organization having some measure of autonomy, even if it cannot exist without the larger whole. It is noteworthy that Schelling here points to disease as proof of the freedom of the body's parts. In disease they assert their independence *against* the good of the whole, and their freedom allows them to do this. Later in the *Freiheitsschrift* he will cite disease as a "profound analogy" for evil (SW VII, 366). In the passage we are considering, therefore, we have a foreshadowing of the "real and living concept" of human freedom as "a capacity for good and evil" (SW VII, 352).

Of course, the analogy with parts of the body is not just one analogy among many. Throughout Schelling's philosophical development he returns again and again to the organism as an image for his philosophy as a whole: the true system is "an organic whole" (SW III, 379; cf. VII, 422), and if God comprehends all that is, God himself is an organism. Besides the wholes-within-wholes structure discussed already, there is another aspect of life that is relevant for God's grounding of free beings: the non-mechanistic nature of organic grounding. Schelling writes: "God is not a god of the dead but of the living. It is not comprehensible how the most perfect being could find pleasure even in the most perfect machine possible" (SW VII, 346). The parts of a machine are the products of a mechanical causality; however, as Kant had observed in the third *Critique*, the life of organisms evades mechanistic explanation, and we are unable to explain so much as a "blade of grass" through the laws of mechanism (KU §77, AA 5, 409). In his *Naturphilosophie* Schelling had instead developed a dynamic account of life in terms of the conflict and interplay of independent forces.[63] Schelling notes in the passage that a mechanistic grounding does not allow what is grounded to be something "for itself." Its entire being is determined through causal laws: the parts have no independence or self-determination, and thus are incapable of the opposition necessary for life. In contrast, what is contained within God has life and independence—God is living, and he "begets" what is living. Indeed, the concept of begetting (*Zeugung*) we have been discussing is not just theological but is used in biological contexts to refer to the generation of offspring.

In the remainder of the passage, Schelling first characterizes God's grounding in terms of self-revelation, then in terms of the relation between the divine mind and what it represents. For God to reveal himself to himself, what he grounds must be "like him" (*ihm ähnlich*). Indeed, this is in accord with the usual understanding of begetting: God begets God, a human begets a human being. Schelling then specifies in what way what is grounded is like God: they are free beings that "act from [out of] themselves" (*aus sich selbst handelnd*) (SW VII, 347). He then adds that for their being "there is no ground other than God." We have been focusing on the grounding relation between God and things; however, one would think that things are grounded by God *and* by other things. In fact, in our discussion of system in chapter 1, we noted that both of these grounding relations are problematic for human freedom. Here Schelling simply denies the existence of a grounding relation among things—at least with respect to their "being" (*Sein*). This presents a number of difficulties, and we will return to this question in chapter 7 when discussing the formal essence of freedom. For now, I will only say that Schelling has in mind God's grounding of things as they are in themselves, outside of their relations to other things.

The end of the passage is a rich characterization of divine knowing and its relationship to its representations. What does the character of divine knowing have to do with grounding? Divine knowing is itself grounding—God grounds by knowing.⁶⁴ This is true because the character of divine knowledge is quite different from ordinary human knowledge, where what is known is either completely dependent or completely independent of knowing. On the one hand, the imagination allows us to generate a rich and almost boundless array of objects, which have no existence independent of the mind. On the other hand, we can also know objects—like the physical world around us—that exist independent of the mind; but in this case, the mind does not generate the objects but only knows them after they already exist.⁶⁵

In the case of divine knowledge, however, God's knowing is at the same time the grounding of independent beings. The objects of divine knowledge are neither completely dependent nor completely independent. It is not the case that the existence of objects in the world is "prior" to God's knowledge of them. As Schelling writes in the *Würzburg System* (1804): "God does not know things *because they exist*, but the other way around: things *exist, because God knows them*" (SW VI, 169). Here Schelling is drawing on the idea of a divine intellectual intuition or intuitive understanding, which Kant developed as a foil for our own cognitive powers in the first and third *Critiques*.⁶⁶ Such a creative understanding is both spontaneous and non-discursive, generating the objects that it knows. But what is produced by divine knowledge, Schelling insists, is independent: "For what is the limiting element in our representations other than exactly that we see what is not independent? God intuits the things in themselves" (SW VII, 347).

In this last line Schelling invokes the famous—or infamous—concept of the things in themselves. Kant also had connected a knowledge of things in themselves with intellectual intuition.⁶⁷ It is true that Schelling, Fichte, and Hegel are often portrayed as rejecting the Kantian distinction between appearances and things in themselves.⁶⁸ For Schelling, however, this distinction is alive and well—at least in his *Identitätsphilosophie*.⁶⁹ What Schelling rejects is an understanding of things in themselves that would make them inaccessible to philosophical knowledge: they are only inaccessible in terms of categories (like empirical causality) that apply to appearances. Absolute knowing, by contrast, is a self-knowledge of the absolute that grants access to things in themselves through our identity with them. In any case, Schelling gives a characterization of things in themselves in the passage in the *Freiheitsschrift*: "Only this is in itself: what is eternal, resting on itself, will, freedom" (SW VII, 347). Through

God's knowledge, God grounds things by bringing them forth as "things in themselves." But as such, they are necessarily like God: independent, self-determining—even eternal. As we will see when discussing the formal concept of freedom, Schelling follows Kant in locating the ultimate act of self-determination outside of time.

Schelling concludes the passage in dramatic fashion: "So little does immanence in God contradict freedom that precisely only what is free is in God to the extent it is free, and what is not free is necessarily outside of God to the extent that it is not free" (SW VII, 347). This statement is a complete reversal of the initial starting point of the discussion, which was the assumption that dependence on God—and more specifically, immanence in God—is a threat to freedom. But here Schelling says that immanence in God, far from being opposed to freedom, is *required* for it. At first, this claim seems to be a non sequitur. We have seen that what is grounded by God must be independent—indeed, as a thing in itself, it must be self-determining and absolute with respect to its essence. In short, the immanence of things in God requires freedom. But why is the converse true—why does freedom require immanence in God?[70]

There is a sense in which this is trivially true: because all things are in God, nothing can exist—or have freedom—without being in God. But if whatever is begotten in God is ipso facto free, this would mean that *everything* is free. There is indeed in Schelling's philosophy a tendency to universalize freedom. Later in the text he writes: "Only one who has tasted freedom can feel the longing to make everything analogous to it, to spread it throughout the whole universe" (SW VII, 351). The danger is that freedom becomes nothing special, something that belongs to everything and thus does not really belong to anything. We should note, however, that Schelling uses the word "analogous" here; it is conceivable that lower life forms (like the parts of an organism) have "a kind of freedom" (SW VII, 346) that falls short of the fullness of human—or divine—freedom.

Despite this tendency to universalize freedom, the second half of the statement points to the possibility of non-freedom: "What is not free is necessarily outside of God to the extent that it is not free" (SW VII, 347). But if God is all things, how is it possible for something to be outside of God? Schelling provides us with a clue somewhat later in one of the most famous passages in the *Freiheitsschrift*: "In the final and highest judgment, there is no other being than willing [*Wollen*]. Willing is primordial being [*Ursein*] to which alone all predicates of primordial being apply: groundlessness, eternity, independence from time, self-affirmation. All of philosophy strives only to find this highest expression" (SW VII, 350). Schelling here gives a characterization of what he had earlier described as "in itself." The predicates are virtually identical: the In-itself was described as "eternal, based on itself, will, freedom." According to this passage, the In-itself alone *is* in the original and highest sense. And because the In-itself is freedom, part of what it means to be is to be free. But Schelling prefaces these remarks with the phrase "in the final and highest judgment." This implies that from a lower standpoint there is a lower form of being that is not in itself: appearance. Indeed, in the *Identitätsphilosophie*, Schelling speaks of appearance as something outside of God or outside of absolute identity.[71]

The status of appearance is problematic for Schelling in the *Freiheitsschrift*: traces of his earlier devaluation of it compete with a new emphasis on the historical unfolding of revelation, which is God's coming-to-appearance. Indeed, this tension in Schelling's later thought is the subject of Habermas's dissertation.[72] But the distinction between appearances and things in themselves does explain the meaning of the passage's conclusion. What is free is in God: through his intuitive understanding, God brings forth the things in themselves, whose essence is freedom. What is not free is outside God: appearance insofar as it is not in itself. To the extent that appearances are externally determined through empirical causality, they lack freedom. This Kantian distinction between appearances and things in themselves will prove decisive in the later discussion of the formal essence of freedom.

There is, however, another sense in which something can be outside God, which Schelling will introduce much later in the text. In this sense, being outside God involves evil, which is a rebellion against the creature's status as creaturely: "For there still remains in the one who has departed from the center the feeling that he has been all things, namely, in and with God; thus, he strives again to attain this—but for himself [alone], not where he could be [all things], namely, in God" (SW VII, 390). Schelling goes on to associate this Fall with a loss of "initial freedom" (SW VII, 391). However, the meaning of the phrase "in God" here seems to go beyond the pantheistic immanence of the passage discussed in this chapter: to be in union with God requires either the original state of unity before the Fall or the condition of moral goodness, which involves the "divine relation" of the principles (SW VII, 365).

Now that we have reached the end of the passage in the *Freiheitsschrift*, we can summarize the results with respect to the nature of God's grounding and the possibility of freedom. (1) Schelling emphasizes repeatedly the sense of ground as conditio sine qua non or condition of the possibility, and he invokes this sense of ground in both his account of dependence and his account of containment. (2) God's grounding involves dependence. But this dependence allows for both independence and freedom, because there need not be determination of the essence of what is dependent. (3) God's grounding involves containment: it is an immanent grounding of things within God. (4) This immanent grounding also involves an internal progression by which God actively generates created things. In this way, Schelling implicitly answers Jacobi's objection to a pantheistic Creator. (5) The concept of "begetting" (*Zeugung*) contains many of the unique features of God's grounding: (a) condition of the possibility, (b) the bringing forth of what is grounded in a progression, (c) immanent grounding or containment, and (d) the preservation of the radical independence or absoluteness of what is grounded. (6) Although Schelling does not give a full account of freedom, it is clear that it requires both independence and life. God's grounding does not jeopardize either of these requirements. Finally, (7) God grounds by means of an intellectual intuition that does not compromise the independence of its objects but requires that they be things in themselves, which essentially involves freedom. Far from jeopardizing the freedom of what is grounded, God's grounding makes this freedom possible.

4
Schelling's Fundamental Distinction between Ground and What Exists

After reading the section on pantheism discussed in the last two chapters, one might be left with the impression that Schelling has solved the problem of a system of freedom to his satisfaction. The immanence of all things in God—the doctrine to which any rational viewpoint is drawn (SW VII, 339)—does not compromise the independence needed for freedom, he argues. On the contrary, God's immanent grounding makes this freedom possible: "Only what is free is in God to the extent it is free, and what is not free is necessarily outside of God to the extent that it is not free" (SW VII, 347). In light of the strength of this conclusion, the opening of the very next paragraph comes as a surprise: "However insufficient [*ungenügend*] such a general deduction is in itself for one who sees deeper, it makes clear enough that the denial of formal freedom is not necessarily connected with pantheism" (SW VII, 347). What was "insufficient" about the previous discussion? And why does Schelling now limit his conclusion to what he calls "formal freedom"?

The answers to these questions lie in what is new about the *Freiheitsschrift*: an account of evil and the dynamic development of nature and history in terms of a dualism within God. In his discussion of pantheism, Schelling had more or less remained at the standpoint of monism characteristic of his previous writings in the *Identitätsphilosophie*. In the section that follows, he presents the contributions of "idealism," a designation referring to the thought of Kant and Fichte as well as Schelling's own earlier writings on the ideal side of philosophy. Chief among the contributions of idealism is "the first complete concept of formal freedom" (SW VII, 351), which is a self-determination outside of time. Schelling in no way wishes to throw out the overarching monism of his *Identitätsphilosophie* or idealism's insights into formal freedom—we will see that he reincorporates them later on in the treatise. However, he recognizes that this "idealistic" standpoint is insufficient to account for the specifically human element in freedom, what he calls "the real and living concept": it is "a capacity of good and evil" (SW VII, 352).[1]

Why does evil make it problematic to understand freedom solely in terms of self-determination within a pantheistic God? If God is all-good, it is not possible for evil—or even the capacity for evil—to be present in him. Schelling thus concludes: "If freedom is a capacity for evil, it must have a root independent of God" (SW VII, 354). Only later does he reveal the identity of this independent root: the ground of God's existence, one of the two principles in God. Accordingly, the freedom to do evil requires Schelling to introduce a dualism within God, thus going beyond a pantheistic monism: God as that-which-exists is distinguished from the ground of his existence.

This fundamental distinction is the subject of the present chapter. Its importance for the *Freiheitsschrift* as a whole cannot be overstated. Schelling remarks that his present investigation is based (*sich gründet*) on it (SW VII, 357), and it plays a central role in his account of the divine nature, evil, human freedom, anthropology, the development of nature and history—in short, the major themes of the text. Accordingly, one simply cannot understand the *Freiheitsschrift* as a whole without first understanding this distinction. It also plays a decisive role in Schelling's answer to the problem of ground. Most obviously, the word "ground" appears as one of the terms in the distinction. Though the sense of ground that applies here is not exactly the same as we have encountered with respect to God's relationship to things, it shares with the latter something essential. A consideration of the distinction will therefore help us to understand the meaning(s) of ground in Schelling. But beyond that, the distinction has systematic implications for grounding: it articulates a structure that is repeated again and again throughout the system at every level. By understanding the grounding relations within the distinction, we can understand the grounding relations that connect the parts of the system as a whole. Indeed, Schelling universalizes these grounding relations, providing what could be considered another version of the principle of ground immediately after reflecting on the priority of the distinction's elements.[2]

Despite the immense importance of the distinction for understanding the *Freiheitsschrift*, its precise meaning is difficult to understand—especially if one relies only on what is said in the *Freiheitsschrift*. As we will see, essential elements of the distinction were misunderstood by Schelling's contemporaries; unfortunately, these same elements are still widely misunderstood today, even by careful readers. Part of the reason for this is Schelling's way of presenting the distinction: he employs common philosophical terms like "existence" and "ground" without indicating he has a special sense in mind, and he supplements the original terminology of his distinction with analogies and rich metaphorical language that can be both illuminating and misleading. Fortunately, Schelling gives us a more direct account of the distinction in his replies to questions and objections from Eschenmayer and Georgii. In these replies, Schelling also corrects misinterpretations of his distinction that are common—both then and now. Accordingly, we can use these texts to orient ourselves when interpreting the more difficult presentation of the distinction in the *Freiheitsschrift*.

It would require an entire book to treat the distinction adequately—tracing its sources in Schelling's earlier writings, parsing the many passages in the *Freiheitsschrift* and related works that shed light on its meaning, drawing out the systematic implications for freedom, evil, and the nature of God. For our purposes, we will focus on the meaning of ground in the distinction and the relationship of interdependence among its terms. But before we can focus on these particular issues, we need to understand the nature of the distinction in general and address common misconceptions. I therefore begin with a general characterization of the distinction, followed by an account of its relation to the doctrine of the potencies. I then address the most common misunderstanding: the failure to recognize what I call the "distinction within the distinction," or the distinction between existence (*Existenz*) and that-which-exists (*das Existierende*). Recognizing this second, implicit distinction will allow us to understand the role of the ground as well as the relations among the distinguished terms. I then conclude with a consideration of the implications of Schelling's distinction for the problem of ground and a system of freedom.

1. General Characterization of the Distinction

It is tempting to think of the distinction in the *Freiheitsschrift* primarily in terms of God. It would therefore concern (1) God insofar as he exists and

(2) the ground of God's existence. This is justified to the extent that the dynamic relationship between God as that-which-exists and the ground of his existence is the central focus of what follows in the text. Moreover, Schelling's initial remarks, intended to provide an "elucidation" (*Erläuterung*) of the distinction, articulate it in terms of God. However, when it is first introduced, God is not mentioned at all: "The philosophy of nature of our time has first advanced in science the distinction being insofar as it exists and being insofar as it is merely the ground of existence" (SW VII, 357). The being (*Wesen*) in question can be God, but it can also be other things, including human beings. Indeed, after Schelling's initial characterization of the distinction in God he adds: "A reflection starting out from things leads to this same distinction" (SW VII, 358). A little later he notes that "both principles are indeed in all things" (SW VII, 363). Accordingly, this distinction articulates a fundamental structure of reality, which can be applied at every level of the system.[3] Indeed, this structure can be applied to philosophy itself, which has a structure that reflects the nature of God. Nonetheless, there is a sense in which the distinction applies preeminently to God. Creation is divine self-revelation: what is created shares the same nature as the Creator (cf. SW VII, 347). Thus, all things have this same structure because they reflect the nature of God, who has this structure. We will return to the structural implications of the distinction shortly.

Before characterizing the distinction further, it is helpful to reflect on the precise language Schelling uses when first introducing it. The distinction is between "being [*Wesen*] insofar as it exists and being [*Wesen*] insofar as it is merely the ground of existence" (SW VII, 357). Although Schelling is explicitly drawing a two-way distinction, within this distinction there are really *four* distinct terms:

1. being (*das Wesen*),

2. that-which-exists (*Existierendes*),

3. the ground of existence (*Grund von Existenz*), and

4. existence (*Existenz*).[4]

The word *Wesen* occurs twice. As I have noted already in other contexts, it is difficult to translate because, like the Greek term οὐσία, it can refer to an individual being as well as essence. The word has as its root sense "what a thing *really* is,"[5] or perhaps "what a thing is at its core."

Besides the word *Wesen*, there is one other word that occurs twice in the original formulation: *sofern* ("insofar as"). The distinction concerns a single *Wesen* that is regarded in two different respects. Accordingly, the word *sofern* marks out the two elements of the distinction: on the one hand, there is being *insofar as* it exists; on the other hand, there is being *insofar as* it is ground of existence. This characterization of the distinction in terms of different aspects of a single *Wesen* recalls our discussion of the "mediated account of the copula" in chapter 2. In this account, Schelling had interpreted the sentence "This body is blue" to mean "the same thing which is this body is also blue, although not in the same respect" (SW VII, 341). The subject and predicate are two aspects of the same X—the unnamed, underlying *Wesen*.[6] We can use Schelling's language in this earlier example to reformulate his distinction: *the same thing* that exists is also the ground of existence, although not in the same respect.

When Schelling applies the distinction to God, he does not use the language of *Wesen* to refer to a single, underlying being/essence—at least in his initial account of the distinction in God. (As we will see in more detail in chapter 6, toward the end of the *Freiheitsschrift* Schelling speaks of the *Wesen* of both (1) God insofar as he exists and (2) the ground of God's existence, and he identifies this *Wesen* with the *Ungrund*.) Instead, "God" takes the place of the word *Wesen* in the original formulation—though the two formulations are not exactly parallel: "Since nothing is prior to, or outside of God, he must have the ground of his existence in himself. . . . This ground of his existence . . . is not God considered absolutely, that is, insofar as he exists; for it is only the ground of his existence" (SW VII, 357–58).

There are several remarkable features of this application of the distinction to God. First, Schelling uses "God" in two senses: (1) In the broad sense, God is all-encompassing. Nothing is outside of him. Therefore, everything—including the ground of God's existence—must be in God. It is in this broad sense that "God" takes the place of *Wesen* in the original formulation. (2) God in a more specific sense is God "considered absolutely" (*absolut betrachtet*), that is, God *insofar as* he exists.[7] Here again we encounter the word *sofern* as a means of differentiating the elements of the distinction. God "considered absolutely" is an aspect of God in the broad sense—namely, the aspect that exists. Sometimes Schelling refers to God insofar as he exists as "he himself." Thus, the ground of existence is "that which in God himself is not He Himself [*Er Selbst*]" (SW VII, 359).[8] The ground is in God (in the broad sense) but not God (in the more specific sense—God "considered absolutely").

As an aside, I will note the structural parallel here with the relationship between the I and the not-I in Fichte. Because nothing exists outside the I, the not-I must be posited in the I, if it is to be posited at all. Accordingly, there is something in the I that is not the I—just as for Schelling there is something in God that is not God himself. Of course, Fichte distinguishes between the absolute I and the I that is opposed to the not-I—just as Schelling distinguishes between two senses of God. Some of the reasons for these parallels will become clearer below.

We have already touched on one of the other remarkable features of this passage: the containment of the ground *within* God. In the passage Schelling uses the word *sofern* only once to demarcate God "considered absolutely" or God *insofar as* he exists. In the case of the ground, Schelling does not refer to "God insofar as he is the ground of his existence," as we might expect. Instead, he says the ground is *in* God. Though Schelling does not directly say that God insofar as he exists is *in* God, this formulation also seems justified. When applied to God, the distinction thus becomes a distinction *within God*. One can therefore refer to it as an "internal dualism" (to use Friedrich Hermanni's apt phrase),[9] provided that the word "dualism" is understood in the correct sense.[10]

Here an interesting question arises: what exactly are we distinguishing when we distinguish that-which-exists and the ground of existence in God? To put it crudely, what is the genus of the two terms, or what are they *both*? As mentioned above, the word *sofern* ("insofar as") indicates they are two aspects of a common *Wesen*. But what "aspect" means precisely is not yet clear.[11] Schelling also applies the word *Wesen* to the two terms—for example, the ground is "a being [*Wesen*] inseparable, yet still distinct, from [God]" (SW VII, 358).[12] Though the word *Wesen* is difficult to translate, its use in these contexts points to more "substantiality" for the two terms than the word "aspect" would otherwise suggest.[13] Schelling also identifies the terms as "two ways of acting" (*Wirkungsweisen*) of a single *Wesen* (SW VII, 409). Elsewhere he refers to them as "forces" (*Kräfte*), and God as the unity of that-which-exists and the ground of existence is a "living unity of forces" (SW VII, 394). Finally, Schelling also refers to the terms as different "wills": that-which-exists is the "universal will" or the "will of love"; the ground of existence is the "self-will" (*Eigenwille*) or the "will of the ground" (cf. SW VII, 363; 375).[14]

However, Schelling's most common designation for the two terms of the distinction is simply the word "principle" (*Prinzip*). For example, he writes that "both principles are indeed in all things" (SW VII, 363).

Since this language is relatively easy to use, I will also refer to them as "principles." But we should note that Schelling is not using the word in precisely the same sense in which the principle of identity is a principle—that is, an ultimate foundation for the system as a whole, which can also be expressed in a fundamental proposition (*Grundsatz*).[15] Instead, he seems to have in mind something closer to the broad meaning of the Greek word ἀρχή as "beginning" or "source." Along these lines, he refers to the two principles as "two equally eternal beginnings of self-revelation" (SW VII, 395). We will return to the theme of revelation below when discussing the meaning of existence.

So far we have concentrated on the language and terminology surrounding the distinction. At this point I would like to step back and make a general observation about Schelling's use of terminology with respect to the two principles. As we have seen, Schelling distinguishes between (1) that-which-exists (*das Existierende*) and (2) the ground of existence. But it would be more accurate to say that Schelling distinguishes between (1) that which he *designates* as "that-which-exists" and (2) that which he *designates* as "the ground of existence." In other words, the expressions that Schelling uses when formulating the distinction are ways of designating the principles, and we should not assume that these designations give an exhaustive characterization of what each principle is in itself. To use an analogy: the phrase "the queen of England in 2021" picks out Elizabeth II as a unique individual. But the designation does not give an exhaustive characterization of who she is; it merely expresses a role she uniquely plays as queen, leaving open the possibility that she plays other roles. In the same way, the phrase "ground of existence" designates one of the two principles by naming a role that it plays: ground of existence. What this phrase means will be examined in more detail below. But Schelling gives a rich characterization of the ground of existence that includes characteristics that are not directly related to its role as ground. The same can be said for "that-which-exists," which designates a principle that also has characteristics not directly related to its status as existing.[16]

Why is it important to distinguish (a) Schelling's designations from (b) those things that are *designated* by the designations? To begin with, this helps us to recognize that Schelling often refers to the same things using very different designations; Hermanni calls this Schelling's "terminological plurality."[17] Unfortunately, Schelling often does not say explicitly when he is using another term for something to which he had referred earlier using a different term. One must therefore be careful not to equate things that merely have similar characteristics but are ultimately distinguished. Nevertheless, with respect to the two principles that Schelling distinguishes in the *Freiheitsschrift*, we are confronted with the possibility that he refers to these same two principles in other works—both before and after the *Freiheitsschrift*—using different designations. Indeed, given the centrality of the two principles in the text, it seems unlikely that Schelling would have pulled them out of thin air without preparing the way in his previous writings.

In fact, when Schelling introduces the distinction between the two principles in the *Freiheitsschrift*, he cites the *Darstellung meines Systems* (1801) as the first text in which this distinction appears (SW VII, 358). However, because the passages that concern the distinction in the earlier text are rather obscure, and Schelling rarely uses the language of "ground of existence" and "that-which-exists" in the texts leading up to 1809,[18] it is tempting to view the distinction as something essentially new to the *Freiheitsschrift*, clothed in terminology he had used earlier.[19] It is my contention, however, that the distinction has long been present in other forms, and it has long served an important role in Schelling's philosophy. What is new in the *Freiheitsschrift* is not the distinction between the two principles as such but rather their dynamic relationship and the emphasis that Schelling places on their relation to existence—especially the "grounding role" of the ground of God's existence.

The key to understanding how the two principles have already played an important role in Schelling's philosophy is to recognize something that Schelling never says straightforwardly in the *Freiheitsschrift*: that-which-exists is the *ideal principle*, and the ground of existence is the *real principle*. Despite the obvious importance of this characterization—both systematically and for connecting the distinction to Schelling's earlier work—there is little explicit acknowledgment of this aspect of the distinction among commentators.[20] Nevertheless, the *Freiheitsschrift* provides an abundance of textual evidence that the distinction is between an ideal and a real principle. Schelling's most direct statement occurs toward the end in the discussion of the *Ungrund*: "Real [*Reales*] and ideal [*Ideales*], darkness and light, or however we otherwise want to designate the two principles . . ." (SW VII, 407). In several passages, Schelling refers to that-which-exists as "the ideal principle." For example, when characterizing the nature of God as personality, he writes: "God is the highest personality through the connection of *the ideal principle* in him with the (relative to it) independent ground, since basis and that-which-exists in him necessarily unify themselves in one absolute existence" (SW VII, 395, emphasis added).[21] And in at least one instance in the *Freiheitsschrift* Schelling also refers to the ground as a "real principle."[22]

If Schelling is less than direct in the *Freiheitsschrift*, the characterization of the two principles as ideal and real is unambiguous in the *Stuttgart Private Lectures* from the following year. He there offers the following summary statement of the principles in God: "The real [*das Reale*] is not God himself, although inseparably connected with him. For [1] the real in God is *being* or existence, [2] the ideal [*das Ideale*] is *that-which-exists*, [3] that in which the real and the ideal are one is the actually-existing, living God" (SW VII, 430). That-which-exists (*das Existierende*) is the ideal principle in God, and the other principle is the real principle. However, as we can see already from this quotation, Schelling adopts a terminology in the *Stuttgart Private Lectures* that differs slightly from that in the *Freiheitsschrift*. In particular, he refers to the real principle as "being" or "existence," not the "ground of existence." Thus, in the *Stuttgart Private Lectures* Schelling most commonly refers to the two principles as (1) that-which-is (*das Seiende*) and (2) being (*das Sein*)— terminology that carries over into the *Ages of the World*.[23] Nevertheless, despite the different designations, the principles have the same essential characteristics as the two principles in the *Freiheitsschrift*. For example, in the quotation Schelling says that the real principle "is not God himself, although inseparably connected with him."[24]

The fact that (1) that-which-exists is the ideal principle and (2) the ground of existence is the real principle has an interesting consequence: the relationship between the two principles corresponds to the relationship between idealism and realism, or the relationship between the "ideal part" of philosophy and the philosophy of nature. Above I noted that the distinction between the two principles articulates the structure of reality as such, and it can be applied at every level—the highest level being God himself, who encompasses the whole of reality. But the structure of philosophy reflects the structure of reality as a whole. Just as God has two principles within himself, so too does philosophy have two parts: a real part (the philosophy of nature)[25] and an ideal part.[26] Indeed, Schelling identifies the ground of God's existence with nature (SW VII, 358), which Schelling had long associated with the real part of philosophy.

As if to confirm the connection between Schelling's distinction and the structure of philosophy as a whole, the passage immediately preceding his initial formulation of the distinction treats the relationship between idealism and realism, or the relationship between the ideal and the real parts of philosophy.[27] In fact, Schelling's description of this relationship is at the same time an excellent description of the relationship between the two principles in God. First, he notes that idealism needs "as its basis a living realism" in order to avoid abstract dogmatism. Modern philosophy is deficient because nature is not present for it, and it therefore "lacks a living ground." Schelling then introduces an analogy for the relationship between idealism and realism: "Idealism is the soul of philosophy; realism is the body; only both together can constitute a living whole. The latter can never provide the principle but must be the ground and medium [*Mittel*] in which the former makes itself real and takes on flesh and blood" (SW VII, 356). We will return to this analogy below when discussing the relationship between that-which-exists and the ground of existence. But already in this quotation we can see certain parallels between idealism and that-which-exists on the one hand, and between realism and the ground of existence on the other. Realism is the ground in which idealism makes itself real or actual. In other words, realism is the *ground of the existence* of idealism—just as the real principle in God is the ground of the existence of that-which-exists. Moreover, the precise character of the grounding in this passage anticipates what we will see below with respect to the ground of God's existence. The ground is not an efficient cause that produces by itself what it grounds. Rather, the ground is a medium (*Mittel*) in which something is actualized.

Schelling's insistence that two sides of philosophy are necessary, and that reality as a whole has two principles or "beginnings," recalls the structure and content of Plato's *Timaeus*. Indeed, Schelling's relationship with the *Timaeus* reaches back to the beginning of his philosophical development, when he wrote an unpublished commentary on that dialogue (1794). In the *Freiheitsschrift* itself Schelling likens the ground to "Plato's matter" (SW VII, 360)—almost certainly a reference to the χώρα in the *Timaeus*—and he later discusses the relationship between "Platonic matter" and God (SW VII, 374).[28] How do the structure and content of the *Timaeus* relate to the two sides of philosophy and the two principles in Schelling? Midway through the *Timaeus*, the character Timaeus makes a new beginning and embarks on a second discourse—the "other side" of his cosmology. Before he had mostly spoken of the way in which things were crafted by intellect (νοῦς). Now he turns to an account of how things came to be through necessity (ἀνάγκη): "For mixed indeed was the birth of this cosmos here, and begotten from a standing-together of necessity and intellect" (47e–48a).²⁹ Two discourses are necessary because of the two "principles" that gave birth to the cosmos—just as two sides of philosophy are necessary for Schelling because of the two principles that structure all of reality. As John Sallis notes, Schelling's distinction in the *Freiheitsschrift* is a "reinscription" of the distinction in the *Timaeus* between νοῦς and ἀνάγκη.³⁰

This is not the first time the distinction in the *Timaeus* has reappeared in Schelling's philosophy. In fact, the subtitle of Schelling's 1802 dialogue *Bruno*, "On the Divine and Natural Principles of Things," refers to this distinction. In an endnote, Schelling states that the following passage from the *Timaeus* is to serve as a "preliminary explanation" for the subtitle: "One should mark off two forms of cause [αἰτία]—the necessary [τὸ ἀναγκαῖον] and the divine [τὸ θεῖον]—and seek the divine in all things for the sake of gaining a happy life, to the extent that our nature allows" (SW IV, 330).³¹ This passage reformulates the distinction that Timaeus had earlier introduced between the intellect and necessity. But in this passage he refers to the intellect as a divine cause: νοῦς is the means by which the divine demiurge crafts the world. Incidentally, Schelling also refers to the divine principle (that-which-is) in the *Freiheitsschrift* using the German word for νοῦς: *Verstand*, "understanding" (SW VII, 350, 360–62). In any case, Schelling uses the phrases "divine principle" and "natural principle" in *Bruno* to refer to the ideal and the real principles, respectively (SW IV, 305–6).³² As I mentioned above, recognizing that the ground of existence is the real principle and that-which-exists is the ideal principle is the key to connecting the distinction in the *Freiheitsschrift* to Schelling's earlier works. By placing this distinction (articulated in the language of the *Timaeus*) in the title of his dialogue *Bruno*, Schelling already stresses the centrality of the distinction several years before the *Freiheitsschrift*.

2. The Distinction in Relation to the Doctrine of Potencies

The characterization of the distinction in terms of an ideal and a real principle is connected to one other aspect of Schelling's distinction: the relation of the two principles to his doctrine of potencies (*Potenzenlehre*). When we express the distinction in terms of potencies, the ground of existence corresponds to the *first potency* (the real moment), that-which-exists corresponds to the *second potency* (the ideal moment), and existence corresponds to the *third potency*³³ (the moment of the identity or indifference of the first two potencies).[34] If there is little acknowledgement in the secondary literature that the distinction involves a real and an ideal principle, there is even less appreciation for its connection to the doctrine of potencies.[35] Accordingly, before addressing in more detail this doctrine in relation to the distinction, I want to justify in a preliminary way the relevance of the potencies. Of course, the ultimate justification will be the success of this characterization: does it help us to understand what Schelling says about the distinction in the *Freiheitsschrift*? Nonetheless, there are three preliminary reasons for applying the *Potenzenlehre* to the distinction:

(1) In the texts of the *Identitätsphilosophie* leading up to the *Freiheitsschrift*, Schelling expresses the relationship of the real and ideal principles in terms of potencies and the accompanying symbolism. If these are the same principles that appear in the *Freiheitsschrift* as that-which-exists and the ground of existence, as I have claimed, then we can also understand the principles in the *Freiheitsschrift* in terms of potencies.

(2) Although the language and symbolism of the potencies are largely absent from the *Freiheitsschrift* (1809), they play a prominent role again in the *Stuttgart Private Lectures* (1810), which present much of the same material using different terminology. In the lectures, Schelling uses the potencies to articulate the principles in God (SW VII, 430; 433–34) and these same principles as they appear again and again on every level of reality.[36]

(3) Finally, in the *Freiheitsschrift* itself, Schelling applies the doctrine of potencies when explaining the relationship between light and gravity—the forces in nature analogous to the two principles in God (SW VII, 358). We will return to this passage below.

What, then, does Schelling mean by *potency*? Unfortunately, despite the importance of the concept and its almost constant presence in the writings of the *Identitätsphilosophie*, Schelling never gives a comprehensive treatment of its meaning; we will have to piece together an account from his occasional remarks and his use of the concept in practice.[37] The potencies are the different forms or degrees of reality grasped within God or absolute identity.[38] They form a "sequence of steps" (*Stufenfolge*) (SW VII, 179), in which each moment retains the moments that preceded it and on which it rests (SW IV, 77). Thus, a higher potency has a higher degree of reality, because it grasps the lower ones within it (SW VI, 213). However, it is also true that a higher potency unfolds or makes explicit what was hidden or implicit in the lower potencies.[39]

The sequence of potencies has a three-step scheme that is repeated over and over at various levels. Hence Schelling will often refer to the first, second, and third potencies—but these designations apply only for a particular level (for example, something that is the third potency at one level is not the third at another level). The first potency (A^1 or $A = B$) is the real moment: its objectivity outweighs its subjectivity. The second (A^2) is the ideal moment: its subjectivity outweighs its objectivity. The third (A^3) is the moment of indifference, or the identity of the first two potencies: its subjectivity and objectivity are balanced.[40] Here the different potencies are described in terms of different relations of subjectivity and objectivity: either one outweighs the other, or they are both balanced. This is Schelling's way of accounting for difference in his *Identitätsphilosophie*. Because everything that exists is absolute identity, there can be no *qualitative* difference, or difference with respect to essence. There can, however, be *quantitative* difference, or difference with respect to the relative balance of subjectivity or objectivity. In the case of quantitative difference, there is still an identity between subject and object (this subject-object identity is the essence of all that is), but one can outweigh the other to varying degrees. The general formula for quantitative difference is $A = B$, which is also the general formula for a potency (SW IV, 124, 135). The concept of potency and that of quantitative difference are therefore closely related: both involve different balances of subjectivity (A) and objectivity (B).

This connection between quantitative difference and the potencies accounts for one of the more interesting features of the *Potenzenlehre*: the relativity of the potencies. In the *Darstellung meines Systems* (1801), Schelling introduces the image of the magnetic line to illustrate this (§46, SW VII, 137–38).

```
    +                                                          +
  A = B ─────────────────────────────────────────────────── A = B
                              A = A
```

Every potency has a place somewhere on this line. At the center ($A = A$), the amount of subjectivity and objectivity is balanced. As one moves to the left, subjectivity (A) more and more outweighs objectivity (B). (The plus sign indicates this relative imbalance.) Conversely, as one moves to the right, objectivity (B) more and more outweighs subjectivity (A). The two end points of the line are called "poles," and the center is called the "indifference point."

This line can be divided into an infinite number of smaller lines simply by picking any two points on the line: these become the poles of a smaller line. As a result, each smaller line itself has (1) an objective pole, (2) a subjective pole, (3) and an indifference point (midway between). As Schelling notes, the fact that the line can be divided into an infinite number of smaller lines has a significant consequence: every point on the line is at the same time an objective pole, a subjective pole, and an indifference point—relative to different parts of the line (SW IV, 138). Thus, if we consider the marked points on the following line:

```
    +                                              +
    A = B                       | | |           A = B
               A = A            e d f
```

Point d is the indifference point relative to points e and f. Point e is the subjective pole, and point f is the objective pole.[41] However, e can be the subjective pole relative to d and f only because it is to the left of these two points. But for all the points to the left of e, e is relatively objective (farther to the right). Thus, relative to other line segments, e can be the objective pole or the indifference point. As a consequence, any single potency is *objective* relative to some potencies (those to its left) and *subjective* relative to other potencies (those to its right).

This helps to explain how the same threefold schema of the potencies can be repeated over and over again at various levels. This threefold schema corresponds (approximately) to the two poles and indifference point that define every line segment. Once again, the first potency (A^1) is the objective moment, the second potency (A^2) is the subjective moment, and the third potency (A^3) is the indifference or identity of the first two. But the particular designations—first, second, and third—only hold for a particular level (represented by a particular line segment). From the viewpoint of a higher level within nature (a more subjective potency), what appears as the third potency (A^3) on a lower level can become the first potency (A^1) of a higher series. Thus, the schema of three potencies can be repeated again and again.

How, then, do these observations about the relativity of the potencies relate to the distinction between that-which-exists and the ground of existence? Because the ground of existence corresponds to the first potency and that-which-exists corresponds to the second potency, the same thing can be that-which-exists *on one level* but the ground of existence *on another level*. In other words, these designations are not absolute but have meaning only in relation to other potencies on a particular level. This allows us to explain the enigmatic passage in the *Freiheitsschrift* immediately following the application of the fundamental distinction to God. To shed light on the relation between the principles in God, Schelling refers to an "analogical" relation in nature between light and gravity. These are not merely metaphors but potencies that have the same relation to each other as the principles in God, only on another level. Thus, gravity is not only analogous to the ground of God's existence but is itself the ground of existence in relation to light. Similarly, light is not only analogous to God insofar as he exists, but is itself that-which-exists in relation to gravity. In the passage in the *Freiheitsschrift*, Schelling explicitly connects gravity with the concept of potency, and goes on to note the relativity of the designations in the fundamental distinction: "[Gravity] *is* absolute identity, namely considered in a particular potency. For, incidentally, that which relative to gravity appears as existing [*als existierend erscheint*] also belongs in itself to the ground, and hence, nature in general is everything that lies beyond the absolute being of absolute identity" (SW VII, 358). Here Schelling describes the same relativity with respect to the designations "ground" and "that-which-exists" that we have seen with respect to the potencies. Relative to gravity, light "appears as existing." However, at a higher level—at the level of the two principles in God—light belongs to the ground: it is part of nature, which is the ground of God's existence.[42]

This quotation is also noteworthy for the way in which it relates gravity to absolute identity. Gravity *is* absolute identity (Schelling's own emphasis), but only when "considered in a particular [*bestimmten*] potency." The potencies are different respects or different ways of regarding absolute identity. This recalls the language in which Schelling originally introduces the fundamental distinction: the distinction concerns a single being (*Wesen*) regarded in two respects—insofar as (*sofern*) it exists, and insofar as it is the ground of existence. The doctrine of potencies allows us to clarify what "insofar as" means: the distinction concerns a single being regarded with respect to two of its potencies.

At the end of the cited quotation, Schelling provides a remarkable definition of nature: "Nature in general is everything that lies beyond the absolute being [*Sein*] of absolute identity" (SW VII, 358). This line may seem like a radical departure from Schelling's previous *Identitätsphilosophie*: if absolute identity is all that there is, how can something lie beyond its absolute being? Actually, this definition of nature appears verbatim in the inaugural text of the *Identitätsphilosophie*, the 1801 *Darstellung meines Systems*.[43] The context is a discussion of the same relativity of the potencies we have been considering: gravity is the ground of the being of absolute identity on one level (as A^2), but light is the ground of being on a higher level (as A^3), and A^3 is the ground of being on a yet higher level. Schelling then concludes with not one, but two definitions of nature: "By nature we understand absolute identity to the extent that it is regarded, not as being [*seiend*], but as ground of its being [*Sein*], and from this we see in advance that we will name nature everything that lies beyond the absolute being [*Sein*] of absolute identity" (§145, SW IV, 203-4). These definitions of nature arise out of Schelling's reflections on the relativity of the potencies. Each of the potencies within nature can be regarded as ground or existing, depending on what level one is considering. But regarded at the highest level, these potencies all belong to the ground of the being of absolute identity, and this ground is nature.

What, then, are we to make of the second definition of nature, which Schelling quotes in the *Freiheitsschrift*? In context, Schelling infers this definition from the previous line. This definition, therefore, cannot mean that nature is outside of absolute identity, since Schelling had just identified nature with absolute identity to the extent that it is the ground of its being. The key phrase for interpreting the definition is "absolute being": nature does not lie beyond absolute identity as such, but beyond the *absolute being* of absolute identity. Just as nature is an aspect of absolute identity (*insofar as* it is the ground of its being), so too is the absolute being of absolute identity an aspect of absolute identity. But in the previous line of this passage Schelling had already identified the aspect of absolute identity that is *not* nature: absolute identity regarded as being (*seiend*). Nature is everything beyond absolute identity to the extent that it *is* or exists. We can conclude that Schelling—in this passage at least—uses the phrase "absolute being" to refer to that-which-exists, which is the ideal principle in God.[44] Indeed, this interpretation is confirmed by Schelling's comments on this line three years later in his polemic against Jacobi (1812).[45]

Now that we have considered the general aspects of Schelling's doctrine of the potencies, we can ask: why does Schelling refer to these forms or steps of reality as "potencies" (*Potenzen*)? Although Schelling never answers this question directly, there seem to be two reasons for his choice of terminology. First, the German word *Potenz* can mean "mathematical power" or "exponent,"[46] and this is reflected in the symbolism that Schelling uses (A^1, A^2, A^3). In fact, the language of "potentiation" (*Potenzierung*) was introduced by the mathematician Carl Friedrich Hindenburg before it was taken up by Eschenmayer, whose use of potencies Schelling both critiques and appropriates.[47] However, in Schelling "potency" is not meant in any strict mathematical sense but as an indication of the relative strength of subjectivity or ideality[48] (thus the exponents accompany the letter *A*, which stands for the subjective factor). The exponents also reflect the fact that there is a "doubling" of the previous potency: A^2 affirms and thereby contains ideally A^1, the potency that precedes it (cf. SW VII, 427).

The other reason Schelling seems to have chosen the term is suggested by the English translation: "potency." Absolute identity contains all the potencies (implicitly) within itself, without being any potency in particular. The potencies are *potentially* present in the absolute, but are not differentiated (SW VII, 428). Through the process of revelation, the potencies are gradually unfolded and come to appearance: what before was implicit and potential becomes explicit and actual. Though the use of the word *Potenz* in this quasi-Aristotelian sense (as a rough equivalent of δύναμις) is mostly implicit in the texts before 1809, it is especially prominent in the *Freiheitsschrift*. In several passages Schelling speaks of something being "raised" (*erhoben*) from potency to act (*Actus*)—for example, light, which is raised from the dark principle (gravity) as ground (SW VII, 377).[49] In lower potencies the higher potencies are present, but in a state of "potency." As nature develops, each is sequentially raised to act.

With this overall characterization of the *Potenzenlehre* in mind, we can return now to the fundamental distinction in the *Freiheitsschrift*. If the ground of existence and that-which-exists correspond to the first two potencies, as I have argued, how does this help us to understand the distinction? Although we will see the usefulness of applying the *Potenzenlehre* in more detail as we proceed, in general we can say that it sheds light on the distinction in two respects.

First, interpreting the distinction in terms of the potencies allows us to see how it articulates the structure of reality on every level. There is a sequence of three potencies on each level, which correspond to (a) the ground of existence, (b) that-which-exists, and (c) existence. Moreover, the doctrine of potencies shows how the terms of the distinction (ground, that-which-exists) are not absolute but have meaning relative to other potencies on a particular level of reality.

Second, the doctrine of the potencies is helpful for understanding the grounding relations among the terms of the distinction. This is true not only with respect to the potencies on a single level, but also with respect to the relation of all of the potencies within the system. In particular, we will see in the final section of this chapter how the concept of potency is connected to another version of the law of ground, which Schelling introduces in the *Freiheitsschrift* after the initial application of the distinction to God.

3. The Distinction within the Distinction

In the introduction to this chapter, I noted the difficulty in interpreting Schelling's distinction, especially if one relies only on what he writes in the *Freiheitsschrift*. As a consequence, the vast majority of commentators make a fundamental mistake when writing about this distinction: they do not distinguish existence (*Existenz*) from that-which-exists (*das Existierende*). When initially introducing the distinction, Schelling writes that it is between "being insofar as it exists and being insofar as it is merely the ground of existence" (SW VII, 358). Since he presents this as a two-way distinction, it is natural to assume that the existence referred to in the phrase "ground of existence" is precisely the first element of the distinction—being (*Wesen*) insofar as it exists. The distinction would therefore concern the existence of something and the ground of its existence. Accordingly, Heidegger and most modern commentators write about a distinction between "ground and existence."[50] In fact, Heidegger's oversight is especially ironic, given the importance of the distinction between *Sein* and *Seiendes* in his own thought.

Admittedly, Schelling never clearly states in the *Freiheitsschrift* that he distinguishes that-which-exists and existence. Indeed, he never treats existence thematically as a topic independent of that-which-exists. Nevertheless, Schelling consistently uses the participial noun *Existierendes* (that-which-exists) throughout the work, despite the fact that *Existenz* would be less awkward. More decisively, he stresses the distinction in his public reply to Eschenmayer's objections to the *Freiheitsschrift*, which Schelling published in 1812. Eschenmayer had objected that, if God has the ground of his existence in himself, then God's existence and the ground of his existence would collapse into one—that is, there would be no real distinction. Schelling in his reply notes that this objection is based on a mistaken interpretation: "I have not spoken at all of a difference between existence [*Existenz*] and the ground for existence, but rather a difference between *that-which-exists* [*dem Existierenden*] and the ground for existence—which, as you see yourself, is a significant difference" (SW VIII, 164). Somewhat later in his reply Schelling refers to existence and that-which-exists as "two concepts that are worlds apart" (*zwei himmelweit verschiedene Begriffe*) (SW VIII, 172). He characterizes that-which-exists as the "subject of existence" and gives the Greek τὸ ὄν in parentheses. (Presumably existence would correspond to the Greek εἶναι.) Since this distinction between existence and that-which-exists is implicit *within* Schelling's fundamental distinction, I will refer to it as the "distinction within the distinction."[51]

Why is this second distinction important? Is it merely a matter of precision without wider implications? We can begin to see its significance if we articulate it in terms of potencies. The ground of existence corresponds to the first potency (the real moment), that-which-exists corresponds to the second potency (the ideal moment), and existence corresponds to the third potency (the uniting of the first two moments). If one confuses existence with that-which-exists, one is actually confusing the second potency with the third.[52] Moreover, a failure to distinguish existence from that-which-exists has two other decisive consequences: (1) The relationship between that-which-exists and the ground of existence is fundamentally misunderstood. (2) The question "what is existence?" is not posed as a question separate from the question "what is that-which-exists?" In the remainder of this section, I will discuss these two consequences. However, my treatment of the first consequence will be comparatively brief here, since I discuss it in more detail in the next section, which deals with the nature of grounding in the distinction.

(1) *The relationship between that-which-exists and the ground of existence.* If one assumes that existence is the same as that-which-exists, this relationship is clear enough: the ground of existence is the *ground* of that-which-exists. However, Schelling denies this in his reply to Eschenmayer: "The ground for existence cannot be ground for anything other than *existing* [*Existieren*], purely as such; [it is] not, however, ground of that *which exists* [*was existiert*], the subject of existence" (SW VIII, 172). The ground is not the ground of that-which-exists, but the ground of the *existence* of that-which-exists: the ground is what allows that-which-exists *to exist*. But here one might object: isn't the ground of the existence of a thing *also* the ground of that thing? This objection presupposes that "existence" has the ordinary sense of "being at all." But Schelling has a different sense in mind.

(2) *The question: what is existence?* Failing to make the "distinction within the distinction" has another consequence: the question *what is existence?* is never really posed. If one assumes that existence is the same as that-which-exists, one will accept Schelling's description of the latter as a sufficient account of the former. This tendency is reinforced by his mode of presentation in the *Freiheitsschrift* itself. Though Schelling has much to say about that-which-exists and its relation to the ground, he never singles out existence as a topic for examination.

Nevertheless, there are passages in the *Freiheitsschrift* where we can discern an indirect characterization of existence. For example, when treating the relationship of the *Ungrund* to ground and that-which-exists, Schelling writes: "The non-ground divides itself into the two exactly equal beginnings, only so that the two . . . become one through love, that is, it divides itself only so that there may be life and love and personal existence" (SW VII, 408). Somehow the uniting of the two principles through love is connected with the coming to be of "personal existence," which is mentioned together with life and love. In another passage, Schelling indirectly associates existence with life and personality: "Only in personality is there life, and all personality rests on a dark ground" (SW VII, 413). From what follows it becomes clear that this dark ground is the ground of existence. Thus, the ground of existence is also the ground of personality. As we can begin to see in these examples, there is a cluster of concepts associated with existence, which Schelling at times seems to identify with existence, even if they are more precisely differentiated in other contexts. This cluster includes life, personality, spirit, revelation, and actualization.

There is, however, a fundamental ambiguity in Schelling's use of the term "existence." On the one hand, it corresponds to the third potency in each series, which unites the first two potencies. We can therefore characterize existence as the unity of that-which-exists (the second potency) and the ground of existence (the first potency). This explains the connection of existence to life and personality, which are also defined in terms of the dynamic unity of the principles. Thus, in the discussion of divine freedom, Schelling characterizes God's "absolute existence" in this way:

> We have explained God as a living unity of forces; and if personality is founded . . . on the connection [*Verbindung*] of something autonomous with a basis independent of it, then, similarly, because both of these completely interpenetrate and are but one being [*Wesen*], God is the highest personality

through the connection of the ideal principle in him with the (relative to it) independent ground, *since basis and that-which-exists in him necessarily unify themselves in one absolute existence.* (SW VII, 394–95, emphasis added)

Both personality and existence involve the connection, unification, and interpenetration of the two principles in God.[53]

On the other hand, Schelling uses the term "existence" to mean *revelation* or manifestation. Although this meaning seems to be very different from the first, the two are closely related: God is fully revealed in the dynamic unity of the two principles. The meaning of existence as revelation can be inferred from certain passages in the *Freiheitsschrift*, but it is more explicit in the replies to Georgii (1810) and Eschenmayer (1812), which correct misunderstandings related to the fundamental distinction. Georgii was the host for the series of lectures Schelling gave in Stuttgart the year following the *Freiheitsschrift*. Referring to the passage in the treatise that introduces the fundamental distinction in God, Georgii asks if God is no longer an *ens a se*—the traditional concept of something that exists "from itself" (*a se*), requiring nothing outside itself to exist. If God has a ground for his existence that is different from God, does this mean that God no longer exists *a se*? In posing this question, Georgii makes the assumption that "existence" in the phrase "ground of existence" simply means "being" in the broadest sense—the sense in which we refer to the "proofs for the existence of God." This assumption would seem reasonable, since Schelling does not give direct indications that he has a special sense of existence in mind.

But Schelling insists that he is not giving up the traditional notion of God as existing *a se*. As that-which-exists or that-which-is,[54] God *is by nature*, and thus God does not require the ground in order simply to *be*.[55] But the ground is necessary for God's existence, understood in a different sense: "That-which-is-*suâ naturâ* [by its nature], thus *a se*, in God is *actu*, that is, it proves itself *as* that-which-is-*suâ naturâ* by seeking to raise that-which-(relatively)-is-not (B) to itself, to assimilate and to divinize it."[56] Here Schelling distinguishes between (i) being and (ii) being *actu*, or "actually" being. The latter is what Schelling means by "existence" in the *Freiheitsschrift*: the ground of God's existence is not the ground for God being at all, but the ground for God being *actu*.[57] But how is being *actu* different from just being? Doesn't being already imply actuality? In the quotation above, Schelling explains that God is *actu* in proving himself *as* that-which-is, and this is accomplished by acting in certain ways on and within the ground. Accordingly, the "actuality" of God's existence has two aspects: (1) the revelation or showing forth of God *as* what he is, and (2) the activity by which this self-manifestation of God occurs.

The word "revelation" (*Offenbarung*) appears throughout the *Freiheitsschrift*, and Schelling uses it as another way of referring to the process of creation. Early in the treatise he begins to use the term in this way: "The procession [*Folge*] of things from God is a self-revelation of God" (SW VII, 347). It is a *self*-revelation because God is both its subject and object, both what reveals and what is revealed in creation. Moreover, when Schelling speaks of the process of creation, he refers to the ground of God's existence as "the will for revelation" (SW VII, 375) and "the ground for revelation" (SW VII, 388)—further evidence that revelation is essential to the meaning of "existence."[58]

The fact that Schelling in his letter to Georgii distinguishes (i) being from (ii) being actual implies that it is at least conceivable for something to be without being actual.[59] Something similar is also implicit in the concept of revelation: what is revealed is not simply identical with its own revelation, but precedes or is in some way independent of being revealed. In other words, revelation always implies a prior state of concealment of the revealed object; otherwise, there would be nothing to be revealed. Thus, Schelling speaks of God as that-which-is "before all manifestation"[60]—although the word "before" cannot indicate a temporal priority, because time is itself part of creation or revelation.[61] In his reply to Eschenmayer, Schelling calls the ground "the only tool of the actualization of the *concealed* essence [*Wesen*] of the deity, which in itself [*an sich*] is *merely in itself* [*in sich selbst*]" (SW VIII, 170, emphasis added). Before being revealed, God is concealed and enclosed within himself. In revealing his previously concealed essence, God shows himself *as* what he is.[62] Thus, we can infer one further consequence of conflating existence and that-which-exists: in effect, it conflates revelation and what is revealed.

In the quotation from his reply to Eschenmayer, Schelling refers to God's concealed essence as "merely in itself." Accordingly, the disclosure involved in revelation would be a coming-out or externalizing of what was previously enclosed. This explains why Schelling chooses the word "existence" to express God's state as revealed and actualized: the Latin verb *exsistere* literally means "to stand out," "to emerge," and thus "to come to appearance."[63] Schelling emphasizes this externality when he refers to existence as "external-being" (*äußerlich-Sein*) and "outwardly effective existence" (*äußerlich wirkende Existenz*) (SW VIII, 173–74).[64] But this raises a question: how can God be externalized? Doesn't this imply that there is something outside of God? But how can that be, if God is all things?

The key to answering these questions is the doctrine of the potencies. As we saw in the last section, the potencies are defined by their quantitative difference, or imbalance of subjectivity and objectivity relative to the whole. But Schelling notes in the 1801 *Darstellung* that quantitative difference is only possible "*outside* of absolute identity" (§25, SW IV, 125). Within absolute identity all of the potencies are (ideally) present, but balance each other out in a state of quantitative indifference. To reveal what is (ideally) present in absolute identity, there is a gradual unfolding of the potencies by which they are pulled apart and differentiated, and thus come to appearance. The complete existence of God is the culmination of this process of unfolding. And yet as unfolded the potencies are outside of absolute identity to the extent that *within* absolute identity the potencies are in a state of enfolded indistinguishability.

This process of the unfolding of potencies is connected to one final aspect of existence, which we noted in the letter to Georgii: it involves activity, by which the agent is revealed. As Schelling notes in the letter, that-which-is proves itself *as* that-which-is by acting on and in the ground. This action is a process, whose end result is the actual existence of God. In the *Freiheitsschrift*, Schelling describes this activity of the ideal principle, which he designates as the "understanding." On the one hand, its activity involves division and unfolding: "The first effect [*Wirkung*] of the understanding in nature is the division [*Scheidung*] of forces, since only thus can the understanding unfold the unity that is unconsciously but necessarily immanent in nature as in a seed" (SW VII, 361). But Schelling also characterizes this activity in terms of the "in-forming" (*Ein-Bildung*) of nature and even the "awakening" (*Erweckung*) of the unity hidden in the ground (SW VII, 362). (Incidentally, although Schelling also designates that which arises from the ground as that-which-exists, he is careful to distinguish this from the ideal principle in God, which is *originally* that-which-exists.[65])

We can now summarize the various ways of characterizing existence in Schelling. (1) Existence is the revelation or manifestation of what exists. (2) As revelation, existence requires the externalization or emergence of what is revealed. (3) This externalization takes place through the activity of what is revealed in something outside itself (the ground). (4) As the end result of this process of revelation/externalization, that-which-exists is unified with the ground. This unity is existence in the fullest sense. (5) As the unity of ground and that-which-exists, existence is related to a cluster of concepts that includes life, personality, and spirit. With this characterization of existence in mind, we are now in a position to examine what it means to be the *ground* of existence.

4. The Grounding Character of the Ground of Existence

In the previous chapters we encountered various senses of ground, especially in the context of God's grounding relationship to things. Now, in considering Schelling's fundamental distinction, the word "ground" appears again. But what is the sense of ground in the phrase "ground of existence"? Does it have the same meaning here that we saw with respect to God's creative activity?

Before addressing these questions, it is important to recall something I noted in the first section of this chapter: "that-which-exists" and the "ground of existence" are two designations or ways of naming the ideal and the real principles. Each designation names its respective principle in terms of a certain aspect or role the principle plays. Accordingly, these designations do not provide an exhaustive characterization of what that principle is: it may have other aspects or roles not directly related to its designation. For example, "ground of existence" is a designation for the real principle, and this designation picks out a role that the principle plays. But not everything that is true of the principle need pertain to its role as ground. Indeed, Schelling provides a rich characterization of the ground of existence in the *Freiheitsschrift*, using metaphorical language derived in part from the mystic Jacob Boehme.[66] In particular, Schelling describes the ground in terms of longing (*Sehnsucht*).[67] The ground is an unconscious but "divining" (*ahnend*) will that yearns to give birth to God (SW VII, 359). But these descriptions do not directly address the question of why the ground of existence is a *ground*. Rather than develop a full account of the ground of existence that would consider all of its aspects, I would like to focus more narrowly on its role as ground. Here again Schelling's replies to Georgii and Eschenmayer will help to orient our interpretation of the *Freiheitsschrift*.

In his letter to Georgii, Schelling responds to a question: if the ground is the "cause of God" (Lat. *causa Dei*), how can God be prior to the ground, as Schelling says in the *Freiheitsschrift* (SW VII, 358)?[68]

First, Schelling notes that he has never spoken of a "ground of God" but rather of a "ground of the *actual existing* of God" or a "ground of the *actual existing* of that-which-is."[69] Here again we see the importance of distinguishing existence from God as that-which-exists: without this distinction, one misidentifies *what* is grounded. Schelling then corrects Georgii's misinterpretation of the word "ground." One should not confuse *ground* with *cause*: "Cause and ground are related as *causa* and *conditio sine qua non*. That I do not understand 'cause' by the term 'ground,' I thought was sufficiently indicated by this: that I also called the ground *foundation* [*Fundament*], substrate [*Unterlage*], groundwork [*Grundlage*], basis [*Basis*]."[70] In this passage, Schelling not only distinguishes ground from cause but begins to define it positively through the phrase conditio sine qua non and a cluster of words that all roughly mean "foundation." Unfortunately, Schelling does not specify the precise sense in which he understands cause: we will have occasion to return to its meaning below. In any case, later in the letter to Georgii, he refers to the ground and writes in parentheses: "means of realization" (*Realisierungsmittel*).[71] The ground of existence is the means (or even tool) for achieving existence. Finally, in the *Freiheitsschrift* itself Schelling uses the language of giving birth and begetting to characterize the grounding of the ground. Accordingly, I will develop these four aspects of the grounding character of the ground of existence: (1) ground as conditio sine qua non, (2) ground as foundation, (3) ground as means or tool, and (4) ground as what gives birth.

(1) Ground as conditio sine qua non. The ground of existence is the "necessary condition" or the "condition of the possibility" of existence. Without the ground of existence, existence would not be possible.[72] We have seen this sense of ground several times before, and I have claimed that it is the central meaning of ground in the *Freiheitsschrift*: it allows for dependence without determination, and thereby leaves room for freedom. In the reply to Eschenmayer, Schelling also characterizes the ground using the word "condition" (*Bedingung*): "The irrational principle in God, which by itself lacks understanding, is for God ground, that is, foundation, *condition*, medium of the revelation of his subject as it is only in itself, or the *condition* of his outwardly effective existence" (SW VIII, 173, emphasis added). The ground is the condition of the revelation of God. Accordingly, if ground means condition and existence means revelation (as we saw in the previous section), we can reformulate Schelling's distinction in an illuminating way: *what is revealed* is distinguished from *the condition of its revelation*.

Toward the end of the *Freiheitsschrift* Schelling refers several times to the ground as condition. In the section that treats the freedom of God in relation to evil, he writes: "What comes from the mere condition [*Bedingung*] or the ground, does not come from God, although it is necessary for his existence" (SW VII, 399). Later he explains that God cannot abolish the will of the ground: "This would be precisely as much as to say that God would abolish the condition of his existence" (SW VII, 403). And in a passage that shows the necessity of having the ground of existence, Schelling uses the word "condition" again and again as his designation for the ground. The passage begins: "All existence demands a condition so that it may become actual [*wirklich*], namely personal, existence. Even God's existence could not be personal without such a condition except that he has this condition *within* and not outside himself" (SW VII, 399). Here it is clear that the ground of God's existence is the necessary condition of God's real, personal existence.

But how is the ground the necessary condition? We have seen the answer to this question in the previous section. Existence essentially involves revelation or manifestation, and Schelling notes in the *Stuttgart Private Lectures*: "Each thing, in order to manifest itself, requires something which is not *itself* in the strict sense" (SW VII, 435). The ground, as something essentially other than that-which-exists, is the necessary condition for the latter's manifestation. Moreover, we saw that Schelling also defines existence as the interpenetrating unity of the two principles. But such a unity would be impossible without the ground, which is the real principle.

(2) Ground as *foundation*. In the letter to Georgii, Schelling cites a cluster of words that he had used to name the ground: *Fundament, Unterlage, Grundlage, Basis*.[73] All of these words mean roughly "foundation." As such, they bring out the spatial element in the word *Grund* and its English equivalent: the ground is what lies *beneath*. In addition to this spatial element, the concept of foundation involves a functional relation: it *supports* what is above it; what is on top *rests on* it. In the context of the letter to Georgii, Schelling cites this characterization of ground as "foundation" as evidence that he does not intend ground to mean cause (*Ursache*). But what is the difference? By "cause," Schelling seems to have in mind something that actively brings forth another thing. But this is not the case with a foundation: a building's foundation does not generate the building but supports it once it is built—and prior to this, it provides the space on which the building is constructed. Because the ground does

not actively bring forth what it grounds, Schelling denies in his reply to Eschenmayer that "ground" is a correlate to "consequence" (*Folge*): it does not have consequences that "follow from it." Schelling refers to this as the "vulgar sense" of ground (SW VIII, 165)—though Schelling himself sometimes pairs ground and consequence, as we have seen in his account of the copula in the *Freiheitsschrift*![74]

Although it is easy to overlook, Schelling's distinction between cause and foundation is a remarkable departure from the metaphysical tradition—and one that signals the basis for his solution to the problem of a system of freedom. As we saw in chapter 1, one of the dominant models for system in the modern period is that of a building. In the *Meditations* Descartes razes the edifice of his knowledge and begins again from the foundations. Fichte also describes the *Wissenschaftslehre* as a building founded on "solid earth" (FW I, 42–43). But the foundation of these systems is also the principle from which all else is derived. The principle not only supports but brings forth what rests on it, and does so with necessity. If we take a step back, it is indeed strange that the architectural metaphor for system should be coupled with the demand to derive everything from the foundation—as if the foundations of a building could produce the building itself! What Schelling in part accomplishes through his emphasis on the foundational character of the ground is a return to the original sense of the language: the ground as foundation is the condition of the possibility of what rests on it, but does not produce it.

I noted that the concept of ground as foundation has two aspects: it is *spatially* what lies beneath and *functionally* what provides support for what rests on it. Both aspects are important in Schelling's characterization of the ground of existence. First, the ground is *lower* in terms of potency: as the first, it precedes the other potencies that are based on it and consequently higher. In the *Ages of the World*, Schelling notes that there is an inverse relation between priority and superiority, because what is "higher" follows what is "lower" (WA I, 26). Moreover, the "proper" or divine relationship between the ground and that-which-exists requires that the ground be subordinate to (or lower than) that-which-exists (SW VII, 365). As we will see in the next chapter, evil is an inversion of this relationship: the self-will (which corresponds to the ground) is elevated instead of serving as the basis (SW VII, 389). Here, incidentally, we can see the importance of distinguishing "ground" as a designation from the real principle it designates: the real principle *should be* a ground or basis, but in evil its proper role is not fulfilled.[75]

Finally, as foundation, the ground of existence supports what rests on it.[76] We have seen in what way this is true with respect to the doctrine of the potencies: the higher potencies rest on the lower ones and contain the lower potencies in themselves. The ground as the first potency supports the potencies that come after it. This "supporting" role of the ground is also evident in Schelling's critique of one-sided idealism, which lacks a living realism as its basis; it thus lacks a "living foundation" and becomes empty and abstract, because it is not grounded in reality (SW VII, 356). Such emptiness and abstraction are also evident in a conception of God that does not include the ground of his existence. The true conception of God "does not hover [*schwebt*] in the air" but rests on firm ground (SW VII, 438).

(3) Ground as *means* or *tool*. Above we saw how the fundamental distinction in Schelling parallels the distinction between νοῦς and ἀνάγκη in Plato's *Timaeus*. Schelling's account of the ground shares another feature of the *Timaeus*: the tension between the model of ποίησις and τέχνη on the one hand, and the model of procreation and birth on the other.[77] The third characterization of the ground reflects the model of ποίησις: a craftsman has an image or paradigm in mind and crafts a product by shaping its material. The difficulty is that Schelling seems to give the ground different roles in this model. This is evident when he first introduces the word "tool" (*Werkzeug*) to describe the ground: "The understanding together with yearning becomes a freely creating and all-powerful will and builds in the initially unruly nature as in its element [*Element*] or tool" (SW VII, 361). On the one hand, nature as ground is the "element" *in which* the understanding builds. Along these lines, Schelling refers to the real principle in God as the material or "stuff" (*Stoff*) out of which everything is created (SW VII, 439). On the other hand, nature as ground is the tool or instrument by means of which the understanding creates.[78] This role of the ground is an important part of the proper relation of the two principles that we noted above. Here again, evil is a reversal of the respective roles: "Man, instead of making his selfhood [i.e., ground] into the basis, the instrument [*Organ*], can strive to elevate it into the ruling and total will and, conversely, to make the spiritual within himself into a means [*Mittel*]" (SW VII, 389).

What are we to make of this ambiguity in the ground's role—on the one hand, stuff or material; on the other hand, tool of production? What seems most important for Schelling is what is common to both: the instrumentality of the ground *in service of* the actualization or revelation of

God. Both material and tools are used as means of production. Thus, in the letter to Georgii he calls the ground of existence "the means of realization" (*Realisierungsmittel*).[79] Incidentally, we have seen that the understanding or the ideal principle (that-which-exists) is what acts on the ground in this process, producing an "effect" (*Wirkung*).[80] Thus, Schelling refers to the ideal principle as "cause" (*Ursache*) in contrast to the real principle as "ground." For example, in describing the reversal of the principles in evil, he refers to the striving "to reverse the relation of the principles, to elevate the ground over the cause" (SW VII, 365).[81] The causality of the ideal principle will appear again in the next characterization.

(4) Ground as *what gives birth*. In contrast to the previous model of technical production, Schelling also describes the ground according to the model of procreation and birth.[82] In the *Freiheitsschrift*, Schelling proposes to characterize the ground in terms "humanly closer to us" (*uns menschlich näher*): "It is the yearning the eternal One feels to give birth to itself. . . . The yearning wants to give birth to God, that is, unfathomable unity, but in this respect there is not yet unity in the yearning itself" (SW VII, 359). It is noteworthy that Schelling here does not yet describe the ground as what gives birth to God but what *wants* or *yearns* to give birth to God. Considered in itself, the ground is not yet fulfilled in this desire. As we will see, it requires something else to give birth: the father.[83] This not-yet-fulfilled character of the ground matches the above characterization of the ground as condition of the possibility. The ground is necessary for there to be birth, but it is not alone sufficient.[84]

In the 1804 *Würzburg System*, Schelling describes the relationship between gravity and light, the forces in nature that are analogous to the two principles in God (cf. SW VII, 358). Here he characterizes gravity (as the ground of existence) in terms of giving birth; in fact, the image of birth contains the whole constellation of ground of existence—that-which-exists—existence:

> To the extent gravity provides the *ground* of reality [*Realität*], in which the particular things first come to be, and from which they emerge with their own life—thus, to the extent that gravity is in general the receiving and motherly principle of things, light is the fatherly principle of all things in nature. Impregnated by light, gravity gives birth to the particular forms of things and releases them from her fruitful womb to their own life. (SW VI, 266)

As the ground of existence, gravity is the "motherly principle" (*mütterliches Prinzip*). Light, on the other hand, corresponds to God as that-which-exists. This is the "fatherly principle" (*väterliches Prinzip*) that actively works in the ground to bring forth existence. (Schelling had referred to light earlier in the passage as the "cause."[85]) Finally, there is the offspring—the particular things with their own life, corresponding to existence. Thus, as the mother, the ground of existence is the necessary condition of existence but is not alone sufficient to bring it forth. This requires that-which-exists (light) as the fatherly principle. Here again we can see one of the consequences of confusing existence with that-which-exists: this would be confusing the fatherly principle (that-which-exists) with the offspring (existence).[86]

In addition to procreation, there is another remarkable image that helps us to understand the constellation of ground of existence—that-which-exists—existence. Schelling introduces it in the *Freiheitsschrift* when describing the relationship between realism and idealism: "Idealism is the soul of philosophy; realism is the body; only both together can constitute a living whole. The latter can never provide the principle but must be the ground and medium [*Mittel*] in which the former makes itself actual [*sich verwirklicht*] and takes on flesh and blood" (SW VII, 356). As we saw above, the relationship between realism and idealism reflects the relationship between the real principle (the ground) and the ideal principle (that-which-exists). Thus, if we apply the image to Schelling's distinction, the soul is the ideal principle (that-which-exists), the body is the real principle (the ground), and the living organism is the unity of the ideal and real principles (existence). In other words, the body is the ground of the existence of the soul by allowing it to be revealed and become visibly manifest. In the *Stuttgart Private Lectures*, Schelling notes that nature reaches a point where it becomes for the ideal principle "its immediate manifestation—its body, as it were" (SW VII, 454). Just as the body is not the ground of the soul, so too is the ground of existence not the ground of that-which-exists—it is the condition of its manifestation.

We have seen that Schelling characterizes the grounding character of the ground of existence in different ways: (1) as condition of the possibility, (2) as foundation, (3) as means or tool, and (4) as what gives birth. However, the first of these is primary and is implicitly contained in each of the others. A foundation is the condition of the possibility of what rests on it; the means is the condition of the possibility of what is produced; what gives birth is the condition of the possibility of what is born. We have already seen numerous instances of this sense of grounding in Schelling, and we will now turn to its implications with respect to a system of freedom.

5. Grounding Relations in a System of Freedom

In the last section, we saw that the real principle is a ground primarily in the sense of a condition of the possibility. In this section, we will see that this sense of ground is not unique to the real principle; indeed, it defines the relationships in the constellation ground—that-which-exists—existence. And, by extension, it defines the relationships among all the parts of Schelling's system.

We can begin to see the wider application of this sense of grounding in the discussion of love in the section on the *Ungrund*, the subject of chapter 6. Through love, the two principles in God become one. After noting the role of love in uniting that-which-exists with the ground, Schelling formulates what he calls *das Geheimnis der Liebe*: "This is the mystery of love, that it links such things of which each could exist for itself, yet does not and cannot exist without the other" (SW VII, 408). Evidently, Schelling regarded this as a powerful insight because he repeats it almost verbatim in several texts during this period.[87] Elsewhere he connects it with the idea of a "divine identity," as opposed to a merely finite identity (SW VII, 174). In this line he says that each of the two principles "cannot exist without the other." In other words, each is the condition of the possibility of the other. Thus, if we understand ground to mean condition of the possibility, the two principles are *mutually grounding*.

But the passage is puzzling because it seems to contain an outright contradiction: on the one hand, each of the principles "could exist for itself" (*für sich sein könnte*); on the other hand, each "cannot exist without the other" (*nicht sein kann ohne das andere*). To resolve this contradiction, we need to turn to other texts, especially the 1804 *Würzburg System*, where Schelling treats the same theme in more detail. But we can note in advance that we have already encountered this apparent contradiction in other forms: it is the same "square circle" expressed in the phrases "system of freedom" and a "derived absoluteness or divinity." Each requires some mixture of dependence and absolute independence.

In the *Würzburg System*, Schelling discusses the "mystery of eternal love" in the context of his treatment of gender or sexual difference. He refers to the relation of those things combined through love as the "highest of all relations" (SW VI, 407), one that can be uniquely represented through the relationship of the sexes.[88] Male and female individuals are each a whole (*ein Ganzes*), possessing perfect substantiality and independence. And yet Schelling adds: "Notwithstanding this independence, each is again a non-whole, that is, something that can only *be* insofar as what is opposed [to it] is as well, and that only truly *is* in identity with what is opposed [to it]" (SW VI, 407). Each individual is both a whole (and thus independent) and a non-whole (and thus dependent). How is this conceivable? Each individual is a whole *within* a whole. In chapter 1, we saw how each part of Schelling's system is a microcosm—a world within the larger world, or a system within the larger system. And in the parallel passage from the 1806 *Aphorisms*, Schelling makes clear that this embedding of wholes within the whole is necessary for love: "If each were not a whole but only part of a whole, there would not be love: there is love, because each is a whole, and is not and cannot be without the other" (SW VII, 174).[89]

As a whole, each has its own independence; Schelling even says in Würzburg that divine identity requires each of the principles be *in itself* absolute. This is the sense in which Schelling says in the *Freiheitsschrift* that each principle united by love "could exist for itself." On the other hand, each is also part of a larger whole and thus capable of being connected to form a higher unity. Although in one sense it *is* as an independent whole, it "only truly *is*" (*wahrhaft nur ist*)—that is, in a higher sense—in a larger whole, in connection with what is opposed to it (SW VI, 407). This is the sense in which Schelling says that each of the principles united by love "cannot exist without the other." Each is the condition of the other's existing in a higher form. Thus, we can resolve the contradiction in the "mystery of love" by appealing to two senses of being: (1) independent existence as an isolated whole and (2) a higher, dependent existence, united by love.[90]

So far we have noted that the two principles in God are reciprocally dependent and thus reciprocally grounding. In fact, Schelling discusses this reciprocal grounding in the passage following his treatment of light and gravity—the forces in nature that are "analogical" to the two principles in God. Schelling had just claimed that "gravity precedes [*vorgeht*] light as its ever-dark ground," and he goes on to clarify the nature of this priority:

> It is to be thought neither as precedence according to time nor as priority of essence [*Wesen*]. In the circle from which everything comes to be, it is no contradiction that that through which the One is generated [*erzeugt*] may itself be in turn

> begotten [*gezeugt*] by it. . . . God has in himself an inner ground of his existence that in this respect precedes him as existing; but, precisely in this way, God is again the *prius* of the ground insofar as the ground, even as such, could not exist if God did not exist *actu*. (SW VII, 358)

In chapter 2, we discussed the sense of priority that Aristotle calls priority "according to nature and substance." In this sense, what is prior is the condition of the possibility of what is posterior. At the end of this passage, we see Schelling make use of this sense of priority: the ground could not exist if God did not exist *actu*. The actual existence of God is the condition of the possibility of the ground's being. But Schelling notes just before this that the ground precedes God as existing: the ground is the condition of the possibility of God's existence and precedes it in potency.[91] Thus, we have a circular grounding relation between God's existence and its ground.

We can see how this works concretely if we return to the image of soul and body as an analogy for the relation between that-which-exists and the ground of existence. The soul corresponds to that-which-exists, the body corresponds to the ground, and the living organism corresponds to existence. On the one hand, just as a living organism cannot exist without a body, God's existence requires the ground of existence as its necessary condition. On the other hand, the body of an organism, qua organic body, cannot exist independently of its combination with the soul; an organic body without a soul or vital principle is a corpse—that is, no longer an organic body. In this sense, the body requires a living organism as its necessary condition. In the same way, the ground could not exist independently of existence: it only exists when it is joined with that-which-exists to form the existence of God. As a result, God's existence and the ground of his existence ground and presuppose each other.

In allowing for this reciprocal grounding, Schelling is departing from the traditional way of conceiving ground as one-directional: x grounds y, but y cannot in turn ground x.[92] Kant, however, had introduced the possibility of reciprocal grounding in his discussion of organic nature in the third *Critique*. Finite human understanding cannot explain the relations within organisms in terms of mechanical causality because the parts "produce one another" in such a way as to produce the whole.[93] Kant's thinking on organic nature had a profound influence on Schelling—an influence not limited to the domain of organic life or even the philosophy of nature. As mentioned in the last chapter, Schelling returns again and again in his philosophical development to the organism as the model for philosophy as a whole. We can expect, therefore, that the reciprocal relation of "organic grounding" is not limited to the two principles in God but extends throughout his system.

Schelling provides a first indication of this universal extension in another line from the passage cited above: "In the circle from which everything comes to be, it is no contradiction that that through which the One is generated may itself be in turn begotten by it" (SW VII, 358). Here he introduces the image of a circle that is all-encompassing: *everything* becomes or comes to be (*alles wird*) from within its circuit. Moreover, he uses the language of generation (*erzeugen*) and begetting (*zeugen*) to express the circle's reciprocal grounding. We have already seen that Schelling describes the grounding character of the ground of God's existence in terms of giving birth, which is a form of generation.[94] And in the last chapter we discussed God's grounding of things as a begetting (*Zeugung*). But this description of grounding raises the same difficulty we encountered before. We have been speaking of ground in the sense of "condition of possibility," but generation and begetting require something more: the "bringing forth" of what is grounded. As we saw in the discussion of God's grounding in the last chapter, the concept of begetting combines the sense of ground as condition of the possibility with a positive generation or bringing forth that does not determine the essence of what is grounded. Nevertheless, it is easier to conceive of a reciprocal conditioning than it is to conceive of a mutual begetting or generation. As Kant notes in his discussion of organic grounding in the third *Critique*, this reciprocal generation goes beyond the understanding's way of conceiving causal relations.

Schelling's image of the "circle from which everything comes to be" reappears in a slightly different form in the dialogue *Clara* (1809–1812?). The remarkable passage in which this image occurs brings together the elements we have been discussing and anticipates the systematic application of reciprocal grounding, to which we will turn next. The pastor, who narrates, discusses with Clara the relationship among the body, spirit, and soul in the human being. Though potencies are not explicitly mentioned, each human element corresponds to one of them: the body is the first (real moment), the spirit is the second (ideal moment), and the soul is the third (what unites the first two). The pastor notes that each of the three is dependent on the other two for its existence: "The whole of the human being represents a kind of living circuit [*Umlauf*] . . . where each [element] requires the others" (SW IX, 46). A little later he adds that body, spirit, and soul are "essentially linked": you cannot take one away without taking them all away (SW IX, 49).

But it is not only the three potencies that form a "living circuit." All potencies, all of the parts of Schelling's system are organically connected to form a living circle, where each part presupposes the others.[95] In the *Freiheitsschrift*, the passage about the circle expresses this powerfully: "Here there is no first and last because all things mutually presuppose each other, nothing is another thing and yet [it] is not without another thing" (SW VII, 358). Because all things "mutually presuppose each other" (*sich gegenseitig voraussetzt*), each thing is the condition of the possibility or the *ground* of everything else. It is impossible to take away one thing without taking away the whole. As a result of this reciprocal grounding, "there is no first and last." Here we have a striking statement of equiprimordiality—part of a larger movement toward equiprimordiality in Schelling's treatise. Nothing is prior to anything else, because the circle has no beginning or end point. Traditionally, one would say that the ground is prior to what is grounded. But if everything grounds everything else, *everything* would have to be prior—that is, nothing is.

Of course, we should note that there are other senses in which there is priority. Although each thing is the condition of everything else, there are different ways in which something can be a condition. The different potencies have different roles to play, and as a result, the grounding function of each takes on a different character. For example, the ground of existence is also ground in the sense of "foundation" or what lies beneath. Thus, it is prior to existence in terms of potency: as a lower potency, it comes first and underlies the other potencies in the sequence. On the other hand, existence as the unity of the ground with that-which-exists is more complete and has a "higher dignity," although it comes later as a potency. It is prior to the ground, to the extent that an organic whole is prior to (and thus the condition of the possibility of) any of its parts.

We are now in a position to address the consequences of reciprocal grounding for the question of a system of freedom. In chapter 1, I identified the "connectedness of parts" as an essential characteristic of system. A system must form a unity out of many different elements, and this can only happen if the system's parts are integrally connected. Traditionally, this connection is accomplished through grounding: each part is grounded by other parts, so that each is tied to the whole. The principle of ground, by demanding that everything be grounded, is the ultimate principle of connection. But this poses a problem for human freedom, insofar as the grounding is deterministic: the human will would be determined by forces outside itself, thus destroying its independence (assuming a non-compatibilist account of freedom).

By prioritizing another sense of ground, Schelling is able to connect the parts of the system through grounding while at the same time preserving the independence necessary for freedom. First, the primary sense of ground in Schelling is non-deterministic. As a condition of the possibility, the ground does not determine the essence of what it grounds. To be sure, what is grounded is dependent on the ground, but dependence is not incompatible with independence—as we saw in the discussion of divine grounding in the last chapter. Second, Schelling extends this non-deterministic sense of ground throughout his system in such a way as to connect all the parts: "All things mutually presuppose each other, nothing is another thing and yet [it] is not without another thing" (SW VII, 358). In this statement, Schelling asserts the same universality of grounding contained in the traditional principle of sufficient reason. In fact, we can consider this statement to be another version of the principle of ground for Schelling. Unlike the traditional principle, however, it does not demand a determining ground for each thing but a necessary condition. Each thing presupposes everything else: this allows for all parts of the system to be integrally connected in a way analogous to the parts of an organism.[96] At the same time, the reciprocal grounding need not determine their essence, thus allowing for the independence and freedom of each.

If we consider the statement "all things mutually presuppose each other" to be another version of the principle of ground, how does it relate to the version we discussed in the last chapter? The latter concerns the grounding relation between God and things: the basic statement of pantheism, "God is all things," means that God grounds all. In contrast, the statement about the universality of mutual presupposition concerns the relations *among* things. All things reciprocally depend on each other. We can therefore consider the two versions as complementary. Though they describe relations among different objects, both versions share the affirmation of a grounding dependence that does not require determination. The space that Schelling thereby creates between groundedness and determination is the space for human freedom. In chapters 5 and 7 we will see more concretely how he fills in this space.

5

Evil and the Irrational

One of the central claims of this book is that the problem of ground underlies the problem of a system of freedom. But one can raise an objection to this thesis: the central problem for a system of freedom in Schelling's text is not the problem of ground but the problem of evil.[1] This objection finds support not only in the amount of space that Schelling devotes to evil in the treatise but also in his statements underscoring the centrality of the problem. Immediately after defining the "real and living concept" of freedom as "a capacity for good and evil," he writes: "This is the point of the deepest difficulty in the whole doctrine of freedom—a difficulty that has always been felt and which does not just affect this or that system but more or less all of them" (SW VII, 352). If the human ability to do evil presents the deepest difficulty for freedom, it seems that the problem of ground is not the fundamental problem after all.[2]

On the contrary, I argue in this chapter that the difficulties that evil poses are all essentially tied to the concept of grounding—that the problem of evil is a problem of ground. Like the more general problem of the possibility of a system of freedom, the problem of evil requires for its resolution a careful consideration of the kinds of grounds and the structure of the grounding relations within the system. How is this true? At the most general level, the problem of evil arises because of the difficulty of answering the question "where does evil come from?" (*unde malum?*). In other words, the problem of evil is the problem of accounting for the origin or ground of evil. Of course, this is only a problem insofar as one presupposes that evil must have an origin, that philosophy cannot simply leave evil unexplained. And this presupposition is a direct consequence of the principle of ground, which states that everything—including evil—must have a ground.

It is clear enough from Schelling's treatment of the problem that he shares the conviction that there must be a ground of evil. We can see this already in his initial outline of the difficulties that evil poses for previous philosophical systems (SW VII, 353–56). A common shortcoming of these systems is their inability to explain the origin of evil: "The first capacity for a God-defying deed remains *unexplainable* in all previous systems" (SW VII, 354, emphasis added). In fact, the verb "explain" (*erklären*) and its cognates appear again and again both in Schelling's critique of other accounts of evil and in his own positive account. For example, Schelling writes of one attempt to preserve the reality of evil: "With this [account] evil does not disappear, although it is also not *explained*" (SW VII, 353, emphasis added). And Schelling makes clear that explaining evil is what he intends to do: "For the *explanation* of evil there is nothing else available to us besides the two principles in God" (SW VII, 375, emphasis added). This demand for an explanation, which Schelling pursues tirelessly throughout his investigation of evil, presupposes that evil is *explainable*—that it is possible to define it and account for its origin.[3]

But why is accounting for the origin of evil a problem? Any account must explain why there is evil in such a way that the nature of God is not compromised; in particular, God must not be made morally responsible for evil's existence. Here too the problem of evil proves to be a problem of ground, because it is precisely God's grounding relation to the world that seems irreconcilable with evil. If God as creator is the ground of all that exists, that would seem to require that God be the ground of evil as well. And if God is the ground of evil, God would seem to be morally responsible for its existence, which would contradict his perfect nature. The resolution of this traditional problem (the problem of theodicy) requires parsing the senses in which God is a ground, including a possible ground of evil. As we will see, the key to Schelling's solution is the fundamental distinction between the two principles within God and the "internal dualism" that this distinction makes possible.

Beyond the problem of theodicy, evil poses a more general difficulty that has to do with ground and the principle of ground. Evil challenges not only belief in God but also the rational ordering of the universe. This is because evil appears to be irrational, senseless, without purpose—in short, groundless (*grundlos*). For this reason, evil has always been a formidable challenge for rationalist thinkers. Though rationalism has taken many different historical forms, in the broad sense it requires that everything have its place in an intelligible order governed by the principle of ground. And yet evil and other (seemingly) irrational phenomena strongly resist integration into an intelligible order. Of course, one possibility when confronted with these phenomena is to give up on the notion that there is a rational ordering of the universe, thus rejecting the traditional principle of ground. My contention is that Schelling does not take this path. As we have seen, he proceeds under the assumption that evil has an explanation, and he rejects at the outset of the *Freiheitsschrift* the possibility of renouncing reason in order to preserve freedom.[4] If there is any remaining doubt about Schelling's commitment to rationalism, he seems to settle it in the section on formal freedom where he emphatically denies the existence of chance and contingency.[5]

But this is not the whole story. Sprinkled throughout the *Freiheitsschrift* are references to chaos, the irrational, and the unruly—especially in Schelling's description of the original state of nature and its subsequent formation. For example, he refers to the "irrational relationship" of nature to the understanding (SW VII, 396) and the "contingent determinations" within nature (SW VII, 376). And in a famous passage, Schelling draws attention to the apparent originality of what is "unruly" (*das Regellose*) and adds: "This is the incomprehensible basis of reality in things, the irreducible remainder [*der nie aufgehende Rest*], that which cannot be resolved in understanding by the most strenuous effort, but always remains in the ground" (SW VII, 359–60). What are we to make of these passages? Is there a way to reconcile Schelling's strongly rationalist statements with the existence of irrational elements in the text?

One response would be to concede that these two strands in Schelling's thought are irreconcilable, and that this is one of the reasons that Schelling's attempt to develop a system of freedom fails—and perhaps must fail. My view, however, is that Schelling's references to irrational elements are not inconsistent with his rationalist orientation in general or the affirmation of the principle of ground (as a principle of sufficient reason) in particular. To show this requires a careful examination of what Schelling means by the words "chaos," "unruly," and "irrational." As we have seen in other contexts, he sometimes uses common philosophical terms (like "existence") without indicating he has a special meaning in mind. But more fundamentally, bringing the rationalist and the irrational elements in the text together requires a reflection on the nature of Schelling's rationalism. Schelling intentionally includes irrational phenomena within his system in a way that other forms of rationalism are unable to do. And the reason they are unable to do this is the same reason they are unable to account for the origin of evil: they lack his fundamental distinction and the resulting appreciation for the dark ground of existence.

The issues raised by Schelling's account of evil are legion, and there is already a formidable body of research devoted to them.[6] I therefore do not attempt in this chapter to provide a full account of evil in the *Freiheitsschrift*. Instead, I focus on the connections between evil and grounding in an attempt to show how the problem of evil for Schelling is fundamentally a problem of ground. I begin by examining how Schelling accounts for the origin of evil. Here we will see that he distinguishes between different kinds of grounds, and that this distinction is at the heart of his solution to the problem of evil. I then tackle a point of controversy among Schelling scholars, namely, the question of whether and to what extent evil is necessary for divine revelation—or, to put it more pointedly, the question of whether evil is a ground of God's existence. In the final sections of the chapter, I consider both the broader challenge that the irrational poses for the principle of ground and the implications of evil and the irrational for the character of Schelling's rationalism.

1. The Ground of Evil

What is the ground of evil? There are multiple answers to this question, depending on how the word "ground" is understood. As we will see, the central distinction between (1) ground as condition of the possibility and (2) determinative ground plays a decisive role in the account of evil in the *Freiheitsschrift*. In this respect, Schelling's approach to the problem of evil reflects his broader approach to the problem of ground and a system of freedom. But before we examine his answers to the question of evil's ground, it is necessary to consider his critique of previous accounts of evil. This will allow us to see more clearly why accounting for its ground is problematic and how Schelling's approach to the question is an attempt to overcome the inherent difficulties.

The initial discussion of evil in the *Freiheitsschrift* occurs in the context of Schelling's critique of one-sided idealism. Although idealism provides the formal concept of freedom (self-determination outside of time), it is unable to account for the "real and living concept" of human freedom as "a capacity for good and evil" (SW VII, 352). (I will treat the relationship between the real and the formal concept of freedom in the final chapter.) After introducing the real concept, Schelling outlines a series of *aporiai*, the purpose of which is to show that evil poses insurmountable difficulties for every kind of system of philosophy developed up to Schelling's time (SW VII, 352–56). Without going into the details, we can observe a pattern in the difficulties that he outlines. Each system of philosophy faces a horned dilemma: Either the system denies the reality of evil, or it affirms it. If the system denies the reality of evil, this denial compromises the real concept of freedom as a capacity for good and *evil*. But if the system affirms the reality of evil, this affirmation compromises the nature of God as an all-perfect being.

Why would acknowledging the reality of evil compromise God's nature? There are two problems here that Schelling seeks to address—one having to do with the "location" of evil, the other having to do with its origin. On the one hand, the *location* of evil is problematic for systems that affirm the immanence of all things in God (the true interpretation of "pantheism"). If evil has reality, this would mean that evil would be in God. But it is a contradiction for an all-perfect being to include evil within itself—and thus to be connected with evil through the kind of grounding identity we discussed in chapter 3. How can God be all-good if evil is part of him?

On the other hand, the *origin* of evil is also problematic, even for those systems that deny the immanence of all things in God in favor of a more distant connection between God and creatures. God is supposed to be the ultimate origin of all positive existence: "The proposition 'Everything positive in the creature comes from God,' must also be claimed in this system" (SW VII, 353). If evil has a positive existence, it too must come from God—and this would make him morally responsible for its existence. Even if evil comes into being indirectly by means of creatures (for example, human beings), these creatures are nonetheless dependent on God for carrying out their actions, and so God becomes complicit in the evil they do (SW VII, 353).[7] Moreover, it does not seem possible that a real capacity to do evil in creatures would originate from a creator that is perfectly good (SW VII, 354). In summary, God as the ultimate ground of all that is real would have to be the ground—directly and indirectly—for the reality of evil.

In light of these difficulties, we can see why it would be attractive to deny the reality of evil. Particularly influential has been the Augustinian thesis that evil is the privation of the good (*privatio boni*), which has its roots in Neoplatonism: evil is nothing positive but the corruption of something positive, or the absence of something that should be there. Everything that exists, insofar as it exists, is good. At first glance, this position seems to solve the problem posed by the universality of God's grounding: even if God is the source of all that exists, he need not be the source of evil, because evil does not exist. And yet even Augustine and other advocates of the privation theory recognize that denying evil's reality cannot by itself resolve the grounding problem. If evil is the absence of something that should be there, this absence itself requires an account.[8] This is especially true when the absence is not original but the result of a process of corruption or *de-privation*. What is responsible for the absence that makes something evil *evil*?

However, Schelling's objection to theories that deny the reality of evil extends further than their inability to resolve the problem of grounding evil. He initially indicates that denying evil's reality would destroy the real concept of freedom as a capacity for good and evil—though he does not explain why (cf. SW VII, 353). Presumably, if evil does not really exist, there cannot be a real capacity to do evil; in effect, it would be a capacity to do nothing, or simply an incapacity. But this is not true to the phenomena. Far from being an incapacity, the ability to do evil is the power to inflict tremendous harm. This points to what I regard as the heart of the problem with denying the reality of evil, as Schelling sees it—a problem that amounts to an inversion of the difficulty concerning evil's ground. One not only has to account for the ground of evil; one also has to account for its *effects*, for the ways in which evil itself is a ground. Ex nihilo nihil fit: "nothing comes from nothing." If one denies the reality of evil, one is saying that the effects of evil come from nothing, and this is untenable. How can something that lacks reality be so effective? And the effectiveness of evil is a central theme in Schelling's account.[9] After treating the possibility of evil, he turns to explaining "its universal effectiveness [*Wirksamkeit*], or how evil could have broken out as an unmistakably universal principle everywhere in conflict with the good" (SW VII, 373). Evil is not simply an absence of the good, but something that actively resists and works against it.

Indeed, later in the text Schelling observes that opposition (*Gegensatz*) to the good is essential for evil and that evil has reality only in opposition (SW VII, 409).[10] But evil cannot oppose the good if it has no positive existence and is merely a lack. Kant illustrates this point mathematically. If the good = a, then an absence of good = 0. This 0 is incapable of counteracting the force of the good ($a + 0 = a$). To resist it, one needs "positive evil" ($= -a$).[11] Evil's resistance to the good runs through the development of nature and history in the *Freiheitsschrift*. In a remarkable passage, Schelling describes the extent of this resistance (here expressed in terms of sin): "Revealed sin does not fill [us] with regret, like mere weakness and inability, but with terror and horror—a feeling that is only explainable by the fact that sin strives to break the word, to touch the ground of creation, and to profane the mystery" (SW VII, 391).

We can now summarize what Schelling wishes to accomplish in his account of evil, in light of the inadequacies of previous approaches. He wishes (1) to affirm fully the reality of evil, since this is necessary to account for the effectiveness of evil and its active resistance of the good. But we have seen that affirming the reality of evil poses difficulties for the nature of God—both in terms of the "location" of evil in God and God's ultimate grounding of all that exists. Thus, Schelling wishes to accomplish two other seemingly paradoxical tasks: (2) to locate evil outside of God while still affirming the immanence of all things within God; and (3) to affirm God as the ultimate ground of all that exists while denying that God is the ground of evil—or even ground of the human ability to do evil.

How does Schelling attempt to carry out this terrifically ambitious— and seemingly impossible—agenda? The key to his solution is the fundamental distinction between that-which-exists and the ground of existence. On the one hand, Schelling defines evil in terms of an inversion of the proper relationship of these two principles in human beings. On the other hand, by distinguishing God insofar as he exists from the ground of his existence, he allows evil to have a basis (the ground of God's existence) that is both independent from God and yet within God.

First, how does Schelling define evil in terms of the two principles? As we saw in the previous chapter, both principles are in all things, not just in God. The real principle (corresponding to the ground of God's existence) is the self-will (*Eigenwille*) of the creature. By virtue of this "dark" will, the creature is separated and independent from God, because the self-will is rooted in the ground of God's existence (SW VII, 362–63).[12] On the other hand, the ideal principle (corresponding to that-which-exists) is the universal will (*Universalwille*), which Schelling also calls the understanding and "the light" (SW VII, 363). Both principles—the self-will and the universal will—together form a living identity, which is spirit (*Geist*) (SW VII, 363–64).[13] And within this living unity, each will has a proper role to play and a proper relationship to the other will: the self-will should be subordinate to the universal will and serve as its tool (*Werkzeug*) (SW VII, 363). In other words, the self-will should be the ground of the existence of the universal will. Schelling designates this "the divine relationship of the principles" (SW VII, 365).

So far, the relationship of the wills in human beings mirrors their relationship in God. But there is a key difference: in God the unity of the two principles is inseparable, but it is separable (*zertrennlich*) in human beings. This accounts for "the possibility of good and evil," according to Schelling (SW VII, 364).[14] But why would this make evil possible? Evil consists in raising the self-will over the universal will, thus producing an inversion (*Umkehrung*) of their true or divine order (SW VII, 365–66). For the order to be reversed, the principles must be separated, and their true unity must be dissolved. In a later discussion, Schelling adds another condition: the self-will of the creature must be aroused or activated so that it strives against the universal will (SW VII, 374–76; cf. 458–59). Thus, we can distinguish three conditions that together constitute evil: (1) activation of the self-will, (2) separation of the principles, and (3) inversion of the principles.

At this point, we can take a step back and ask what Schelling is doing in defining evil in this way. It is noteworthy that he does not refer to evil actions and their effects on other human beings—the things that normally come to mind when thinking about evil in the world. Instead, his focus is on the ontological disposition of the human being who commits evil acts. Here Schelling seems to be drawing on Kant's account of evil in *Religion within the Limits of Mere Reason*, to which he will later refer when discussing radical evil (SW VII, 388). According to Kant, human beings have two kinds of incentives (*Triebfedern*) when acting: (1) the incentive to follow the moral law and (2) incentives to follow the impulses of our sensibility through the principle of self-love. A human being is good when self-love is subordinated to the moral law. Evil, on the other hand, consists in the subordination of the moral law to self-love. Thus, Kant also defines evil as a "inversion" (*Umkehrung*) of the human being's incentives (AA 6, 36).[15]

Like Kant, Schelling conceives of evil as an inversion—though for him the inverted elements are not incentives but fundamental principles (or wills) that constitute the human being. The two accounts are also similar with respect to their treatment of the universal versus the particular in good and evil. Goodness involves subordinating the self in its particularity to the universal principle (which takes the form of the moral law for Kant). For Schelling, the tendency to universalize is tied to the will of love and a drive toward unity with all things (cf. SW VII, 381). In contrast, evil is the domination of the particular self over the universal. In effect, Schelling is saying that all evil is a form of self-centeredness—and thus a rebellion against unity and love.

If Schelling's account of evil is focused on the ontological structure of evil in the human being, how precisely does this relate to evil *actions*? Curiously, the *Freiheitsschrift* has little to say about this relationship, perhaps because action follows naturally from the (more fundamental) relationship of the principles. In the *Stuttgart Private Lectures*, Schelling defines a one-to-one correspondence between action and disposition: "Depending on whether [the human spirit] makes either the lower or the higher its principle, it acts [for] good or evil" (SW VII, 471). This seems to suggest that the good or evil relationship of the two wills does not have permanence and can change from action to action. In other places, however, Schelling implies a more permanent disposition related to character, which would therefore require a fundamental conversion to change (cf. SW VII, 386–87; 389; 392–93). In any case, his focus is the evil disposition of the wills, because this is more foundational than evil actions—and thus the primary locus of human evil. The freedom to do evil is not simply the freedom to act in an evil way; on a deeper level, it is the freedom to place one's will to self over one's will to love.

Returning to the larger argument: Schelling believes that this ontological account allows him to show how evil can be a substantive force that resists the good—something that privation theories were unable to do. The same elements (the two principles) are in both good and evil. What is distinctive about evil is the form of the principles, or how they are disordered, and this form is itself the result of a positive force—the striving of the self-will to subordinate the universal will (SW VII, 370). One might object that Schelling retains an element of the privation theory, insofar as he still defines evil in terms of a lack—in this case, a lack of unity on account of the separation of principles. However, Schelling emphasizes that the disharmony in evil is still a unity, even if it is a false unity. A single note cannot produce disharmony; only a *clash* of notes can do that, but a clash requires something positive, not just an absence (SW VII, 371).[16] Indeed, the false unity of the two principles still forms a kind of spirit—evil has a spiritual reality: "[We do not] have to struggle just with flesh and blood but with an evil within and outside of us that is spirit" (SW VII, 388). Schelling even calls the "other spirit" that comes to be in us through evil "the inverted god" (SW VII, 390).

If Schelling defines evil as something real and highly positive, how does he account for its existence without making God responsible? Here Schelling develops a two-pronged approach, effectively removing God twice from evil. The first prong takes advantage of the fundamental distinction between (1) God insofar as he exists and (2) the ground of God's existence. The location and ground of evil (and the human ability to do evil) is not God insofar as he exists but the ground of his existence—that which in God is not "God himself." The second prong involves defining the precise sense in which the ground of existence is a ground of evil. The ground makes evil possible, but only the free decisions of human beings can make it a reality.[17]

Before exploring each of these prongs in more detail, it is important to answer a potential objection to Schelling's overall strategy. If the ground of evil is not God but the ground of God's existence, doesn't this mean that God is no longer the ground of all that exists? Yes and no. Although Schelling never says so explicitly, his solution to this problem relies on his implied distinction with respect to the term "God." As we saw in the last chapter, there are two senses of God implied in the account of the fundamental distinction. In the broad sense, God is all-encompassing, and includes both the ground and that-which-exists. But Schelling also defines God more narrowly: God "considered absolutely" (*absolut betrachtet*) is God insofar as he exists, not the ground of his existence (SW VII, 358). By defining God in these two senses, Schelling is able to accomplish the seemingly paradoxical tasks I mentioned earlier. First, he is able to locate evil outside of God while still affirming the immanence of all things in God. All things—including evil—are in God in the broad sense; however, evil is located outside of God in the narrow sense. In the same way, God in the broad sense is the ultimate ground of all that exists; in the narrow sense he is neither the ground of evil nor the ground of the human ability to do evil.

One way to understand what Schelling is doing is to think of his solution as combining pantheism and dualism. Indeed, an impetus for writing the *Freiheitsschrift* was his reading of Friedrich Schlegel's *On the Language and Wisdom of the Indians* (1808), which treats three systems in Indian thought: emanation, pantheism, and dualism. According to Schlegel, pantheism affirms an ultimate unity of all things, but thereby eliminates the distinction between good and evil: if God is all things, and God is all-good, there is no place for evil.[18] Dualism, on the other hand, easily accounts for the existence of good and evil in the world, but at the cost of the ultimate unity of the system, which reason demands.[19] Schelling intends to avail himself of the advantages of both systems while avoiding their drawbacks.[20] Insofar as he distinguishes *two principles* within God, his system is a dualism and can accommodate evil while affirming God's goodness (to the extent that God is that-which-exists). Insofar as Schelling distinguishes these two principles *within God*, his system is pantheistic and ultimately forms a unity.[21] However, this solution—as innovative as it is—has costs that Schelling does not fully acknowledge. If evil exists in God in the broad sense, this means that God in the broad sense is not perfectly good.[22] And if evil is not grounded by God insofar as he exists, this means that the existing God (whose goodness is preserved) is no longer the ground of all that is—a significant concession.[23]

Returning to Schelling's two-pronged strategy, we can ask: how does the ground of God's existence provide the location and ground of evil? As we saw in Schelling's account of the human capacity for evil, the self-will is rooted in the ground of God's existence (SW VII, 362–63). In this way, the freedom to do evil has a "root independent of God" (SW VII, 354). More generally, created things (not just human beings) have their ground in the ground of God's existence, which provides the place for their "becoming" (*Werden*) (SW VII, 359) and supports them in their existence—even when doing evil. Schelling makes this clear when addressing the theodicy question later in the text. He confronts the traditional objection that God, even if he does not will evil directly, continues to work in the evil person—holding in existence the arm that stabs an innocent victim, for instance. Schelling concedes that this applies to the ground: "The primal ground of existence also continues to be active in evil as health continues to be active in disease, and even the most dissolute and false life still remains and moves within God to the extent that he is the ground of existence" (SW VII, 403). However, what happens in the ground is not subject to God's free will (SW VII, 401), and thus God is not responsible for the evil that happens there.

Beyond providing the "location" of evil and supporting its existence, the ground is involved in evil in a more active way. As we saw in the account of evil, one of the conditions for realizing evil is the activation or excitation (*Erregung*) of the self-will—a term with roots in Schelling's *Naturphilosophie*. Drawing on the work of the Scottish physician John Brown, Schelling had developed a theory of life in which "excitation through external influences" was a necessary condition for a living organism (SW III, 81).[24] In the *Freiheitsschrift*, excitation is also a condition of life, but the category of life applies more broadly—even to the principles within human beings that constitute good and evil: "The activated selfhood is necessary for the sharpness [*Schärfe*] of life; without it there would be complete death, a falling asleep of the good; for, where there is no struggle, there is no life" (SW VII, 400). In other words, the excitation of selfhood prompts it to resist the understanding (or universal will), thus creating a conflict between principles that makes life possible. But that same resistance makes evil possible as well: only if the universal will prevails in the resulting conflict do we have a "living good" (cf. SW VII, 467); however, if the self-will overpowers and subordinates the universal will, evil is the result.

The excitation necessary for both life and evil is accomplished by the ground of God's existence, which awakens (*erweckt*) or stirs up the self-will throughout creation, thus inspiring a drive toward the particular that resists the will to love (SW VII, 375). Beyond the general connection to life, Schelling gives two reasons for the ground's activity. First, human beings are in a state of "indecision" (*Unentschiedenheit*) with respect to good and evil, because both are possibilities. The activation of the self-will provides a "ground of solicitation" or temptation to evil, which draws human beings out of their indecision (SW VII, 374, 381).[25] Second, the ground's arousal of the self-will is necessary for the revelation of God (SW VII, 373). This is because "each being [*Wesen*] can only reveal itself in its opposite" (SW VII, 373), and the self-will actively opposes the love and goodness of God. In response to the activated self-will, divine goodness becomes activated to resist it, and God's goodness reveals itself by striving against and prevailing over the self-will.[26]

By activating the self-will, the ground of God's existence serves as both the ground of evil and the ground of life and revelation. But in what precise sense does it serve as a *ground* of evil? Addressing this question is the second prong of Schelling's strategy for distancing evil from God. The ground of God's existence is not a determinative cause of evil's existence but makes it possible. Only the free decision of human beings can provide the determinative ground. Schelling makes this clear in a passage that nicely captures both prongs of his theodicy-strategy: "What comes from the mere condition or the ground does not come from God, although it is necessary for his existence. But it also cannot be said that evil comes from the ground or that the will of the ground is the originator [*Urheber*] of evil. For evil can only arise in the innermost will of one's own heart and is never accomplished without one's own deed" (SW VII, 399). The activation of the self-will comes from the ground, not God (the first prong).

But by activating the self-will, the ground is not causing evil; it is only making evil possible by establishing one of its necessary conditions (the second prong). As Schelling explains succinctly: "The ground does indeed arouse the possible principle of evil, yet not evil itself" (SW VII, 401).[27]

In the other senses in which the ground can be said to "ground" evil, it also does so in the sense of making evil possible. As we have seen, the ground provides a space for evil that is independent of God. It also grounds evil by continuing to work in the evildoer. But in both these cases its grounding alone is not sufficient to produce evil. Ultimately, it is human freedom that provides the determining ground: "Evil remains always an individual's own choice; the ground cannot make evil as such, and every creature falls due to its own guilt" (SW VII, 382). These lines occur immediately before the section on the formal concept of freedom, which accounts for how the decision for good or evil is made (see chapter 7). In any case, Schelling in his account of evil once again employs the key distinction between (1) condition of the possibility and (2) determining ground, thus reflecting his broader approach to the problem of ground. In this instance, the distinction, beyond making freedom possible, serves to distance God from the consequences of that freedom.

2. Evil as a Ground of Revelation?

One of the disputed questions in Schelling scholarship concerns the relationship between evil and revelation—specifically, whether evil is necessary for revelation. At first glance, there seems to be an abundance of textual evidence that it is. Schelling draws attention to the "universal effectiveness" of evil as a universal principle in conflict with the good, and he declares that it is necessary for revelation, "at least as a universal opposition" (SW VII, 373). Later he notes that God as spirit reveals himself in the "conflict of good and evil" (SW VII, 380). And Schelling formulates the general principle that struggle is necessary for life (SW VII, 400),[28] and that opposition is necessary for revelation: "For every being [*Wesen*] can reveal itself only in its opposite, love only in hate, unity in conflict" (SW VII, 373). If we apply this principle to God, it follows that divine goodness can reveal itself only in evil. Accordingly, Heidegger, Habermas, and many other commentators have asserted that evil is necessary for Schelling.[29]

However, there is another way of reading most, if not all, of these passages, so that evil is not necessary—at least, not evil in the strict sense.

This alternative interpretation is suggested by a remarkable passage at the end of Schelling's treatment of the theodicy problem:

> The Leibnizian concept of evil as *conditio sine qua non* can only be applied to the ground [to the extent] that the latter arouses the creaturely will (the possible principle of evil) as the condition under which alone the will to love could be realized. We have already shown why God does not resist the will of the ground or abolish it. This would amount to God abolishing the condition of his existence, that is, his own personality. Thus, in order that there be no evil, God himself would have to not be. (SW VII, 402–3)

If we concentrate on the last sentence, Schelling seems to be claiming that one cannot abolish evil without abolishing God's existence, and thus evil is necessary for God to exist at all. However, when we examine the sentences that precede it, we can notice that a key word appears twice: condition. The ground is the *condition* of God's existence. The ground's activation of the self-will (the possible principle of evil) is the *condition* of the realization of love. But we saw in the last section that the ground's activation of the self-will is also the condition of evil. Thus, the ground is the condition of both evil and God's existence. The meaning of the last sentence in the passage is therefore the following: one could eliminate evil by eliminating its condition (the ground), but this would also eliminate God's existence, because the ground is its condition as well. Once again, the key sense of ground as condition plays a decisive role in understanding the grounding relations in the system.

How does this help us to understand the relationship between evil and revelation? The passage suggests the following relationship: evil is not necessary for revelation; instead, the same thing that is a necessary condition of evil is also a necessary condition for revelation—the ground's activation of the self-will. But what about the passages cited above where Schelling says that evil is necessary for revelation? In many (if not all) of these passages, Schelling is using the term "evil" to refer to the activated self-will, which is necessary—but not sufficient—for the full realization of evil in the inversion of the principles. Sometimes Schelling refers to evil in this sense as "universal evil," presumably because it is a general principle in battle with the good throughout creation and is not unique to human beings (SW VII, 373, 380–81). But Schelling later makes clear that this is not evil—at least not in the strict or fullest sense: "For evil is not aroused selfhood in itself but only to the extent that it has completely torn itself away from its opposite, the light or the universal will" (SW VII, 399–400).

As this analysis already indicates, Schelling uses the term "evil" in a number of senses. In fact, we can distinguish at least three:

1. Evil is the false unity or disharmony produced through the inversion of the principles.[30]
2. Evil is the real principle (self-will) insofar as it separates itself from the ideal principle.[31]
3. Evil is the real principle (self-will) insofar as it is activated and strives against the good/universal principle.[32]

In the second and third sense, evil is the real principle considered in a certain respect (*sofern* . . .). This has implications for understanding evil's grounding function, as we will see. In any case, one can argue that only evil in the third sense (universal evil) is necessary for revelation, and Schelling admits that this is not evil, strictly speaking. Accordingly, Hermanni and Buchheim both contend that the evil that results from human freedom—evil in the first and second senses—is not necessary for revelation.[33]

I am sympathetic to this interpretation for systematic reasons in addition to the textual ones. It is difficult to see how the evil that results from human freedom can be necessary without compromising that freedom. As we will see when examining freedom's formal concept, the ultimate decision for good or evil is made through a timeless act of freedom, determined by nothing outside itself (SW VII, 382–88). But if evil is necessary for revelation, and revelation is itself necessary,[34] then the decision for evil would have to be determined by something other than freedom in order to guarantee the result. Moreover, interpreting Schelling in such a way that evil is not necessary helps distance him from the teleological justification of evil, which we find in Hegel's philosophy of history. Hegel famously asks: "When we regard history as the slaughter bench on which the happiness of peoples, the wisdom of states, and the virtue of individuals are sacrificed, the question necessarily arises for our thought: for whom, for what ultimate purpose have these tremendous sacrifices been made?" (HW 12, 35). One should avoid a caricature of Hegel's perspective here: he does not think that history is *merely* a slaughter bench. Nonetheless, he does offer a clear answer to the question he raises: the negativity of evil in history is necessary for the realization of spirit—and thus his philosophy of history is a "theodicy" or justification of God (HW 12, 28). In light of the atrocities of the twentieth century, however, it is difficult to stomach the notion that evil is in service of the realization and revelation of God or spirit.[35]

Nevertheless, it seems to me that the solution of Buchheim and Hermanni is a little too tidy, and that elements of the text are in tension with it. Their case is based largely on the distinction between universal and moral evil. But there are two other issues to consider with regard to this question: (1) the consequences of Schelling's principle that something can only be revealed in its opposite; and (2) his remarks on the moral necessity of creation. With respect to the first issue, one can ask: if universal evil is not evil in the fullest sense, would it be sufficient to provide the opposition needed to reveal divine goodness? Most of the textual evidence suggests that Schelling's answer is yes, thus supporting Buchheim and Hermanni. In the passages that mention a "struggle" (*Kampf*) or a "conflict" (*Streit*) between good and evil, the evil in question is universal evil (the activated self-will), not moral evil (SW VII, 373, 380–81). In fact, Schelling introduces the principle that opposition is needed for revelation in the first of these passages. I suspect that Schelling calls the activated self-will "evil" precisely because of its role in revealing the good through conflict, in accordance with his principle.

Moreover, Schelling offers an analogy confirming that evil in the fullest sense is not needed to fulfill the principle: "Were there no root of cold in the body, warmth could not be felt" (SW VII, 400). Here Schelling does not say that cold *as such* is needed to feel warmth, but only "a root [*Wurzel*] of cold." The same applies to evil in relation to the good. In order for the good to be "capable of being sensed" (*empfindlich*), there needs to be a root of evil—the self-will activated by the ground (SW VII, 400). In fact, as we saw in the last section, this activation of the self-will is necessary not only to reveal the good but to bring it to life: "A good, if it does not have within it an evil that is overcome, is not a real, living good" (SW VII, 467). But an evil *overcome* is only a root of evil and not fully actualized.[36] Schelling even describes evil in this limited, potential state as a ground of the good (in the foundational sense of ground): "For evil is only evil to the extent that it exceeds potentiality, but, reduced to non-being or the state of potency, it is what it always should be, basis, subordinate" (SW VII, 405). This makes sense if we think of evil as the real principle insofar as it is activated (the third sense defined above), which should serve as the ground of the existence of the ideal principle.

This textual evidence all supports the thesis that only potential or universal evil is necessary for revelation and life. However, if we accept Schelling's principle that revelation happens through opposition, isn't it the case that the existence of moral evil—evil in the fullest sense—allows God to reveal his goodness in a way that he wouldn't otherwise? The virtues of heroes are displayed most powerfully when they do battle against real evil—wouldn't the same hold for God? In fact, in at least one passage, Schelling seems to claim that God's power is only fully revealed through actual evil: "Were there no separation [*Zertrennung*] of principles, unity could not prove its omnipotence" (SW VII, 373-74). Hermanni suggests that the language here is imprecise, and notes that in a similar passage Schelling uses the word "separability" (*Zertrennlichkeit*) (SW VII, 364).[37] But from a purely theoretical standpoint, doesn't triumphing over real evil better reveal God's power? Indeed, one might go further and say that the greater the evil, the more the power of the good is revealed in overcoming it.

The key word here is "more." The revelation of God need not be a matter of all or nothing. God can be revealed in different ways and in different degrees. Thus, one can concede that moral evil allows God to reveal himself in ways that he would not otherwise, without having to affirm that moral evil is necessary for God to be revealed at all. When human beings freely choose to do evil, God can reveal himself through his victory over it. Had they not chosen to do evil, God could reveal himself in other ways.[38] Indeed, this is essentially the Christian understanding: the fall of man was a *felix culpa*, a "happy fault,"[39] because it made necessary the Incarnation and Christ's victory over sin through his passion and resurrection. But God could have revealed himself through other means had the Fall not taken place. Thus, moral evil is not necessary for revelation.

But there is a problem for this interpretation: Schelling's remarks on the moral necessity of creation call into question the notion that God could have revealed himself in other ways—and, by implication, the notion that moral evil is not necessary. These remarks occur in a section of the text devoted to the question of theodicy (SW VII, 394-403). Specifically, Schelling poses the question of how God relates to revelation as a "moral being." On the one hand, Schelling clearly denies that God wills evil directly: "The will to creation was therefore immediately only a will to give birth to the light and the good along with it; evil, however, did not come into consideration in this will either as means or even, as Leibniz says, as the *conditio sine qua non* of the greatest possible perfection in the world" (SW VII, 402).⁴⁰ He also denies that everything follows from God with a blind, abstract necessity. On the other hand, he does affirm that creation is the result of another kind of necessity—a moral one, which is also absolute and metaphysical (SW VII, 397).

What does Schelling mean by this? He borrows the term "moral necessity" (*sittliche Notwendigkeit*) from Leibniz, whom he quotes at length (SW VII, 396). In fact, much of this section is a critical engagement with Leibniz's *Theodicy*, which Schelling had read shortly before beginning the *Freiheitsschrift*.⁴¹ Leibniz is confronted with a dilemma. On the one hand, he is committed to the principle of sufficient reason, which requires everything to have a reason determining that it occur. On the other hand, he wishes to preserve the freedom of God in choosing which world to create. He attempts to resolve this dilemma by distinguishing two kinds of necessity: (1) geometrical necessity, which he also calls logical, metaphysical, and absolute; and (2) moral necessity. Only geometrical necessity is incompatible with freedom and contingency. Although God's wisdom and goodness determine his choice of which world to create, this determination is a form of moral necessity, which does not compromise freedom.⁴²

As we will see, Schelling does not adopt all the details of Leibniz's account; however, we can identify two defining features of moral necessity that are important for Schelling. First, moral necessity presupposes something that goes beyond the divine understanding and what can be established through geometrical proof. In Leibniz's case, this is divine goodness, which motivates God to choose the best of an infinite number of options, all of which were equally possible from a "geometrical point of view." In Schelling's case, this is the ground of existence, which is independent from the understanding (that-which-exists) and forms a living unity with it. In the passage immediately preceding the quotation from Leibniz, Schelling gives an account of divine personality (*Persönlichkeit*), which is constituted by the dynamic unity of both principles or wills. God is not a logical abstraction from which everything follows with blind necessity, and yet everything does follow from God in another sense: "The person of God is the general law, and everything that happens, happens by virtue of the personality of God" (SW VII, 396). Thus, we might say that moral necessity for Schelling is a *personal necessity*.⁴³

The second defining feature of moral necessity is that it is teleological—directed toward the good. According to Leibniz, God's infinite goodness motivates him to choose the best of all the possibilities. The passage from the *Theodicy* that Schelling cites has to do with the determination of the laws of nature: different laws are logically possible, but God chooses what is most fitting.[44] Schelling refers to this teleological aspect in his own account when he notes that the act of revelation is "necessary morally or in reference to goodness and love" (SW VII, 397). God's love and goodness were necessary to counteract the tendency toward hiddenness and self-enclosure so that there would be a revelation at all. This makes creation "a conscious and morally free deed" (SW VII, 397). Moreover, God foresaw the consequences of his revelation (SW VII, 396), and thus he was fully aware of what he was doing and acted with purpose.

However, Schelling breaks decisively with Leibniz on the question of alternative possibilities. For Leibniz it is important that there be other possible worlds that God could have chosen; although his choice was morally necessary (given divine goodness), it was not absolutely necessary, because other worlds were logically possible. Schelling denies the distinction between moral and absolute necessity. He rightly notes that this distinction in Leibniz depends on an abstract, formal concept of possibility, according to which something is possible if it is not self-contradictory. On these terms, a world that is worse than ours is still possible because it does not entail a contradiction *when considered in itself*. However, such a concept of possibility is artificial, because it requires that one disregard God's nature, which would not be compatible with the creation of an inferior world. When one considers God's nature, there is no avoiding the conclusion that there is only one possible world, "just as there is only One God" (SW VII, 398).[45]

Schelling draws the consequences of this identification of possibility and actuality when considering the divine nature:

> As soon as the closer determination of a moral necessity is added, the proposition is utterly undeniable: that from the divine nature everything follows with absolute necessity, that everything which is possible by virtue of this nature must also be actual, and what is not actual also must be morally impossible. Spinozism is by no means in error because of the claim that there is such an unshakable necessity in God, but rather because it takes this necessity to be non-living and impersonal. (SW VII, 397)

There is no doubt that this passage poses significant challenges—not only with respect to the necessity of evil but also with respect to the possibility of human freedom.[46] "From the divine nature everything follows with absolute necessity." The key word here is "everything" (*alles*). If this includes moral evil and other free acts, all evil would be necessary, and human freedom would be an illusion. Instead of understanding God's grounding primarily in terms of making possible, as I have argued, Schelling would seem to be falling back into the traditional conception of deterministic grounding relations proceeding from a single principle.

Despite the strong-sounding language in this passage, there are aspects of the text that point to an alternative interpretation. To begin with, Schelling's primary intention in the passage is not to define *what* follows from God, but rather to define *how* it follows. In fact, already at the beginning of this section of the text he had specified what follows from God: *revelation*. Schelling asks: "How does [God] relate to this revelation as a moral being? Is it an act that ensues with blind and unconscious necessity or is it a free and conscious deed?" (SW VII, 394). Immediately before the problematic passage, Schelling gives an answer: "The act of revelation in God is necessary only morally or in regard to goodness and love." He also affirms that revelation is a "conscious and morally free deed" (SW VII, 397). He then dismisses the notion that God chooses among possible worlds, affirming instead that everything follows from God with absolute necessity.

In light of this context, when Schelling writes "everything" here, we can take him to mean "everything that follows from God," thus referring primarily—if not exclusively—to revelation, which is morally (and therefore absolutely) necessary. Revelation includes creation, and Schelling uses the terms more or less interchangeably. For example, he refers to the "deed of self-revelation as creation" (SW VII, 401). Moreover, Schelling provides clear indications that acts of human freedom—and moral evil in particular—are not included in revelation and God's creative activity, nor do they follow necessarily from them. In the course of considering an objection, he mentions that God foresees that evil would follow from self-revelation "at least by way of accompaniment" (*wenigstens begleitungsweise*), thus indicating that the two are only incidentally connected (SW VII, 402).[47] Schelling affirms once again that evil comes to be only through "one's own deed" (SW VII, 399) and not from the ground or that-which-exists—the two "eternal beginnings of self-revelation" (SW VII, 395). Creation itself involves the ordering of nature, and "the will to creation was therefore immediately only a will to give birth to the light and the good along with it" (SW VII, 402).

Even if we understand Schelling to be referring only to revelation and creation in his statement about absolute necessity, at least two problems remain. First, Schelling also states that there is only one possible world: "[There is an] archetype in the ground containing the only possible world according to God's essence, which in the actual creation is raised from potency into act only through division [and] regulation of forces" (SW VII, 398). But if evil is part of the only possible world, then evil is necessary. One could avoid this consequence by interpreting "world" here not as the totality of what exists (including free acts) but only what God has created.[48] This would seem to find support in the passage, which describes the only possible world coming into being through the division of forces—God's primary creative activity, which does not directly bring forth evil. However, this would be a departure from Leibniz's use of the term "possible world," and Schelling presents himself as critically engaging with Leibniz.[49]

Second, even if it is not human action but only revelation that follows necessarily from the divine nature, this revelation is not completely independent of human action. How God reveals himself depends at least in part on what human beings do and whether they abuse their freedom. Because moral evil has entered the world, God reveals himself through the Incarnation, which Schelling describes in highly orthodox terms. The light of spirit appears in "personal, human shape" to confront "personal and spiritual evil" and to restore the relationship of creation to God. "For only what is personal can heal what is personal, and God must become man so that man returns to God" (SW VII, 380).[50] But this presents a problem, in light of Schelling's statement that God's action in the world follows from the divine nature with absolute necessity. How could some of this action also be in response to moral evil—unless moral evil itself follows from the divine nature? A similar problem arises with respect to the course of history, which Schelling presents as a revelation of a higher order than the unfolding of nature (cf. SW VII, 377ff.). If the course of history is determined through free human actions, how can God's revelation in history follow necessarily from the divine nature?[51]

One might resolve these difficulties by saying that God foresees the free decisions of human beings (or takes note of their eternal acts of freedom[52]) and orders his revelation and actions in the world accordingly.[53] However, this would require an emendation of Schelling's original statement. Instead of writing: "everything follows from the divine nature," he would have to write: "everything follows from the divine nature and human freedom."[54] In any case, these difficulties point to what I regard as the central weakness of the *Freiheitsschrift*. Although Schelling succeeds in defining the grounding relations in the system in such a way that a form of absolute freedom is possible for both God and human beings, he does not show how the consequences of independent acts of freedom can be brought together and integrated within nature to form a coherent whole. This would seem to require providence or a form of preestablished harmony—a fact that Schelling himself recognized earlier in his career. We will return to this question in the book's conclusion.

3. The Irrational and the Irreducible Remainder

So far we have considered how evil is grounded and how it fits within the grounding relations in Schelling's system. But evil is just one of a constellation of concepts that challenge the rational ordering—and grounding—of the universe; others include chance, contingency, chaos, and the irrational. Such terms appear with some frequency in the *Freiheitsschrift*, especially in the description of nature's origins in the ground and its subsequent formation. As a consequence, one might say that Schelling has recovered an appreciation for the irrational that sets him apart from the other German Idealists as well as the larger rationalist tradition.[55] This is true, but it can easily lead to a misunderstanding. One might think that Schelling is affirming that there are "gaps in reality"—random events and groundless phenomena to which the principle of sufficient reason does not apply.[56] But if this were the case, then Schelling would be abandoning his commitment to system, which by its nature does not allow gaps in reality; this is precisely why formulating a "system of freedom" is such a challenge. Schelling himself justifies his strong denial of chance by citing its threat to the systematic character of reality: "Chance is impossible; it contests reason as well as the necessary unity of the whole" (SW VII, 383).

But if Schelling does not allow for groundless and random phenomena, what do we make of the irrational elements in the text? Answering this question requires a careful examination of the meaning of the irrational and related concepts, which Schelling does not define directly. My overarching thesis in this section is that the irrational elements are not opposed to reason in the sense of being groundless; instead, they are opposed to the understanding and its way of knowing, which requires division before elements can be ordered.[57] This, of course, presupposes the distinction between reason (*Vernunft*) and understanding (*Verstand*), which has its roots in Kant and is operative in Schelling's previous writings. For example, in the *Philosophy of Art* (1802–3) he notes that in the higher levels of nature and art there is a higher lawfulness, "which is irrational for the *understanding* and is conceived and grasped only by *reason*" (SW V, 576, emphasis added). In the *Identitätsphilosophie*, the understanding is associated with what Schelling calls "reflection," which separates and opposes what is originally one.[58] Reason, on the other hand, is another name for intellectual intuition, which alone can see things in their original unity.[59]

The status of understanding and reason is not precisely the same in the *Freiheitsschrift*: Schelling no longer devalues the contribution of the understanding as he does in many of his earlier writings, and intellectual intuition is present only implicitly—if at all. Nevertheless, the primary activity of the understanding is still division and separation, as we will see. Moreover, one of the remarkable things about the understanding in the *Freiheitsschrift* is that it functions as an ontological principle as well as an intellectual capacity.[60] The understanding is one of Schelling's designations for that-which-exists or the ideal principle in God; he calls it "the original understanding" (*der ursprüngliche Verstand*) (SW VII, 362) to distinguish it from the understanding of creatures, which is raised from the ground (SW VII, 360).[61] By contrast, the ground or the real principle is what lacks understanding (*das Verstandlose*) (SW VII, 360, 402). In a revealing passage, Schelling also calls the ground the "irrational principle": "The preceding reflections clarify in what sense, nonetheless, one could say of the irrational principle that it resists the understanding or unity and order, without thereby supposing it to be an *evil* fundamental being" (SW VII, 374). This confirms that the irrationality of the ground is to be thought in reference to the understanding. Moreover, the passage provides us with another way of formulating Schelling's fundamental distinction: if the real principle (the ground) is the irrational principle, then the ideal principle (the understanding) is the rational principle.[62] We will return to this point below.

In this passage we can also see that the irrational does not simply lack understanding—it actively resists the understanding, as well as the unity and order associated with it. If this is the case, then we can determine more precisely the meaning of the irrational by examining the understanding's activity and how it brings about unity and order. In fact, the primary activity of the understanding can be summed up in a word that occurs again and again in the text: division (*Scheidung*).⁶³ The first effect of the understanding in nature is the division of forces (SW VII, 361). This process of division is repeated over and over, and at each level of the division a new being emerges (*entsteht*) from out of nature (SW VII, 362). If the irrational is defined as what lacks understanding and resists its activity, then the irrational is also what is undivided and resists division.

How does the understanding's division give rise to the forms of nature? Schelling describes the process: "Something comprehensible and individuated first emerges in this manner . . . through genuine impression [*Ein-Bildung*], since that which arises in nature is impressed [*hineingebildet*] into her, or still more correctly [something emerges] through awakening, since the understanding brings to the fore the unity or idea hidden in the divided ground" (SW VII, 361–62). Since Schelling begins the second part of the passage by indicating that its description is more correct than the first part, something about the first description of nature being formed through impression is inadequate. But what? The language of "impression" suggests that form is something outside of nature and must be impressed upon it. According to the second, more accurate description, form—the "unity or idea"—is already in nature, but hidden. Through division, this hidden form is unfolded and revealed. Form comes to nature from within, not from outside.

In addition to division and the unfolding of what is hidden, there are two other key moments in the understanding's ordering of nature. They appear in a passage that relates to the unruly (*regellos*), one of the terms closely associated with the irrational: "By no means is this unruliness [of the ground] to be thought as if there were no archetype in the ground containing the only possible world according to God's essence, which in the actual creation is raised from potency to act only through division, regulation of forces and exclusion of the unruly, which hinders and darkens the archetype" (SW VII, 398). In addition to dividing and revealing forces, the understanding orders nature through (1) the regulation (*Regulierung*) of these forces and (2) the exclusion of the unruly. When the forces are divided, they are not yet ordered. Their regulation or ordering is a hierarchical arrangement in which the self-will or ground-like principle is subordinated to the universal will or the principle of the understanding—the "divine relationship of the principles," which is reversed in evil (SW VII, 365; cf. SW VII, 439).

The final moment, the exclusion (*Ausschließung*) of the unruly, is not developed in the *Freiheitsschrift*, but Schelling discusses it extensively in the *Stuttgart Private Lectures* (1810). He notes that every *krisis* or division is accompanied by an ejection (*Ausstoßung*) or exclusion. Each division is a court of judgment, and the last division is the "last judgment" (SW VII, 483). But what is excluded or ejected in each division? That which is dark, unconscious, and not divine (the real) is excluded from that which is conscious and divine (the ideal). But this exclusion is not an abandonment of what is excluded. The dark and unconscious part contains hidden within itself other conscious and divine elements that can be revealed only through further division. Another division is necessary, in which the dark and unconscious element is once again excluded from the conscious and divine. And so on. Each division excludes or ejects an element that requires further division.

The activity of the understanding in creation is therefore an iterative process. This process would go on ad infinitum if there were not finally an excluded element that can no longer be divided. Schelling refers to this element in his description of the "final, total division" at the end of the *Freiheitsschrift*. He compares it to the *caput mortuum* (literally "dead head"), the worthless substance left over after a chemical process in alchemy.[64] For Schelling, however, the indivisible element at the end of the process of creation is not worthless: it serves as the "eternally dark ground of selfhood," which remains behind as potency that can never be raised to act (SW VII, 408). It provides the "root of evil" needed for the good to be vital (cf. SW VII, 400; 405).

In light of the above analysis, we can turn to the most decisive passage for understanding the irrational in the *Freiheitsschrift*—the famous passage on "the irreducible remainder" (*der nie aufgehende Rest*).[65] It is my contention that what Schelling calls the irreducible remainder is precisely the *caput mortuum* at the end of the process of creation. The full passage reads:

> After the eternal act of self-revelation, everything in the world is, as we see it now, rule, order and form; but the unruly still lies in the ground, as if it could break through once again, and nowhere does it appear as if order and form were what is original but rather as if something initially unruly [*ein anfänglich Regelloses*] has been brought to order. This is the incomprehensible base of reality in things, the irreducible remainder, that which with the greatest exertion cannot be resolved in understanding but rather remains eternally in the

> ground. The understanding is born in the genuine sense from that which is without understanding. (SW VII, 359–60)

At first glance, this passage seems to be a statement of an extreme irrationalism. If we look more carefully, however, we can see many of the features that we have already encountered with respect to the irrational and its relationship to the understanding. To begin with, Schelling is describing nature from a standpoint *after* its formation by the understanding has run its course ("after the eternal act of self-revelation"). At the end of the process there remains an irrational element, the "incomprehensible base of reality." In what sense is it "incomprehensible" (*unergreiflich*)? Schelling makes clear that this is in reference to the *understanding*: it cannot be resolved or dissolved in *Verstand*.[66] This leaves open the possibility that this irrational element can be accessed from another standpoint; indeed, Schelling's philosophical discussion of the element presupposes such a standpoint, even if he never explicitly characterizes it.

We have already seen what the understanding's resolving or dissolving activity looks like: it divides the forces in the ground, thereby unfolding the forms that were previously hidden. If the final element at the end of the process cannot be divided, it is incomprehensible for the understanding. The alternative translation of *der nie aufgehende Rest* as "indivisible remainder" is therefore appropriate, if somewhat free.[67] In the passage Schelling seems to treat *aufgehen* and *sich auflösen* ("to be dissolved") as synonyms; this is also the case in his discussion of the irrational in the published reply to Eschenmayer (1812), where he refers to the chemical process of dissolving something. Dissolution requires that a heterogeneous element become homogeneous (SW VIII, 163–64). In the formation of nature, this is accomplished when the understanding (the ideal principle) divides the real from the ideal in the ground, unfolding the ideal elements that are homogeneous with it. But at the end of the process, a heterogeneous (real) element remains that cannot be so dissolved. Other meanings of *aufgehen* are relevant as well. For example, in arithmetic the verb is used to express the divisibility of one number by another without remainder.[68] It can also refer to the opening up and unfolding of a seed when a plant grows or a flower blossoms.[69] Schelling himself uses this image when describing the division of forces in nature: "Only thus can the understanding unfold the unity that is unconsciously but necessarily immanent in nature as in a seed" (SW VII, 361). The irreducible remainder, on the other hand, cannot be further unfolded; it is an empty or exhausted seed.

The passage on the irreducible remainder has one other theme: the non-originality of order and understanding. The initially unruly is what is original. Understanding is born from what lacks understanding.[70] This seems to suggest that order and rationality are derived from disorder and irrationality, which would call into question the very foundation—and legitimacy—of rationality.[71] Indeed, many have interpreted Schelling along these lines, beginning with Eschenmayer (cf. SW VIII, 152–53). However, this interpretation overlooks two things. First, the passage is treating the origin of understanding and order *in nature*, not in general. The understanding in created beings arises from the unruliness of the ground, but this is not true of God's understanding, which Schelling also calls "the original understanding" (SW VII, 362).[72] In fact, this original understanding is implicitly invoked in the passage through the passive voice: "something initially unruly has been brought to order"—namely, by the divine understanding. This leads to a second point: the sense in which the unruly is a ground. Order and form in nature are not derived from disorder and formlessness. Instead, forms are already present within the ground in an undifferentiated state, and the understanding reveals these forms through the division and ordering of forces. As we saw in the last chapter, the ground is not the cause but the condition of the existence of order in nature.[73] It gives birth, but only with the help of the understanding.

In what sense, then, is the unruly original? And what does "unruly" (*regellos*) even mean? The unruly is original in the sense that it defines the original state of nature or the ground before the process of creation. We can therefore discover its meaning by working backward from what the understanding has accomplished in nature. As we have seen, the understanding divides, unfolds, and raises up what is in the ground. If we reverse this process, the initial state of nature is a condition in which all the forms that will later appear are present, but hidden and undifferentiated. In what way is this *unruly*? That which is unruly (*regellos*) lacks a rule (*Regel*) or regulation. As we have seen, the divided forces are regulated by being placed in a hierarchy. Order and rule require division; that which is not yet divided is not yet ordered and thus unruly.[74]

This may seem like a strange conception of nature's "anarchy," if one thinks of the latter as a state of chaos that involves random movement, in violation of the principle of sufficient reason. However, the conception of the unruly as an undifferentiated unity matches Schelling's discussion of "chaos" in both the writings of his *Identitätsphilosophie* and his much later *Philosophy of Mythology*. In *Further Presentations* (1802), Schelling defines chaos as a state in which nothing is distinguishable; all things are in-one-another (*im absoluten Ineinander*), perfectly merged or intertwined (SW IV, 447). In fact, Schelling uses the concept to characterize absolute identity itself, the principle of his system (cf. SW IV, 445). In the *Philosophy of Art* (1802–3), he writes: "The inner essence of the absolute, in which all lies as one and one lies as all, is the original chaos itself" (SW V, 465). Elsewhere he refers to "that almost divine chaos" (*jenes fast göttliche Chaos*) (SW IV, 402).[75] This reveals something remarkable: Schelling not only places chaos at the deepest level of nature; he also recognizes a "divine chaos" in the absolute. Chaos is both below and above the rational ordering of things. One can therefore say that the absolute, like the ground, is irrational—in the sense of being beyond comprehension by the understanding, which knows through division. But this does not mean that it cannot be known some other way.[76]

However, this account of the irrational and the unruly in terms of an undifferentiated state of concealment is missing a key element: resistance to order. After all, there are two possible ways that the irrational can relate negatively to the understanding: (1) it can lack understanding (the non-rational) and (2) it can resist understanding (the anti-rational). In the passage on the irreducible remainder, Schelling alludes to such resistance when he notes that the unruly still lies in the ground "as if it could break through once again" (SW VII, 359). And when describing the process by which the understanding unfolds what is in the ground, Schelling adds that the ground "strives now to retain the glimpse of life seized within itself and to close itself up in itself so that a ground may always remain" (SW VII, 361). Just as the understanding is a drive toward disclosure of what is hidden, the ground as the irrational principle is a drive toward concealment. But this resistance to disclosure is not arbitrary or "without reason." Indeed, it serves to make the formation of nature a dynamic process: creation is not the product of mechanical causality but the result of the living interplay between opposed forces. As Schelling writes in the *Stuttgart Private Lectures*, "No life without opposition" (SW VII, 435).

There is one other characteristic of the irrational that is closely tied to its association with the ground or real principle in opposition to the understanding or ideal principle. As we saw in the last chapter, these two principles are defined relative to each other at a particular level of the system. Thus, the same thing can be that-which-exists on one level and the ground of existence on another level. If irrationality is understood in terms of the relationship between the principles, this means that something can be rational on one level and irrational on another: irrationality is itself *relative*. This is confirmed by Schelling's identification of the irrational with non-being (*das Nicht-Seiende*) in his reply to Eschenmayer (SW VIII, 163). Elsewhere he emphasizes the relativity of non-being: "All non-being is *only relative*, i.e., with reference to a higher being [*Seiendes*]" (SW VII, 437). If irrationality, like non-being, is relative, what does that mean exactly? If the irrational is what lacks division and order, something can be more or less irrational depending on the degree to which it has been divided and ordered. Thus, greater and greater rationality emerges as the understanding divides and orders the ground.

I have argued in this section that the irrational elements in the *Freiheitsschrift* are not "gaps in reality" that lack a sufficient reason. But there is one final irrational element to account for: the "contingent determinations" (*zufällige Bestimmungen*) in nature (SW VII, 376). These seem to introduce gaps, contradicting Schelling's subsequent rejection of contingency and chance for the sake of the unity of the whole (SW VII, 383). I would argue, however, that the contingency to which Schelling refers in this passage is compatible with grounding—and even compatible with a form of necessity. In effect, Schelling's distinction between forms of grounding allows him to combine necessity and (relative) contingency.

To see why, we need to return to the nature of necessity. Just as the irrational is defined by reference to the understanding, the contingent is defined by reference to the necessary—it is precisely what is *not necessary*. This means that different senses of necessity correspond to different senses of contingency. As we saw in the last section, Schelling follows Leibniz in distinguishing different senses of necessity: revelation does not follow from God with a geometrical necessity, but it does follow with a moral and absolute necessity. Accordingly, Schelling can allow for contingency with respect to geometrical necessity (what we might call "geometrical contingency"), even as he denies it with respect to absolute necessity. In fact, Schelling cites geometrical necessity in the passage referring to nature's contingency: "The irrational and contingent, which show themselves to be bound to that which is necessary in the formation of beings, especially the organic ones, prove that it is not merely a *geometrical necessity* that has been active here, but rather that freedom, spirit and self-will were also in play" (SW VII, 376, emphasis added). Thus, the contingent elements in this passage are not *geometrically* necessary (they are geometrically contingent), but they can still be products of a higher necessity—provided that that necessity is living and personal.

But what does geometrical necessity mean here? The passage gives us a clue by implying that freedom, spirit, and self-will go beyond it. Similar clues are provided in a passage that immediately precedes the discussion of moral necessity in Leibniz:

> The whole of nature tells us that it in no way exists by virtue of a merely geometrical necessity; in it there is not undiluted pure reason but personality and spirit. . . . Otherwise the geometrical understanding that has ruled for so long would have long ago had to penetrate into nature and prove its idol of general and eternal laws of nature to a greater degree than has occurred thus far, whereas [geometrical understanding] has had to recognize the irrational relation of nature to itself more every day. (SW VII, 395–96)

Here again Schelling implies that personality and spirit go beyond geometrical necessity, which he associates with the geometrical understanding and general laws of nature. One cannot comprehend nature by using the understanding alone.[77] As Kant points out in the third *Critique*, the form of a living organism is contingent for our understanding, which can only know nature in terms of the laws of mechanical causality: "Nature, considered as mere mechanism, could have structured itself differently in a thousand ways without hitting on precisely the unity in terms of a principle of purposes" (KU §61, AA 5, 360). In the treatise *On the World Soul* (1798), Schelling follows Kant in interpreting the contingency of living organisms as being *relative to* the necessity of mechanical laws (SW II, 515).

I would therefore interpret "geometrical necessity" in these passages to mean the necessity of mechanical causality, which requires deriving natural phenomena from universal laws. Organic elements in nature are contingent (and ungrounded) relative to this mechanical necessity, even though they *can* be grounded non-mechanically. As we will see in the next section, they are products of the dynamic interplay of two forces, which correspond to the two principles in God; personality and spirit, evident even in nature, are precisely the living unity of the two principles. Thus, Schelling combines a (relative) contingency with a "living" necessity (cf. SW VII, 397) resulting from the dynamic interaction of forces. Indeed, this combination reflects a larger pattern with respect to his treatment of the irrational: he admits elements that are contingent and irrational relative to the understanding and its way of knowing, even as he incorporates them into a rational order defined by new forms of grounding.

4. The Living Character of Schelling's Rationalism

In light of the place of evil and the irrational in Schelling's thought, what can we say about his philosophy as a whole? Is he abandoning the tradition of continental rationalism that stretches back through Leibniz to Descartes? On the contrary, I would argue that he is seeking to transform it into a *living rationalism*. To understand what this involves as well as its motivations, we need to recall the polemical context of the *Freiheitsschrift*, which Schelling mentions at the beginning and returns to at the end (SW VII, 336–38; 412–14). According to an "old but in no way forgotten legend" that goes back to Jacobi, any system of reason requires the denial of freedom (SW VII, 336). More recently, Friedrich Schlegel had claimed that pantheism is "the system of pure reason," which involves an annihilation of difference and individual existence (SW VII, 338).[78] The critics of reason had also claimed that any purely rational system is incompatible with the existence of a personal God; at best, reason can know God in the form of an abstract "absolute."[79]

In response to these critics, Schelling never wavers in his defense of reason or in his conviction that it is possible to include freedom and personality in a rational system.[80] He quips that renouncing reason is "more like flight than victory" (SW VII, 338), and later compares abandoning reason to the self-castration of the priests of the Phrygian goddess Cybele (SW VII, 356–57). At the end of the treatise, he affirms the sufficiency of reason even for concepts—like the personality of God—that others claim go beyond reason: "We are of the opinion that a clear, rational view [*Vernunfteinsicht*] of even the highest concepts must be possible insofar as only in this way can they really be our own, accepted in ourselves and eternally grounded" (SW VII, 412).[81]

And yet Schelling concedes that the critics of reason have a point with respect to previous philosophical systems, which lack the resources to account for a personal God and the existence of evil.[82] The problem with these systems is not their rationality but their *one-sidedness*: "All modern European philosophy since its beginning (with Descartes) has the common defect that nature is not present for it and that it lacks a living ground. Spinoza's realism is thereby as abstract as the idealism of Leibniz. Idealism is the soul of philosophy; realism is the body; only both together can constitute a living whole" (SW VII, 356). Both sides of philosophy—the real and the ideal—are necessary if philosophy is to avoid abstraction and do justice to the living, dynamic character of reality. This passage also hints at the key to Schelling's living rationalism: unlike previous philosophy, it has a "living ground." This, of course, is nature as the ground of God's existence; Schelling's fundamental distinction is the basis for his living rationalism.

Let me back up and develop the meaning of that phrase more precisely, beginning with the word "rationalism." First, I should clarify that I am not referring to an anti-empiricist, a priori approach to philosophizing confined to "pure thinking"—a form of rationalism that Schelling will later reject in his critique of negative philosophy (cf. GPP 238–49). Instead, I am using the term to designate Schelling's commitment to the rational order and intelligibility of the world, as articulated in a "system of reason." This commitment to rational order, in turn, involves a commitment to explanation, to answering the question *why*? As we saw in Schelling's treatment of the problem of evil, he proceeds under the assumption that evil can be explained; previous accounts that leave evil unexplained are ipso facto inadequate. And this commitment to explanation reflects a more general commitment to grounding and the principle of ground. Thus, we might sum up this general sense of rationalism in the line: nothing is without a ground.

What makes Schelling's rationalism different, however, is the kind of grounding involved. He recognizes that the ordinary understanding of grounding relations cannot account for the irrational elements in reality, including evil. This is where the *living* character of his rationalism comes in. Previous systems are unable to account for evil and other irrational phenomena for the same reason they are unable to account for life. By introducing a dynamic approach to grounding that can explain life, Schelling intends to provide his rationalism with the resources to account for evil and the irrational as well. In effect, life becomes the paradigm for a new approach to grounding. It is therefore no coincidence that the word "living" appears again and again in his critique of one-sided philosophies that cannot account for evil and a personal God: modern philosophy lacks a "living ground" (SW VII, 356); idealism is missing the "real and living concept" of freedom (SW VII, 352); Spinoza's version of necessity is "non-living and impersonal" (SW VII, 397).

What, then, is Schelling's "living" approach to grounding? At its core, it is the "dynamic mode of explanation" (*dynamische Erklärungsart*) in terms of the conflict between two forces (cf. SW VII, 396). To appreciate the significance of this way of explaining life, it is helpful to contrast it with two other approaches popular at the turn of the nineteenth century.[83] The first is to explain life in terms of Newtonian mechanics—in effect, treating organisms like complex machines. However, Kant in the third *Critique* had recognized that mechanics (at least, as understood by human beings) could not account for the unique features of organisms—in particular, the way the parts depend on the whole for their possibility: "Absolutely no human reason . . . can hope to understand, in terms of nothing but mechanical causes, how so much as a mere blade of grass is produced" (KU §77, AA 5, 409). As noted above, Schelling seems to be referring to this mechanical approach in the *Freiheitsschrift* when he notes the inadequacies of the "geometrical understanding" and its attempts to derive natural phenomena from universal laws (SW VII, 395).

If mechanical explanations of life are insufficient, one might be tempted to say life is essentially *inexplicable*—at least in terms of more basic natural forces. This is the position of vitalism, which posits a special "life force" to distinguish organisms from inorganic nature. However, Schelling in his 1798 treatise *On the World Soul* emphatically rejects this approach as well: "It is an old delusion that organization and life are unexplainable [*unerklärbar*] in terms of the principles of nature" (SW II, 348). Schelling thus seeks to explain life, but to do so dynamically, not mechanically—in effect, steering a middle course between mechanism and vitalism. In fact, this formulation of his *via media* nicely captures his larger approach to evil, nature, and God in the *Freiheitsschrift*: he is committed to explanation in terms of dynamic (not mechanical) principles. He thus rejects both the irrationalism of Jacobi (corresponding to vitalism) and the abstract rationalism of Spinoza (corresponding to mechanism) in favor of a living rationalism.

What, then, does a dynamic explanation of life involve? Essentially, it is a matter of showing how life is constituted through the conflict of two opposed forces. "The essence of life," Schelling writes in *On the World Soul*, "does not consist in a *force*, but in a *free play of forces*" (SW II, 566). And in the *Freiheitsschrift* he notes: "Where there is not struggle, there is not life" (SW VII, 400). The roots of this dynamic mode of explaining are in Kant's *Metaphysical Foundations of Natural Science* (1786), with its construction of matter from the forces of attraction and repulsion.[84] In Schelling's mature *Naturphilosophie*, however, the two basic principles are gravity and light—life is constructed from their interaction (cf. SW VI, 396–97).[85]

Now the key to applying this dynamic explanation of life to the *Freiheitsschrift* is to recall that light and gravity are the natural forces analogous to the two principles in God: light corresponds to that-which-exists, gravity corresponds to the ground of existence (SW VII, 358). But they are not simply analogous. As we saw in the previous chapter, the distinction between two principles in God reflects a basic structure of reality that appears at different levels, including at the level of light and gravity. Because of this parallel structure, the same dynamic explanation of life in terms of light and gravity can be extended to other levels of the system, using whatever principles correspond to the two forces at that level. Thus, the divine life and personality are explained dynamically in terms of the opposition and unity of the two principles in God. And human life and the possibility of evil are explained dynamically in terms of the union (and potential reversal) of the two wills in human beings.

This wide application of dynamic explanation in the *Freiheitsschrift* corresponds to an extension of the concept of life far beyond what are normally considered "organisms." Indeed, variations on the words "living" and "life" occur more than eighty times in the text in a variety of contexts. At the highest level, the system is itself a life. As we noted in chapter 1, Schelling had long thought of system as "an organic whole" (SW III, 279), an idea with roots in his early reading of Plato's *Timaeus*, which characterizes the cosmos as a "living being" (T 29–33). Thus, the dynamic explanation in terms of two complementary forces applies to the overarching structure of his philosophical system: "Idealism is the soul of philosophy; realism is the body; only both together can constitute a living whole" (SW VII, 356).

We can now understand Schelling's critique of modern philosophical systems in light of his application of the dynamics of life to the whole of philosophy. Those systems are missing nature as a "living ground" (SW VII, 356). In particular, idealism does not have "a living realism as its basis" and thus lacks a "living foundation" (SW VII, 356). The word "living" in all these phrases is applied to the real element—either nature or the realism focused on nature. The real element is a *living* ground by virtue of its dynamic opposition to the ideal element: only both together can constitute life as a "play of forces." Any one-sided philosophy that lacks the real element is therefore missing one of the essential ingredients for life.

With this in mind, we can return to the famous line "God is not a system but a life" (SW VII, 399). One might argue that Schelling is here rejecting rationalism (in the sense of a comprehensive rational order), because life necessarily falls outside any rational order. However, as I argued in chapter 1, Schelling is referring to a narrower sense of system in this passage: the (ideal) system "in the divine understanding." The line is saying in effect: God is not just his understanding (that-which-exists), because he has within himself a living ground as well. Both together form the divine life, which is a living system or organic whole. In light of the theme of this section, we might therefore paraphrase the famous line as follows: "To do justice to God, philosophy must not be an abstract or one-sided rationalism, but a living rationalism."

So far I have emphasized the "dynamic mode of explanation" as central to Schelling's organic understanding of grounding. I would now like to round out the discussion by briefly placing this mode of explanation in the context of the larger problem of ground and the features of organic grounding we discussed in the last chapter. First, dynamic explanation clearly aligns with Schelling's general departure from the all-from-one model of grounding, in which a single ground or cause determines what follows from it. Light and gravity are both *conditions of the possibility* for life, but neither is sufficient on its own to produce it—just as we saw with respect to the two principles in God. Second, life as a conflict or "play of forces" involves their interaction and *reciprocal grounding*. On the one hand, each acts on the other (and resists the other's action). On the other hand, each is the condition of the possibility of the other qua part of an organic whole. Again, we have already seen dramatic examples of this organic reciprocity in the "living circuit" (SW IX, 46) and "the circle from which everything comes to be," where "all things mutually presuppose each other" (SW VII, 358).[86] There is, however, a final organic structure that goes beyond dynamic explanation as such. As we saw in the mystery of love, the parts of the organism are *wholes within a larger whole*. Each part depends on the larger whole for its possibility, but it is also "its own world" that reflects the larger world. We will see the importance of this microcosmic aspect of Schelling's thought in the next chapter.

In any case, I hope to have shown how the grounding structures of life allow Schelling to maintain a commitment to rationalism while accommodating phenomena that seem to defy rational explanation—including evil and the irrational. Expressed in another way, new grounding structures allow Schelling to combine reason and mystery. It is a common assumption that mystery is incompatible with reason, which flattens reality into something comprehensible and essentially unmysterious. And yet one of the distinctive features of Schelling's philosophy is its blend of rationality and a sense of mystery or the uncanny, particularly in the *Freiheitsschrift*, *Clara*, and the *Ages of the World*. Examples include his reference to "derived absoluteness or divinity" (SW VII, 347) and his haunting description of the ground of God's existence, especially the irreducible remainder (SW VII, 359–60).

It is true that these mysterious elements are irrational with respect to our ordinary ways of thinking—in particular, our ordinary understanding of grounding relations. A living rationalism, however, is able to integrate such elements within a rational order by introducing new forms of grounding—including dynamic explanation, begetting, and self-grounding. In other words, a more capacious rationalism that is able to accommodate life is also able to accommodate mystery.

But wouldn't these elements cease to be mysterious as soon as they are integrated into a rational order of grounds? It depends, of course, on how one defines "mystery." I believe it is possible to define it meaningfully in terms of four characteristics that Schelling preserves within his living rationalism. (1) Mystery is hidden from our everyday way of knowing. Schelling, for example, notes that the intelligible deed of freedom is "incomprehensible for the common way of thinking" (SW VII, 386). (2) It is therefore imperfectly captured by our ordinary language. For this reason, Schelling draws on the language of mysticism, and at times his language has a poetic or paradoxical quality.[87] (3) Even though it is integrated into an order of grounding, mystery has infinite depth and thus inexhaustibility. Indeed, the "mysterious" grounding structures in the *Freiheitsschrift*, like "derived absoluteness," have infinity built into them. (4) Finally, mystery is an object of wonder, which is reflected in the uncanny feeling evoked by Schelling's language.[88]

And feeling can itself be revelatory of mystery. Schelling refers to the feeling that we are what we are from all eternity (SW VII, 386), and he begins the treatise by noting the feeling of freedom (SW VII, 336). But feeling by itself is not sufficient for the philosopher: Schelling emphasizes the need to treat the concept of freedom and "the connection of this concept with the whole of a scientific worldview" (SW VII, 336). Nonetheless, he never leaves feeling behind, as evidenced by the language that evokes wonder throughout the treatise—though he stresses the need to recognize feeling's proper place: "Feeling is glorious if it remains in the ground" (SW VII, 414). Thus, we can say that Schelling's living rationalism also unites reason and feeling.

This all has implications for the nature of reason. To combine feeling, mystery, and the irrational in a living whole, Schelling's rationalism must be founded on a conception of reason that is similarly comprehensive. Reason cannot be reduced to the geometrical understanding or a merely ideal capacity. At the end of the treatise, Schelling describes the kind of system that would satisfy—and not satisfy—the demands of reason in its comprehensiveness:

> A system that contradicts the most holy feelings, character, and moral consciousness, can never be called, at least in this respect, a system of reason, but rather only one of non-reason. To the contrary, a system in which reason really recognized itself would have to unify all demands of the spirit as well as those of the heart, and those of the most moral feeling as well as those of the most rigorous understanding. (SW VII, 413)

Reason only recognizes itself in a system that does justice to both the head and the heart, intellect and feeling—one might add: the rational and the irrational. Only both sides together can form a living whole. Joining them does not require denying that everything is grounded—even evil and the irrational have their grounds. But it does require a grounding that is sufficient for life.

6

The *Ungrund* as the Ultimate Origin

We come now to the section in the *Freiheitsschrift* that Schelling calls "the highest point of the entire investigation" (SW VII, 406). This is the section concerning that being or essence (*Wesen*) that Schelling designates—somewhat hesitantly—as the *Ungrund*. This name itself, together with the unusual manner in which Schelling introduces it, already suggests that this concept is decisive for the problem of ground in the *Freiheitsschrift*. When Schelling first mentions the *Wesen* that was "before the ground and before that-which-exists," he leaves its name an open question: "How should we designate it?" (SW VII, 406).[1] After a short intervening discussion, he finally names it, but only in the form of a question: "How can we call it anything other than the original ground [*Urgrund*], or rather the *non-ground* [*Ungrund*]?" (SW VII, 406). This question contains not one but *two* possible designations, and they seem to be at odds with one another. Is this *Wesen*[2] the original ground, or a non-ground? Expressed more directly: is it a ground or not? My thesis is that the *Ungrund* is a ground in one sense, but not a ground in another. As we will see, its ambiguous relation to grounding is another expression of the theme we have encountered before: the distinction between (1) the historically dominant sense of ground as "determining ground" and (2) ground as conditio sine qua non.

In the *Freiheitsschrift* Schelling clearly prefers the designation *Ungrund* ("non-ground") to *Urgrund* ("original ground"). In the passage introducing these terms, this is indicated by means of italics and the phrase "or rather . . . ," and he never uses the word *Urgrund* in what follows. Nevertheless, by introducing the term in the form of a question,

Schelling displays a certain hesitancy regarding the name. In the works that immediately follow the *Freiheitsschrift*, the term *Ungrund* rarely appears (cf. WA I, 93). And even when he refers to this passage in his reply to Eschenmayer (1812) and his polemic against Jacobi (1812), he does not call the *Ungrund* by that name.[3] I suspect that his hesitation in using the term is a reflection of the inadequacy of any name for what the word *Ungrund* designates.[4] One of its "characteristics" is the "lacking of a predicate" (*Prädikatlosigkeit*) (SW VII, 406). It therefore resists the determination that any name would provide.[5]

One thing, however, is certain: Schelling borrows the designation *Ungrund* from the German mystic Jacob Boehme (1575–1624), whose works Schelling studied with Franz von Baader beginning in 1806.[6] The word *Ungrund* in Boehme refers to the primordial aspect of God that precedes divine revelation and lacks any determination.[7] For example, in the text *On the Election of Grace*, Boehme writes: "One cannot say that he is this or that, good or evil, [or] that he has differences in himself. . . . He is in himself the non-ground [*Ungrund*] without his own will."[8] Moreover, some of the language in Schelling's passage on the *Ungrund* seems to echo Boehme—for example, his remark that the *Ungrund* "divides itself into the two equally eternal beginnings" (SW VII, 408).[9] Nevertheless, it is possible to exaggerate the role of Boehme in Schelling's thought on the *Ungrund*, as well as in the *Freiheitsschrift* in general. For example, Schopenhauer—perhaps to downplay his own debt to Schelling—accuses him of taking "the whole fable" from Boehme's *Gründlicher Bericht* (ASW III, 29).

But what is the precise relationship between Boehme and Schelling's thought on the *Ungrund*? Even if Schelling uses language drawn from Boehme, and many of his ideas resemble things Boehme says, this does not necessarily mean that he "appropriated many of Boehme's ideas" or adopted Boehme's categories in a way that transformed his previous philosophy, as Robert Brown argues.[10] Indeed, we will see that much of what Schelling says about the *Ungrund* was developed years earlier in Schelling's writings about the nature of absolute identity. My own view is that Schelling saw in Boehme's writings certain affinities with his own thought and adopted some of Boehme's language to express his own ideas in a new way; however, that language takes on a meaning determined by Schelling's own philosophical reflections, which need not match its original meaning in Boehme. For this reason, an examination of Boehme's writings on the *Ungrund* has only limited usefulness for understanding what is at stake philosophically in this passage in the *Freiheitsschrift*.

Nevertheless, the connection with Boehme does raise an issue that has significant implications for the meaning of ground in Schelling. This is the use of the word *Grund* and its cognates in the tradition of German mysticism, going back to Meister Eckhart. Although as a mystical term *Ungrund* appears to originate with Boehme, the German mystics had long used the words "ground" (*Grund*) and "abyss" (*Abgrund*) to designate the innermost being of God. Indeed, the preeminent scholar of the history of mysticism, Bernard McGinn, gives the name "mysticism of the ground" to the distinctive brand of mysticism represented by Eckhart and his followers.[11] According to McGinn, ground is their "master metaphor," with a rich array of meanings—both concrete and abstract.[12] Above all, for Eckhart the word "ground" signifies the indistinct identity of God and the human soul.[13]

One of the interesting features of the use of "ground" in Eckhart and his followers is its paradoxical combination with what seems to be its opposite: *Abgrund*.[14] The ground of God and of the human soul is also an "abyss." Similarly, Schelling in the *Freiheitsschrift* designates the same *Wesen* as both *Urgrund* (original ground) and *Ungrund* (non-ground).[15] But this raises the question of the precise relationship between these terms: (1) *Grund*, (2) *Abgrund*, (3) *Ungrund*. In particular, what is the meaning of the prefixes *ab-* and *un-* when applied to *Grund*? They seem to indicate a privation or a negation. The word *Abgrund* ("abyss") is common in German, and the sense of the privative prefix *ab-* is easy to understand. The abyss is what lacks a ground; it is therefore "bottomless."[16] Similarly, we can think of the prefix *un-* as privative: *Unruhe*, for example, means "unrest."[17] The word *Ungrund* would therefore refer to something that lacks ground. But there is an ambiguity with respect to the negation: Does the "absence of ground" mean (1) that the *Ungrund* does not ground anything else? Or does it mean (2) that the *Ungrund* does not *have* a ground, that the *Ungrund* is itself ground*less*?

In the case of the word "abyss" (*Abgrund*), these two possible negations are combined. The abyss is bottomless. It therefore (1) cannot be a ground of anything else, because (2) it itself has no ground. In fact, the *Deutsches Wörterbuch* of the Brothers Grimm lists one of the meanings of *Ungrund* as "abyss."[18] However, one of the interesting aspects of the passage on the *Ungrund* in the *Freiheitsschrift* is that the question of whether and how the *Ungrund* is itself grounded never arises. Instead, Schelling's focus is the relationship between the *Ungrund* and what comes after it (that-which-exists and the ground of existence). The general orientation of the passage toward the priority of the *Ungrund* strongly suggests that the designation concerns the role of the original *Wesen* as a possible subject of grounding. The prefix *un-* would thus deny that it is a ground (in a certain sense), not necessarily that it has a ground.

But one can nevertheless pose the question: is the *Ungrund* itself grounded? Somewhat after his initial discussion, Schelling states that the *Ungrund* or indifference is the "beginning point" (*Anfangspunkt*) of the system (SW VII, 412). There would therefore be nothing *before* it that could serve as its ground: it is the ultimate origin. Accordingly, two possibilities remain open: (1) the *Ungrund* is groundless, or (2) it is *self*-grounding. As we will see below, the *Ungrund* has many of the same features that Schelling had ascribed to absolute identity in his earlier writings, and he even identifies the *Ungrund* with absolute identity in his 1812 polemic against Jacobi (SW VIII, 81).[19] To be sure, earlier works characterize absolute identity as self-grounding or self-affirming.[20] And yet Schelling elsewhere indicates that what is self-affirming can nonetheless be groundless. In the famous line in the *Freiheitsschrift* about willing as primordial being, Schelling lists both "groundlessness" and "self-affirmation" as its predicates (SW VII, 350). I will return to the relationship between groundlessness and self-grounding when discussing the concept of *causa sui* in the next chapter. Moreover, we will see below in what way the *Ungrund* is also integrated into a circle of mutual presupposition or grounding, along the lines I discussed in chapter 4.

The section in the *Freiheitsschrift* that treats the *Ungrund* (SW VII, 406–12) is one of the most demanding passages in an already difficult text. A certain modesty is therefore required when approaching this theme: what follows is my attempt to make sense of Schelling's thought on the *Ungrund*, with a special emphasis on the implications for the problem of ground and system. Because of the complexity of the topic, I would like to emphasize three points in advance, so that they can guide our discussion. First, the *Ungrund* is a ground in the sense of a condition of the possibility. It precedes and makes possible the duality of the principles in God, which inaugurate the process of creation and revelation. Second, the *Ungrund* is not a ground in the sense of a first principle from which everything else can be derived. There is no "transition" from what is without opposition to opposition. Third, the *Ungrund* is nevertheless integrated within the system, and Schelling's discussion of it arises out of systematic considerations.

The *Ungrund* as the Ultimate Origin | 187

Because the placement of the *Ungrund* within the *Freiheitsschrift* as a whole is important for understanding what Schelling says about it, I begin with the context. I then consider in what way the *Ungrund* is a *Wesen* that underlies the development of the principles in God. The consideration of its "attributes" and a comparison with characteristics of the absolute in previous works sets the stage for a closer examination of the *Ungrund* as indifference. This, in turn, will allow us to determine in what sense it is and is not a ground. Finally, I end with a more speculative proposal concerning the relation of the *Ungrund* to the distinction between essence and form in Schelling's *Identitätsphilosophie*.

1. The Context of Schelling's Treatment of the *Ungrund*

At first glance, the discussion of the *Ungrund* seems to come out of nowhere.[21] At the very least, it appears to fit uneasily into the surrounding context. Schelling had been discussing the endpoint of the process of revelation and creation. At the end of this process God is love, which is "all in all." This invocation of love prompts Schelling to turn to the—as yet unnamed—*Ungrund*: "[Love] is what was, then, before the ground and before that-which-exists (as separate), but not yet as *love*, rather—how should we designate it?" (SW VII, 406). Instead of answering this question immediately and developing the concept of the *Ungrund*, Schelling formulates the objection of an (imagined) opponent to his fundamental distinction between ground and that-which-exists. Only after this objection does he finally designate and develop his thought about the *Ungrund*—first in what he calls a "dialectical discussion," with reference to objections and misunderstandings; then finally in what he identifies as a "completely determinate" (*ganz bestimmt*) explanation (SW VII, 407).

Why does Schelling discuss the *Ungrund* at this point in the *Freiheitsschrift*? Is it an unnecessary addition or afterthought that has little to do with the rest of the treatise—or even a step back from insights he had developed in the preceding pages, as Heidegger claims?[22] Although Schelling does not clearly present the connection with the surrounding context, a close reading of this context reveals that the section is thematically integrated into its surroundings. These surroundings can be characterized above all through the keyword *process*. In fact, the long paragraph before the introduction of the *Ungrund* begins with a series of process-related questions: "Will evil end and how? Does creation have a final purpose at all, and, if this is so, why is it not reached immediately, why does what is perfect not exist right from the beginning?" (SW VII, 403). These questions concern the necessity of process, which cannot be taken for granted: it is conceivable that the endpoint could be reached immediately, and no development (with the accompanying evil) would be necessary. Schelling's reply is that a process is necessary "because God is a life, not merely a being [*Sein*]" (SW VII, 403). God as life involves becoming and development. In the remainder of the paragraph Schelling gives a résumé of this process, which culminates with spirit and the subordination of spirit to love, which is "all in all." Toward the end of the discussion of the *Ungrund*, he reprises the final stages, beginning with the last division and ending again with love (SW VII, 408). This again emphasizes the connection of the process with the *Ungrund*.

But what does it have to do with this process? We can begin to see the answer to this question, if we note what Schelling says about being: "God is a life, not *merely* a being [*ein Sein*]" (SW VII, 403, emphasis added). Here Schelling does not deny that God is a being—only that he is *merely* a being. He goes on to describe the relationship between being and becoming: "Being becomes sensitive to itself [*sich empfindlich*] only in becoming. In being there is admittedly no becoming . . . but in [its] actualization [*Verwirklichung*] there is necessarily a becoming" (SW VII, 403). The process of becoming is at the same time the process of the realization and the coming-to-consciousness of being. Being therefore *begins* as unconscious and unrealized and *ends* as conscious and realized. As we will see in the next section, this is precisely the role of the *Ungrund* vis-à-vis the process of creation. In anticipation of the discussion in the next section, we can say that the *Ungrund* relates to the process of revelation in three ways:

1. The *Ungrund* is the *Wesen* that underlies, unifies, and makes possible the process. The process itself is the unfolding of what is concealed in this *Wesen*.

2. The *Ungrund* as indifference is the "beginning point" of the process. As indifference, the *Wesen* is not yet unfolded and thus not yet conscious and personal.

3. The *Ungrund* is the same *Wesen* as love. This *Wesen* is the *Ungrund* at the beginning point of the process, while this

Wesen is love at the endpoint. Thus, Schelling says the *Ungrund* is the same *Wesen*, but "not yet" (*noch nicht*) as love (SW VII, 406), and love is the same *Wesen*, but "no longer" (*nicht mehr*) as indifference (SW VII, 408).

We can now explain why Schelling turns to a discussion of the *Ungrund* after an account of the process of revelation, ending with love. Even if it is not "part" of the process, the *Ungrund* underlies the process in such a way that any account is incomplete without considering it. Moreover, an account of the process of revelation is also incomplete without an account of *what* is being revealed. But what is revealed is precisely the *Wesen* that is both the *Ungrund* (at the beginning) and love (at the end).

Immediately after alluding to the *Wesen* that he will eventually call the *Ungrund*, Schelling notes that we have finally reached the "highest point of the entire investigation" (SW VII, 406). Why the "highest point"? First, because of the relationship between the *Ungrund* and love, which Schelling had just identified as highest, adding: "Love is what was, then, before the ground and before that-which-exists (as separate) but not yet as love" (SW VII, 406). Thus, the *Ungrund* is the same *Wesen* that becomes love at the end of the process of revelation, and love is "the highest."

Second, the discussion of the *Ungrund* is the highest point because it assumes the "highest standpoint." In the middle of the passage, Schelling claims that the *Ungrund* "posits and confirms" the distinction between the two principles in God. He then adds that the distinction "has shown itself as a very real distinction that from the *highest standpoint* was first correctly proved and fully grasped" (SW VII, 407, emphasis added). The standpoint of the *Ungrund* is the highest, because it involves seeing things from the perspective of the absolute origin. The last line of the *Freiheitsschrift*[23] even identifies this perspective as the goal of our striving: "It is not the time to rouse old oppositions once again, but rather to seek that which lies outside of, and above, all opposition" (SW VII, 416). The standpoint of the *Ungrund* is precisely what is above and prior to all opposition.[24] And twice Schelling labels the *Ungrund* "das schlechthin betrachtete Absolute" (the unconditionally absolute, or the absolute regarded absolutely) (SW VII, 407–8, 409).[25]

Finally, the discussion of the *Ungrund* is also the highest point of the investigation in that it treats the ultimate structure of Schelling's system. It answers the question: is the system ultimately a monism or a dualism? The process mentioned above consists in the development and interaction of the two principles in God. But is the twoness of the principles ultimate? Or is there a higher "principle" that would bring unity to the process and thus to the system as a whole?

Schelling raises these questions in the form of an imagined objection to his fundamental distinction: "What end [*Wozu*] should be served by that first distinction between being [*Wesen*] insofar as it is ground and insofar as it exists?" (SW VII, 406). The objection that follows takes the form of a "horned dilemma": either there is a common middle point for the two principles, or not. If not, then the system is ultimately a dualism. Earlier in the text Schelling had declared the non-viability of a (certain kind of) dualism: "If [this system] is really thought as the doctrine of two absolutely different and mutually independent principles, [it] is only a system of the self-destruction and despair of reason" (SW VII, 354).[26] As we saw in chapter 1, reason requires an ultimate unity for knowledge. But the alternative appears undesirable as well. If there *is* a common middle point for the two principles, the two collapse into one. There is no longer any genuine twoness in the system, and everything is blended together.

As we will see below, the indifference of the *Ungrund* is Schelling's answer to this dilemma. With this concept, Schelling aims to create a combination of monism and dualism. Earlier, in an important footnote on the fundamental distinction, he makes this intention clear: "This is the only correct dualism, namely that which at the same time permits a unity" (SW VII, 359n). Accordingly, the *Ungrund* has a double, seemingly paradoxical function. First, it ensures the ultimate unity of the system. The system is not *ultimately* a dualism, but is *one* in the final analysis, despite the two principles in God. Second, the *Ungrund* guarantees the genuine *twoness* of the principles, because it allows each to exist *for itself* and as an independent whole. In this way, the *Ungrund* ensures the genuineness of the fundamental distinction within God at the same time that it avoids an ultimate dualism.

2. The *Ungrund* as the *Wesen* of the Two Principles in God

Already in the last section we saw that Schelling's discussion of the *Ungrund* is closely connected to the fundamental distinction between that-which-exists and the ground of existence. In fact, I would argue that Schelling had already referred to the *Ungrund* in relation to the distinction much earlier in the *Freiheitsschrift*, albeit without using the designation

Ungrund.²⁷ The first formulation of the fundamental distinction reads: "The philosophy of nature of our time has first advanced in science the distinction between being [*Wesen*] insofar as it exists, and being insofar as it is merely the ground of existence" (SW VII, 357). One of the interesting features of the distinction is the "silent presence" of the word *Wesen*. The distinction concerns a single "being" (*Wesen*) regarded in two respects, marked each time with the word *sofern* ("insofar as"). The two respects are the two principles: that-which-exists and the ground of existence. But what about the *Wesen* of which these principles are aspects? In the subsequent development of the distinction, Schelling says nothing more about it—though we noted that the word "God" appears in place of *Wesen* when the distinction is applied to God.²⁸ Considered in itself, it is an unnamed X that underlies the two principles.

Only in the passage on the *Ungrund* does Schelling identify what it is: "The *Wesen* of the ground, as of that-which-exists, can only be that which comes *before* all ground, thus, the unconditionally absolute, the *Ungrund*" (SW VII, 408). The *Ungrund* is itself that *Wesen*, of which the two principles are aspects—and thus the same *Wesen* Schelling had already mentioned in his first formulation of the fundamental distinction. In the reply to Eschenmayer (1812), he formulates the relationship of the two principles to the *Ungrund* in more detail. Noting that they "belong to a single *Wesen*" (*zu Einem Wesen gehören*), he explains:

> God has the ground of his existence *in himself*, in his own original being [*Urwesen*]; thus, this ground belongs to the same original being to which the existing God (God as subject of existence) also belongs. In my treatise I designate clearly enough this original being, from which God himself emerges [*hervortritt*] only through the act of his manifestation (p. 497 [SW VII, 406])—just as I have otherwise called it, not God, but the unconditionally *absolute*, to distinguish it from *God* (as the mere subject of existence). (SW VIII, 165)

The passage from the *Freiheitsschrift* that Schelling cites is the very passage we have been considering. There can be little doubt that the *Urwesen* to which both principles belong is the *Ungrund*.

But what does *Wesen* mean when applied to the *Ungrund*? As we have seen in other contexts, it can refer to both (1) the essence and (2) a being. With respect to the *Ungrund*, both meanings apply. On the one hand, Schelling attributes to the *Ungrund* a substance-like character that fits with the sense of "being." Thus, he refers to the *Ungrund* as a *Wesen* ("being") before all ground and before all that exists (SW VII, 406). On the other hand, the phrase "*Wesen* of the ground" is more naturally translated as "essence of the ground" (SW VII, 407). And we will see below that each of the principles shares the same *essence* of the absolute, and that this allows each to be an independent whole.[29]

I mentioned that Schelling attributes a substance-like character to the *Wesen* that is the *Ungrund*. This is confirmed by his treatment of predication in the passage. The two principles cannot be predicated of the *Ungrund* as opposites (*Gegensätze*), but they can be predicated of the *Ungrund* as non-opposites (SW VII, 407). I discuss what this means below. Regardless of how Schelling distinguishes the two kinds of predication, the fact remains that the two principles relate to the *Ungrund* as its *predicates*, and thus it functions as their substrate (ὑποκείμενον).

At first glance, it seems strange to think of the principles in God as predicates, because this seems to deny their substantiality, and Schelling even says that each principle is "its own being" (*ein eignes Wesen*) (SW VII, 408). We can better understand this relation of predication if we return to the mediated account of the copula discussed in chapter 2. Recall that subject (A) and predicate (B) are identified, not because they are immediately one, but because each is an aspect of "the same thing" (= X). A is B, because X is (in one respect) A and (in another respect) B. In his elaboration of this account in the *Ages of the World*, Schelling refers to this X as "that not always named *same thing* [*dasselbe*], of which subject and predicate are both predicates" (WA I, 28). This is precisely the relationship between the *Ungrund* and the principles. The same *Wesen* (X) that is that-which-exists (in one respect) is the ground of existence (in another respect), and this *Wesen* is the *Ungrund*.[30]

But there is a difficulty with simply equating the *Ungrund* and the *Wesen*. We can see why when we apply the same logic of the copula to the relationship between (1) the *Ungrund* as indifference and (2) love—one of the most difficult aspects of this passage in the *Freiheitsschrift*, and easy to overlook. As we saw above, it is precisely Schelling's invocation of love that allows him to pivot to a discussion of indifference and the *Ungrund*. Here Schelling identifies love with what he will later designate as the *Ungrund* and indifference. And yet he qualifies this identification: the *Ungrund* is "not yet" love (SW VII, 406). Later on in the passage, Schelling makes the same identification, but from the opposite direction: "Above spirit, however, is the initial *Ungrund*, which is no longer indifference (equipollence [*Gleichgültigkeit*]) and yet not the identity of both principles, but rather a general unity that is the same for all and yet gripped by nothing; a beneficence that is free from all and yet acting in all; in a word, *love*, which is all in all" (SW VII, 408, emphasis added). Here Schelling identifies the "initial *Ungrund*" with love but again qualifies the identification: love is "no longer" indifference.

How are we to make sense of this identity of love and the *Ungrund*? If we apply the mediated account of the copula, the nature of this identity becomes clearer: the same *Wesen* (X) that is the *Ungrund* is also love. As the *Ungrund*, this *Wesen* is not yet love. And as love, this *Wesen* is no longer indifference (the *Ungrund*)—but this means that the *Wesen* and the *Ungrund* cannot simply be equated.[31] The two phrases "not yet" and "no longer" clearly indicate a process: *Ungrund* and love designate two "states" or "moments" of the same *Wesen*. At the beginning, before the process of revelation, this *Wesen* is the *Ungrund* or indifference. At the end, at the completion of the process of revelation, this *Wesen* is love, which is "all in all."[32]

These statements seem to suggest that the *Wesen* is part of a process and therefore *changes* from indifference into love. I would instead say that the *Wesen* underlies and makes possible the process, which involves an unfolding of what was already implicit in this *Wesen*. In the strict sense, it is outside the process, because it remains what it always has been even as it comes to be revealed. This is the sense in which I interpret Schelling's earlier discussion of the relation of being (*Sein*) and becoming (*Werden*). "In being there is of course no becoming" (SW VII, 403). In this sense, the *Wesen* is always the same and outside the process. But Schelling adds: "Being becomes sensitive [*empfindlich*] to itself only in becoming. . . . In its actualization [*Verwirklichung*] through opposition there is necessarily a becoming" (SW VII, 403). Though the *Wesen* is beyond all becoming, it is unfolded in such a way that it becomes realized and conscious of itself in what is unfolded.

Here Schelling's thought is especially difficult, because he attempts to hold together the traditional metaphysical conception of God as immutable being (*Sein*) with a radically new conception of a personal God that involves life and becoming. It is perhaps helpful to think of God in the *Freiheitsschrift* on two levels. The first level is the level of being (*Sein*) or the underlying *Wesen*. This is the level for the *Ungrund* (indifference) and love. The second level is the level of becoming or the unfolding of the potencies. This is the level at which the principles in God develop and interact. The first level underlies and makes possible the second but remains beyond the latter's process of becoming. But one can object: isn't there also becoming on the first level? After all, the transition from indifference to love is a kind of becoming. One (partial) answer would be to say that this transition is not a change in the underlying *Wesen* in itself but a change in its relation to the state of the potencies on the second level—on the one hand enfolded and undeveloped, on the other hand unfolded and developed.[33] As we will see below, the designations "indifference" and "love" are essentially relational, and thus they say something both about the underlying *Wesen* and that which "belongs" to this *Wesen* on the second level.

A related question concerns the relationship between (1) the indifference of the *Ungrund* and (2) the personality (*Personalität*) or personhood (*Persönlichkeit*) of God that results from the process of revelation. Schelling evidently regarded the discussion of the latter as one of the original achievements of the *Freiheitsschrift*: "We believe that we have established the first clear concept of personality in this treatise" (SW VII, 412). But how can the personality of God be reconciled with Schelling's account of the *Ungrund*, which he labels the unconditionally absolute? This question has deep roots in Schelling's own philosophical development,[34] and it is essentially connected to the objections of Jacobi and Eschenmayer to conceiving God as an impersonal Absolute. Schelling himself admits that in the *Ungrund* there is no personality (SW VII, 412), but he restricts the place of the *Ungrund* within the system: "We have shown the particular point of the system where the concept of indifference is indeed the only possible concept of the absolute. If it is now taken generally [*allgemein*], the whole is distorted" (SW VII, 411–12).[35] The indifference of the *Ungrund* only applies to a "particular point" (*bestimmter Punkt*) of the system. But where in the system is this point? Schelling gives a reply in the form of a question: "In the *Ungrund* or indifference there is admittedly no personality. But is the beginning point really the whole?" (SW VII, 412). The *Ungrund* is the "beginning point" (*Anfangspunkt*), not the system in its totality.

But the designation "beginning point" is ambiguous. On the one hand, it could refer to the status of the *Ungrund* as the underlying *Wesen* of the two principles. Thus, Schelling repeatedly refers to the *Ungrund* as *before* the ground and that-which-exists (SW VII, 406; 407–8), indicating its priority as what underlies all that comes after it. On the other hand, "beginning point" could refer to the *Ungrund* as the enfolded *Wesen*, which is "not yet" love (the same *Wesen* as unfolded). We can formulate these two possible meanings of "beginning point" in terms of the two levels mentioned above. In the first meaning, the *Ungrund* is the beginning point, because it is on the first level, which underlies and makes possible the second (the level of the unfolding potencies). In the second meaning, the *Ungrund* is the beginning point, because *within* the first level (the level of the underlying *Wesen*) the *Ungrund* precedes love.

This discussion of the system's starting point highlights two ways in which Schelling's treatment of the *Ungrund* differs remarkably from his treatment of the absolute in previous works. First, though he refers to the *Ungrund* as the starting point, it does not come at the beginning of the *Freiheitsschrift*—in fact, it comes almost at the end.[36] In all of the previous works in the *Identitätsphilosophie*, Schelling begins with the unity of the absolute, and difference emerges only later.[37] Part of the reason for the inversion of the order is certainly the special focus on human freedom and the question of evil, which shapes the order of treatment. But I would also suggest that Schelling wishes to avoid the impression that everything, including human freedom, is derived *more geometrico* from the first principle (the all-from-one model of grounding).

The second way the discussion differs from the treatment of the absolute in previous works is the restriction of the concept to a *particular point* in the system. Previously, the absolute precisely is the whole, because God is All.[38] Nevertheless, the restriction of the *Ungrund* to a particular point is less radical a departure from his previous thought than it might seem. To begin with, Schelling continues to regard the single *Wesen*, which he identifies with the *Ungrund*, as all-comprehensive. He concedes this in response to an imagined objection: "Whoever thus would want to say (as before): there is in this system one principle for everything; it is one and the same *Wesen* that rules in the dark ground of nature and in eternal clarity . . . although he says that all entirely correctly, he should not forget that the one *Wesen* divides itself into two *Wesen* in its two ways of acting" (SW VII, 409). Though Schelling concedes here that the *Wesen* of the *Ungrund* is a comprehensive principle of unity, there is nonetheless the need to go "beyond" it in the process of revelation: this is the only way to arrive at a personal God. Similarly, though Schelling begins other works in his *Identitätsphilosophie* with the absolute, he also goes "beyond" the absolute, considered in itself, in order to construct the various forms of reality.³⁹ Here there is also a sense in which the concept of the absolute is the beginning point but not the whole: otherwise, these works would end after the account of the absolute!⁴⁰

In his 1812 polemic against Jacobi, Schelling again emphasizes the place of the *Ungrund* at the beginning of the system, while clarifying its relationship to the process of revelation. In the passage, Schelling denies that reason can have an immediate knowledge of a personal God: it can only know absolute identity immediately, and this is not yet personal. As evidence, Schelling cites the very passage in the *Freiheitsschrift* in which he states that there is no personality in the *Ungrund* or indifference (SW VII, 412). To be sure, knowledge of the absolute is knowledge of God, but only "to the extent that the *Wesen* of that absolute identity is *implicite* already God, or to speak more precisely, is *the same Wesen* that is transfigured into the personal God" (SW VIII, 81). Here again we see an application of the mediated account of the copula. The same *Wesen* (= X) is both absolute identity/the *Ungrund* (A) and the personal God (B).

Schelling then gives an overview of the development of this *Wesen*, which he refers to as God (considered in a broad sense): "I posit God as first and as last, as A and as Ω, but as A he is not what he is as Ω. To the extent that he is only God in the eminent sense as Ω, he cannot be God in the same sense as A, nor strictly speaking can he be called God; he would be [as A] the *undeveloped* God, *deus implicitus*, since he is *deus explicitus* as Ω" (SW VIII, 81). In this passage I interpret God as A to be the *Ungrund*, which is *implicitly* already what God will be *explicitly* at the end of the process.⁴¹ Accordingly, the process of revelation is the development or unfolding of what is enveloped or enfolded in God as the *Ungrund*. But what is unfolded? In chapter 4 we saw that the potencies are implicitly contained in the absolute and that the development of creation is the unfolding of these potencies.⁴² Indeed, in the *Stuttgart Private Lectures* Schelling designates the "original state" of God as the "indifference [*Gleichgültigkeit*] of potencies in him" (SW VII, 433). Before they are unfolded in a sequence, "the potencies lie in the absolute in complete indifference [*Indifferenz*] or indistinguishability" (SW VII, 428). Elsewhere Schelling describes the absolute as "free from potency" (*potenzlos*)—it is the substrate of the potencies, but not a potency itself (SW VI, 212; VII, 185–86).

We can now summarize the place of (a) the original *Wesen*, (b) the *Ungrund* or indifference, and (c) love in relation to the process of revelation and the unfolding of the potencies. (1) The original *Wesen* is the substrate underlying the process. It is also what is revealed, since the unfolded potencies belong to this *Wesen*. (2) The *Ungrund* is this *Wesen* in its initial state, before the process of revelation. It contains all the potencies within itself, but they are in a state of indifference. (3) Love is this *Wesen* at the end of the process, after all of the potencies have been unfolded and united. Everything that God was implicitly in the *Ungrund* he is explicitly in love.[43]

3. Characteristics of the *Ungrund* and Its Relation to Schelling's Previous Descriptions of the Absolute

We already encountered characteristics of the *Ungrund* in the last section: it is the *Wesen* of the two principles in God and the "beginning point" of the system. In this section, I examine its other characteristics, relating them to his previous descriptions of the absolute. Schelling characterizes the *Ungrund* in the following ways:

1. In relation to opposites or opposition (*Gegensatz*). (a) The *Ungrund* precedes all opposites. (b) The opposites are not distinguishable (*unterscheidbar*) in it. (c) The opposites are in no way present (*vorhanden*) or implicitly contained in it.

2. In relation to "absolute identity." Schelling repeatedly denies that the *Ungrund* or absolute indifference is the absolute identity of the two principles in God (SW VII, 406; 407).

3. As the absolute indifference of the two principles. Here the *Ungrund* relates to the principles, not only as Either-Or (disjunction), but also as Neither-Nor. It is in each principle in the same way (*gleicherweise*), and it is neutral toward both (*gegen beide gleichgültig*).

4. In relation to predication. On the one hand, Schelling says that the *Ungrund* has no predicate except for being without predicates (SW VII, 406). On the other hand, Schelling allows for the two principles to be predicated of the *Ungrund* as non-opposites (*Nichtgegensätze*).

As we will see, these characteristics correspond in nearly every respect to characteristics of the absolute in Schelling's works from the preceding years, especially *Philosophy and Religion* (1804).[44] But any attempt to assimilate the *Ungrund* in the *Freiheitsschrift* to Schelling's previous accounts of the absolute encounters an obvious objection. Schelling's preferred designation for the absolute in previous works is "absolute identity." But Schelling repeatedly denies in the *Freiheitsschrift* that the *Ungrund* or indifference is absolute identity. At the same time, he claims twice that the *Ungrund* is "das schlechthin betrachtete Absolute" (the unconditionally absolute, or the absolute regarded absolutely) (SW VII, 407–8; 409; cf. SW VIII, 165). Is this not clear proof that Schelling is departing from his previous conception of the absolute as absolute identity?[45]

However, what Schelling designates as "absolute identity" in the *Freiheitsschrift* is significantly different from some of his characterizations of "absolute identity" in both earlier and later works. We have already seen examples of ways in which the fluidity of Schelling's terminology poses a challenge to understanding his thought. It is therefore necessary to consider precisely how Schelling uses the expression "absolute identity" in the text before proceeding with a characterization of the *Ungrund*. Examining absolute identity in the *Freiheitsschrift* will also shed light on the nature of the *Ungrund* by way of contrast, insofar as Schelling says it is *not* absolute identity.

The first thing to note about absolute identity in the *Freiheitsschrift* is that Schelling identifies it with spirit (*Geist*). He makes this clear when reprising his account of the end of revelation: "Then everything is subordinated to spirit. In spirit that-which-exists is one with the ground for existence; in spirit both really are present at the same time [*zugleich*], or it is the *absolute identity of both*. Above spirit, however, is the initial *Ungrund* . . ." (SW VII, 408, emphasis added).[46] Elsewhere Schelling describes spirit as the "living unity" of the two principles (SW VII, 395). By identifying absolute identity with spirit, Schelling places it on the level of the development of creation and revelation. Absolute identity as spirit is the result of a process in which the two principles are developed and finally united. In terms of the potencies, spirit corresponds to the third (existence),[47] which unites the first (the ground of existence) with the second (that-which-exists). But Schelling in his earlier writings had emphasized that absolute identity is *not* the result of a process (SW IV, 348) or a synthesis of lower elements that are previously separate (SW IV, 134; IV, 235).[48] Moreover, in response to claims by Eschenmayer, Schelling had denied that the absolute is a potency, even the highest (SW VII, 185–86).

Absolute identity in the passage on the *Ungrund* also differs from absolute identity in certain previous works (as well as from the *Ungrund*) in its relation to opposition (*Gegensatz*). Indeed, the concept of opposition plays a decisive role in this passage. Schelling describes the relation of absolute identity to opposition in a counterfactual statement: "If the *Ungrund* were the absolute identity of [the two principles], it could only be both *at once* [*zugleich*], that is, both would have to be predicated of it *as opposites* and thereby would themselves be one again" (SW VII, 407). Here Schelling describes absolute identity in terms of the unification of opposites. The two principles are opposed, and this opposition is essential to the production of their absolute identity.[49] Opposition is what allows spirit as absolute identity to be a "living unity" of that-which-exists and the ground of existence (cf. SW VII, 395). As Schelling writes in the *Stuttgart Private Lectures*, "Without opposition there is no life" (SW VII, 435). Moreover, because the two principles are predicated of absolute identity *as opposites*, they continue to be opposites even in their identity.

In contrast to absolute identity, the *Ungrund* is devoid of opposition. Schelling first notes that it precedes all opposites (*Gegensätze*).[50] From this precedence he draws two consequences: (1) opposites are not distinguishable (*unterscheidbar*) in the *Ungrund*; (2) they are not in any way present (*vorhanden*) in it. A few lines later he adds that (3) opposites are not even implicitly contained in the indifference of the *Ungrund*. Incidentally, Schelling remarks that most people, "when they come to the point of examination where they have to recognize a vanishing of all opposites," forget that the opposites have vanished (SW VII, 406). This reference to "most people" suggests that the concept of the *Ungrund* as indifference is not something new; it has been around long enough for people to misunderstand it. Indeed, he may be speaking about misinterpretations of his own previous descriptions of the absolute. In earlier works he also attributes non-distinguishability to absolute identity (cf. SW IV, 127) and denies the presence of opposition.[51]

The non-presence of opposition in the *Ungrund* is related to another feature: it has no predicate. Indeed, Schelling introduces this feature as a consequence of the utter non-presence of opposites: "[Indifference] is nothing other than the non-being of opposites, and for this reason it has no predicate other than being-without-predicates [*Prädikatlosigkeit*], without for that reason being a nothing or a non-thing" (SW VII, 406). But what does the lack of predicates have to do with the lack of opposition? Schelling makes this connection clear when developing the idea of the absolute in the 1806 *Aphorisms*:

> The proposition that the absolute has no predicates is completely correct, [1] to the extent that a predicate itself is only possible in opposition to a subject (an opposition that is unthinkable in God), and [2] to the extent that for every possible predicate another predicate can be opposed to it. But nothing that is in relation [*in Beziehung*], thus nothing that can stand in opposition, is affirmable through reason and of God. (§64, SW VII, 153–54)

Predication presupposes opposition on two levels. On the one hand, attributing a predicate to a subject presupposes an opposition between the predicate and the subject to which it is attributed. The predicate is not the subject but belongs to it. On the other hand, in order for the predicate to be meaningful, it must involve the negation of its opposite. For example, if I attribute to God the predicate "perfect," I am implicitly denying the opposite, "imperfect." As Spinoza famously wrote, *omnis determinatio est negatio*: "All determination is negation."[52] But if there can be no opposition in the *Ungrund*, then it is not possible to attribute to it a predicate that would be opposed to another predicate. It is therefore without predicates, or, following the principle articulated by Spinoza, without any determination—which is also true of the *Ungrund* in Jacob Boehme.[53]

But Schelling's claim that the *Ungrund* has no predicate raises substantial difficulties. First, as we will see in more detail in the next section, he goes on to predicate the two principles in God of the *Ungrund*, despite denying it has predicates. Second, Schelling's claim is self-referential and therefore self-contradictory: "Indifference has no predicate except for that of having-no-predicate." In attributing *Prädikatlosigkeit* to the *Ungrund*, Schelling is both claiming that it has a predicate and that it does not. A third, more general difficulty is related to this. How is an account or any kind of description of the *Ungrund* possible if it has no predicate? Indeed, in the passage on the *Ungrund*, Schelling says many things about it—for example, that it precedes the ground and that-which-exists. But these descriptions of the *Ungrund* are only intelligible if they presuppose the negation of their opposite, and therefore the opposition of the *Ungrund* to what it is *not*.

We will be in a better position to address the first difficulty in the next section, which treats Schelling's account of indifference in relation to the two principles as predicates. But here we can note that in the 1806 *Aphorisms* he does not flatly state that the absolute has no predicates, but instead says that the absolute has no predicates *insofar as* predication involves opposition. This at least leaves open the possibility of another kind of predication that would not involve opposition. It is this alternative kind of predication that Schelling introduces to relate the two principles to the *Ungrund*.

The other two difficulties arise out of the problematic and even contradictory nature of language about the absolute. Although Schelling occasionally refers to this problem in his writings, he never treats it in a sustained way. Why is language about the absolute problematic? Language makes use of concepts, which belong to the domain of the understanding (*Verstand*), or what Schelling calls "reflection" in his *Identitätsphilosophie*. The understanding or reflection pulls apart and places in opposition what is originally one in reason (*Vernunft*).[54] Because the absolute is beyond opposition, it can only be known through reason; and yet this knowledge of the absolute can only be expressed in language through concepts derived from the understanding. Schelling notes the necessity of making use of reflection in a passage from the *Further Presentations* (1802). Essence and form are not at all opposed in the absolute. However, we oppose the two to each other "in reflection or in the concept [*im Begriff*]" because "this is necessary in order for us to express ourselves at all concerning the matter, but with full awareness of the mere subjectivity of this opposition" (SW IV, 380). Although the means of expression is necessarily inadequate, it does reflect in some fashion the nature of the absolute; language is necessary as an instrument for philosophizing,[55] but one must always keep in mind its limitations.[56]

Schelling also emphasizes the role of reflection in the section on the absolute in *Philosophy and Religion* (1804). In fact, his characterization of how the absolute is "expressed" (*ausgesprochen*) in reflection corresponds directly to several of the features of the *Ungrund* in the *Freiheitsschrift*. He notes that all of the forms in which the absolute can be expressed "are reducible to the three possible forms that lie in reflection" (SW VI, 23). These forms in turn correspond to the three kinds of syllogisms (categorical, hypothetical, disjunctive), although Schelling does not clearly explain the connections with the syllogisms.[57] The first form (categorical) in which reflection expresses the absolute is the form "Neither-Nor" (*Weder-Noch*).

In itself the absolute is *neither* the one *nor* the other of two opposites.[58] In the passage in the *Freiheitsschrift* Schelling uses the phrase "Neither-Nor" in apposition to indifference: "Duality breaks forth immediately from the Neither-Nor or indifference" (SW VII, 407).

In the second form (hypothetical), reflection expresses the absolute as "the same *Wesen*" of both the subject and the object (SW VI, 23). Schelling also expresses this as the "In-itself" (*An-sich*) of the two, which is neither subjective nor objective. This second form corresponds to Schelling's characterization of the *Ungrund* in the *Freiheitsschrift* as the *Wesen* of the ground and of that-which-exists (SW VII, 407–8). Finally, the third form is disjunctive: "[The absolute] is only One, but this One can be regarded in completely the same way—now wholly as ideal, now wholly as real" (SW VI, 24). Since this form is "disjunctive," we can reword it in terms of either-or: the absolute can be regarded in the same way as *either* wholly the one principle *or* wholly the other. This also corresponds to Schelling's account of the *Ungrund* in the *Freiheitsschrift*. The two principles can be predicated of the *Ungrund* "in disjunction and each *for itself*" (SW VII, 407). We will examine what this means in more detail in the next section. Moreover, in describing the third form in *Philosophy and Religion*, Schelling writes that the absolute can be regarded as either of the two principles "not at once [*zugleich*], but in the same way [*auf gleiche Weise*]" (SW VI, 24). This also corresponds to what Schelling says in the *Freiheitsschrift*: "[The *Ungrund*] is not both at once [*zugleich*], but it is in each in the same way [*gleicherweise*]" (SW VII, 408).

But doesn't this third form of expressing the absolute contradict the first? How can the absolute be (1) neither *A* nor *B*, and (2) either *A* or *B*? A subtlety in Schelling's language is decisive here: the one absolute can be regarded (*betrachtet*) as either wholly ideal or wholly real. The two principles are ways of regarding, or "aspects," of the absolute—as we saw above. But in itself (*an sich*), as the underlying *Wesen*, the absolute is neither one of these principles.

In any case, Schelling is more forthright in *Philosophy and Religion* about the inadequacy of language about the absolute than anywhere else in his writings on absolute identity. He states bluntly: "All possible forms of expressing the absolute are only modes of appearance [*Erscheinungsweisen*] of the absolute in reflection" (SW VI, 25). These forms can only explain (*erklären*) or describe (*beschreiben*) the absolute using the concepts of reflection, but the absolute can only be *known* through intuition (SW VI, 25–26). And yet philosophical writing—including the passage on the *Ungrund*—must approach the absolute through explanations and descriptions! At the end of the section in *Philosophy and Religion*, Schelling observes that "every human language is too weak to describe that evidence that lies in the idea of the absolute" (SW VI, 27). This is the situation that gives rise to Schelling's paradoxical statement in the *Freiheitsschrift* that the only predicate of indifference is the lacking of predicates.[59] On the one hand, any predicate that we ascribe to the absolute will be inadequate. On the other hand, philosophical discourse requires predication through language, which—however imperfect—allows us to approach, if not know, the absolute.

4. Indifference and the Grounding Character of the *Ungrund*

We now turn to an examination of the concept most closely associated with the *Ungrund*: indifference. Through this examination we can determine more precisely in what sense it is a ground and in what sense it is not. On the one hand, Schelling states very directly in what sense the *Ungrund* as indifference is a ground: "*Without* indifference, that is, *without* an *Ungrund*, there would be no twoness of principles" (SW VII, 407, emphasis added). Indifference is a ground in the sense of being a conditio sine qua non or necessary condition for the twoness of principles. The difficulty, however, is in (1) determining in what way the *Ungrund* is a necessary condition of twoness, and (2) relating this sense of ground to other statements about the relation of the *Ungrund* to what comes "after" it—for example, Schelling's statement that duality "breaks forth" immediately from indifference (SW VII, 407).

Schelling first introduces indifference as an alternative to absolute identity as a way of designating the *Ungrund* in its relationship to the principles in God: "Since [the *Ungrund*] precedes all opposites, these cannot be distinguished in it nor can they be present in any way. Therefore, it cannot be designated as identity, but only as the absolute *indifference* of the two" (SW VII, 406). In what follows, Schelling emphasizes the utter absence of opposition in indifference. But what does "indifference" mean in this context? Schelling had long used the term, beginning with his early works in the philosophy of nature (cf. SW II, 52), and it plays an important role in his characterization of the absolute in the *Darstellung meines Systems* (1801).[60] In Schelling's writings the term has at least three meanings, which are not mutually exclusive. The first two concern the relationship *between* things within the absolute; the third meaning concerns the relationship of the absolute *toward* the things within it.

1. The first meaning is simply the lack of difference—the prefix *in-* functions privatively. In the *Darstellung*, he writes: "Since in the sentence $A = A$ it is one and the same A that is posited in the position of the predicate and in the position of the subject, without doubt there is *no difference*, but rather *absolute indifference* posited between the two" (SW IV, 124, emphasis added).

2. The second meaning is balance or equilibrium (*Gleichgewicht*). In the section on the potencies in chapter 4, we discussed Schelling's image of the magnetic line, which represents the relations of the potencies: at one end is the subjective pole, and the objective pole is at the other. In the middle is the "indifference point," where the subjective and objective factors are in a state of equilibrium. Sometimes he will refer to indifference in this sense as "quantitative indifference," because it concerns the quantity of subjectivity and objectivity relative to each other.[61]

3. Unlike the previous two meanings, the third does not concern the relation of two or more things on the same level (lack of difference, equilibrium), but the comportment of something on one level toward two or more things on another level. This will become clearer if we consider the everyday use of the word "indifference" in English, which corresponds to a possible meaning of *Indifferenz* in German. If I am considering two choices, and my attitude toward them is one of *indifference*, the word here does not describe the relation between the choices but *my* relation or comportment toward them. I relate to them both *in the same way*. From my perspective, both of them are "equally valid" (*gleichgültig*). Indeed, in the *Freiheitsschrift* Schelling gives *Gleichgültigkeit* in parentheses after one of his uses of the word *Indifferenz* (SW VII, 408; cf. SW IV, 322).

The second meaning of the word (equilibrium) does not appear to play a role in the passage on the *Ungrund*. The first meaning (lack of difference) is more promising: Schelling describes indifference as the "non-being" of opposites and opposition, and he says that opposites cannot be distinguished in the *Ungrund* (SW VII, 406). This seems to suggest that *nothing* is distinguishable in it, and thus it lacks all difference. The problem is that he does not define the relationship between opposition and difference. To be sure, opposition requires difference: for two things to be opposed, there obviously must be some difference between them. The question is whether difference requires opposition. It is at least conceivable that two things be different, but not opposed—in the sense of actively working against each other.[62] Sometimes Schelling uses the term "opposition" in a stronger sense that goes beyond mere difference; for example, he notes that the two principles have to be "in opposition, in conflict [*Kampf*]" to produce a living human being (SW VII, 424). But he sometimes uses the terms "opposition" and "difference" interchangeably—for example, in the dialogue *Bruno* (1802).[63] In any case, if Schelling, when characterizing the *Ungrund*, has in mind the absolute as he had presented it in his previous writings, we can conclude that the *Ungrund* is also indifference in the sense of lacking all difference.[64] Nevertheless, we will see below that something resembling difference plays a role in the *Ungrund*.

As for the third meaning of indifference, it is unambiguously present in the passage in the *Freiheitsschrift*. Moreover, it will allow us to determine how indifference can be a condition of the possibility of the "twoness of principles." Used in this sense, the word "indifference" does not describe the relationship *between* the two principles in God, but the comportment of the absolute *toward* these principles: it relates to both in the same way. Schelling makes this clear when explaining how the principles can be predicated of the *Ungrund* as non-opposites: "For, precisely because [the *Ungrund*] relates to both [*gegen beide verhält*] as total indifference, it is neutral [*gleichgültig*] toward both" (SW VII, 407). The indifference of the *Ungrund* is directed toward (*gegen*) the principles.[65]

But what is the precise relationship to the principles? To answer this question, we need to interpret the difficult passage regarding predication and the *Ungrund*, at the end of which Schelling makes the claim about indifference. He begins by denying that the two principles can be predicated of the *Ungrund* as opposites. He then introduces another possibility for their predication: "Nothing hinders that they be predicated of it as non-opposites [*Nichtgegensätze*], that is, in disjunction and each *for itself* whereby, however, precisely duality (the actual twoness of principles) is posited" (SW VII, 407). Here Schelling introduces the unusual term "non-opposite," and attempts to clarify what it means by adding two additional phrases: (1) "in disjunction" and (2) "each *for itself.*" Both clarifying phrases indicate that the principles can be predicated of the *Ungrund* only if they are completely independent of one another—and thus without relation. This is why Schelling later denies that the *Ungrund* can be both principles "at once" (*zugleich*). If it were both principles at once, the two would be together and in relation. Instead, the *Ungrund* is *either* the one *or* the other (in disjunction)—or, as Schelling formulates it in *Philosophy and Religion*, "now as the one, now as the other" (SW VI, 24). But if the principles are completely independent and unrelated to each other, they cannot be opposites: opposition requires relation. Thus, they are predicated of the *Ungrund* as "non-opposites."

This lack of relation follows from the nature of God or the absolute, as Schelling characterizes it in earlier writings. In the 1806 *Aphorisms* he writes, "Nothing in relation [*Beziehung*], thus nothing that can stand in opposition, is affirmable through reason and of God" (§64, SW VII, 154). Why? It is a result of what we might call the microcosmic aspect of Schelling's *Identitätsphilosophie*. Because there exists no qualitative difference,[66] or difference with respect to essence (*Wesen*), everything in the system shares the nature of the absolute. "Not only the whole as whole is divine," he notes in the 1806 *Aphorisms*. "Even the part and the individual is for itself divine." The form of the absolute is "an inner organic connection, where every part is of the nature of the whole" (§18, SW VII, 143).[67] And if the part shares the nature of the whole, this means that the part is itself a whole or "its own world" (§120, SW VII, 165). But a whole, insofar as it is a totality, has nothing outside of it—and thus nothing to which it can relate.[68]

Accordingly, the two principles in God are without relation in the *Ungrund*, because each shares the nature of the absolute, and thus each for itself is a whole—"as if there were nothing outside it" (§88, SW VII, 160). Later in the passage in the *Freiheitsschrift*, Schelling confirms the "totality" of each of the principles, when predicated of the *Ungrund*. The *Ungrund* "is in each *in the same way* [*gleicherweise*], thus in each the whole [*das Ganze*], or its own *Wesen*" (SW VII, 408). Being in each "in the same way" is another means of expressing indifference, as we have seen.[69] Indifference in this context thus means that the absolute relates to each principle in the same way: each shares the nature of the absolute, and thus each is a whole for itself. To use a line from the mystic St. Teresa of Ávila, it is "as if there existed only God and itself."[70] This mystical perspective captures perfectly the manner in which each of the principles is "for itself" in the *Ungrund*.

I began this section by noting Schelling's statement that indifference is the conditio sine qua non of the twoness of principles. Moreover, in the passage where Schelling allows for the principles to be predicated of the *Ungrund* as non-opposites, he adds that duality is thereby posited. What, then, is the connection between predicating the principles as non-opposites and the positing of duality? And how is indifference the necessary condition of the twoness of the principles?

The answers to these questions depend on the precise meaning of twoness (*Zweiheit*) and duality (*Dualität*). Schelling uses the terms more or less interchangeably in the passage. When first introducing "duality," he adds in parentheses: "the actual [*wirkliche*] twoness of principles" (SW VII, 407). Later he gives a second definition: "Duality is where really two *Wesen* stand opposite each other [*entgegenstehen*]" (SW VII, 409). Finally, he emphatically distinguishes it from opposition: "[Duality] is something entirely different from opposition, even though we might have used both synonymously up to now since we had not yet reached this point in the investigation" (SW VII, 407). Unfortunately, he does not spell out how the two terms are "entirely different."

The key to interpreting the meaning of duality and connecting it to indifference is the word *wirklich* in the cited lines. Duality is an "actual" twoness of principles—that is, the principles are "actually" two. In order for two beings to be *actually* two, they have to be truly independent from each other: each has to exist *for itself*. This is what sets duality apart from opposition. There can be opposition between two things that are not *actually* two because one or both do not have any existence independent of the opposite. Evil, for example, only appears in opposition to the spirit of love; nonetheless, evil is not part of a duality, because it is not its own being (*Wesen*) and thus does not have an independent existence (SW VII, 409). Moreover, Schelling suggests that opposition, as such, compromises the independent existence of what is opposed. In the case of what Schelling here calls "absolute identity," the principles would be predicated as opposites, "and thereby would themselves be one again" (SW VII, 407). This automatic uniting of opposites in absolute identity compromises their genuine twoness. In order for opposites to be genuinely two, they must exist independently before they are brought into opposition.

This meaning of duality as the genuine twoness of completely independent beings is essentially connected to the "mystery of love," which we discussed in chapter 4, and which arises in this passage on the *Ungrund*. In fact, in the *Stuttgart Private Lectures*, Schelling explicitly connects love with duality: it is "the mediator in this duality that does not exclude identity and in this identity that does not exclude duality" (SW VII, 453). On the one hand, love requires duality: it unites two things, "each of which could exist for itself" as an independent whole in the absolute (SW VII, 408). On the other hand, love requires identity: it unites two things, each of which "is not and cannot be without the other" (SW VII, 408). In other words, each is dependent on the other for its "existence" (which involves being in relation), but independent with respect to its being in the absolute (out of relation).

We are now in a position to explain why Schelling claims, "*Without* indifference, that is, *without* an *Ungrund*, there would be no twoness of principles" (SW VII, 407). As we have seen, the indifference of the *Ungrund* allows the principles to exist for themselves as independent wholes—and thus to be *actually* two. Without indifference, they would only exist in relation (not in disjunction) and thus mutually restrict and oppose each other, compromising their independence. The indifference of the *Ungrund* is therefore a necessary condition for the duality of the principles—as two, truly independent wholes. And because they must be truly independent in order to be united by love, the *Ungrund* is also the necessary condition of love. (This is why Schelling includes the mystery of love in the passage on the *Ungrund*.) Thus, we can see in what way the *Ungrund* is a ground: it is a necessary condition or conditio sine qua non. Once again, this sense of ground is decisive for Schelling's thought in the *Freiheitsschrift*.

By grounding duality, the *Ungrund* also ensures the ultimate reality of Schelling's fundamental distinction between ground and that-which-exists. Recall that Schelling begins his discussion of the *Ungrund* with an imagined objection to the ultimacy of this distinction: either (1) there is no common middle point between the principles, and the system is ultimately a dualism; or (2) there is a common middle point—then the principles collapse in the end, and the distinction is not a genuine one. Schelling attempts to resolve this dilemma through the unique character of the *Ungrund* as indifference. Immediately after stating that the *Ungrund* is a necessary condition of the twoness of the principles, Schelling returns to the fundamental distinction and concludes: "Far from the distinction between the ground and that-which-exists having been merely logical, or one called on as a heuristic aid and again found to be artificial in the end, it has shown itself rather as a very real distinction that from the highest standpoint was first correctly proved and fully grasped" (SW VII, 407). The distinction has shown itself as "very real," because of the genuine twoness of the principles rooted in the *Ungrund*: they cannot be collapsed into one.

Accordingly, the *Ungrund* as the "common middle point" performs the seemingly paradoxical dual function mentioned earlier. On the one hand, it ensures the ultimate unity of the principles and thus the ultimate unity of the system. Each principle belongs to a single *Wesen*, which is the absolute. The *Ungrund* is in each of the principles *in the same way*, and thus each shares the *same* nature of the absolute. On the other hand, the *Ungrund* ensures the ultimate reality of the distinction of the principles by ensuring their ultimate "twoness" and irreducibility. The *Ungrund* is in *each* of the principles in the same way: each for itself is the whole, and thus they are really two. This allows for what Schelling had earlier called "the only correct dualism, namely that which at the same time permits a unity" (SW VII, 359n).[71]

If the *Ungrund* is a condition of the possibility of the duality of the principles, it also their ground in this respect: it is the underlying *Wesen* of which the principles are predicated, and thus they would not be possible without it. This is confirmed by the priority Schelling ascribes to the *Ungrund*: it is "before" the ground and that-which-exists, and we can interpret this priority in terms of being the condition of their possibility. We have also seen that the *Ungrund* is the "beginning point" of the system, before the process of revelation. But now the question arises: How do we leave that beginning point? How does that which comes after the *Ungrund* come to be?[72]

These questions presuppose a certain understanding of the grounding relations within the system: the all-from-one model of grounding. According to this model, the system forms a linear progression, beginning with an absolute starting point. Each moment in the progression must be sufficiently grounded by—and therefore arise out of—what came before it. From this perspective, if something comes after the *Ungrund*, the *Ungrund* must cause or otherwise sufficiently determine it: otherwise, it would never come to be. Indeed, this is an application of the traditional principle of sufficient reason, which demands that everything have a ground that sufficiently determines that it is precisely the way that it is. Ex nihilo nihil fit: nothing comes from nothing.

It is my contention, however, that Schelling, by making *conditio sine qua non* the primary sense of ground in the *Freiheitsschrift*, fundamentally departs from this understanding of grounding relations. As we saw at the end of chapter 4, everything in the system is connected because all things reciprocally presuppose one another (SW VII, 358). The *Ungrund* is also connected in this way to what comes "after" it. Schelling says explicitly that it is the necessary condition of duality. As the underlying *Wesen* of the two principles, it is also the condition of the possibility of these principles and their subsequent development in the process of creation. And I will suggest in the next section a way in which what follows the *Ungrund* is a condition of the possibility of the *Ungrund* itself. If this is correct, then the *Ungrund* is itself part of the circle of presupposition, to which Schelling had referred earlier in the *Freiheitsschrift* (SW VII, 358).[73]

It is true that Schelling uses various formulations in the passage on the *Ungrund* that can be interpreted to mean that "at some point" the *Ungrund* inaugurates the process of creation by spontaneously producing what follows from it. For example, before the passage on the mystery of love, he writes: "The *Ungrund* divides itself [*teilt sich*] into the two equally eternal beginnings, only so that the two, which could not exist simultaneously or be one in it as the *Ungrund*, become one through love" (SW VII, 408). The difficulty is that there is nothing in the nature of the *Ungrund* that would prompt it to "divide itself," if we understand this as a precipitous act by which the *Ungrund* transforms itself from a previous state of non-division to a state of division.[74] Accordingly, such an act would have to be utterly spontaneous or random.[75] But Schelling rules out this kind of "chance occurrence" without grounds, as we will see in the next chapter. One might also attempt to account for the self-division of the *Ungrund* through an act of divine freedom, anticipating Schelling's position in later works. There are, however, no hints of freedom in the passage, and it is unclear what it would mean for the *Ungrund* to exercise freedom.[76] Moreover, the previous discussion of divine freedom (SW VII, 394–98) had emphasized divine personality and consciousness, which presuppose the dynamic relationship of the principles that are *unrelated* in the *Ungrund*.

I therefore do not interpret the above quotation to refer to a precipitous act but rather to the immediate relation of the *Ungrund* (as *Wesen* of the absolute) to its form. What this means will become clearer in the next section. But the problem is connected to Jacobi's famous line about the impossibility of a "transition from the infinite to the finite," which was a strong motivation for Schelling's *Identitätsphilosophie*. As we saw in chapter 3, if there cannot be a transition from the infinite to the finite, the two must be immediately one: the finite is in the infinite. In the same way, there is no transition from the *Ungrund* to its various forms—in particular, the two principles in God. Rather, the *Ungrund* is immediately one with its forms. Indeed, the German reflexive construction that Schelling uses ("teilt sich") could be translated using the passive voice, which fits this interpretation better: the *Ungrund* "is divided" into two equally eternal beginnings.[77]

Before pursuing the relationship to form in the next section, I would like to make a remark about the historical significance of the grounding character of the *Ungrund*. We have seen that it is a ground in the sense of condition of the possibility, but not in the sense of a productive cause of creation. Schelling thereby severs two senses of ground that have almost always been thought together in the history of philosophy when considering the "ultimate origin." Plotinus's doctrine of the One is a good example of how these two senses often sit uneasily together. On the one hand, Plotinus argues for the ultimacy of the One by showing that it is the condition of the possibility of all that is, and thus ἡ ἀρχὴ τῶν πάντων.[78] On the other hand, he confronts the seemingly insurmountable problem of how the diversity of the world can arise from the supreme unity of the One. But these two senses of ground need not always be joined together. The ultimate origin can be the condition of the possibility of all things without being their productive cause.

But if the ultimate origin is not a productive cause, how can this be reconciled with the claim earlier in the *Freiheitsschrift* that the unity of the law of identity is progressive and immediately creative (SW VII, 345)? As we saw in chapter 3, God as creative unity grounds all things, not just in the sense of being the condition of their possibility, but by bringing them forth in a progression. For this productive activity, the *Ungrund* does not suffice: the form is needed as well.

5. The *Ungrund* and the Relationship between Essence and Form

In this final section, I would like to offer a speculative proposal that relates the *Ungrund* to the distinction between essence and form in Schelling's *Identitätsphilosophie*. We have already seen the importance of the word

Wesen in the account of the *Ungrund*. Schelling first introduces it as a *Wesen* before the ground and that-which-exists (SW VII, 406) and later calls it the *Wesen* of the two principles (SW VII, 407–8). My proposal involves yet another connection to the word: the *Ungrund* corresponds to what he had earlier called "the essence of the absolute," in distinction from its form. This proposal can only be a sketch: a full argument would require the consideration of a number of texts and a range of issues. Nevertheless, understanding the *Ungrund* as the essence of the absolute helps to clarify its grounding relations with what comes "after" it.

First, we can begin with Hegel's famous bon mot in the *Phenomenology of Spirit*—apparently targeting Schelling—that the absolute is like the night in which all cows are black (PhG §16; HW 3, 22). Indeed, this seems to be an apt description of the *Ungrund*: it contains no opposition, and because nothing is in relation, nothing can be compared and distinguished within it. What is remarkable is that Schelling had already used a similar image in 1802, five years before the publication of the *Phenomenology*. In the *Further Presentations*, he concedes that "most see in the essence of the absolute nothing but pure night" (SW IV, 403). The only way this essence can be known is through the form. In a remarkable passage, Schelling describes the necessity of the form for knowledge of the essence of the absolute:

> The essence of the absolute in and for itself reveals nothing to us. It fills us with representations of an infinite withdrawnness [*Verschlossenheit*], of an unsearchable quiet and concealment, like the oldest forms of philosophy describe the state of the universe before the one who is life, through the act of his self-intuiting knowledge, emerged *in his own shape* [*Gestalt*]. This eternal form, equal to the absolute, is the day in which we grasp that night and the wonders concealed within it; the light, in which we clearly recognize the absolute; the eternal mediator, the all-seeing and all-revealing eye of the world, the source of all wisdom and knowledge. (SW IV, 404–5)

In poetic language Schelling refers to an "act of self-intuiting knowledge" by which God emerges in his own shape or form. Before this act, God is in a state of concealment: this is the essence of the absolute, considered in itself—which I interpret as the *Ungrund* in the *Freiheitsschrift*. As a result of the act of self-knowledge, God comes to be revealed (cf. SW VII, 57).

What precisely is this act of self-knowledge, and how does it relate to the form of the absolute on the one hand, and the essence of the absolute on the other? In the act of self-knowledge, the absolute is both the subject (what knows) and the object (what is known). In other words, there is an identity of subject and object (S = O). Schelling identifies this subject-object identity as the *form* of the absolute: "The pure absoluteness [or essence] for itself is necessarily pure identity, but the *absolute form* of this identity is: being for itself subject and object in an infinite manner" (SW V, 281, emphasis added). Schelling has various ways of expressing this form or "way of being" (*Art zu sein*)[79] of the absolute. Symbolically, it can be expressed as A = A: the same *A* is both subject (the first position) and predicate or object (the second position).[80] And, since only in self-knowledge are subject and object the same, Schelling also identifies the form of the absolute as self-knowledge (*Selbsterkennen*).[81] Finally, because knowledge is fundamentally an affirming,[82] Schelling also identifies the form as self-affirmation (SW VI, 162).

What, then, is the relationship of the essence to the form of the absolute? In addressing this question, we should note that Schelling designates what he calls "the essence of the absolute" in different ways. Sometimes he uses the phrase "the absolute" to refer just to the essence of the absolute,[83] even though we might expect him to reserve the phrase for the inseparable unity of the essence and form of the absolute.[84] (Recall that Schelling also refers to the *Ungrund* as "the unconditionally absolute.") The same applies to the phrase "absolute identity" (cf. SW IV, 122). Finally, Schelling also uses the word "being" (*Sein*) interchangeably with "essence," referring to the relationship between "being and form" when he would normally refer to "essence and form" (SW VI, 161).[85] In any case, the fundamental meaning of "essence" or *Wesen* is the inner being of a thing (its essential core); the form is the shape that this inner being takes.[86]

Accordingly, the form is the form *of* the essence; the essence of the absolute *has* a form or is *in* a form. But this relationship between essence and form has consequences for their grounding. The two are mutually dependent—each presupposes the other. On the one hand, the essence cannot exist without the form: "Absolute identity *is* only under the form of the knowledge of its identity with itself" (§19, SW IV, 122). On the other hand, the form cannot exist without the essence: as self-knowledge, the form requires that *something* know itself, and this something is the essence of the absolute. Accordingly, essence and form are mutually grounding (in the sense of ground as conditio sine qua non).[87] One might also say that they are equally original or "equiprimordial."[88] Indeed, their relationship corresponds to that between the form and content of the first principle, as described in the *System of Transcendental Idealism* (1800): "The principle of philosophy must be such that in it the content is conditioned by the form, and conversely the form is conditioned by the content . . . and both reciprocally presuppose each other" (SW III, 360).

If my suggestion that the *Ungrund* is the essence of the absolute is correct, then the *Ungrund* is part of a circular grounding relationship—the same kind of grounding relationship that integrates the system as a whole, as we saw in chapter 4. By means of its grounding dependence on the form of the absolute, the *Ungrund* is itself integrated within the system. Moreover, because the form is just as original as the *Ungrund*, there is not a single ultimate origin from which everything is derived. If this interpretation is correct, the essence-form relationship is one of the most striking instances of the movement toward equiprimordiality in the *Freiheitsschrift*, which we have already seen in Schelling's designation of freedom as "derived absoluteness or divinity." The *Ungrund*'s non-deterministic grounding allows for more than one absolute starting point.

How, then, does the form connect the essence to the rest of the system? In particular, how does the form relate to the two principles, which play such an important role in the passage on the *Ungrund*? The answers to these questions lie in a closer examination of the self-knowledge of the absolute, which Schelling identifies as its form. The self-knowledge of the absolute is an act of "subject-objectification" (*Subjekt-Objektivieren*) (SW IV, 391; V, 324; II, 62). This means that the absolute in its act of self-knowing becomes both the subject and the object of its knowledge. This act has two sides: a "real" side in which the absolute becomes its own object, and an "ideal" side in which it returns to itself as subject (SW V, 281, 460).[89] These two sides are the basis for the distinction between the "real All" (nature) and the "ideal All" (the spiritual world), which very roughly correspond to the two principles in God in the *Freiheitsschrift*. Indeed, I interpret Schelling to be referring to the two sides of the act of absolute self-knowing in the passage on the *Ungrund*: "In its two ways of acting the one *Wesen* divides itself into two *Wesen* [and] it is in the one *merely* ground for existence, in the other merely *Wesen* (and, for that reason only ideal)" (SW VII, 409). The "two ways of acting" (*Wirkungsweisen*)[90] would be the two sides of the act of self-knowing, each corresponding to one of the principles in God.

Through the form, the essence of the absolute takes on a "double" character: it is both subject and object, ideal and real, affirming and affirmed. But because the knowledge of the absolute is *self*-knowledge, the subject of this knowledge is the whole absolute, and the object of this knowledge is the whole absolute. The same essence (*Wesen*) is in both. But, as we have seen, this essence cannot exist without the form of self-knowledge (subject-objectivity). As a consequence, if the absolute as subject contains the whole essence, it also has the form of self-knowledge: the subject is not just a subject, but a subject-object (S = O). The same is true for the absolute as object. Because it also contains the whole essence of the absolute, it also has the form of subject-object. Thus, what was originally the form S = O becomes (S = O) = (S = O). As we discussed in chapter 3, the same process can be repeated again and again: each of the subjects and each of the objects contains the whole essence of the absolute, and thus it shares the form of self-knowledge and self-affirmation. In this way, we can see how the essence of the absolute becomes infinitely productive through its form. What it produces are the ideas, which are the true objects of philosophy as a science of "things in themselves."[91]

My proposal that the *Ungrund* corresponds to the essence of the absolute (regarded as independent of the form) is only a sketch, but it explains both the character of the *Ungrund* as ground and its connection to the system as a whole. As the essence of the absolute, the *Ungrund* is the ultimate ground: everything that is shares the essence of the absolute, and *without* this essence, there would be nothing else. And yet the *Ungrund* is not a ground in the sense of a productive cause: as Schelling writes in the poetic passage from the *Further Presentations*, the essence of the absolute (in itself) reveals nothing; it is a withdrawn God, before all revelation.[92] This revelation—which is also an infinite producing—comes only through the form of absolute self-knowledge. And yet the *Ungrund* is not completely independent of this revelation through the form: the form is *its* form; the essence and the form of the absolute presuppose each other. This circle of presupposition connects the *Ungrund* to the system by means of the form, even as it allows it to maintain a tranquil independence, "indifferent" toward what follows after it.

7

Freedom, Necessity, and Self-Grounding

Up to this point we have seen that the predominant sense of ground in the *Freiheitsschrift* is condition of the possibility: the ground makes possible what it grounds without determining what it is. The two versions of the principle of ground that we have considered employ this sense of the term. (1) In chapter 3 we saw that all things are grounded by God, and this grounding both (a) makes possible the things that are grounded and (b) brings them forth (begets them) in such a way that they remain independent and undetermined. (2) And in chapter 4 we saw that all things are grounded by everything else, insofar as all things reciprocally presuppose each other as the condition of their possibility. Like the traditional principle of sufficient reason, these two versions of the principle of ground affirm the universality of being grounded. Unlike the traditional principle of sufficient reason, however, the grounding does not sufficiently determine what is grounded.

But this raises the question: what is the status of the traditional principle of sufficient reason in Schelling's *Freiheitsschrift*? By offering these alternative statements of universal grounding, does he mean to deny the traditional principle, and thereby affirm that not everything has a *sufficient* reason—and thus, that there is not always a complete answer to the question why? On the contrary, we will see that Schelling affirms the traditional principle in the section on the "formal essence" of freedom. Though somewhat indirect, this affirmation of the principle is decisive: he declares contingency impossible; and because nothing can be contingent or random, everything requires a determining ground (cf. SW VII, 383).[1]

But if Schelling affirms the traditional principle, this seems to create a problem for human freedom. The other versions of the principle of ground make room for freedom because their sense of grounding is not *deterministic*, thus allowing for a combination of dependence (being grounded) and independence (being undetermined). In the traditional principle, however, grounding *is* deterministic. Far from compromising freedom, however, this determinism belongs to its ultimate form. This is because the ground that determines a free being is not something external to it but that very being itself. Formal freedom is essentially self-grounding as self-determination.

Like the passage on the *Ungrund*, the passage on the formal concept of freedom—the focus of this chapter—has the feel of an excursus. Though it is thematically connected to its surroundings in the text, these surroundings treat the *universality* of evil in the context of the process of revelation and the dynamic relationship between the two principles in God. By contrast, the section on the formal essence of freedom focuses on freedom at the level of the *individual's* eternal decision, beyond and independent of the unfolding of revelation and the interplay of forces.

It might therefore be tempting to overlook this section, or to write it off as Schelling's pro forma nod to his earlier, more rationalist idealism, while maintaining that the heart of his thought on freedom lies elsewhere. But he stresses the centrality of the topic from the very beginning of the *Freiheitsschrift*, when he insists that "it is time that the higher or, rather, the genuine opposition emerge, that of necessity and freedom, with which the innermost center point of philosophy first comes into consideration" (SW VII, 333).[2] The relationship between freedom and necessity is, after all, another way of formulating the relationship between freedom and deterministic grounding, the central theme of this section. It therefore treats the "innermost center point of philosophy."

Nonetheless, because the connection to the rest of the work is not obvious, I devote the first section of this chapter to situating the formal concept of freedom in context. This requires treating its relationship to the "real concept of freedom." We will then consider the role of the principle of sufficient reason, as this plays out in the relationship between freedom and necessity. Up to this point Schelling follows the path of idealism, uniting freedom and necessity at a higher standpoint, beyond appearance. We will then see how he further develops the idealistic conception of freedom in terms of an "intelligible deed" outside of time. This deed is self-determining: accordingly, we will consider the meaning of this reflexive grounding in relation to the traditional concept of *causa sui* and draw out its consequences for moral responsibility. This will set the stage for returning to the question of a system of freedom in the book's conclusion and assessing Schelling's answer to the question.

1. The Formal vs. the Real Concept of Freedom

One of the most famous lines from the *Freiheitsschrift* is a definition of freedom: "The real and living concept [of freedom] is that it is a capacity for good and evil" (SW VII, 352). This definition comes at the end of Schelling's initial treatment of the concept of freedom in what he calls "idealism." Schelling seems to be quite critical of idealism: though it provides us with the first complete concept of "formal freedom," it "leaves us at a loss [*ratlos*] in the doctrine of freedom as soon as we wish to enter into what is more exact and determinate" (SW VII, 351). The concept of freedom provided by idealism is "the most general" and "merely formal." In contrast, the concept of freedom as a capacity for good and evil is "the real and living concept" (SW VII, 352).

From these lines, one might come away with the impression that the "real and living concept" surpasses and therefore replaces the "formal concept" offered by idealism. It would therefore come as a surprise that Schelling reintroduces this formal concept much later in the treatise: "We have generally focused up to this point less on the formal essence of freedom, although insight into it seems to be joined with difficulties no slighter than the explication of the real concept" (SW VII, 382).[3] In what follows, he develops this formal concept of freedom—a clear indication that the "real and living concept" does not simply replace it. But then the question arises: how do the two concepts of freedom relate to each other?

There are in fact two related answers to this question. The first is that the formal concept is a *general* account that applies to all free beings, while the real concept applies *specifically* to human beings. Schelling makes this clear when discussing the relationship of idealism's formal concept of freedom to things in themselves. According to Schelling, Kant had distinguished things in themselves only negatively, in terms of their independence from time.[4] And yet in the second *Critique*, Kant treats independence from time and (formal) freedom as correlative concepts. If things in themselves are independent from time, and independence from time correlates with freedom, then freedom is also characteristic of things in themselves. Indeed, Schelling calls freedom the "only possible positive concept of the In-itself" (SW VII, 352). But he emphasizes that this concept, as it applies generally to the In-itself, is not sufficient to define *human* freedom:

> On the other hand, however, if freedom really is the positive concept of the In-itself, the investigation concerning human freedom is thrown back again into what is *general*, insofar as the intelligible on which it was alone grounded is also the essence of things in themselves. Mere idealism does not reach far enough, therefore, in order to show the *specific difference*, that is, precisely what is the distinctiveness of human freedom. (SW VII, 352, emphasis added)

Earlier in the *Freiheitsschrift* Schelling had himself associated freedom with things in themselves when discussing the character of divine grounding (SW VII, 347).[5] (We will return to the connection with things in themselves below.) In any case, Schelling makes clear in this passage that the formal concept of freedom only defines freedom *in general*. It applies to whatever is "in itself," and only what is "in itself." This of course includes human beings to the extent that they have an existence in themselves—what Schelling later calls "the intelligible essence" of each human being (SW VII, 384). But it would also apply to God and any other nonhuman thing in itself.[6]

Accordingly, Schelling states that the formal concept provided by idealism does not give the "specific difference" of human freedom (SW VII, 352). This Aristotelian phrase helps us to define more precisely the relationship between the formal and the real concept of freedom. In the Aristotelian tradition, a complete definition requires the genus and a specific difference—for example, the famous definition of human being as *animal rationale*. Similarly, a complete account of human freedom requires both an account of the genus (what it means to be free in general) and an account of the specific difference (what distinguishes human freedom from other kinds of freedom—for example, divine freedom). The formal concept of freedom provides the genus; the real concept provides the specific difference. Only for human beings is freedom a capacity for good and evil (the real concept). The two concepts are therefore complementary: neither one is sufficient, because a complete account of human freedom requires both.

In light of this analysis, we can understand more precisely what Schelling is doing in his critique of idealism in the *Freiheitsschrift* (SW VII, 351–52). Idealism is only problematic insofar as it regards itself as self-sufficient. Indeed, idealism makes a necessary contribution to our understanding of freedom by providing us with its formal concept. But what exactly does Schelling mean by "idealism"? He uses the term in two overlapping senses. On the one hand, it is a historical designation for the philosophies of Kant and Fichte. On the other hand, it refers to the "ideal side" of Schelling's own philosophy, which builds on the fundamental insights of Kant and Fichte. In this second sense, he describes the relationship between the two in terms of body and soul: "Idealism is the soul of philosophy; realism is the body; only both together can constitute a living whole" (SW VII, 356). Just as idealism and realism are each necessary but complementary sides of philosophy, the formal and real concepts are each necessary but complementary.

The second answer to the question of the relation between the two concepts has to do with the word "formal" in the phrase "formal concept." We have seen in other contexts the importance of the distinction between form and content, or form and essence (*Wesen*). Expressed succinctly, the content or essence concerns the *what* and the form concerns the *how*.[7] The real concept concerns the *what*, or the possible content of human freedom.[8] According to the real concept, human freedom is a capacity for good and evil, the possible contents of a free decision. The formal concept concerns the *how* or form. It answers the question: how is the free decision made (regardless of what its content is)?

This helps to explain the placement of Schelling's discussion of the formal concept of freedom within the work as a whole. After introducing the real concept as a capacity for good and evil, he seeks to show the possibility of evil within the system. As we saw in chapter 5, this requires the development of the fundamental distinction between that-which-exists and the ground of existence. After discussing evil's possibility, Schelling turns to its actuality (SW VII, 373ff.). At first, he is only concerned with its actuality at a general level, not at the level of the individual. Thus, he seeks to explain evil's "universal activity" (*universelle Wirksamkeit*) and the natural inclination of human beings toward evil. Nevertheless, in the midst of this discussion of evil's universality, Schelling acknowledges that the individual plays the decisive role in making it actual: "Notwithstanding this general necessity, evil remains always an individual's own choice; the ground cannot make evil as such, and every creature falls due to its own guilt. But just *how* in each individual the decision for good or evil might now proceed—this is still shrouded in complete darkness and seems to demand a specific investigation" (SW VII, 381–82, emphasis added). This passage serves as the transition to the treatment of the formal concept of freedom, which immediately follows. Here he clearly states the function of the formal concept: it provides an answer to the question of *how* the individual makes a decision for good or evil. By embedding his discussion of formal freedom in the section on the actuality of evil, Schelling emphasizes the interconnection between the formal and the real concepts. The real concept provides the formal concept with a concreteness it would otherwise lack: it not only addresses the general question "how is the decision made?" but also the more concrete question "how is the decision *for evil* made?"

2. The Unity of Freedom and Necessity beyond Appearance

Schelling proceeds dialectically in his discussion of formal freedom. He begins by presenting "the usual concept of freedom" as the power to choose between alternatives without a determining reason.[9] After criticizing this conception (SW VII, 382–83), he briefly presents the position of empirical determinism, which denies the possibility of freedom in the world (SW VII, 383). In response to both positions, Schelling expresses the need for a higher standpoint that would unite necessity and freedom in a "higher necessity" (SW VII, 383). This higher standpoint is provided by "idealism," which claims the existence of an "intelligible essence" (*intelligibles Wesen*) outside of time: this being is free insofar as it acts according to the laws of its inner nature (SW VII, 383–84). Finally, Schelling builds on the insights of idealism to articulate his own position, which identifies an "eternal deed" as the locus of freedom (SW VII, 384–89).

In certain respects, Schelling's dialectical presentation resembles the Kantian antinomies in the *Critique of Pure Reason*. In the third antinomy, Kant famously presents a proof that freedom must exist (the thesis) and that freedom is impossible (the antithesis). Both proofs are compelling. According to the thesis, freedom as the absolute beginning of a series of causes must be assumed: otherwise, there would be an infinite regress in the series of causes, and thus no cause would be sufficiently determined. According to the antithesis, such an absolute beginning of a series of causes is impossible: each cause is subject to the causal law, which requires each cause to have its own prior cause (A 444-51/B 472-79).

Like Kant, Schelling presents the opposed positions of freedom and causal determinism and then resolves the opposition by assuming a higher standpoint. But his dialectical presentation differs from Kant's to the extent that it follows one of the fundamental insights of his *Identitätsphilosophie*—something that has gone unnoticed by commentators. According to this insight, what is opposed in appearance or reflection is originally one for reason or in itself. In other words, appearance separates and opposes what is really united. But the two opposites, qua opposed, do not have the same character that they do when they are united—they are distorted. Thus, freedom and necessity are originally one for reason, but are opposed and thereby distorted in appearance. These *distortions* of freedom and necessity are the subject of Schelling's initial antinomic presentation.

Accordingly, his presentation differs from Kant's in two ways. First, for Kant both of the opposed positions are *right*—or in the case of freedom, potentially right. They just apply to different domains. Causal necessity applies to appearances; freedom applies to things in themselves. For Schelling, on the other hand, both of the opposed positions are *wrong*: they represent distorted versions of freedom and necessity.[10] Second, the structure of their respective solutions is different. Schelling's solution is to unite freedom and necessity: true freedom is also necessity, and true necessity is also freedom. In contrast, Kant resolves the conflict by maintaining the separation: each has its own domain (sensible or intelligible), free from interference by the other.

At the beginning of Schelling's dialectical presentation, the discussion of the "usual concept of freedom" is noteworthy for our purposes, because it includes an indirect but decisive endorsement of the traditional principle of sufficient reason. According to the usual concept, freedom is the completely undetermined capacity (*Vermögen*) to will one of two contradictory alternatives "without determining grounds" (SW VII, 382). This is, of course, a direct violation of the principle. Schelling may have in mind Reinhold, who had developed a Kant-inspired theory of freedom centered around *Willkür* or the power of choice.[11]

In any case, Schelling is unequivocal in his assessment of this concept of freedom: "When applied to individual action, it leads to the greatest absurdities" (SW VII, 382). He has three objections, the first two of which are fairly standard. One objection is that it is not worthy of being called freedom; when taken in this sense, freedom loses its dignity, because it is "just a prerogative to act completely irrationally" (SW VII, 382). This is because those who act rationally have definite reasons for what they do. If there are compelling reasons to act in a certain way, but one nevertheless acts in a different way *for no reason*, one is simply acting irrationally. Schelling here dismisses the famous example of Buridan's ass, which is supposed to illustrate the difference between human beings, who have free will, and nonhuman animals, who do not.[12] Standing exactly halfway between two bales of hay, the animal starves because there is no reason to choose one bale over the other. A human being—so the argument goes—possesses freedom and thus could avoid starving by arbitrarily picking a direction. Schelling remarks sardonically that this "would not distinguish man [from the animal] in exactly the best way" (SW VII, 382).

Schelling's second objection to the usual concept is that it lacks any positive proof. If one attempts to demonstrate the reality of this kind of freedom by arbitrarily raising one's left or right arm "for no reason," this only shows that one *does not know* the reason why the one arm was selected over the other. But one cannot infer from the ignorance of a determining reason that there is no such reason.[13] Indeed, Schelling points out that when we do not know the determining reason why we do something, we are "all the more certainly" determined (SW VII, 382–83). Presumably, this is because we would be determined by unconscious forces, and this is a cruder, more machine-like form of determination than acting out of conscious motives.

The third objection to the usual concept is the "main issue" (*Hauptsache*), according to Schelling, and he gives here an indirect but decisive endorsement of the traditional principle of sufficient reason. The usual concept "introduces a complete contingency [*Zufälligkeit*] of individual actions" (SW VII, 383). By "contingency," he does not mean the modal category, according to which a fact is contingent if its negation is not impossible.[14] Rather, he means randomness: something occurs precipitously, and thus without any reason. This becomes clear in his subsequent comparison of this concept with the infamous "swerve" of atoms in Epicurus. To avoid fatalism, Epicurus taught that atoms do not always follow determined paths but randomly swerve for no reason at all. Schelling categorically denies the possibility of such randomness: "Chance [*Zufall*] is impossible; it contests reason as well as the necessary unity of the whole; and, if freedom is to be saved by nothing other than the complete contingency [*Zufälligkeit*] of actions, then it is not to be saved at all" (SW VII, 383). By denying randomness, Schelling is implicitly affirming that everything is sufficiently determined: nothing comes from nothing. But this is precisely what is claimed in the principle of sufficient reason.[15] A little later, in the section on "idealism," Schelling adds that "there is no transition from the absolutely undetermined to the determined" (SW VII, 384).[16] This is because there is *no sufficient reason* for something completely undetermined to determine itself. Everything requires a sufficient reason: the traditional principle holds universally.

Schelling's explanation of why chance is impossible recalls a point I developed in chapter 1 with respect to the concept of system. He claims that chance "contests reason as well as the necessary unity of the whole." Chance disrupts the system's unity, because it severs the connections between phenomena and creates gaps in reality. Something arises ex nihilo and thus is not integrated with what came before. But reason demands that all things be unified to form a whole.[17] The principle of sufficient reason provides the connectedness needed to unify all things by requiring that everything be grounded (and thereby connected). The denial of the principle through the affirmation of chance amounts to the denial of the connectedness and unity of the whole.

Schelling's discussion of empirical determinism—the position opposed to the usual concept of freedom—is quite brief. According to empirical determinism, all actions are empirically necessary, because each is determined either by representations (*Vorstellungen*) in the mind or by other causes that precede the actions in time (SW VII, 383). Kant formulates this position powerfully in the second *Critique*: "If it were possible for us to have so deep an insight into a human being's way of thinking . . . that we would become acquainted with every incentive to actions . . . and likewise with all external promptings affecting these incentives, then we could calculate a human being's conduct for the future with certainty, just like any lunar or solar eclipse" (KpV, AA 5, 99).

Schelling notes that both positions—empirical necessity and the usual concept of freedom—"belong to the same standpoint" (SW VII, 383). As noted above, both positions presuppose the separation and opposition of freedom and necessity. In the language of the *Identitätsphilosophie*, they belong to the standpoint of reflection or appearance, which pulls apart and opposes what is originally united in reason or in itself. Thus, both positions have in common that they cannot account for what is absolute, which is both absolutely free and absolutely necessary. One of the consequences of this failure is that *both* positions affirm a kind of contingency—even empirical necessity, which Schelling claims is really only a "disguised contingency" (SW VII, 384–85). How can this be true, if empirical necessity requires everything to be determined by prior causes? Here Schelling is drawing on the critique of the causal law that he developed in the early years of his *Identitätsphilosophie*. The causal law requires that every phenomenon be determined by a prior cause. But the prior cause is also a phenomenon, and so it must also be determined by a prior cause. Thus, the causal law requires an infinite regress to prior causes without ever reaching what is absolute and unconditioned.[18] True necessity, however, requires that everything be *sufficiently* determined, which is impossible in a causal series that never reaches completion.[19] If it fails to determine anything sufficiently, the empirical necessity of the causal law is really a disguised contingency.

Since both empirical necessity and the usual concept of freedom belong to the same standpoint, we need a higher perspective in order to know true freedom and true necessity. Remarkably, Schelling notes that if there were no such higher standpoint, empirical necessity would have the upper hand. This echoes what I regard as the most powerful line in the *Critique of Pure Reason*: "If appearances are things in themselves, then freedom cannot be saved" (A 536/B 564). Appearances are all governed by the causal law; if there is nothing beyond appearance, then all things are determined by external forces reaching far in the past, and thus freedom is impossible.[20]

But what is this higher standpoint from which freedom *is* possible? Schelling notes that "idealism first raised the doctrine of freedom to that very region where it is alone comprehensible" (SW VII, 383). The higher standpoint is that of "idealism." A few lines later he makes clear that he has primarily Kant in mind: he is expressing the "Kantian concept" in such a way as to make it comprehensible, but without using his exact words (SW VII, 384).[21] How does Kant raise the doctrine of freedom to idealism's higher perspective? By affirming this basic position: "The intelligible essence of each thing and especially of the human being is outside all causal connectedness as it is outside or above all time" (SW VII, 383). This line contains three aspects that are essential to the possibility of freedom for Kant: (1) the intelligible being or essence (*Wesen*) of a thing, (2) independence from time, and (3) independence from causal connectedness.[22]

1. Kant defines the word "intelligible" in the *Critique of Pure Reason*: "What in an object of the senses is not itself appearance I call *intelligible*" (A 538/B 566).[23] The intelligible essence of a thing is that thing insofar as it is not appearance but *in itself*. The higher perspective of idealism is therefore the perspective of things in themselves. We will see that by locating freedom in the intelligible essence, Schelling gives freedom an essential unity: in its origin, it is concentrated in a single point, in contrast to the multiplicity of human actions within appearance.[24]

2. As we saw in the last section, Schelling already discusses "independence from time" as a characteristic of things in themselves in his treatment of Kant earlier in the text (SW VII, 351–52). As one of the pure forms of sensible intuition, time is merely a condition of our knowledge of things as they appear, not in themselves.

3. For Kant, independence from causal connectedness is a direct consequence of independence from time: empirical causality requires time, and outside of time the causal law does not apply. Indeed, Schelling notes that Kant's (more accurate) designation for empirical determinism is "pre-determinism" (SW VII, 383). If time is a condition of the causal law, then what is timeless—the thing in itself—is not subject to this law. This is the heart of Kant's solution to the conflict between freedom and empirical necessity. The latter applies universally within appearance, where everything arises in time and thereby falls under the causal law. But beyond appearance, the things in themselves are outside of time; they therefore can provide the "absolute beginning" needed for freedom, as they need not be determined by a prior cause.[25]

Before continuing with Schelling's further characterization of the "idealist" position, it is worth bringing together three passages dispersed throughout the *Freiheitsschrift* that provide a succinct statement of that "higher perspective" needed for freedom—that of things in themselves. The first occurs in Schelling's characterization of God's grounding relation to things early on in the text: "God intuits the things in themselves. In itself is only: what is eternal, based on itself, will, freedom" (SW VII, 347). The second passage is famous, but perhaps not for the right reasons.[26] It occurs after the discussion of Spinoza's philosophy as a "one-sidedly realist system" and is meant to articulate the fundamental position of idealism, which complements the real side of philosophy. Indeed, immediately following the famous passage Schelling remarks that philosophy "has been raised up to this point by idealism" (SW VII, 350–51). "In the final and highest judgment, there is no other being [*Sein*] than willing [*Wollen*]. Willing is primordial being [*Ursein*] to which alone all predicates of the same apply: groundlessness, eternity, independence from time, self-affirmation. All of philosophy strives only to find this highest expression" (SW VII, 350).[27] Finally, in the section we are considering on the formal concept of freedom, Schelling mentions "genuine being" (*das eigentliche Sein*), which precedes consciousness, insofar as it is merely subjective cognition (*Erkennen*): "This being, presumed to be prior to cognition, is, however, not being,[28] though it is likewise not cognition: it is real self-positing, it is an original and fundamental willing [*Ur- und Grundwollen*], which makes itself into something and is the ground and the basis of all essentiality [*Wesenheit*]" (SW VII, 385).

Taken together, these three passages present the following characteristics of what is *in itself*: (1) eternity or independence from time, (2) original or genuine being (*Sein*), (3) fundamental willing or will, (4) self-grounding or self-determination. We have seen the importance of the first (eternity) for avoiding the empirical necessity that characterizes appearance. The second characteristic (being) indicates that the In-itself is "what ultimately is" (τὸ ὄντως ὄν), as opposed to appearance.[29] The third and fourth aspects will play an important role below, especially in our discussion of freedom in relation to the concept of *causa sui*.

So far we have concentrated on the negative aspects of idealism's doctrine of freedom: being outside of time and being outside of causal connectedness. The positive aspects concern two grounding relations: (1) the grounding of individual actions (*Handlungen*) by the intelligible essence (*Wesen*), and (2) the self-grounding of the intelligible essence. Schelling does not always clearly distinguish these two relations in his presentation, perhaps because they essentially belong together. Nonetheless, their distinction is important for seeing the precise connection between grounding and freedom. The first grounding relation is the focus of the idealist doctrine; the second is the focus of Schelling's subsequent reflections, to be treated in the next two sections.

He begins to describe the first relation as follows: "[The intelligible essence] can never be determined by any sort of prior thing, since it itself precedes all else that is or becomes within it, not so much temporally as conceptually, as an absolute unity that must always already exist fully and complete so that particular action or determination may be possible in it" (SW VII, 383). Here the relationship between the intelligible essence and individual action is described in terms of being-in. The intelligible essence is an "absolute unity" *in which* individual action is possible. And it precedes conceptually that which is or becomes *within it*. It is as if it were a concept that contains all the individual actions of a human being within it.[30] As a whole, it makes possible what it contains. Accordingly, it grounds individual actions as the condition of their possibility.

And yet the grounding relation goes beyond merely making individual actions *possible*: actions follow *with necessity* from the intelligible essence of each human being. Schelling describes this in terms of acting according to the laws of its inner nature:

> Hence, the intelligible essence can, as certainly as it acts as such freely and absolutely, just as certainly act only in accordance with its own inner nature; or action [*Handlung*] can follow from within only in accordance with the law of identity and with absolute necessity which alone is also absolute freedom. For free is what acts only in accord with the laws of its own being and is determined by nothing else either in or outside itself. (SW VII, 384)

Every human act is completely determined and therefore necessary, but this does not compromise freedom because of the unique kind of determination that is involved. In the case of empirical determinism, freedom is compromised because the necessity is *external*: one is compelled to act by forces outside oneself. This is true even if one is driven to act by "inner," psychological forces, because they are still part of a causal chain that ultimately reaches far beyond oneself. In the case of the intelligible essence, however, the necessity is *internal*: it acts in accordance with its own inner laws.[31] Its action is not random or arbitrary but determined already in its inner being.

But what are these inner laws, according to which the intelligible essence acts? As we have seen, it is an absolute unity that contains the many individual actions within itself. The inner laws, which belong to the essence of each human being, govern the necessary unfolding of the individual actions. Though Schelling only mentions Kant in this passage, the language of acting according to inner laws recalls the concept of "spontaneity" in Leibniz.[32] Indeed, in the introduction to the *Ideas on a Philosophy of Nature* (1797), he had praised just this aspect of Leibniz's thought, proclaiming: "The time is come when one can reinstitute his philosophy. . . . When Leibniz said this he was speaking to philosophers" (SW II, 20–21). And yet, despite his evident enthusiasm, Schelling comes to recognize a deficiency in Leibniz's account, which we will discuss in the next section.

Finally, there is one other philosopher in the background of this "idealist account" of freedom: Spinoza. Indeed, the account so far closely resembles the definition of freedom at the beginning of the *Ethics*: "That thing is called free which exists from the necessity of its nature alone, and is determined to act by itself alone."[33] Friedrich Hermanni has therefore suggested that Schelling's thought is a synthesis of Kant and Spinoza.[34] Nevertheless, there is a difference in Spinoza that has significant implications: it is not only actions that are determined through the inner necessity of the free being but also its very existence. Thus, only God can be free in the absolute sense for Spinoza, because only God exists by virtue of his own nature (as *causa sui*). In contrast, Schelling only speaks of *actions* following from the inner nature of the intelligible essence. This leaves open the possibility that this being is still dependent on another (God) for its existence, even though it is independent with respect to the determination of its being or essence (*Wesen*).[35] We will return to this issue below in the section on the concept of *causa sui*.

The idealist account thus unites absolute freedom and absolute necessity in the concept of "inner necessity." At the lower level of reflection and appearance, necessity is merely external determination (force) and freedom is merely random choosing. The inner necessity of the free being, by contrast, combines an unfailing obedience to the principle of sufficient reason with a self-determination that originates in what is innermost in the being itself. Though Schelling's account does not end there, his subsequent reflections build on this fundamental insight.

3. The Intelligible Deed

After discussing the idealist doctrine of freedom, Schelling begins his own account with a question: "What then is this inner necessity of the being

[*Wesen*] itself?" (SW VII, 385). Evidently, he poses the question because something in the idealist explanation of inner necessity is not sufficiently developed. But what? We have already seen Schelling's indirect invocation of the traditional principle of sufficient reason. Since everything must be sufficiently determined, individual actions do not arise randomly but follow necessarily from the intelligible essence. But now the question arises: where does that intelligible essence come from? If all things are sufficiently determined, then so must that essence. But what determines it? In the passage, Schelling implicitly rejects the two most obvious answers. First, it could be determined by something outside itself (for example, God). But this would lead to the same external determination that the concept of "inner necessity" was meant to avoid. A second answer seems more promising, and one might even mistake it for Schelling's actual solution: the intelligible essence is not determined *by* anything. Because it is eternal, it is always already determined. Indeed, the causal law only applies to appearances because they arise in time. But from the perspective of eternity, nothing arises in time, and therefore nothing needs to be caused or determined by something else. Everything simply is the way that it is.

One could object to this answer on the grounds that the principle of sufficient reason is not the same as the causal principle; at least for Leibniz, the former is not limited to appearance but applies even to eternal truths. For example, it is eternally true that the sum of the interior angles of a triangle is equal to the sum of two right angles, but there must nonetheless be a sufficient reason for it. But Schelling's objection to this approach raises another concern, which lies at the heart of the problem of freedom: "Were this [intelligible] essence [*Wesen*] a dead being [*Sein*] and a merely given one with respect to the human being, then, because all action resulting from it could do so only with necessity, responsibility and all freedom would be abolished" (SW VII, 385). If my intelligible essence were always simply the way that it is without anything determining it, it would be something merely given (*gegeben*) to me. I would have no active role, no freedom with respect to it. But if my essence is just a "given," I cannot have responsibility (*Zurechnungsfähigkeit*) for it. All my actions follow with necessity from an essence that I have no role in determining. It therefore does not matter whether the intelligible essence is (1) determined by something outside itself, or (2) determined by nothing: in both cases *I* have no role in determining it.

This is the problem that Kant had already identified with respect to Leibniz's account of freedom as spontaneity. According to Leibniz, everything that happens in the human soul arises by virtue of its inner principle, determined by its inner being alone. But what determines this inner being? For Leibniz, it is created and determined by God, who ensures that the inner representations of each monad correspond to those in other monads (the doctrine of preestablished harmony).[36] But this means that human beings have no role to play in determining their inner being. Kant quips that their freedom would be "no better than the freedom of a turnspit, which once it has been wound up, also performs its motions on its own" (KpV, AA 5, 97).

How, then, does Schelling account for the determination of the intelligible essence if the obvious answers lead to a denial of freedom and moral responsibility? Schelling's answer is a radical *self-determination* through an eternal deed (*Tat*). The intelligible essence can only be responsible for what it is if it constitutes itself. Thus, in one of the passages cited above, Schelling characterizes genuine being (*Sein*) as "real self-positing . . . original and fundamental willing, which makes itself into something" (SW VII, 385). In order to be free, the human being must be *causa sui* in a sense more radical than Spinoza's.

Before exploring the radicality of what Schelling is claiming, it is worth noting briefly how his account of the intelligible deed draws on both Fichte and Kant. Schelling himself cites Fichte when introducing the concept (SW VII, 385), and he uses the same language of self-positing that Fichte had used to express the activity of the absolute I. Unlike Fichte's *Tathandlung*, however, the intelligible deed for Schelling ultimately determines the moral actions of the individual human being, since these follow necessarily from the intelligible essence constituted by the deed. By contrast, the self-positing of the absolute I in Fichte does not seem to have features that would distinguish one human being from another and thus cannot determine individual moral actions.

The other source for the intelligible deed is Kant, who introduces the concept in *Religion within the Limits of Reason Alone* to account for how human beings can be morally accountable for an original propensity for evil (i.e., radical evil) in human nature (AA 6, 31, 39). Schelling likewise traces radical evil and original sin back to the intelligible deed, citing Kant (SW VII, 388). However, his account has two features that are absent from Kant's—or at least not clearly present. First, the single eternal deed is comprehensive in scope, including within itself not only an original propensity to evil, but all morals acts, including repentance and the acceptance of grace (cf. SW VII, 389).[37] Second, to ensure ultimate responsibility, Schelling follows Fichte in making the deed radically circular and reflexive in its self-determination.

Because we are so used to the language of self-determination, it is easy to miss the radical nature of what Schelling is claiming. Our ordinary understanding of self-determination is implicitly temporal: when I determine myself, I am already determined in the present and from that state determine what I will be in the future. This presupposes a distinction between my future self that is determined and my present self that does the determining. But for the intelligible essence there is no such temporal distinction. It determines itself, but in order to do so it must already be determined. This is because "there is no transition from the absolutely undetermined to the determined" (SW VII, 384). Accordingly, in order for the intelligible essence to determine itself it must already be determined by itself.[38] This requires that the self-grounding of absolute freedom be radically circular and reflexive,[39] like the *Tathandlung* in Fichte, which Schelling himself cites.[40]

Schelling himself admits that this idea is "incomprehensible" (*unfaßlich*) for the ordinary way of thinking (SW VII, 386). This is to be expected: the usual way of thinking assumes the perspective of reflection and appearance, which can only think of freedom under the conditions of time and empirical causality. More specifically, Schelling's account of the eternal deed departs from ordinary ways of thinking about freedom in three ways: (1) it does not involve choice; (2) it is pre-conscious—at least in terms of our present form of consciousness; and (3) it is not a human capacity but the human being itself. Let me develop these points in more detail.

(1) One of the curious features of the section on the formal concept of freedom (SW VII, 382–89) is that the word "choice" (*Wahl*) does not appear at all.[41] Instead, Schelling refers to an eternal "decision" (*Entscheidung*), which is also an intelligible deed (*Tat*) that determines the temporal life of the human being (SW VII, 385). Often in ordinary language we use "choice" and "decision" interchangeably. However, Schelling contends that not every decision involves a choice, even if every choice involves a decision.[42] A choice requires a moment of indecision, during which one weighs the options before making a decision. But the eternal decision, precisely because it is eternal, is always already decided.[43] In the *Stuttgart Private Lectures* (1810), Schelling criticizes the idea of "free choice" with respect to the role of knowledge: "Usually one only sees freedom where a choice has taken place, a state of doubt precedes [it], and finally the decision follows. But

the one who knows what he wills seizes it without choice. The one who chooses does not know what he wills, and thus he does not [really] will. All choice is a consequence of an unilluminated will" (SW VII, 429). In what follows, Schelling describes the grounding of one's character (*Charakter*)[44] as an absolute action (*Handlung*). Although no one would claim that human beings choose their character, it is still "imputable" to the human being by virtue of this absolute action (SW VII, 430).

It is also important to note the uniqueness of the eternal decision. In our life in time, we make many discrete decisions, most of which are unrelated. But the eternal deed is a single decision that wholly determines our intelligible essence: as we have seen, all of the individual actions that unfold in time are necessary consequences of this essence, which is an absolute unity. Although we experience our life in separate moments, Schelling notes that nothing is as separated and successive as it seems—everything happens simultaneously "in one magic stroke" (SW VII, 387; cf. VII, 206, 241). All of our actions in this life are wrapped up in that single primordial act.[45]

(2) The intelligible deed is also unconscious or pre-conscious. Schelling does use the evocative phrase "life before this life" to describe the eternal deed (SW VII, 387).[46] This may seem to suggest a prior conscious state, analogous to our present life. But Schelling excludes the eternal deed from consciousness—at least insofar as this is the merely subjective consciousness that distinguishes subject from object: "That free deed . . . admittedly cannot appear in consciousness to the extent that the latter is merely self-awareness and only ideal, since it precedes consciousness" (SW VII, 386). As we know it, consciousness is essentially temporal and belongs to appearance, but the eternal deed transcends all appearance. But here one can object: how can we be morally responsible for an unconscious act? After all, we only impute responsibility to those who act with awareness of what they are doing. Schelling does not address this objection directly. However, we should note that in two of the passages that mention consciousness, he adds a restricting phrase: the eternal deed is beyond consciousness "to the extent that the latter is merely self-awareness and only ideal" (SW VII, 386) and "to the extent that it is thought merely as self-conception or knowledge of the I" (SW VII, 385). This at least leaves open the possibility that the eternal deed is accessible to a more original form of consciousness, to which responsibility could be imputed.

Indeed, Schelling notes that a trace of this eternal deed remains in consciousness, evidently left over from a "prior" state.[47] As a result, those who do wrong are conscious of the fact that they are who they are through their own fault (SW VII, 386). He also speaks of a "feeling" in each human being that "he has been what he is from all eternity and has by no means become so first in time" (SW VII, 386). Heidegger expresses this eloquently: "Thence comes that uncanny and at the same time friendly feeling that we have always been what we are, that we are nothing but the unveiling of things long since decided."[48] Despite the changes that take place in our lives, we identify with and feel responsible for who we were in the past and who we will be in the future. The moments of our lives are not so discretely separated, and "in what is earlier that which comes later is also already active" (SW VII, 387). Schelling expresses this consciousness of eternal self-identity, embracing the different moments of time, in an unpublished quatrain:

Ich bin der ich war.   I am who I was.
Ich bin der ich sein werde.   I am who I will be.
Ich war der ich sein werde.   I was who I will be.
Ich werde sein der ich bin.   I will be who I am.[49]

These haunting lines are an expression of God's consciousness of his eternal self-identity through time—Schelling's interpretation in the *Ages of the World* of the untranslatable name of God given to Moses (cf. SW VIII, 263–64). However, they express equally well the feeling that the moments of our lives essentially belong together, that we are who we are for all eternity.

(3) Finally, Schelling's account of the intelligible deed differs from ordinary conceptions of freedom in not regarding freedom as a capacity (*Vermögen*). As commonly conceived, freedom is an ability that human beings *have* to act on their own. Thus, three things are usually distinguished: (a) the human being, (b) freedom (as the capacity to act), and (c) the act itself. Schelling, in contrast, unites all three: "The being [*Wesen*] of the human being is essentially *his own deed* [*Tat*]; necessity and freedom are in one another as one being [*Ein Wesen*] that appears as one or the other only when considered from different sides—in itself freedom, formally necessity" (SW VII, 385). The human being is his own deed; the human being is freedom.[50] In order for the deed to be something other than the

human being, the latter would have to exist "before" and independent of the deed. But the deed is what constitutes the innermost essence of each human being. It is not something the human being *does*, because the human being is *the doing* of the deed. This recalls the character of the I as *Tathandlung* in Fichte, whom Schelling cites in this context. According to Fichte, the I is also "its own deed," which is a self-positing. "But the I is nothing different from this self-positing, rather it is precisely self-positing itself" (SW VII, 385).[51] Later Schelling affirms that the human being is originally "act and deed" (*Handlung und Tat*) (SW VII, 388)—the two words Fichte joined together to express the unique character of the I (FW I, 96).

If the human being is itself an eternal deed, it would make little sense to say that freedom is a *capacity*: this would presuppose that the human being exists independently of the deed and has the capability to perform it, which may or may not be realized. But if the human being is nothing other than this deed, it is not a mere possibility, but a necessity. Here freedom and necessity are again united: the deed is necessary insofar as it could not be otherwise for the human being;[52] the deed is free insofar as it alone determines itself.

If human freedom is not a capacity, why does Schelling earlier define it as "a capacity for good and evil" (SW VII, 352)? We have seen that the latter is the real concept: it provides the possible content (the *what*) of freedom, while the formal concept provides the form (the *how*). The word "capacity" in the real definition should therefore be interpreted in relation to freedom's content, not its form. It indicates that good and evil are possible contents: the human being is *capable* of both. But these contents are *determined* in accordance with the formal concept of freedom, which is not a faculty for deciding how to act. Moreover, Schelling dismisses an understanding of freedom as *Willkür* or the "power to choose" (cf. SW VII, 382, 392; VIII, 199–200; IX, 39).[53]

In fact, Schelling's conception of freedom as an eternal deed and not a capacity is part of his general tendency to move away from an anthropology of capacities or faculties. In the 1806 *Aphorisms*, he boldly proclaims: "Reason is not a capacity or tool, and it cannot be used; it is not as if there is a reason that we *have*, but only a reason that *has us*" (SW VII, 148–49, emphasis added).[54] Something similar can be said about the language of will, which plays an important role in the *Freiheitsschrift*; for example, that-which-exists and the ground of existence are called wills (SW VII, 363; 375). One is tempted to interpret the word "will" (*Wille*) as the capacity of an agent to will, which would therefore be prior to the activity of willing (*Wollen*). But Schelling famously proclaims: "In the final and highest judgment, there is no other being than willing [*Wollen*]. Willing is primordial being" (SW VII, 350). This is echoed in the section on the formal essence of freedom: true being is "original and fundamental willing" (*Ur- und Grundwollen*) (SW VII, 385). Here there is no capacity to will prior to the activity of willing. The same is true in the case of freedom. In fact, it is clear in context that Schelling is describing the self-positing character of freedom when he refers to "original and fundamental willing." The act of freedom by which the intelligible essence is determined is a fundamental willing, which is also a self-grounding.

All these ways that the intelligible deed is "incomprehensible" for our ordinary thinking point to the essentially *mysterious* character of freedom (in the sense developed at the end of chapter 5). This mysterious character is reflected in the sense of wonder evoked by Schelling's language, especially his reference to "a life before this life" (SW VII, 387). In fact, there are remarkable connections between his treatment of our "preexistence" and the mystical tradition—in particular, the famous *Armutspredigt* of Meister Eckhart.[55] To have true poverty, Eckhart says, the human being must be "as he was when he did not yet exist."[56] Here Eckhart is referring to our original state of being as an eternal idea in the mind of God before creation—what he elsewhere calls our "virtual being" (*esse virtuale*) as opposed to our "formal being" (*esse formale*) as creatures in time.[57] Eckhart even states: "I was my own cause [*sache mîn selbes*]" in this original state of existence.[58] The statement probably does not refer to an act of self-determination like the intelligible deed; instead, Eckhart seems to have in mind his uncreated status as a divine idea. Nevertheless, the parallels to the "life before this life" in the *Freiheitsschrift* are striking and show the affinities of Schelling's thought with mysticism, even if he is not drawing here from mystical sources.[59]

4. Self-Grounding and the Concept of *Causa Sui*

We have seen that the formal concept of freedom involves two grounding relations. The first is the grounding of individual actions, which follow with necessity from the intelligible essence. The second is the self-determination of the intelligible essence through an eternal deed. In this section, we will consider the character of this self-grounding as it relates to the concept of *causa sui*.

The notion of a *causa sui* has been problematic throughout the history of philosophy. To understand why, we have to recognize a fundamental problem connected to the principle of ground, especially in its traditional form. As we noted in chapter 3, the movement of the traditional principle is regressive, moving from something that exists to its ground. But its ground is something that also exists, and thus it must have a ground as well. The principle thereby inaugurates a regress to more and more original grounds. How does this regress end? There are three possibilities.[60] The first is that it does not: there is an *infinite regress*. However, as we saw above with Schelling's critique of the causal law, an infinite regress does not allow any of its members to be sufficiently grounded. One thing rests on another, which rests on yet another thing. But without an absolutely first ground, the whole series remains suspended in mid-air.[61]

The second and third solutions both affirm an absolutely first ground but have different ways of accounting for its possibility. The second solution is that there is an absolutely first ground in the series, but this first ground is itself *ungrounded*. When ground is understood to mean "cause," the first ground is the uncaused, first cause. This solution is perhaps the most popular throughout the history of metaphysics, especially in the Aristotelian tradition, but it comes at the price of the universality of the principle of ground. All things are grounded, except the first.[62] But this raises the question, why should it not require a ground as well? Kant expresses this objection powerfully in the first *Critique*. Assuming the voice of God, he writes: "I am from eternity to eternity, and apart from me there is nothing except what is something merely through my will; *but whence, then, am I?*" The question, presumably, is unanswerable. Kant thus refers to the unconditioned as "the true abyss" for human reason—it is an *Abgrund* ("abyss") precisely because it is groundless (A 613/B 641).

Finally, the third solution is that there is an absolutely first ground in the series, and this first ground is *self-grounding*. When ground is understood to mean "cause," the first ground is the cause of itself, *causa sui*. One advantage of this solution is that it preserves the strict universality of the principle of ground. Everything, including the first ground, is grounded. The difficulty is that it introduces a concept that is outside our experience and may well be incomprehensible. How can something be the ground of itself or the cause of itself? Would this not require that it exist before it exists, if a cause exists before its effect?

Throughout most of the *Freiheitsschrift*, Schelling uses expressions that align freedom and the In-itself with the third of these possibilities. Thus, he describes the In-itself as "what is based on itself" (*das auf sich selbst Beruhende*) (SW VII, 347). In the context of the eternal deed, Schelling identifies genuine being as "real self-positing" and "original and fundamental willing, which makes itself into something" (SW VII, 385). And yet Schelling also ascribes a groundlessness to freedom and "what ultimately is." In the famous passage where he identifies being and willing, Schelling lists the predicates of primordial being: "groundlessness [*Grundlosigkeit*], eternality, independence from time, self-affirmation [*Selbstbejahung*]" (SW VII, 350). Self-affirmation is yet another expression for self-grounding.[63] Thus, in the very same passage, Schelling says that primordial being is groundless and self-grounding. How is this possible?

In the years following 1809, Schelling makes similar statements that shed light on the possibility of thinking groundlessness and self-grounding together. In the dialogue *Clara* (1809–1812?), the physician explains the nature of freedom to the title character: "Necessity is the inner [character] of freedom. For this reason, no ground can be provided for a truly free action. It is so, because it is so. It simply is [*ist schlechthin*]; it is unconditioned and thus necessary. But as such, freedom is not of this world" (SW IX, 39; cf. WA I, 93). On the one hand, the physician says that no ground can be provided for freedom. On the other hand, he gives a ground. It is so, because it is so: it is its own ground.[64] Moreover, he emphasizes the necessity involved. Freedom is not without a ground in the sense of being arbitrary or a matter of chance. The passage in the *Stuttgart Private Lectures* (1810) is very similar, but with an important addition: "All true, that is, absolute freedom is again, of course, an absolute necessity. For no further ground [*kein weiterer Grund*] can be given for an action of absolute freedom. It is so, because it is so—that is, it simply is, and to that extent [it is] necessary" (SW VII, 429). Here Schelling does not say that no ground can be given, but that no *further* ground can be given. Thus, the act of freedom is groundless with respect to a ground outside itself but grounded with respect to its self-grounding.[65] As I argue below, this allows Schelling to combine necessity with a form of contingency: the eternal deed is necessary with respect to itself but contingent with respect to anything beyond it.[66]

But what is really at stake in saying that the free act is self-grounding? Is this really any different from saying that it is ungrounded or uncaused? To answer these questions and discover what is innovative in Schelling's account, we need to situate it within the history of the concept of *causa sui* as a competitor to an uncaused first cause.[67] The first explicit use of the concept is in Plotinus. In the *Ennead* on free will, he refers to the One as αἴτιον ἑαυτοῦ, "cause of himself" (VI.8.14).⁶⁸ Despite the apparent boldness of this expression, it has a primarily negative meaning. Because the One is prior to all else, it cannot have its being from anything else: it must be "from itself" (*a se*). In its negative interpretation, the concept of *causa sui* has essentially the same meaning as the concept of an uncaused first cause. This negative interpretation of *causa sui* was widespread among the Neoplatonists, and it reappears in modernity.⁶⁹

On the other hand, the positive interpretation of *causa sui* has been subject to harsh criticism throughout the history of philosophy. St. Thomas Aquinas offers the classic argument against it: "But we neither find nor is it possible for something to be the efficient cause of itself; for then it would be prior to itself, which is impossible."⁷⁰ It is noteworthy that Aquinas here specifies *causa sui* as "efficient cause" of itself. In the case of efficient causality, the cause is prior to the effect.⁷¹ Therefore, an efficient cause of itself would have to be prior (as cause) to itself (as effect), which is contradictory. But this—potentially—leaves open the possibility of self-grounding, if grounding is understood as something other than efficient causality. Indeed, it is noteworthy that Schelling almost never uses the phrase *causa sui*,⁷² even though it is an important concept in Spinoza, from whom he draws heavily in the *Identitätsphilosophie*. The avoidance of the phrase is certainly related to Schelling's critique of causality in general and the wish to make a clear distinction between grounding in the In-itself and the causality characteristic of appearance.⁷³

For Descartes and Spinoza, the most prominent modern philosophers to use the phrase *causa sui*, the positive concept is closely linked to the ontological proof for the existence of God. This proof is based on the fact that God's essence includes his existence: God is that being whose nature it is to exist. Spinoza begins the *Ethics* with this definition of *causa sui*: "By cause of itself I understand that whose essence involves existence, *or* that whose nature cannot be conceived except as existing."⁷⁴ Because God's existence follows necessarily from his essence, one can say that—in a certain sense—his essence causes his existence. And because the divine essence is indistinguishable from the divine existence, God can be called the cause of himself. Of course, this causality is very different from efficient causality as it is usually understood—although Descartes claims it has "a great analogy with efficiency."⁷⁵

This is just a brief sketch of some of the moments in the history of the concept of *causa sui*. Nevertheless, we can see that, despite what appears to be a significant difference with the concept of uncaused first cause, historically the difference mostly concerns language and emphasis rather than substance. The proponents of the concept of *causa sui* either (1) interpret it negatively, in which case it simply means that God does not have his being from another but is *a se*; or (2) interpret it positively in terms of the necessary existence of God. Despite the provocative language, both interpretations of the concept affirm conventional metaphysical views about God.

Schelling's doctrine of the intelligible deed is significantly different from the traditional interpretations, and in a particular respect it is more radical. Of course, the first difference concerns what it is that is self-grounding. In the case of the intelligible deed, this is not just a single *causa sui* (God), but all free beings. This is in accordance with Schelling's general tendency to divinize freedom, which we have seen already. Early on in the treatise, he had noted that a "derived absoluteness or divinity" is the middle term of all philosophy (SW VII, 347). Schelling sets the bar for freedom so high that to be free is to be both absolute and divine.[76]

The second difference concerns the word "derived" in the striking phrase "derived absoluteness." Although free beings are absolute, they are also dependent. This cannot be said of the traditional concept of God as *causa sui* or uncaused cause. In chapter 3, we discussed the possibility of combining dependence with absolute independence—in particular, the following decisive lines from the early part of the *Freiheitsschrift*: "But dependence does not abolish independence, it does not even abolish freedom. Dependence does not determine the essence [*Wesen*] and says only that the dependent, whatever it also may be, can be only as a consequence of that of which it is a dependent; dependence does not say what the dependent is or is not" (SW VII, 346). In this passage, Schelling distinguishes between the being and the essence of a thing. What is free can be dependent with respect to its being: God is its ground, both in the sense of conditio sine qua non and in the sense of bringing forth what is grounded through begetting (*Zeugung*). Nevertheless, it is independent with respect to its essence: *what it is* is not determined by its dependence.

If we interpret the account of formal freedom in accordance with this earlier passage, we can say that the eternal deed of freedom determines the *essence* of each human being, even though each is dependent on God with respect to *existence*.[77] It is curious, however, that God is almost entirely absent from the discussion of the formal concept of freedom, although Schelling does make indirect references to the Creator. On the one hand, the human being is "created [*erschaffen*] into the beginning of creation" (SW VII, 385). On the other hand, through the eternal deed the human being is "outside the created, being free and eternal beginning itself" (SW VII, 386). I interpret the first line to refer to the dependence of human beings with respect to their existence: they are created by God. The second line would then refer to their absolute independence with respect to their essence: to the extent that they are radically self-determined through the eternal deed, they are uncreated.[78]

The third and final difference from traditional interpretations of *causa sui* is the most decisive aspect of Schelling's account. Because free beings determine their own essence, they are responsible for who they are. The intelligible deed is intended to account for ultimate moral responsibility. In this respect, the human being is *causa sui* in a more radical sense than Spinoza's God. In the case of Spinoza—and for that matter, the larger metaphysical tradition—the essence of God is not something that God determines. It is something that is simply given. God is *causa sui* only with respect to his existence, not with respect to determining his essence. But this means that God is only responsible for the fact *that he is*, not *what he is*.[79] And if everything that God does follows from what he is, God would not really be responsible for what he does.

This connection between responsibility and self-determination of essence is at the heart of Schelling's account of the formal concept of freedom, as we discussed in the last sections.[80] Individual actions follow with necessity from the intelligible essence of the human being. If we are not responsible for what we are as intelligible essences, we cannot be responsible for our actions. This makes clear what is at stake in choosing between self-grounding and groundlessness, or between *causa sui* and uncaused first cause. If my essence is not something that I cause or determine, then I am not responsible for it. Indeed, the Greek word αἴτιον ("cause") is derived from the adjective αἴτιος, which means "responsible." What causes something is responsible for it: to be responsible for who I am, I must cause who I am. It is not enough that who I am is not determined by something outside myself (and thus ungrounded, uncaused). This is a merely negative sense of freedom, a "freedom from . . ." Moral responsibility requires a genuinely positive freedom, and this in turn requires that I positively determine who I am.[81]

To contemporary philosophers, this account of eternal freedom may seem wildly speculative—a good example of the excesses of German Idealism. Nevertheless, an influential thinker in the contemporary analytic debate on free will reaches conclusions strikingly similar to Schelling's. In the essay "The Impossibility of Moral Responsibility," Galen Strawson argues that "in order to be truly morally responsible for one's actions one would have to be *causa sui*, at least in certain crucial mental respects."[82] This is because "if one is to be truly responsible for how one acts, one must be truly responsible for how one is,"[83] and this can only happen if one brings it about that one is the way that one is. Saying that we can determine who we are through our previous actions does not resolve the problem but merely pushes it back, because our previous actions arose from who we were in the past. Only the truly circular self-determination of a *causa sui* can provide ultimate responsibility. Strawson intends the invocation of the concept of *causa sui* to be a reductio ad absurdum. For him it is clearly impossible that a human being should be *causa sui*. Nevertheless, his argument is compelling and reflects Schelling's fundamental insight: in order to be responsible for what we do, we must cause or ground what we are.[84]

But is Strawson right that this is impossible? Schopenhauer evidently thought so. In his dissertation on the principle of ground, he calls the notion of a self-grounding *causa sui* a "contradiction in terms" and compares it to the Baron Münchhausen's attempt to lift himself and his horse out of the swamp by pulling on his own hair (ASW III, 28)—an image Nietzsche will borrow in his critique of freedom in *Beyond Good and Evil* (§21). Certainly self-grounding or self-causality is absurd when conceived in purely physical terms, or more generally when conceived in time, where effect must follow cause in temporal succession. Schelling himself admits that the eternal deed is "incomprehensible" for our common way of thinking (SW VII, 386), which pulls apart what belongs together and separates in temporal succession what is eternally one. Thus, according to our usual way of thinking, I cannot ultimately determine who I am, because I would have to be *already* determined in order to determine myself.

This logic applies to appearance and within time, and Schelling readily concedes the impossibility of ultimate freedom within appearance. As Kant says so powerfully, "If appearances are things in themselves, then freedom cannot be saved" (KrV, A 536/B 564). Freedom, if it exists, belongs to the things in themselves. Here self-grounding is possible—or at least conceivable—because it need not follow the linear and temporal succession of empirical causality. In any case, if Kant and Schelling are right that the conditions for freedom and moral responsibility can only be fulfilled by going beyond our ordinary, time-bound view of the world, then we are faced with a choice. We can stick with a view of the world that is close to experience and common sense but does not leave room for freedom. Or we can entertain a more mysterious picture of reality that allows for the self-grounding necessary for us to be accountable for who we are.

Conclusion

Ground in a System of Freedom

Now that we have examined Schelling's solution to the problem of freedom and necessity, we can take a step back and assess his overall approach to the problem of ground—the central problem of the treatise, as I have argued. How does Schelling sort out the different kinds of grounds and the structure of the grounding relations in the system? How does this resolve the difficulties related to a system of freedom? And what are the strengths and weaknesses of his approach?

At the core of Schelling's solution is his—largely implicit—identification of different senses of grounding. Although "ground" has an array of meanings in the treatise, we have seen that three are most prominent: (1) ground as condition of the possibility, (2) ground as what determines, and (3) ground as what begets (that is, brings forth without determining). Moreover, I have argued that the first sense is primary. In the letter to Georgii, Schelling himself identifies it as the core meaning with respect to the ground of God's existence, and we have seen it appear in a number of other contexts—including the meaning of the copula, the solution to the problem of evil, and the characterization of the *Ungrund*.

Corresponding to the three senses are three versions of the principle of ground, each of which expresses the universality of being grounded: nothing is without ground. The third sense (together with the first) is used in the version of the principle that Schelling himself calls the "law of ground" (SW VII, 346). In chapter 3, I argued that this can be formulated: *God is all things*. This means that all things are in God, who thus grounds them by making them possible. But this principle also expresses God's creative unity with all things: he brings them forth within himself through a begetting (*Zeugung*) that does not determine what is begotten but allows for its "derived absoluteness." A second version of the principle is implied in the passage on the fundamental distinction: "In the circle from which everything comes to be . . . all things mutually presuppose each other" (SW VII, 358). Here the first sense of ground is applied universally: *All things reciprocally ground each other*. Each thing is the condition of the possibility for all the others. Finally, we saw that Schelling implicitly endorses the traditional principle of sufficient reason when ruling out arbitrary or random occurrences in the section on formal freedom (SW VII, 383). This version of the principle uses the second sense of ground: *Everything has a ground that sufficiently determines it*.

Each of the three versions helps articulate the structure of the grounding relations within the system—one of the tasks needed to address the problem of ground, as I have defined it. In fact, each has as its focus one of three key relationships for a system of freedom. (1) For the first version, this is the relationship between God and the world: God grounds all things insofar as they are in God and begotten by him. (2) The second version concerns the relationship among things, which mutually presuppose each other. (3) And, as we saw in the last chapter, the third version applies to the self-relation of the intelligible essence in the act of freedom: it sufficiently determines itself.

Beyond the three versions of the principle, we have seen Schelling articulate other grounding relations—above all, in the fundamental distinction between that-which-exists and the ground of God's existence. The ground is the condition of the possibility of God's revelation (his existence) through the unfolding of creation. But the "cause" in this process is not the ground but the understanding (that-which-exists), which actively divides forces within the ground and raises them to new life (SW VII, 361–62). Moreover, the same basic structure of ground and that-which-exists recurs throughout the system, because "both principles are in all things" (SW VII, 363). Their "divine relationship" obtains when the ground serves as *ground*, that is, as foundation for that-which-exists (SW VII, 365), but this relationship is reversed in evil (SW VII, 366). Finally, we have seen how the *Ungrund* is the ultimate ground. As indifference, it is the condition of the possibility of the two principles' duality. And as the essence of the absolute, it makes possible all that exists. And yet it is not a productive cause of creation, the kind of ground traditionally associated with the ultimate being.

With the different senses of ground and the principal grounding structures in mind, we can summarize how Schelling resolves the three main problems associated with a system of freedom: the problem of pantheism, the problem of evil, and the problem of determinism (freedom and necessity). The first of these problems concerns the relation of the system's parts to the whole (that is, God, from the perspective of pantheism). If all things are one in God, they do not seem to have the independence necessary for freedom: they are swallowed up in a divine whole. We saw in chapters 2 and 3 that Schelling affirms the immanence of all things in God but denies that this compromises their independence. Here the first version of the principle of ground comes into play: "God is all things," which means "God grounds all things," according to the account of the copula. The immanence of things in God is therefore not a monolithic sameness but a grounding identity that requires difference within it. But divine grounding also allows for the independence—even the absoluteness—of what is grounded. This is because it involves grounding in the third sense: God produces things through begetting (*Zeugung*), which brings them forth within himself without determining what they are.

The second problem, that of evil, arises because of the difficulty of accounting for evil's reality—and the human freedom to do evil—within a system in which God is the ground of all things. How can the reality of evil be affirmed without making God responsible for its existence? The resolution of the problem requires sorting out the ways in which God is and is not a ground of evil. As we saw in chapter 5, Schelling's answer rests on his fundamental distinction: by distinguishing God insofar as he exists from the ground of his existence, he allows evil to have a basis (the ground of God's existence) that is not "God himself" and yet within God. Moreover, the central sense of ground in the treatise—condition of the possibility—plays a decisive role in his solution: the ground of God's existence makes evil possible, but it does not determine that evil should exist. Only human freedom can do that.

Finally, by reconceiving the grounding structures within the system, Schelling is able to provide an answer to the problem of determinism, which he formulates in terms of the opposition between freedom and necessity. As we saw in chapter 1, he places this opposition at "the center of philosophy" (SW VII, 333) and associates it with the task of uniting freedom and system (SW VII, 338). I argued that the principle of ground is the link between this task and the opposition between freedom and necessity: a system requires connectedness, which the principle of ground provides by requiring that everything be grounded; however, this seems to jeopardize freedom if the principle of ground requires everything to follow deterministically (or with necessity).

Schelling's overall solution to this problem consists in distinguishing deterministic and non-deterministic senses of ground: non-deterministic grounding can provide the connectedness needed for system without compromising freedom. This is clear in the first two versions of the principle of ground that we identified. According to the first version, all things are grounded by God and thus linked to the ultimate principle of the system. However, this grounding does not determine what they are for themselves, only *that* they are. According to the second version of the principle, all things are connected to each other insofar as they reciprocally presuppose each other. Indeed, because the grounding is reciprocal, the parts are arguably more integrated than they would be in the conventional understanding of grounding relations as linear and one-directional. But since the grounds are conditions of the possibility, what is grounded is not determined. All things relate to each other like the parts of an organism, which maintain their independence despite their integration within the living whole.

These two versions of the principle of ground help resolve the problem by connecting the parts of a system while *avoiding* necessity. In a final step, Schelling defines the formal essence of freedom in such a way that necessity is united with freedom in an "inner necessity." As we saw in the last chapter, this involves an original deed of self-determination outside of time. Each of our actions in time follows with necessity from our intelligible essence, which is determined by that original deed. Here a deterministic sense of ground is operative. But this does not compromise freedom, because it is a self-grounding. In fact, Schelling recognizes that if the free being did not determine itself in the strictest sense, if it remained undetermined (either by itself or by something else), it could not be ultimately responsible for its actions. Here grounding is essential for freedom; indeed, freedom is a kind of grounding.

In light of this overview of Schelling's solution to the problem of ground and his attempt to construct a system of freedom, what can we say about his ultimate success? It is a commonplace among Schelling commentators that the *Freiheitsschrift* fails in one way or another—even if it is a heroic failure.[1] Certainly, the work has shortcomings and unresolved difficulties, which we will turn to presently. But it is also a major achievement in the originality of its approach, its ambitions, and the extent to which those ambitions are carried out. Let me develop the principal aspects of that achievement, as I see it.

The most general aspect is what we might call Schelling's contextualization of the problem of human freedom. Already in the full title of the treatise he announces that it is not just about freedom: it also investigates "the matters connected therewith." This reflects his fundamental insight that freedom cannot be treated in isolation, but only in connection with the treatise's many other themes: the meaning of identity, God's nature and relation to the world, creation, the development of nature and history, the problem of evil, redemption, the end of the world—in short, the entire system. But why? Certainly Schelling, like the other German Idealists, is a systematic philosopher, and we have seen that he affirms the organic connectedness of all things, even if their connection to human freedom is not always obvious. But in Schelling's case, I am claiming that the reason is more specific: he treats the problem of freedom as part of the larger problem of ground. He recognizes that freedom can only be understood—and the problems connected to it can only be resolved—by rethinking the meaning of ground and the network of grounding relations that make up the system. One cannot address the problem of determinism, for example, without considering the nature of God's grounding or the role of the principle of ground in connecting the system's parts. Whatever one makes of Schelling's specific philosophical positions, in eighty pages he succeeds in placing freedom in the context of the problem of ground and thus articulating the full range of grounding problems that any complete theory of freedom must address.

From within this general approach, several of Schelling's more specific achievements are tied to his introduction of non-deterministic senses of ground—especially "condition of the possibility," which I have argued is its central meaning in the *Freiheitsschrift*. This is a departure from Spinoza, Leibniz, and the larger metaphysical tradition, which tends to privilege deterministic causality when articulating grounding relations. As a consequence, Schelling is able to combine dependence with an extremely strong sense of independence, a combination captured in the phrase "derived absoluteness" (SW VII, 347). Free beings can be dependent on other beings—and ultimately God—as the conditions of their possibility, but this leaves them undetermined and absolute with respect to what they are in themselves.

Making "condition of the possibility" the central sense of ground has other significant consequences. First, it allows Schelling to move decisively away from the all-from-one model of grounding relations, toward which rationalist philosophies gravitate. In fact, his earlier *Identitätsphilosophie* can be interpreted to fit this model: all that exists can be traced back to absolute identity as the single starting point from which everything follows necessarily—though there are problems with applying this model, especially with respect to the relationship of absolute identity to finite appearances. However, if God in the *Freiheitsschrift* is a ground primarily in the sense of condition of the possibility, not everything is derived deterministically from a single absolute. This opens up the space for multiple starting points and a plurality of absolutes. Indeed, every eternal deed of freedom is an absolute starting point. Schelling himself observes that through this deed, the human being is "outside the created, [and thus] free and eternal beginning" (SW VII, 386). Likewise, the two principles in God are "two equally eternal beginnings of self-revelation" (SW VII, 395).

Multiplying the starting points has two additional consequences: the decentralization of the system and a movement toward equiprimordiality. At the beginning of the treatise, Schelling had referred to freedom as one of the "ruling center points of the system" (SW VII, 336).[2] If there are multiple free beings, one can infer that there are multiple centers. The introduction of a dualism within God—the two principles—also has a decentering effect: with respect to the development of nature and history, both are relatively independent focal points. Moreover, the move away from a single center and starting point is reflected in the organization of the *Freiheitsschrift*, as I argued in chapter 6. Unlike previous presentations of the system, Schelling does not begin with the absolute and proceed from there—an order that gives the impression that all is derived from a single principle. Instead, "the absolute without qualification," the *Ungrund*, is only introduced toward the end of the treatise. Of course, the relative "disorder" of presentation is partly due to the form that Schelling intentionally adopts: "everything arises as in a dialogue," as he notes in a footnote (SW VII, 410n). But the form also matches the decentralized content.

The decentralization of the system goes hand-in-hand with the movement toward equiprimordiality. In the introduction, I noted that Heidegger connects the all-from-one model of grounding to the failure to recognize phenomena that are "equally original." Schelling's movement away from this model thus allows him to move *toward* equiprimordiality, the best image for which is the circle from which everything comes: "Here there is no first and no last, because all things mutually presuppose each other" (SW VII, 358). As another example, one could cite again the principles in God, which are "two equally eternal beginnings" (SW VII, 395). Moreover, I suggested in chapter 6 that the *Ungrund* corresponds to the essence of the absolute, which is in a relationship of reciprocal dependence (and thus equiprimordiality) with its form.

Perhaps the most striking feature of Schelling's movement toward equiprimordiality is his tendency to divinize freedom. He boldly refers to freedom as "derived absoluteness or divinity" (SW VII, 347) and claims that through the eternal deed, free beings are "outside the created" (SW VII, 386). Indeed, with respect to our eternal essence, this deed is an act of self-creation—in Fichte's words: "I am my own creature."[3] As things in themselves, free beings assume the place that Schelling had given the ideas, which "are themselves gods, for each for itself is absolute, and yet each is grasped in the absolute form" (SW IV, 405). One might therefore say—to use a pointed formulation—the system of freedom turns out to be a "polytheism of freedom." This divinization reflects Schelling's recognition that the extremely high demands of ultimate moral responsibility require absoluteness and attributes (like *causa sui*) traditionally reserved for God.

Nonetheless, at the end of the day, Schelling *moves* toward equiprimordiality, but does not embrace it completely. He still wishes to affirm the priority of God as the creator and ground of all that is, even if free beings extend beyond creation with respect to their freedom: their absoluteness is a derived absoluteness, as paradoxical as that sounds. Although all things are mutually dependent, they are all still *in* God who brings them forth in an act of begetting. The unfolding of nature and history are revelations of God, who manifests himself by acting through the ground of his existence. And the full realization of God in the reign of love is the goal of the entire process. In these respects, Schelling's philosophy is still very much theocentric. However, there are difficulties with combining multiple absolutes with God, to which we will return below.

A final aspect of Schelling's achievement is a consequence of the distinctive way he rejects the all-from-one model. The usual way is to introduce contingency: not everything is derived from an absolute starting point, because there are gaps or places in the system where something happens—for example, an act of freedom—with no sufficient reason. But we saw that Schelling rules out absolute contingency, precisely because it introduces gaps, which destroy the unity of the whole that reason demands (SW VII, 383). Instead, he affirms that everything has a sufficient reason and thus follows with necessity—but not from a single starting point. Each eternal act of freedom is its own absolute beginning and, because of its self-determination, has a sufficient reason as well. Thus, Schelling affirms a unique form of determinism, one that does not require free beings to be externally determined because they are self-determined—each its own "eternal beginning" (SW VII, 386).

Along these lines, we could say that Schelling, by introducing multiple absolute starting points, is able to combine necessity and (relative) contingency in a creative way. On the one hand, he endorses the necessity of all things: even the eternal act of freedom is self-determining and thus could not have been different—at least when considered with respect to itself.[4] However, from the perspective of *other* things, including God, it is contingent. It cannot be deduced from anything beyond itself. This explains why Schelling uses the language of both groundlessness and self-grounding, as we discussed above: freedom is groundless and contingent with respect to other things, but self-grounding and necessary with respect to itself. Incidentally, there are parallels here with our discussion of necessity and contingency in chapter 5. We saw that Schelling draws attention to contingent elements in nature, even though he affirms an overarching necessity. This is because they are contingent *with respect to* the understanding and its way of knowing. The same concept of a relative (but not absolute) contingency applies to freedom. In any case, Schelling's combination of necessity and contingency allows him to preserve the absoluteness needed for freedom while retaining the determinism demanded by reason.

These are some of Schelling's achievements with respect to the problem of ground. But what about the remaining problems? As it turns out, what I regard as the central weakness of the *Freiheitsschrift* is directly tied to some of the creative innovations we have just been discussing. Expressed in the most general terms, it is the problem of coordination. Decentering the system by introducing multiple starting points makes it more difficult to ensure that everything fits together, which is, of course, a requirement of system. In particular, we can pose the question with respect to freedom: how can the consequences of independent eternal acts be brought together and integrated within nature and history to form a coherent whole?[5] One advantage of the all-from-one model of grounding is that it makes coordination relatively simple. Because all things flow out from a single starting point, everything can be ordered in advance. But once you introduce multiple starting points and make them radically independent, there is no guarantee that the results will harmonize. Chaos seems inevitable.

The problem can be formulated more concretely in terms of the connection between our two lives: (1) our temporal life as it unfolds within appearance and (2) our "life before this life" (SW VII, 387), the locus of the eternal deed of freedom. As we have seen, Schelling follows Kant in ensuring the radical independence of this deed by placing it outside of time as something "intelligible" or in itself. And part of what it means to be "in itself" is to be without relations to other things.[6] In fact, in the section on the eternal deed, the focus of the discussion is the intelligible essence's self-relation with no mention of other intelligible essences to which it relates or with which it interacts. In chapter 6, we saw that being without relation is also a characteristic of what is in the *Ungrund*, and Schelling even refers to the eternal deed as "acting from the *Ungrund*" in the *Ages of the World* (WA I, 93). In passing, we can note a significant irony here with respect to the principle of sufficient reason. Schelling endorses it because of its integrative function: to deny it would introduce gaps and compromise the "necessary unity of the whole" (SW VII, 383). Moreover, I have argued that Schelling maintains the universality of the principle by making the eternal deed self-grounding. But because the grounding is self-directed, it no longer serves the principle's function of integrating what is grounded within the system. Each eternal deed is an island or, to borrow Spinoza's phrase, a "kingdom within a kingdom" (*imperium in imperio*).[7]

The problem arises when we consider the consequences of the eternal deed in this life, which unfolds in time and in relation. All of our actions in this life are supposed to follow with necessity from our intelligible essence, as determined by the eternal deed. And yet these actions are not isolated phenomena but involve interaction with both nature and other human beings, whose actions are also determined through freedom. How, then, can our actions be coordinated with the actions of other human beings, if they are all determined outside of relation? Moreover, in appearance (under conditions of time), these actions are part of a chain of causality that involves both other human beings and the forces of nature. How is it that what is freely self-determined through the intelligible deed fits perfectly within the complex chain of causality?[8] It is true that Schelling is ambivalent about empirical determinism in general; though he acknowledges it is preferable to introducing randomness in nature, it still belongs to an inferior standpoint (SW VII, 383). Nonetheless, even if the chain of causality is merely a part of appearance, the fact that appearances are perfectly coordinated still requires an explanation.[9]

Schelling himself had drawn attention to this and other problems of coordination in earlier texts—for example, *On the I as Principle of Philosophy* (1795), which he republished in 1809 in the very same volume as the *Freiheitsschrift*. His solution is a preestablished harmony in the absolute, by which freedom and nature are united. But this is significantly different from Leibniz's version of the doctrine, which had involved God coordinating substances (monads) "outside" of him. Instead, Schelling affirms an *immanent* preestablished harmony. By this he means that the harmony is within the absolute: both natural causality and freedom are manifestations of a single ultimate principle, and their coordination is the result of their common origin (SW I, 239–41). In fact, this might be what Schelling has in mind early on in the *Freiheitsschrift* when he interprets the sentence "What is necessary and what is free are one." Its true meaning, according to the first (mediated) account of the copula, is: that which is the essence (*Wesen*) of the moral world is also the essence of nature (SW VII, 342).[10]

But Schelling's most sustained treatment of preestablished harmony is found in the *System of Transcendental Idealism* (1800). It is the central theme of the final divisions of the text, particularly the section on practical philosophy, which culminates in a discussion of providence. As in previous texts, Schelling traces the harmony of independent agents and causes back to their "common source" in "something higher"—absolute identity, which is "the invisible root of which all intelligences are the potencies" (SW III, 600). Even if this provides a basis for explaining the harmony, it seems to come at a cost: a reversion to the all-from-one model of grounding. All independence of free agents would seem to be sacrificed. What appears to be freedom is already decided by the original identity in the absolute.

To determine whether this really is the case (and what recourse Schelling might have in the *Freiheitsschrift*), it is helpful to consider the remarkable metaphor developed in the 1800 *System* (SW III, 602). History is a play in which human agents each have a part to play—and do so freely, acting as they will. Despite the independence of the actors, the play develops rationally toward the goal foreordained by providence. This is because there is a single poet—God—who authors the entire drama. But wouldn't this destroy our freedom, if we are merely actors playing the parts assigned to us? Schelling's answer lies in our precise relationship to God. If God were independent of the drama and us as actors, our freedom would be compromised. Instead, we are "fragments" (*Bruchstücke*) of the divine poet, who reveals himself through our freedom. As a result, we are "co-authors" (*Mitdichter*) of the whole, inventing for ourselves the roles we play. Schelling seems to have the following in mind. Our freedom is not illusory but a reflection of divine freedom: "The absolute acts through that individual intelligence" (SW III, 602). This divine freedom is also *our* freedom, insofar as we are fragments of the absolute. We are therefore co-authors by virtue of our original unity with God, who is author of the whole. Our free acts are fragmented appearances of the original unity, as is the natural causality with which they are in harmony.

Whether one finds this solution satisfying or not, it is clear that the *Freiheitsschrift* gives human beings a more radical independence from God through the eternal deed. In any case, the passage allows us to formulate the problem succinctly in a way that also applies in 1809: the harmony of the whole requires a single author, but freedom requires "co-authors." Any solution depends on formulating how these competing authorships relate to each other. To be sure, this is an underdeveloped theme in the *Freiheitsschrift*, which contributes to its weakness in addressing the problem of coordination. Indeed, one of the curious features of the text is that the account of the eternal deed says practically nothing about its relation to God, while the section on divine freedom and the necessity with which all things follow from God does not directly address the compatibility of this necessity with human freedom (SW VII, 394–98).[11] It is also curious that Schelling does not address the relationship of providence and freedom,[12] even though this is a classic problem in the history of philosophical theology and has such a prominent place in the 1800 *System*.

Though the relationship between human freedom and God's ordering of the world is underdeveloped, I do not agree with Michael Theunissen, who argued in an influential essay that Schelling gradually gives up his intention to account for the "derived absoluteness" of human freedom, affirming in the end an *underived* eternal deed that leaves no room for God as creator.[13] It is true that Schelling says that human beings are "outside the created" by virtue of this deed (SW VII, 386). However, in the same passage he notes that they are "created into the beginning of creation" (SW VII, 385). Though he does not make the connection, I believe we can interpret this in light of the much earlier passage on derived absoluteness, which we treated in chapter 3. God generates the things in themselves—including the intelligible essences of human beings—through a process of begetting (*Zeugung*), which brings them forth without determining what they are. They are derived from God with respect to their generation, but absolute with respect to their essence (SW VII, 346–47).

But where does that leave us with respect to the coordination problem? Even if Schelling does not address it directly, I do not believe that it is in principle insoluble. What is needed is a preestablished harmony that allows for the absoluteness of the eternal deed—which does not seem to be the case for the version found in the 1800 *System*. God would need to act as a mediator between the self-determining intelligible essences and the world order. In fact, it seems as if Schelling already assigns him this role: God yields "the ideas" that were in him to the ground so that they can be raised up to independent life (SW VII, 404).[14] Thus, God's creation of human beings in the world actually unfolds in three stages: (1) the eternal begetting of their intelligible essences (ideas), (2) the transference of these essences to the ground, and (3) raising them up out of the ground as nature and history unfold. It would be possible for a harmony to be "preestablished" at the second or third stages—and thus "after" the eternal deed, which would remain independent of the divine ordering of the world. Establishing harmony might involve selecting from an infinite menu of intelligible essences[15] those that are compatible with each other, the natural order, and the goals of providence. In many ways, this would resemble Leibniz's understanding of creation,[16] although the ideas in the mind of Schelling's God would already be living and self-determining.[17] No doubt there are difficulties with this proposal: it requires that some intelligible essences are never actualized in the world, and it raises additional questions about God's involvement in evil through the process of selection. Nevertheless, it seems to me that something like this account is needed to reconcile God's "authorship" of the world with the co-authorship of human freedom.

The coordination of our absolute freedom and the world order is connected to the more general problem of the relationship between the "two levels" of Schelling's philosophy: the level of the In-itself and "primordial being" (*Ursein*) on the one hand, and the level of appearance and becoming on the other.[18] Of course, the problem is not new to the *Freiheitsschrift* but runs through his earlier writings, with roots in Fichte and Kant. On this score, one could formulate a criticism of Schelling in terms of the unity of system: he maintains a Kantian dualism—and more fundamentally, a Platonic dualism—between the sensible and the intelligible. But this makes impossible the integration needed for a unified system. There is something to this criticism, especially with respect to much of the *Identitätsphilosophie*, which tends to devalue appearance. In the *Freiheitsschrift*, the situation is more complicated, as we have seen. On the one hand, Schelling gives priority to the In-itself in the passages on "primordial being," the eternal deed, and the *Ungrund*, which provides the system with its ultimate unity. On the other hand, the treatise has a new emphasis on the importance of historical becoming—both for the process of revelation and for the personality and life of God, which is the result of this process. Indeed, the fundamental distinction on which so much of the treatise is founded is articulated in terms of "existence," which is the revelation or coming to appearance of what is in itself in the absolute. To be sure, it is not always clear how the two levels relate—or even which we are discussing in a particular passage.[19] Nonetheless, the *Freiheitsschrift* offers a framework for integrating the two in a more satisfactory way, precisely by making condition of the possibility the primary sense of ground. Appearance is not simply derived from the In-itself, but each domain is the conditio sine qua non of the other.[20] Without the In-itself, appearance would not have its "content," that is, its essence and fundamental unity. Without appearance, the In-itself would not be revealed—and it belongs to God's nature to be revealed as a living, dynamic personality. In this way, being and becoming are essentially connected, both part of a circle of presupposition (cf. SW VII, 358).

One could point out other shortcomings of the treatise. Despite his intention to introduce a personal God into his philosophy (cf. SW VII, 412), Schelling does not develop a truly personal relationship between human beings and their creator. This is connected, I believe, with his emphasis on the ontology of revelation over its role as an act of personal communication. Even divine love in the *Freiheitsschrift* is treated primarily as a metaphysical principle, with Schelling only rarely specifying the human being or any other creature as the object of love (cf. SW VII, 363). Moreover, commentators have often drawn attention to the gap between the phenomenological dimensions of human action and the eternal deed. So much of our experience of freedom relates to changing circumstances and the development of our characters—features that are hard to reconcile with an act that decides everything once and for all. Schelling himself mentions the objection that the eternal deed makes repentance, conversion, and self-improvement impossible: these require temporal distance between one's past free act of doing wrong and one's present free act of returning to the good. His answer is that both are included within that eternal deed that constitutes one's essence (SW VII, 389).[21] But this seems unsatisfying: how can one decide in the very same act to do wrong *and* to repent?[22] If we think of the eternal deed as analogous to decisions within our own experience, this is indeed absurd. Schelling's point is, it is not like anything in our experience. This single deed involves enormous complexity, reaching into every corner of our existence. Like other things in the treatise, it is "incomprehensible to the common way of thinking" (SW VII, 386).

One might consider this a weakness; however, it is essentially connected to what I regard as one final strength—something hardly ever discussed by commentators, though it is an undeniable part of the treatise. This is the sense of mystery that pervades the work. The word "mystery" itself only appears a handful of times, most prominently in the expression "mystery of love," which refers to the paradoxical grounding relationship between the two principles in God: each could be for itself, but it is not and cannot be without the other (SW VII, 408).[23] But the language of the treatise continually evokes a sense of mystery, a sense that the ultimate reality is sublime and a little strange, but somehow familiar. A striking example is a line from the passage on formal freedom, "the daring statement of Schelling," as Ralph Waldo Emerson will call it: "There is in every man a certain feeling that he has been what he is from all eternity, and by no means became such in time" (SW VII, 386).[24] In the same section, Schelling refers to a "life before this life" and notes that everything happens at once "in a magic stroke" (SW VII, 387). Much earlier, in the section on creative unity, Schelling calls "derived absoluteness or divinity" the middle term of all philosophy (SW VII, 347). Finally, the descriptions of both the ground of God's existence and the *Ungrund* use language that evokes a sense of wonder, much of it derived from the mystic Jacob Boehme and theosophist Friedrich Christoph Oetinger. The ground is the longing of the eternal One to give birth to itself; it is like a whirling, billowing sea (SW VII, 359; 360). The term *Ungrund*, which comes from Boehme, is introduced haltingly as the name for the absolute, as if Schelling is revealing a secret that can only be expressed imperfectly (SW VII, 406).

Why is this sense of mystery a strength? One might be tempted to regard it as a matter of style that has no direct relevance for the philosophical content of the work. In the case of the *Freiheitsschrift*, however, the style is intended to reflect the nature of reality, which is ultimately mysterious. It also serves to remind the reader that ordinary language and ways of viewing the world are not adequate for understanding the objects of the treatise—freedom, evil, and the nature of God. There is, of course, a long tradition of negative or apophatic theology, which recognizes the limitations of conceiving God in human terms. Though less developed, another line of thought regards evil as a mystery, the *mysterium iniquitatis* (cf. 2 Thessalonians 2:7). And a strong philosophical case can be made that freedom, if it exists, must be something mysterious: *la liberté est un mystère*.[25] In the last chapter, I argued that Schelling anticipates Galen Strawson's argument that ultimate moral responsibility requires the human being to be a *causa sui*—something that cannot be accommodated by a non-mysterious account of freedom. Interestingly, Peter van Inwagen, another analytic metaphysician with little in common with Schelling's approach to philosophizing, also claims that "free will remains a mystery." This is because there are compelling arguments that free will is incompatible with determinism *and* indeterminism, and yet it somehow exists.[26] If Schelling is correct, this is because the usual conceptions of determinism and indeterminism are both wrong: our intelligible essences are self-determined, and so they are neither undetermined nor determined by something else. In any case, in light of the mysterious nature of its objects of inquiry, I would claim that the sense of mystery in the *Freiheitsschrift* is one of its strengths and something that sets it apart from other works of philosophy. Indeed, one could go still further and say that a philosophical account of freedom, evil, and God that does not have a place for mystery is not true to the phenomena.

But if freedom is something mysterious, where does that leave us with respect to a system of freedom? After all, mystery would seem to go beyond what is rationally knowable—and thus beyond what can be integrated within a system of reason. Certainly Schelling would concede that it is impossible to integrate freedom into a system that has a narrow conception of rationality. As we saw in chapter 5, he rejects a one-sided rationalism that reduces everything to the "geometrical understanding" (cf. SW VII, 395) and thus cannot account for evil or the irrational elements in nature. What is needed is the (real) ground of God's existence, which joins with the (ideal) understanding to provide philosophy with a body and soul. I argued that Schelling, instead of rejecting rationalism, advocates a *living rationalism* with a more comprehensive conception of reason: "A system in which reason really recognized itself would have to unify all demands of the spirit as well as those of the heart, and those of the most moral feeling as well as those of the most rigorous understanding" (SW VII, 413). In light of the mysterious elements in the text, I would maintain that Schelling's living rationalism also combines reason with mystery. A system of reason can include what is inaccessible to the understanding and its usual way of knowing, which pulls apart and opposes what is originally one beyond appearances. Thus, what is unfathomable for finite human knowledge can be known from a higher perspective—and Schelling is not shy about claiming to have such a higher perspective, even if it comes in glimpses.

Perhaps no word better captures Schelling's combination of rationalism and mystery than "ground." As we have seen, it is essentially connected to the rationalist elements in the treatise: God as the ultimate ground and principle of unity, the need to explain or find the "ground" of evil, the various forms of the principle of ground, which connect the parts of the system. But the term is also tied to the mysterious elements, such as the accounts of the *Ungrund* and the ground of God's existence, which draw on the language of ground in the mystical tradition. And these rationalist and mysterious currents are united in the phrase "derived absoluteness or divinity," which expresses the mystery of human freedom as a combination of being grounded and being first in the order of grounding. By developing a richer understanding of ground and its various meanings, Schelling offers us a way to resolve this apparent contradiction—and thus bring together rationalism and mystery. No doubt problems remain in his system of freedom; this is perhaps inevitable, given its ambitions and the mysterious nature of its objects. Nonetheless, Schelling has shown us that rethinking ground is the key to the whole enterprise. Only by addressing its meaning and structure can one satisfy the demands of reason while providing a place for the mystery of freedom.

Notes

Introduction

1. McGinn 2005, 84–86.
2. McGinn 2005, 121.
3. GA 42, 3; Heidegger 1985, 2.
4. Translations of the *Freiheitsschrift* are based on the excellent edition of Love and Schmidt (2006), though I freely modify their translation. Translations of other Schelling texts are my own. I cite the page numbers in the edition edited by Schelling's son (SW), since it is more easily accessible than the historical-critical edition, and its pagination is typically included in other editions. The historical-critical edition of the *Freiheitsschrift* was published in 2018 (HKA I/17).
5. HW 20, 444; cf. 453. In both passages Hegel concedes that the treatise is "deeply speculative." For Heidegger's treatment of Hegel's remark, see GA 42, 21–22; Heidegger 1985, 13. See also Schwab 2018, 132–33.
6. GA 42, 169; Heidegger 1985, 98.
7. Hermanni 1994, 18.
8. Gabriel 2015, 96. See Hogrebe 1989. Gabriel also contends that the word "essence" (*Wesen*) in the title refers to the *Ungrund*, thus making it the principal subject of the treatise (Gabriel 2015, 96; Gabriel 2020, 137). I find this line of interpretation unconvincing. It is true that the word *Wesen* refers to the *Ungrund* at important moments in the treatise; however, the opening lines make it clear that the title is referring to the concept of freedom (cf. SW VII, 336).
9. Kosch 2014, 152–53; 158.
10. Theunissen 1965, 179. Cf. "Thinking through the contradiction [of derived absoluteness] is the *intention* of the *Freiheitsschrift*" (180).
11. By *a* problem of ground, I mean a problem that requires for its resolution the sorting out of the different kinds of grounds and the structure of the grounding relations within the system. Thus, the different problems of ground are part of the larger problem of ground: each requires a systematic approach to grounding relations.

12. As we will see in chapter 1, Jacobi identifies a version of the principle of ground as "the spirit of Spinozism" (JW IV/1, 55–56; Jacobi 1994, 187).

13. Cf. "Even at the outset the question of a system of freedom is posed in reference to ground. . . . Everything depends on determining the precise character of this grounding" (Sallis 1995, 222). In fact, the final chapter of Sallis's *Delimitations* gathers together the major themes of the *Freiheitsschrift* under the title "Ground." My project is very much in this spirit.

14. Heidegger, for example, begins his essay "On the Essence of Ground" with the different senses of principle and cause in Aristotle (Heidegger 1949, 5–6).

15. Freedom is the *ratio essendi* of the moral law, and the moral law is the *ratio cognoscendi* of freedom (KpV, AA 5, 4n). For a discussion of Wolff and Crusius in relation to Kant, see Eidam 2000, 4–5.

16. Schelling to Georgii, July 18, 1810 (Plitt II, 220–21). One could also translate *conditio sine qua non* as "necessary condition." I will be using "necessary condition" and "condition of the possibility" interchangeably, because their meanings overlap in most contexts.

17. This model would seem to be included in what Franks calls "Holistic Monism," which he regards as a general commitment of the German Idealists. One thing this position entails is that "the absolute first principle both necessitates its derivatives and is impossible without them" (Franks 2005, 85). To the extent that Schelling rejects the all-from-one model, I would argue that he does not adopt Holistic Monism, even if his position is monistic in other respects.

18. The relationship between the infinite and the finite and the lack of a "transition" between the two is addressed in chapter 3.

19. Krug 1801, 74. For Hegel's dismissive treatment of Krug's challenge, see HW 2, 194–96.

20. This is not to say that the text lacks a clear argumentative structure, which Buchheim has made clear in his analysis of the treatise's organization (Buchheim 2011a, 169–88).

21. Sturma 1995, 150.

22. Bracken (1972, 121–22) has identified an interesting ground-consequence pattern in Schelling's works starting in 1809: the first part of his philosophy provides the logical or historical "ground," the second part provides the consequences, and between the two is placed divine or human freedom, which provides the transition. Bracken regards this as a problem insofar as the ground either determines freedom or renders it redundant, because the second part follows necessarily from the first. My claim is that the problem vanishes if we interpret ground as condition of the possibility.

23. I owe to Peetz (1995, 110–13) the initial inspiration for connecting equiprimordiality to Schelling's thought. Peetz focuses primarily on the relationship between the essence and form of absolute identity and similar structures in Schelling's *Identitätsphilosophie*. Moreover, Freydberg (2008, 23–24, 37) calls attention to the equiprimordiality of the laws of identity and ground, which I

discuss in chapter 3. However, it is my contention that the concept has a much more extensive application within the *Freiheitsschrift*, because it is directly connected to Schelling's rejection of the all-from-one model.

24. Heidegger 2010, 128; Heidegger 2006, 131.
25. See the *Monadology*, §32 (Leibniz 1989, 217).
26. For example, see Gardner 2017, 151–53.
27. Strawson 1994 and Van Inwagen 2000. See the last section of chapter 7 and the conclusion.
28. Vetö 1977, 20.
29. Von Balthasar 1947, 240.
30. These include *Darstellung meines Systems* (1801) (SW VII, 357n), *Lectures on the Method of Academic Study* (1803) (SW VII, 380n), *Philosophy and Religion* (1804) (SW VII, 404n), and *Aphorisms on the Philosophy of Nature* (1806) (SW VII, 408n). In the preface, he notes that *Philosophy and Religion* treats themes belonging to the "ideal side" of philosophy (SW VII, 334).
31. Vetö 1977, 17. The significant work of Rang (2000) is an exception to the relative neglect of the *Identitätsphilosophie*. Rang, however, only occasionally refers to the *Freiheitsschrift*.
32. For a summary of the debate, see Höfele 2019, 103n.
33. In fact, it is explicitly criticized and rejected. See SW VII, 397–98.
34. For a discussion of the "often held view of the failure of the *Freiheitsschrift*," see Hennigfeld 2001, 142.
35. See Bruneder 1958, Brown 1977, and McGrath 2012.
36. For Schelling's later assessment and critique of Boehme and the theosophists, see SW X, 184–89 and GPP 261–66. Schelling describes the theosophists as falling back into a pre-scientific viewing of the source of creation. True science requires understanding, which involves knowing through distinctions and the successive unfolding of elements that are undifferentiated in mystical vision. Though these texts come much later, their methodological considerations apply also to the difference between Boehme's writings and Schelling's thought in the *Freiheitsschrift*, which distinguishes and defines more precisely elements that are blurred in Boehme.
37. Cf. "In the end, all research into common motifs finds its limits in the fact that every independent thinker transforms the motifs that he adopts according to his own fundamental question, and he never simply reproduces a traditional doctrine. With Schelling, this is especially true" (Marx 1984, 92n9).

Chapter 1

1. Works that have a systematic form include the *System of Transcendental Idealism* (1800), *Darstellung meines Systems* (1801), and the *Würzburg System* (1804). By "systematic form" I mean a comprehensive treatment of the whole

or a major part of philosophy, with an order determined by a rigorous method of development (such as demonstration of later propositions from earlier ones).

2. In the most comprehensive exposition of his *Identitätsphilosophie*, the 1804 *Würzburg System*, Schelling orders the parts according to the sequence (1) God, (2) nature, and (3) spirit. He follows the same basic order in the 1810 *Stuttgart Private Lectures*. See Danz 2018.

3. When Schelling uses the word "contradiction" (*Widerspruch*) here, he is not claiming that the two terms are irreconcilable. Instead, they are opposed terms in need of reconciliation, which provides the "driving force" to which he refers in the passage. Cf. the use of the word "contradiction" in the *System of Transcendental Idealism* (SW III, 594). In the preface to the *Freiheitsschrift*, he had identified the opposition between necessity and freedom as the "higher, or rather, the genuine opposition [*Gegensatz*]" and the "innermost center point of philosophy" (SW VII, 333).

4. In what follows, I develop the essential features of system as such, using Schelling's remarks as a guide. For a treatment of the specific structural and methodological features of Schelling's own system during this period, see Danz (2018), who argues that the features of the system in the *Freiheitsschrift* are in continuity with the writings of the *Identitätsphilosophie*.

5. See Rescher 2003.

6. As I indicate below, I do not believe that Schelling is being entirely fair on this point. Jacobi, though rather unfocused in his writing, does have an essential insight into the nature of reason.

7. Schelling goes on to note that Fichte unsuccessfully attempts to achieve unity through a moral ordering of the world. See FW I, 101.

8. Sallis (2005, 11) has given a reading of the Transcendental Dialectic that shows how this movement reflects the older sense of the Greek word λέγειν that means "to gather, to collect": "Λόγος, as the gathering of opposed elements, composes them *all* into *one*, yet without suppressing their mutual opposition."

9. Cf. A 299/B 356. Cf. "The transcendental ideas thus express the peculiar vocation [*Bestimmung*] of reason as a principle of the highest unity of the use of the understanding" (AA 4, 350).

10. One can pose the question: why is it the nature of reason to strive for unity? For Schelling's *Identitätsphilosophie*, the answer has to do with its relationship to absolute identity: reason is the knowledge of absolute identity and of things as expressions of this identity. As we will see in chapter 3, "identity" in Schelling can be understood as "unity."

11. Cf. Heidegger's commentary on the etymology (GA 42, 44–45; Heidegger 1985, 25). See also his general remarks on the concept of system and the historical context of system projects in the modern era (GA 42, 44–59; Heidegger 1985, 25–33).

12. Cf. "The connection [*Zusammenhang*] of the concept of freedom with the whole of a worldview [*Weltansicht*] will always remain the object of a necessary task" (SW VII, 338).

13. In *On the Divine Things and Their Revelation* (1811), Jacobi calls Fichte's *Wissenschaftslehre* the "first daughter of the critical philosophy" and Schelling's *Alleinheitslehre* the "second daughter." Schelling's last substantial publication was a polemic against Jacobi, which quotes extensively from this work. See SW VIII, 23ff. and Jacobi 1811, 117–18.

14. "The two sciences are thus one science, distinguished only by the opposed directions of their tasks" (SW III, 272). "Because nature is a system, there must be a necessary connection, in some principle binding together the whole of nature, for everything that happens or comes about in it" (SW III, 278–79).

15. Though Schelling's understanding of the structure of his philosophy evolves, in the *Freiheitsschrift* he continues to distinguish a real and an ideal part, each forming its own (relatively autonomous) system. In the preface, he claims that the treatise is the first of his writings to present "his concept of the ideal part of his philosophy with complete determinateness" (SW VII, 334).

16. See especially KU §65, AA 5, 372–76; cf. KrV, A 832–33/B 860–61. The discussion of "natural purposes" and the treatment of an intuitive understanding in relation to organic nature would prove especially influential on German Idealism in general and Schelling in particular.

17. Cf. Schelling's *Darstellung meines Systems* (1801): "I will call totality *relative totality* to the extent that the individual exhibits totality in relation to itself—not as if such a totality were not absolute in relation to the individual, but because such a totality is merely relative in relation to the absolute totality" (§42, SW IV, 133).

18. This language recalls Leibniz's monadology. Cf. Schelling's 1804 *Würzburg System*: "Matter itself, as well as every part [of matter] is its own world, microcosm, in which the world at large is copied and reproduced" (SW VI, 385).

19. Schelling also includes self-grounding in his definition of system in the *System of Transcendental Idealism* (1800): "It is assumed as a *hypothesis* that in our knowledge there is a system, i.e., there is a whole that supports itself and harmonizes with itself" (SW III, 353–54).

20. Cf. "*System* means such a whole that supports *itself*, which, enclosed in itself, does not presuppose any ground outside of itself for its movement and its connection" (SW I, 400).

21. Kant says "ungrounded" and "unconditioned," because he claims that the notion of a being that is self-grounding or *causa sui* is unthinkable (cf. AA 1, 394). We will return to this question in chapter 7.

22. Kant often uses the words *Grund* (ground) and *Bedingung* (condition) interchangeably. Cf. A 332/B 389.

23. Although Kant does not connect this principle of pure reason to the principle of ground, there are striking connections between the two. Kant both criticizes the principle of ground (AA 28, 551–52) and reinterprets it as the law of causality within appearance (cf. A 200–201/B 245–46).

24. Cf. "Since, then, the antithesis [of each antinomy] nowhere grants anything first, and grants no beginning that could serve absolutely as the structure's ground, a complete edifice of cognition is—on such presuppositions—entirely impossible. Hence reason's architectonic interest . . . carries with it a natural commendation for the assertions of the thesis" (A 474–75/B 502–3).

25. Introduction to *Ideas on a Philosophy of Nature* (1797, second edition 1803).

26. Schelling also refers to an ideal sense of system when he mentions the connection of the concept of freedom "with the whole of a scientific worldview [*Weltansicht*]" (SW VII, 336; cf. 338). Schelling leaves ambiguous who the knowing subject of the worldview is—God or human beings.

27. Kierkegaard 1992, 109–25.

28. Fichte, for example, draws attention to the difference between the content of a system and its—often imperfect—presentation (cf. FW I, 420).

29. In these writings, reason is not merely *human* reason, as it is for Kant's first *Critique*. When reading Schelling, it would therefore be a mistake to interpret reason's demands for system subjectively and conclude that the requirement of system is merely an imposition on reality (which may or may not be systematic independent of reason).

30. See *Posterior Analytics*, book 1, chapter 2.

31. Kant refers to such a chain of rational inferences (*ratiocinatio polysyllogistica*). One constructs the series upward (from consequences to grounds) through a series of *prosyllogisms* (A 331/B 387–88; AA 9, 133–34).

32. GA 42, 52–53; Heidegger 1985, 30.

33. Particularly in the Platonic school—for example, Proclus's *Elements of Theology*.

34. Fichte 1988, 101.

35. Although Fichte distinguishes system as only one aspect of science (its form, independent of its content—in particular, independent of its groundedness), other philosophers, including Schelling, use the two terms interchangeably: science is precisely the system of knowledge.

36. Fichte 1988, 104.

37. Fichte 1988, 116.

38. See the Schopenhauer passage quoted above. As Hermanni (1994, 144) notes, the principle of ground guarantees the connection of all events, and its denial results in their "atomization."

39. At other points in the treatise, Schelling mentions the existence of irrational and contingent elements, especially in the original formation of nature. In chapter 5, I attempt to reconcile Schelling's conflicting statements on contingency.

40. At least in its traditional formulation as the "principle of sufficient reason." As we will see, Schelling offers alternative versions of the principle of ground that involve other kinds of grounding besides the determinative kind.

41. I should note that there is another possible interpretation of the statements about freedom and necessity in the opening pages of the *Freiheitsschrift*. Beginning with the *Stuttgart Private Lectures* and continuing in the *Ages of the World*, Schelling associates necessity with the real principle and freedom with the ideal principle, referring to their unity as the "identity of freedom and necessity" (cf. SW VII, 424; SW VIII, 239). As we will see in chapters 4 and 5, the dynamic relationship between the two principles is at the heart of the *Freiheitsschrift*. One could therefore interpret Schelling's references to the centrality of the opposition between freedom and necessity as referring to these principles. However, I believe the juxtaposition of the "contradiction of necessity and freedom" and the task of connecting freedom with the whole (SW VII, 338) fits more naturally with my interpretation in terms of the principle of ground, especially in light of Schelling's later statements about the formal concept of freedom (the subject of chapter 7).

42. Cf. Schlegel 1808, 141. In a footnote, Schelling mentions Schlegel after noting that "earlier claims of the kind are well-known" (SW VII, 338n). Polemical remarks targeting Schlegel are found throughout the text, especially at the end. For an excellent treatment of Schlegel's role in the *Freiheitsschrift*, see Whistler 2021.

43. For a discussion of the background of the controversy, see Beiser 1987, 44–91.

44. Schelling to Hegel, February 4, 1795 (Plitt I, 76).

45. This is also the interpretation of Beiser (1987, 83): "The guiding principle behind Spinoza's philosophy, Jacobi tells us, is the governing principle behind all mechanistic or naturalistic philosophy: the principle of sufficient reason."

46. JW IV/1, 55–56; Jacobi 1994, 187. Normally this principle is rendered "ex nihilo nihil fit."

47. JW IV/1, 125–26; Jacobi 1994, 205. "Nothing can come to be from nothing; nothing can return to nothing."

48. Förster (2012, 79–80; 92–93) disputes Jacobi's claim that the principle expresses the spirit of Spinoza's philosophy. As Goethe saw, the principle is mechanical and cuts off intuitive knowledge, which is Spinoza's higher concern.

49. JW IV/1, 63, 65; Jacobi 1994, 190, 191.

50. JW IV/1, 223; Jacobi 1994, 234.

51. JW IV/1, 216–23; Jacobi 1994, 233–34.

52. JW IV/1, 56–57, 172–76; Jacobi 1994, 187–88, 217–18.

53. Note that this is a different claim from the orthodox Christian doctrine that creation is ex nihilo. The latter is meant to deny the Platonic view that God created the world out of preexisting matter. Instead, God posits the world absolutely, without presupposing anything other than God—and in this sense it is ex nihilo. However, creation is not ex nihilo in the sense of lacking a sufficient reason, since God's will is the sufficient reason for the created world.

54. JW IV/1, 56; Jacobi 1994, 188.

55. For a classic discussion, see Thomas Aquinas, *Summa Theologiae*, I, q. 46, a. 1.

56. See SW I, 367; II, 37; IV, 282.

57. Note that Spinoza himself allows for a kind of human freedom—a point that Jacobi himself acknowledges. See JW IV/1, 150-51; Jacobi 1994, 212. But this freedom is not freedom of the will, which Spinoza denies in Part I of the *Ethics* (proposition 32) and the Appendix to Part I.

58. Why does Schelling reject a "compatibilist" position? His full reasons will become clear in chapter 7. External determination does not allow for the ultimate moral responsibility that is required for genuine freedom.

59. Heidegger summarizes the argument thus: "Freedom excludes the recourse to grounding. The system, however, demands the thoroughgoing connection of grounding. A 'system of freedom'—that is like a square circle" (GA 42, 37-38; Heidegger 1985, 21). He also refers to this understanding of system as "geschlossener Begründungszusammenhang" (GA 42, 107; Heidegger 1985, 62).

60. Spinoza defines substance as "what is in itself and is conceived through itself, that is, that whose concept does not require the concept of another thing, from which it must be formed" (*Ethics*, Part I, Def. 3; Spinoza 1994, 85).

61. JW IV/1, 153; Jacobi 1994, 212.

62. George di Giovanni gives an excellent discussion of the implications for individuality in his introductory essay to his translation (Jacobi 1994, 76-77).

63. AT VII, 17; Descartes 1996, 12, emphasis added.

64. Fichte 1988, 104-5.

65. Cf. the early Schelling: "It is a perverted undertaking to want to ground theoretical philosophy through theoretical philosophy. So long as it is only a matter of erecting a philosophical *building* . . . we may be content with such a foundation—just as, if we are building a house, we are content that it stands firm on the earth. But if it is a *system* that we are discussing, the question arises: on what does the earth rest?" (SW I, 399-400).

66. JW IV/1, 75-76; Jacobi 1994, 196.

67. Cf. Schelling's reference in the 1806 *Aphorisms* to scientific form as "an inner organic connection, where every part is of the nature of the whole" (SW VII, 143).

68. See 30b6-c1 of the *Timaeus* (Plato 2001, 61). In his commentary, Schelling cites §65 of Kant's third *Critique*, applying what Kant says about the parts of an organism to Plato's cosmos (T 33).

69. Heidegger makes a somewhat similar point about different meanings of system: "The inner possibility of wavering between jointure [*Füge*] and manipulation and framework always belongs to system, [and] every genuine system always remains threatened by the decline into what is spurious" (GA 42, 45; Heidegger

1985, 26). To a certain extent, one could identify "framework" here with the building metaphor, since the structure is more external and does not arise internally.

70. One could rightly object here that real architects, as artists, do have an idea of the whole in mind, and they cannot simply make additions after their buildings are completed. But I would argue that architecture as art already borrows from the organic model of system, and that art and organic nature are essentially connected—a point confirmed by the structure of Kant's third *Critique*. Cf. Schelling's statement in *Further Presentations* (1802): "The universe is formed in the absolute as the most perfect organic being and as the most perfect work of art" (SW IV, 423).

71. Cf. Jacobi: "It is hard to understand how anyone could have objected to Spinoza that . . . his infinite substance is only an absurd aggregate of finite things. . . . *Totum parte prius esse necesse est* was already a universal principle of Aristotle. . . . Spinoza adheres to this sublime and fruitful principle throughout" (Jacobi 2000, 108–9; Jacobi 1994, 227).

72. This relates to the line cited above from Jacobi, a line that Schelling will quote multiple times in his writings: "There is no transition between the infinite and the finite." In this context this means that the infinite is not part of the grounding series of finite things. Its relationship to the finite is of a different order. We will return to this topic in chapter 3.

73. Cf. this passage from the *Darstellung meines Systems* (1801): "Since all potencies are simultaneous, there is no reason to begin at one or another [of them]" (§44, *Anmerkung*; SW IV, 135).

74. In this respect, he is similar to Leibniz, who has many entry points into his system and also never formulated a definitive statement of his entire system. This is one of many connections between Leibniz and Schelling.

75. Schindler (2012, 199) rightly notes that this line shows "the depth of Schelling's desire not to sacrifice order in the end to freedom."

76. GA 42, 278–79; Heidegger 1985, 161. Other commentators have followed this interpretation. Ohashi (1995, 244) writes that this remark "places the entire preceding investigation in question."

77. In section 1 we saw that there can be "relative systems," which allow for something outside of them. But a relative system is not system in the highest sense, which is demanded by reason.

78. In light of his interpretation of the line quoted above, it is curious that Heidegger writes: "At this stage of the treatise on freedom it is not yet clearly evident to Schelling that precisely positing the jointure of Being as the unity of ground and existence makes a jointure of Being as system impossible" (GA 42, 279; Heidegger 1985, 161). If his interpretation of the above line is correct, it would be nothing other than a statement of this impossibility.

79. For the interpretation of this line, see also Hennigfeld 2001, 119–20. Buchheim (1999, 183–91) interprets the system in the divine understanding to be

the "best condition of all things, to the extent they are in free unity with God." In this sense, evil and history—insofar as evil is a part of history—necessarily fall outside a system of freedom (186–87).

80. Cf. SW VII, 421–22; III, 279; V, 145; V, 399. Freydberg (2008, 89–90) makes this point as well.

81. The reflection of the system of the world in the divine understanding is more explicit in the passage before the line that God is a life. Schelling affirms that all the consequences of self-revelation were foreseen by God—i.e., he has perfect foreknowledge. Within God there is a reflexive image (*Bild*) of everything implicitly contained in his essence. In this image God "ideally actualizes" himself (SW VII, 396–97). The line "God is not a system but a life" therefore means: God is not just this ideal actualization, but he is also *really* actualized. In the line immediately before the statement about God as a life, Schelling also refers to this ideal actualization: "In the divine understanding itself, however, as in primordial wisdom in which God actualizes himself ideally or as archetype, there is only one possible world" (SW VII, 398). See also SW VII, 360–61, where Schelling characterizes the understanding as an "inner, reflexive representation" (*innere reflexive Vorstellung*), in which God is actualized, but only "in himself."

82. See the discussion of the fundamental distinction within God in chapter 4. Schelling does use different language in the *Stuttgart Private Lectures* to articulate the ground of God's existence, but this language is in continuity with what he says in the *Freiheitsschrift*.

83. Heidegger also notes that the language is polemical and the target is the conception of the absolute in idealism (GA 42, 278; Heidegger 1985, 161).

Chapter 2

1. In his late lecture course on the principle, Heidegger refers to its two thousand three-hundred year "incubation period" (Heidegger 1957, 15; Heidegger 1991, 4).

2. This is the passage that introduces the distinction between that-which-exists and the ground of existence (SW VII, 357).

3. It also retains this position in the *Stuttgart Private Lectures* (1810). He states that the principle of his system is expressed in three ways: (1) the principle of absolute identity, (2) the absolute identity of the real and the ideal, and (3) the absolute or God (SW VII, 421–23).

4. Surprisingly little has been written about the statement about the "law of ground," and, to my knowledge, no one has raised the problem I am addressing here. Heidegger and Hennigfeld do not mention the law of ground at all when treating the relevant passage (GA 42, 136–37; Heidegger 1985, 78–79; Hennigfeld 2001, 44–46). Freydberg (2008, 23–24), however, calls attention to the boldness

of Schelling's statement. Marquet (1973, 214–15) has a brief but important discussion of the relationship of the principle of identity to the principle of ground, focusing on the 1801 *Darstellung*, but he does not draw the connection to the passage in the *Freiheitsschrift*.

5. *Monadology*, §§31–32 (Leibniz 1989, 217).

6. See Parkinson 1965, 62. Leibniz seems to have regarded the principles of identity and contradiction as equivalent. For example, see Leibniz 1985, 419.

7. For an overview of this development, see Kahl-Furthmann 1976, especially 110–15.

8. Schelling later identifies this material as part of a "correction of essential concepts that have always been confused, but especially in recent times." The remarks are meant as "an introduction to our genuine investigation" (SW VII, 357).

9. Schlegel 1808, 141. Schelling mentions Schlegel in a footnote (SW VII, 338), but leaves open whether his claim could be interpreted in a way that diverges from Jacobi. He is harsher in his correspondence, interpreting Schlegel's treatment of pantheism as a hidden polemic against his own philosophy (Schelling to Windischmann, May 9, 1809 [Plitt II, 156–57]).

10. Cf. the footnote in the earlier *Aphorisms on the Philosophy of Nature* (1806) where Schelling also discusses the meaning of the sentence *Gott ist alle Dinge* (God is all things) (SW VII, 205n).

11. In a letter from the same year, Schelling refers to his "conviction of the full truth of genuine pantheism" (Schelling to Schubert, May 27, 1809 [Plitt II, 161]).

12. Schelling might seem to reject this doctrine later on: "The concept of immanence is to be set aside completely insofar as [*inwiefern*] thereby a dead containment of things in God is supposed to be expressed" (SW VII, 358). However, the word *inwiefern* should be interpreted as limiting the rejection of the concept to a certain false interpretation of immanence as *dead* containment. Earlier he had described a *living* freedom of things that is compatible with the doctrine of immanence, or the containment (*Begriffensein*) of things in God (SW VII, 346).

13. See Krause 1828, 256.

14. Cooper 2006, 90.

15. This is in contrast to the "existential" use of the word "is." For example: "There is a God."

16. Schelling later includes even tautological propositions, "if they are not to be utterly without meaning" (SW VII, 342).

17. See "Primary Truths" (Leibniz 1989, 31). It is not at all obvious that the copula always expresses the *identity* of subject and predicate. Schelling refers to this as an "assumed explanation [*Erklärung*]" (SW VII, 341).

18. Most of what has been written about Schelling's philosophy of the copula focuses on the account in the *Ages of the World*, which is a development of the first account in the *Freiheitsschrift*. The most influential treatment is that of Hogrebe (1989, 81–83), though I find aspects of his interpretation problematic.

For a synthetic treatment of Schelling's accounts of the copula after the *Freiheitsschrift*, see García 2015.

19. For a more extensive treatment of this account and its wider implications, see Thomas 2014.

20. I believe "auch nur ein unvermittelter Zusammenhang" should be translated "even an unmediated connection," instead of "even *only* an unmediated connection." *Nur* is here a modal particle.

21. In what follows, I focus on the account in the first draft (WA I), but Schelling gives similar explanations of this account of the copula in all three drafts of the *Weltalter*. See WA I, 27–29; WA II, 128–29; SW VIII, 212–15.

22. *Defensio trinitatis per nova reperta logica*, "Defense of the Trinity by Means of New Logical Discoveries" (1669), Leibniz 1875–90, vol. I, 10–16. For a discussion of the context and content of this treatise, see chapter 2 of Antognazza 2007.

23. Schelling uses the word *Band* as a German equivalent of the Latin *copula*. Cf. SW VIII, 213.

24. Schelling also uses Trinitarian language later on in the treatise. For example, he refers to the divine understanding as "the Word" and notes that it is "in the beginning with God" (SW VII, 361), language that echoes the Prologue to John's Gospel. In the same passage, he refers to the "eternal spirit." See Brouwer 2011, 171–75. For a discussion of Schelling's treatment of the Trinity in his later philosophy, focusing on the philosophy of revelation, see O'Regan 2011, 262–65.

25. See Antognazza 2007, 24.

26. See Frank (2014, 135–36; 140–41) for a discussion of the relevance of Schelling's account of the copula for the mind-body problem.

27. "Reduplication" is the term for specifying one of these respects. For an account of "reduplicative identity" in Schelling's philosophical development, see Frank 2014 and Frank 2018.

28. This uniting of different elements in a single substratum recalls the task resolved by the third principle in Fichte's *Wissenschaftslehre*. For Fichte, the principle of ground is the logical principle that corresponds to the third principle. See FW I, 107–11.

29. This movement toward the "substantiation" of the copula is already found in Leibniz and Johann Raue (1610–79), one of Leibniz's sources. The "real copula" includes pronouns that introduce a substance. See Antognazza 2007, 24.

30. GA 42, 129–30; Heidegger 1985, 74–75.

31. Rang (2000, 19) also notes this symmetry in Schelling's account. By contrast, Hogrebe (1989, 81ff.) interprets the account asymmetrically, translating it into predicate logic thus: $Fa \rightarrow (\exists x)(x = a \wedge Fx)$, where $A = a$, $B = F$, and $X = x$. I do not believe this interpretation has an adequate basis in the text: by identifying X and A ($x = a$), the mediating function of X is undermined.

32. As we will see in the third account of the copula, the predicate is also enfolded in the subject. Here again the copula shares features of the subject.

33. In Schelling's dialogue *Clara* (1809–12?) the pastor asks: "In this bodily state is [not] the essence [*Wesen*] of the human being, or what is really human in man [*das eigentlich Menschliche im Menschen*], the soul?" (SW IX, 51).

34. The only instances of the application of *antecedens* and *consequens* to subject and predicate that I have found before Leibniz were in the early modern period—for example, in Petrus Ramus (1555, 72).

35. For this reason, Buchheim's statement that Leibniz used the two pairs of concepts (subject-predicate, antecedent-consequent) as synonyms is not quite correct (2011a, 97, §39).

36. "Principium scientiae humanae" (1685/86?), *Philosophische Schriften* (Leibniz 1999), vol. 4, part A, 671. My translation, emphasis added.

37. Cf. "Primary Truths": "The predicate or consequent is always in the subject or antecedent, and the nature of truth in general or the connection between the terms of a statement, consists in this very thing, as Aristotle also observed" (Leibniz 1989, 31).

38. It may refer to "superiority" or higher "dignity." Elsewhere Schelling notes that there is an inverse relationship between superiority/dignity and priority of potency (SW VII, 427; WA I, 26).

39. A third moment where the question of priority arises is in the discussion of the *Ungrund*. The *Ungrund* is before the ground and before that-which-exists (SW VII, 406).

40. *Metaphysics*, book 5, chapter 11. As Ross notes (Aristotle 1924, 317), there is another classification of the senses of prior in the *Categories* (chapter 12), and Aristotle mentions various senses of priority in passages scattered throughout his work.

41. Cf. SW VII, 427–28; VIII, 247. We will discuss the doctrine of potencies in chapter 4.

42. Cf. SW XIII, 55, 127, 161. *Prius* is the neuter form of the Latin word *prior*.

43. *Categories*, chapter 12, 14^a 30–34.

44. *Categories*, chapter 12, 14^b 11–13.

45. We also say that a conclusion "follows from" the premises: if the premises are true, the conclusion must be true. Here the word "follows" indicates a *logical necessity*—just as the word "follows" in the case of causality indicates a causal determination.

46. Buchheim sees a connection here with Hegel's theory of the "speculative sentence" in the preface to the *Phenomenology of Spirit*, according to which the form of the sentence expresses a movement of thought. Such a movement thus requires a difference between subject and predicate (2011a, 97, §40). See PhG §§61–62, HW 3, 59–60.

47. "Principium scientiae humanae" (1685/86?), *Philosophische Schriften* (Leibniz 1999), vol. 4, part A, 671.

48. Leibniz 1989, 31.

49. *Categories*, chapter 5, 2ᵃ 11ff. Cf. *De Interpretatione*, chapter 3, 16ᵇ 10ff.; *Categories*, chapter 2, 1ᵃ 24ff.

50. *Metaphysics*, book 5, chapter 11, 1019ᵃ 3ff.

51. According to the doctrine of immanence, what is grounded by God is "something contained within him" (*ein in ihm Begriffenes*). SW VII, 346.

52. See "Primary Truths" (Leibniz 1989, 31). See also Leibniz 1903, 518-19. For a discussion of how a priori proof works (through finite or infinite analysis), see Adams 1994, 25-30.

53. Heidegger 1984, 54.

54. At the end of the *Stuttgart Private Lectures* (1810), Schelling observes that the end point of creation comes back to the beginning, "only that now everything is explicitly what it was before [only] implicitly" (SW VII, 483-84).

55. Schelling also refers to the "unfolded copula" or the "unfolded bond" in the same sense. Cf. SW VII, 64.

56. For the connection between the word "*actu*" and appearance (*Erscheinung*), see SW VI, 390, 391 (§§197-98). The term already appears in the *Darstellung meines Systems* (1801).

57. Though Schelling here refers to the *concept* of God, what he says applies to God as well, because of the parallelism between things and concepts in Spinoza. Cf. Part I of the *Ethics*: "D3: By substance I understand what is in itself and conceived through itself, that is, that whose concept does not require the concept of another thing" (Spinoza 1994, 85). Cf. Part II, Proposition 7: "The order and connection of ideas is the same as the order and connection of things" (119).

58. Later on in the same essay, Schelling uses "affirm" in apposition to "posit" (SW I, 220).

59. The German words *setzen* and *aufheben* are literal translations of the Latin *ponere* and *tollere*. These words literally mean "to put down" and "to raise up," but when applied to logic, they mean "to affirm" and "to deny." Thus, *modus ponens* is an argument form that involves *affirming* the antecedent of a conditional; *modus tollens* is an argument form that involves *denying* the consequent of a conditional. Of course, the word "thesis" comes from the Greek word τίθημι, which has the same concrete literal meaning as *setzen* and *ponere*.

60. For example, Schelling writes: "The only being [*Sein*] that is posited [*gesetzt*] through this principle [A = A] is that of *identity itself*, which is thus posited completely independent of A as subject and A as predicate" (§6, SW IV, 117).

61. Around this time Schelling also begins to use the Latin cognate *Position*, which I translate as "positing," but which Schelling uses as a synonym of "affirming." Cf. "The absolute *positing* [*Position*] of the idea of God is in fact nothing else than the absolute negation of the nothing, and as certain as reason

eternally negates the nothing . . . so is it certain that reason affirms the *All*, and thus God exists [*ist*] eternally" (SW VI, 166).

62. For a discussion of Schelling's identification of knowledge with affirmation, see Rang 2000, 41–42. Rang traces this claim to Spinoza's doctrine of the unity of the will and the intellect. To know something involves affirming it as true.

63. Schelling moves very quickly from (1) talking about the subject and object of knowledge to (2) talking about the subject and predicate of sentences. It is not at all obvious that the relationship is the same. The basis for this move from (1) to (2) seems to be the unique character of the law of identity (A = A). Because the principle expresses self-knowledge, the subject of the sentence (A) is also the subject of self-knowledge (A). Thus, because the absolute is self-affirming in its self-knowledge, and the absolute is both subject and predicate in the principle of identity, in this law the subject affirms the predicate. But Schelling claims that the subject affirms/posits the predicate in other sentences as well: "How do subject and predicate relate to each other? The predicate is only posited through the subject." He gives the example, "The circle is round." "I posit round only to the extent that *circle* is posited" (SW VI, 146). Because the subject contains the predicates within itself, positing the subject also involves positing its predicates.

64. However, we will see that the word "evil" has different senses in the *Freiheitsschrift*, and it sometimes refers to what might be more precisely designated "potential evil"—the activated selfhood that is overcome by the good. Cf. "Thus, one can say that the good contains evil within itself. A good, if it does not have an evil overcome within itself, is not a real, living good" (SW VII, 467; cf. SW VII, 400). On the senses of evil, see chapter 5, section 2 below.

65. Not all of these sentences are strictly in the form S is P, e.g., "The soul is one with the body" (SW VII, 342). Nevertheless, one can fairly easily translate these exceptions into this form.

66. If correct, this would require significant translation for sentences that are not obviously in the form S is P. In particular, it would be challenging to translate conditional sentences (in the form "If A, then B") into that form.

67. Cf. "The absolute is the ground and the principle of all truth" (SW VI, 173).

68. Cf. "Absolute identity is in the individual under the same form as it is in the whole" (§39, SW IV, 132).

Chapter 3

1. Already in the 1801 *Darstellung* Schelling had noted that the being (*Sein*) of absolute identity is posited through the law of identity (§6, SW IV, 117). See Marquet 1973, 214.

2. Cf. "For reason, opposition is just as original and true as unity: only by grasping both in the same way, and itself as one, does reason know living identity" (SW VII, 52). I believe this sentence should be interpreted to mean that opposition is just as original as the unity *opposed to it*, i.e., the lower unity. Reason grasps both "in the same way" and itself "as one." This means there is a higher unity that holds unity and opposition together within it. This would be similar to Hegel's description of absolute identity in the *Differenzschrift* ("the identity of identity and non-identity," HW 2, 96), and Schelling's formula in *Bruno* ("the unity of unity and opposition," SW IV, 236).

3. For a brief discussion of the debate with bibliographical references, see Höfele 2019, 103n.

4. As mentioned in chapter 2, Schelling refers to the principle in the 1794 *Formschrift* (SW I, 102–4). He also refers to it in one of the *Weltalter* fragments, but its meaning in that context is tied to the grounding relation among potencies, which does not seem to fit with the reference in the *Freiheitsschrift*. The principle of ground states "that one and the same thing can be something and also its opposite if it is, as the first thing, ground of itself as the second" (WA II, 175; cf. SW VIII, 301). The grounding relation among potencies is treated in the next chapter.

5. One may object: the statement "God is the ground of all things" does not really attribute "being grounded" *universally* because it does not say anything about whether God is grounded. This is true. However, God also has an ambiguous status vis-à-vis the traditional principle of sufficient reason. Sometimes he is included within the principle's application (as self-grounding, *causa sui*). Sometimes he is exempted (as uncaused first cause). We will return to this all-important question when discussing the concept of *causa sui* in chapter 7. In any case, we will see below that it is through God's self-affirmation (or self-grounding) that he grounds or affirms all things.

6. In *Bruno* (1802), the title character asks: "Do you not see that *the unity of the finite and the infinite* is also contained in that which we are calling the unity of intuiting and thinking, and vice versa? And thus, under different expressions we have made one and the same principle the highest?" (SW IV, 242, emphasis added).

7. Emphasis added. In the original, the phrase that is emphasized is "the eternal copula . . . in and for itself."

8. This is similar to what Marquet (1973, 214) says about the implicit relationship between the principles of identity and ground in the 1801 *Darstellung*: the former contains the content of the latter "potentially and in embryo."

9. For example, the law of identity also expresses the absolute identity of the real and the ideal. Cf. SW VII, 422.

10. SW VII, 59; 203. In *Bruno* (1802), however, Schelling had identified "the eternal" as the third potency, which unites the first two (the finite and the

infinite) (SW IV, 229). Elsewhere he warns against identifying the absolute with the eternal, if the latter is considered to be a potency (SW VII, 186-87).

11. Cf. "Thus, the *copula* or absolute identity in each thing is the *eternal*, through which the thing is immediately dissolved [*ausgelöst*] into the creating substance" (SW VII, 204).

12. Cf. "The bond, if it is a bond of unity and multiplicity, is necessarily again the *copula of itself* and that which is bound together from the one and the many; and only *this* bond is the effective and completely real absolute identity" (SW VII, 60). Emphasis added to the phrase "of itself."

13. Cf. "It is formalism to present everything as a series, superficial determination without necessity; instead of concepts we find formulas" (HW 20, 444). Even if Schelling does not always show how this formal variation is adequate to the richness of reality, this does not mean that it is impossible for the latter to arise out of the former. As an analogy, one might consider binary code, which consists entirely of 0 and 1, but which is capable of encoding incredibly rich phenomena.

14. This formulation recalls the doubly infinite character of what follows from God in Spinoza. Cf. Spinoza's *Ethics*, Part I, Proposition 16: "From the necessity of the divine nature there must follow infinitely many things in infinitely many modes, (i.e., everything which can fall under an infinite intellect)" (Spinoza 1994, 97).

15. From the essay "On the Relation of the Ideal and the Real in Nature," attached to the 1806 revision of *On the World Soul*. This is why it appears in SW II, despite its later date.

16. Cf. Schelling's reference to *Wesen* in the 1806 *Aphorisms*: "For reason, the affirmation of infinite unity and totality is not contingent, but reason's entire essence [*Wesen*], which is expressed in the law . . . of identity" (§38, SW VII, 147).

17. Emphasis added to "immediately" (*unmittelbar*) in each of these statements.

18. JW IV/1, 56–57; Jacobi 1994, 187–88.

19. Cf. In *Treatises in Elucidation of the Idealism of the Wissenschaftslehre* (1796–97), Schelling repeats the claim that there is no transition and associates this with the "most original unification of infinity and finitude" (SW I, 367).

20. According to Schindler, Schelling is critical of Spinoza in this passage because he cannot account for the transition and thus denies the existence of the finite (Schindler 2012, 183). However, Schelling explicitly states that such a transition is impossible for *all* philosophical systems; Spinoza's solution of an immanent unity also provides the outlines of Schelling's solution.

21. The terms "leap" (*Sprung*) and "fall" (*Abfall*) appear in *Philosophy in Religion* (1804) in the section on the origin of finite things from the absolute (SW VI, 38ff.). This seems to confirm the need to go beyond the absolute to reach the finite. In my interpretation of this text, Schelling is still affirming the immediate identity of the infinite and the finite. The question is how the finite comes to be (falsely) abstracted from the infinite in appearance and reflection.

22. See Beiser 2002, 573–76. Snow's treatment of the issue is subtle, but she also assumes the need for difference to emerge out of unity: "As was the case in the identity philosophy, Schelling must account for how this groundless identity utterly spontaneously divides into two equally eternal beginnings. . . . The emergence of difference out of primordial unity is *the* defining question for the rest of Schelling's philosophical life" (1996, 177).

23. For a discussion of this view of Schelling's development, see Danz 2018, 98–99. I agree with Danz that this view rests on a misunderstanding.

24. One can, of course, object that Schelling's solution does not solve the problem it was introduced to solve. But one cannot simply cite the problem itself as an objection to the *Identitätsphilosophie* without considering the *Identitätsphilosophie* as an attempt to answer the problem.

25. Cf. "That an emergence of the absolute from itself . . . is absolutely unthinkable is . . . a further axiom of the true philosophy" (SW IV, 390).

26. Creation is based on a deed (*Tat*) of an absolutely free spirit, who "remains the same whether he does the deed or not" (GPP 115). Spirit is "what is free to express itself or not to express itself" (GPP 112).

27. See the discussion of divine freedom and necessity in chapter 5, section 2.

28. This might be considered the "real" formulation of the principle, since it is expressed in terms of being, not truth. The objects of grounding are *things*, not propositions. Alternatively, one could formulate the principle in terms of the truth of propositions: "Every true proposition is grounded."

29. Leibniz 1989, 210.

30. In Heidegger's treatment of the principle in Leibniz, he also notes that "the principle of ground is valid to the extent that God exists" (1957, 55). Moreover, he claims that there is a circle here, because God only exists to the extent that the principle of ground is valid. However, the latter claim seems to confuse the reason for knowing that God exists (*ratio cognoscendi*) for the reason for God's existence (*ratio essendi*).

31. Aristotle, *Physics*, book 1, chapter 1, 184^{a}16ff.

32. Aristotle, *Nicomachean Ethics*, book 1, chapter 4, 1095^{a}30–1095^{b}1.

33. Cf. "Lift from the universe whatever piece you like and recognize that it is of infinite fertility [*Fruchtbarkeit*] and impregnated with the possibilities of all beings [*Wesen*]" (SW IV, 400).

34. Kant claimed to have provided a "proof" for the principle of sufficient reason in his second analogy of experience, which establishes the principle of causality (KrV, A 200–201/B 246).

35. Parkinson writes that Leibniz means "nothing is without a *sufficient* reason" even when he says, "nothing is without a reason," and that the dropping of the adjective "seems to have no philosophical significance" (Parkinson 1965, 63–64). However, as Mercer (2001, 74–75) notes, the adjective makes explicit what is meant by *ratio* in the fullest sense (*ratio plena*), which is a complete or

sufficient reason of a thing that does not itself require a *ratio* of the same type.

36. "The Principles of Nature and Grace, Based on Reason" (Leibniz 1989, 210).

37. Cf. the parallel passage in the 1806 *Aphorisms* (SW VII, 174).

38. I borrow this phrase from the title of Wippel 2011. I should note that Schelling's position on this question changes quite dramatically in his late philosophy. Reason's perspective (negative philosophy) is no longer sufficient to explain why things actually exist (cf. GPP 222–23). Something beyond reason is needed: the free act of creation.

39. In his late Berlin lectures, Schelling connects the human need for philosophy to the question "why is there something rather than nothing?" It is "the last and most general question," which only philosophy can answer (SW XIII, 7–8). For a discussion of this passage and an overview of Schelling's treatment of the ultimate why question at various stages, see Bruno 2020, 187–91.

40. Though not completely absent: "Mere existence [*Dasein*], without regard to its kind and form, must appear as a miracle to the one who beholds it, and it must fill the mind [*Gemüth*] with astonishment [*Staunen*]" (SW VII, 198).

41. Though only an appendix, this text contains an abundance of rich material, including a summary of Jacobi's critique of reason. Schelling clearly knew the text, having cited a line from it in an earlier work (SW VII, 148–49). For a discussion of Jacobi's critique of reason, including his distinction between ground and cause, see Sandkaulen 2000.

42. Giordano Bruno is one of Jacobi's sources for this distinction. In Appendix I, he paraphrases extensive passages from Bruno, including a passage where he distinguishes "principle" from "cause": "*Principle* is the *inner* ground of a thing, the source of its possible existence; *cause* is the *external* ground of a thing, the source of its actual, present existence" (JW IV/2, 6). Cf. Bruno 1998, 36–37.

43. See *Ethics*, Part I, Propositions 15, 16, 33 (Spinoza 1994, 94–97, 106–9).

44. JW IV/2, 146; Jacobi 1994, 372.

45. For a somewhat different response to Jacobi, see the discussion in Schelling's 1833 lecture *Grundlegung der positiven Philosophie* (GPP 331–32). There he argues that God must be ground in order to be cause, and vice versa.

46. It is noteworthy that Schelling does not use the other German word for independence, *Unabhängigkeit*. The latter word, like the English word "independence," is formed by added a privative prefix to the word *Abhängigkeit*, "dependence." In contrast, *Selbständigkeit* expresses a positive meaning: the condition of "standing on one's own."

47. I would argue that Schelling often uses *Wesen* in such a way that it combines aspects of both (1) essence (universal) and (2) being (particular). Insofar as the *Wesen* pertains to a particular thing, it has the second sense. But insofar as it concerns "what a thing is" and thus is the *essence* of the individual thing, it has the first sense.

48. This would be similar to the "individual notion of a thing" in Leibniz, which includes everything that can truly be said of it. See his *Discourse on Metaphysics*, §13.

49. Buchheim (2011a, 101, §55) notes that Schelling is referring to Leibniz's "Defense of the Trinity," a text that is also in the background of his treatment of the copula, as we saw in chapter 2.

50. See Kant's *Logic* (AA 9, 115), where he also gives the Latin *terminus medius*.

51. See also SW VIII, 188; XI, 270; XIII, 340. In the *Ages of the World*, Schelling emphasizes the importance of "intermediate concepts" (*mittlere Begriffe*) like non-being: they are the only truly explanatory concepts in all science (SW VIII, 286; WA I, 44–45). I thank an anonymous reviewer for drawing my attention to the nuances of the word *Mittelbegriff*.

52. Fichte 1988, 109. For Schelling's early treatment of these principles, see SW I, 96–111.

53. Cf. the opposition between being and becoming later in the treatise (SW VII, 403) where being (*Sein*) is clearly eternal. On the ambiguity of *Sein* in the *Identitätsphilosophie*, see Rang 2000, 95–103.

54. As we will see, the essence of each human being is determined by an eternal act of self-grounding, which precedes the coming to be of the human being in time.

55. In chapter 2, I noted that Schelling sometimes uses the language of affirmation to articulate the self-positing of the I. He also uses the word *Position* as a synonym for *Affirmation* (cf. SW VII, 159–64).

56. Snow (1996, 169) also connects self-affirmation to the intelligible deed that determines one's essence.

57. I owe the discovery of this passage to Hennigfeld. For a brief discussion of *Zeugung*, see Hennigfeld 2001, 44–45. Schelling also discusses *Zeugung* in the *Weltalter* (WA I, 56).

58. Cf. Schelling's earlier statement that freedom must be "one of the ruling center points of the system" (SW VII, 336).

59. Heidegger refers to a system of freedom as a "square circle" (GA 42, 38; Heidegger 1985, 21). Theunissen claims that the "main problem" of the *Freiheitsschrift* is explaining how the absoluteness of freedom is not absolute but posited (1965, 179).

60. Being contained is in fact a specific kind of dependence. Thus, we can say that Schelling discusses dependence in general before treating a more specific kind of dependence, viz. containment.

61. The "ideas" play an important role in the *Identitätsphilosophie* as well as the *Weltalter* drafts (1811–15), though Schelling only explicitly mentions them once in the *Freiheitsschrift* (SW VII, 404). An idea is the unity of a particular

form with the absolute (SW IV, 394) or the essentiality (*Wesenheit*) of a thing as grounded in the eternity of God (SW VI, 183). The ideas are the true "things in themselves." At the end of the present passage in the *Freiheitsschrift*, Schelling writes: "God intuits the things in themselves" (SW VII, 347). This is perhaps a reference to the doctrine of ideas developed in the preceding years. See also WA I, 31; WA II, 162–63; SW VIII, 289–90.

62. In other contexts, Schelling refers to begetting to explain the relation among the ideas. Cf. *Philosophy and Religion* (1804): "Even the ideas are necessarily productive in the same way; even they produce only what is absolute, only ideas. . . . This is the true transcendental theogony" (SW VI, 35; cf. II, 189). I owe the discovery of these passages to Buchheim (2011a, 101, §56).

63. For a discussion of Schelling's dynamic theory of life, see chapter 5, section 4.

64. This is also connected to the structure of self-affirmation that we discussed above. In the *Würzburg System*, Schelling notes that self-affirmation is an act of self-knowing (SW VI, 168–70). In other words, the act of affirming all things (through his self-affirmation) is at the same time an act of knowing all things (through his self-knowledge).

65. Schelling summarizes this in the *Würzburg System* (1804): "All merely finite representation [*Vorstellen*] is either *real* or merely *ideal*. If it is real, then what is known appears as the *prius*, and what knows appears as the *posterius*. If it is ideal, no [independently existing] *object* corresponds to the representation" (SW VI, 170).

66. Cf. KrV, B 72; KU §§76–77, AA 5, 402–8. For an extensive discussion of the relationship between the human cognitive powers and an intuitive understanding, see Sallis 2005, chapter 1.

67. Cf. the section "Phenomena and Noumena" in the first *Critique*, A 255–56/B 310–12.

68. Cf. Pinkard 2002, 196n.

69. In the 1801 *Darstellung meines Systems*, Schelling writes, "Through all other laws [besides the law of identity] . . . nothing is determined as it is in reason or in itself, but only as it is for reflection or in appearance" (SW IV, 117).

70. Heidegger emphasizes Schelling's earlier statement that many are brought to the viewpoint of immanence "through the most lively feeling of freedom" (SW VII, 339). See GA 42, 118–19; Heidegger 1985, 68–69. However, even if the *feeling* of freedom requires that one accept the viewpoint of immanence, this does not yet show *how* freedom requires immanence.

71. As Schelling notes in the *Darstellung meines Systems* (1801), quantitative difference—the condition of appearance—is only possible outside of absolute identity (§25, SW IV, 125).

72. Habermas 1954.

Chapter 4

1. For the relationship between the formal and real concepts of freedom, see chapter 7, section 1.

2. According to Buchheim (1996), the principle of ground has an even more essential connection to Schelling's distinction: the latter has its origins in the principle of ground in Leibniz. His argument, however, is based on a non-deterministic reading of Leibniz's version of the principle. I do not believe this interpretation of Leibniz is correct, and it goes against the consensus of Leibniz scholars, who regard him as a determinist. See Adams 1994.

3. According to Heidegger, Schelling's distinction constitutes the basic structure (*Grundgefüge*) or determination of "self-contained beings." Heidegger thus labels the distinction the "jointure of Beyng" (*Seynsfüge*) (GA 42, 188; Heidegger 1985, 108).

4. Jörg Jantzen identifies three of the four in his careful parsing of the distinction, but he does not recognize that *Existierendes* and *Existenz* are distinct for Schelling (1995, 77–79). This mistake is common among Schelling commentators. We will examine its consequences below.

5. Buchheim identifies "what a thing really is" as the traditional Greek sense of *Wesen*, but he adds that this is an "ensemble of defining characteristics" (2006, 184). I would say that *Wesen* in this context lies at the ground of any possible characteristics and therefore is at a deeper level than their ensemble.

6. Schelling also uses the word *Wesen* in connection to X in the account of the copula in the *Weltalter* (SW VIII, 213). See Thomas 2014, 26–27.

7. Schelling uses the phrase "God considered absolutely" in a different sense in the *Stuttgart Private Lectures*. There this phrase refers to the union or identity of that-which-exists (the ideal principle) and the real principle (SW VII, 430). This union is what Schelling calls "absolute existence" in the *Freiheitsschrift* (SW VII, 395). However, in a letter to Georgii (July 18, 1810), Schelling refers to the ideal principle (= A) or "that-which-is" (*das Seiende*) as "God in the eminent sense" (Plitt II, 220). This corresponds to his usage of "God considered absolutely" in the *Freiheitsschrift*.

8. Cf. the similar formulation in the *Stuttgart Private Lectures* (1810), SW VII, 458. See also the passage in the dialogue *Clara*: "*Clara*: how often have I heard you say that everything is part of [*gehöre zu*] God, and nothing is outside of God? *Pastor*: Of course—similarly, much is part of us that nonetheless isn't *we ourselves*" (SW IX, 74).

9. See chapter 4, "Die Deutung des Internen Dualismus," in Hermanni 1994, 85–98.

10. In an illuminating footnote, Schelling writes: "This is the only correct dualism, namely that which at the same time permits a unity" (SW VII, 359n). The sentence that is footnoted is the one that describes the ground as that which

is in God but not God himself. Cf. Schelling to Windischmann, June 17, 1809 (Plitt II, 164).

11. In the account of the unfolding of creation, Schelling writes: "Each being [*Wesen*] having emerged in nature . . . has a dual principle in itself which, however, is basically but one and the same considered from both possible sides" (SW VII, 362). This would mean that the two terms of the distinction are *sides* of a single being.

12. Cf. "The one being [i.e., the *Ungrund*] divides itself into two beings [*Wesen*] in its two ways of acting" (SW VII, 409).

13. I therefore do not fully agree with Krings's statement that the principles are "not metaphysical entities but transcendental-logical categories" (1995, 178–79).

14. One has to be careful when interpreting the meaning of "will" in Schelling. In the *Freiheitsschrift*, he famously states that "in the final and highest judgment there is no other being than willing" (SW VII, 350). Here willing does not refer to a blind impulse but the fundamental act of self-positing or self-affirming (cf. SW II, 362). When referring to the ground as will, he notes that it is only will in the fullest sense *with* the understanding (SW VII, 359)

15. Cf. the discussion of "the principle of my system" at the start of the *Stuttgart Private Lectures* (1810) (SW VII, 421–23).

16. Buchheim makes a similar point when he says that "ground of existence" and "that-which-exists" refer to *roles* something plays. However, he specifies that these are roles that the underlying *Wesen* plays (2006, 184–85). This is true, but one should not overlook the fact that the phrases designate principles that cannot be reduced to the roles to which these phrases refer.

17. Hermanni 1994, 85.

18. After the 1801 *Darstellung*, Schelling does refer to the "ground of reality" in the following passages: SW IV, 416; IV, 456; VI, 250–51; VI, 261; VI, 266; VI, 386.

19. Tilliette's assessment is more measured: "It is improbable that this distinction possessed at the time [1801] that significance that it would later receive [in the *Freiheitsschrift*]" (2004, 205).

20. Kosch is an exception, but she leaves out all reference to existence in her account of the distinction (2006, 98ff.).

21. Cf. "For this reason, as duality comes to be in the non-ground, love comes to be as well, linking that-which-exists (that which is *ideal*) with the ground" (SW VII, 408, emphasis added).

22. "But if the duality is destroyed through separation, the word, or the ideal principle, subordinates itself, and the *real principle* that has become one with it, communally to spirit" (SW VII, 405, emphasis added).

23. It seems strange that what is (a) the ground of existence in the *Freiheitsschrift* becomes (b) simply being or existence in subsequent texts. In his correspondence with Eschenmayer, Schelling explains that there are multiple senses of existence in play: Existence can be (1) pure existence, in which case it

is not different from the ground of existence. Or it can be (2) existence as the whole, which includes *both* the ground and that-which-exists. This is the sense of existence in the phrase "the ground of existence" (SW VIII, 164). We will discuss existence in more detail below.

24. Cf. "[The ground is] a being indeed inseparable, yet still distinct, from [God as that-which-exists]" (SW VII, 358).

25. Schelling associates the ground with the real side of philosophy in his criticism of Spinoza: his system only grasps one side of the absolute, "namely the real one or the extent to which God functions only in the ground" (SW VII, 397).

26. In the preface, Schelling claims that this treatise "puts forth [the] concept of the ideal part of philosophy with complete determinateness" (SW VII, 334).

27. In this section, Schelling sometimes uses the words "realism" and "idealism" to refer to historical instances of the two kinds of philosophy, which are one-sided. At other times, he understands "realism" and "idealism" as *potentially* adequate sides of philosophy, which need each other. This is the sense in the quotation cited below.

28. For a discussion of Schelling's appropriation of the *Timaeus* in his early commentary and the *Freiheitsschrift*, see Sallis 1999, 154–67. Sallis identifies "Plato's matter" with the χώρα (158).

29. Plato 2001, 79–80. Schelling quotes and comments on this line in his 1794 commentary (T 50).

30. Sallis 1999, 164–65.

31. 68e–69a (Plato 2001, 104). This same passage appears as a motto in one of Schelling's notebooks from 1792 (though added later). For a transcription of the notebook, see Franz 1996, 283–305 (the motto is at 284). For a discussion of the connection between *Bruno* and Schelling's early Plato studies, see Franz 1996, 262–69.

32. In the *Further Presentations*, published the same year (1802), Schelling refers to light as the "divine principle" and gravity as the "natural principle" (SW IV, 421). In the *Freiheitsschrift*, he draws an analogy between the two principles in God and light and gravity (SW VII, 358).

33. There is, however, an ambiguity in the meaning of "existence," discussed below.

34. Schelling had used both terms for the third potency in previous writings. The meaning of "indifference" and its relation to identity are problematic, and we will discuss its meaning in more detail below and in chapter 6.

35. For an exception, see Schwenzfeuer 2012, 253–57.

36. He connects potency and ground in his 1812 polemic: "How else can God lower himself but by making *himself*—i.e., a part (potency) of himself—into the *ground*, so that creatures are possible and we have life in him?" (SW VIII, 71).

37. For an excellent discussion (and qualified defense) of the concept of potency in Schelling's early *Identitätsphilosophie*, see Berger and Whistler 2020, 94–116.

38. Cf. "Absolute identity grasps all potencies, without itself being one of them" (SW VI, 213). Schelling also defines the potencies as "ideal determinations" (*ideale Bestimmungen*) or ideal forms of one and the same essence (SW IV, 416).

39. Cf. "In the initial B the A^3 also lies enfolded" (SW VII, 451).

40. In some works—for example, *Bruno* (1802)—Schelling refers to the three potencies as (1) the finite, (2) the infinite, and (3) the eternal. See also SW VII, 186–87n.

41. This diagram with the three points is based on the diagram in Schelling's *Aphorisms as an Introduction to the Philosophy of Nature* (SW VII, 184n2).

42. This relativity reappears in a later passage: just as there is a ground for the birth of light, there must be a ground for the birth of spirit that is "just as much higher than the first [ground] as spirit is higher than the light" (SW VII, 377).

43. Schelling in fact cites this passage in a footnote in the *Freiheitsschrift* (SW VII, 358n3).

44. As we will see in the next section, Schelling later comes to distinguish existence from that-which-exists, and being (*Sein*) from that-which-is (*das Seiende*). However, in this passage—and perhaps now and again in later texts—Schelling does not seem to distinguish *Sein* from *Seiendes*.

45. "But the words also determine what is outside of nature. Nature, they claim, is everything that (from the highest standpoint of existing [*seienden*] absolute identity) lies *beyond* its *absolute*—i.e., subjective—being" (SW VIII, 26).

46. Cf. "The ego-ness is only the potency or exponent under which the divine essence is posited" (SW VII, 440).

47. For the historical background and a discussion of Schelling's critical distance from the over-mathematization of potency, see Berger and Whistler 2020, 94–97, 110.

48. In Stuttgart he also distinguishes the "higher" and "lower" potencies with respect to "dignity" (*Dignität*): "According to dignity, the ideal is higher than the real" (SW VII, 427; cf. 434).

49. For other instances of the same language in the *Freiheitsschrift*, see SW VII, 390, 398, 404.

50. A handful of commentators acknowledge the distinction between existence and that-which-exists. For example, see Schwenzfeuer 2012, 252–53, 260; Hermanni 1994, 87–88. To my knowledge, however, no one has fully developed the consequences.

51. Vetö notes that Schelling first thematizes this distinction in 1812 and that he does not make the distinction in the 1801 *Darstellung meines Systems*. See Vetö 1977, 167–68.

52. There is, however, an ambiguity in the meaning of existence that is addressed below.

53. Cf. "Existenz eben ist tätige Einung eines bestimmten Seienden mit einem bestimmten Sein" (WA II, 131).

54. That-which-exists (*das Existierende*) in the *Freiheitsschrift* and that-which-is (*das Seiende*) in the *Stuttgart Private Lectures* refer to the same thing, viz. the ideal principle in God.

55. Cf. "God alone—as the one who exists—dwells in pure light since he alone is *from himself*" (SW VII, 360, emphasis added).

56. Schelling to Georgii, July 18, 1810 (Plitt II, 220).

57. In the *Freiheitsschrift*, Schelling sometimes uses the Latin word *actu* when speaking about the existing of that-which-exists. See SW VII, 358, 364. Cf. the use of the word *actu* in the 1801 *Darstellung meines Systems* (SW IV, 124–25).

58. Schelling also connects "actual being" to revelation in his 1806 anti-Fichte polemic: "Being—actual, real being [*das aktuelle wirkliche Sein*]—is precisely self-revelation" (SW VII, 54).

59. The distinction of two levels of being is one of the defining features of what I elsewhere call Schelling's "ontology of revelation." See Thomas, forthcoming.

60. Schelling to Georgii, July 18, 1810 (Plitt II, 220).

61. On the question of the beginning of time, see the *Stuttgart Private Lectures*, SW VII, 430.

62. Schelling underscores the preposition "as" (*als*) each of the three times he uses it in his letter to Georgii, July 18, 1810 (Plitt II, 220, 221). Cf. SW VII, 54.

63. Hermanni mentions this etymological connection (1994, 88), as does Heidegger: "Schelling uses the word existence in a sense which is closer to the literal etymological sense than the usual long prevalent meaning of 'existing' as objective presence" (GA 42, 187; Heidegger 1985, 107).

64. I do not believe Schelling is qualifying the meaning of "existence," even if he uses modifiers. The expressions are pleonasms: the modifiers bring out what is already implied by "existence."

65. "What is *in itself* is the *cause* (what effects) of what is (derivatively or *secundario modo*) in the *ground*" (Schelling to Georgii, July 18, 1810 [Plitt II, 221]). Along these lines, in the *Freiheitsschrift* Schelling specifies an "original understanding" (SW VII, 362; cf. VII, 360–61), which should be distinguished from the (derivative) understanding that is born from what lacks understanding (cf. SW VII, 360).

66. See Brown 1977, 127ff.

67. See Heidegger's discussion of longing (GA 42, 216–24; Heidegger 1985, 124–29).

68. Schelling to Georgii, July 18, 1810 (Plitt II, 218).

69. "Grund *des actualen Existierens* Gottes, d. h. des Seienden" (Plitt II, 220).

70. Schelling to Georgii, July 18, 1810 (Plitt II, 221).

71. Schelling to Georgii, July 18, 1810 (Plitt II, 221).

72. In the *Further Presentations* (1802), Schelling refers to nature as the "possibility or ground of reality" (SW IV, 416).

73. He uses *Fundament* in the *Freiheitsschrift* to describe realism in relation to idealism (SW VII, 356) and in Stuttgart to describe the real principle as the principle of God's individuality (SW VII, 438). *Unterlage* is used numerous times to describe the real principle in Stuttgart (cf. SW VII, 437, 454). And Schelling refers to the ground several times as *Basis* in the *Freiheitsschrift* (cf. SW VII, 389, 391, 394).

74. Cf. SW VII, 340, 345–46.

75. In a colorful passage in the *Stuttgart Private Lectures*, Schelling emphasizes the spatial aspect of nature as ground: "God himself is *above* nature; nature is his throne, his subordinate [*Untergeordnetes*]" (SW VII, 437).

76. Cf. Schelling's reference to God making the real principle into "the ground and, so to speak, the carrier [*Träger*] of all things" (SW VII, 391). He also refers to the dark principle as the "carrier and, as it were, the 'receptacle' [*Behälter*] of the higher principle of light" (SW VII, 364). "Receptacle" is another connection to the χώρα in the *Timaeus*.

77. See Sallis 1999, 109ff. and Krell 2005, 81.

78. Cf. Schelling's reply to Eschenmayer: "This [real] principle is the only tool of the actualization of the hidden essence of the divinity" (SW VIII, 170). He also refers to the ground as "organ" (*Organ*) and "tool" in Stuttgart (SW VII, 437).

79. Schelling to Georgii, July 18, 1810 (Plitt II, 221).

80. Cf. "The first effect of the understanding in nature is the division of forces" (SW VII, 361).

81. Schelling himself cites this passage when distinguishing ground and cause in his letter to Georgii (July 18, 1810 [Plitt II, 221]). My interpretation of this passage is therefore very different from that of Peetz (2006, 518–21), who reads it in light of Jacobi's distinction between ground and cause, each representing a different form of knowledge: the ground (timeless logic) is elevated over the cause (temporal experience). See also Peetz 1995, 167.

82. For a discussion of the grounding relation as giving birth in the *Freiheitsschrift*, see Sallis 1995, 227–28 and Krell 2005, 81–83. In the *Ages of the World*, Schelling refers to "eternal nature" as "the potency of giving birth" (*die gebärende Potenz*), which is also the means and tool of eternal birth into being (SW VIII, 269).

83. In the *Freiheitsschrift*, this is the role of the understanding. On the cooperation of "longing" and the understanding in the production of the world, see Steigerwald 2015, 192. Cooperation (*Mitwirken*) is also an important theme in Schelling's 1794 commentary on the *Timaeus*. See T 29, 32, 48. Plato even has a word for this kind of co-ground: συναίτιον (46c; Plato 2001, 78).

84. A related image is the earth from which a plant grows: "All birth is birth from darkness into light; the seed kernel must be sunk into the earth and die in darkness so that the more beautiful shape of light may lift and unfold itself in the radiance of the sun" (SW VII, 360). He uses similar imagery in the 1802

Further Presentations: "Gravity in and for itself would be merely an eternal ground of reality without actual reality and enclose in itself all forms, but in complete indistinguishability, merely as seeds, if it did not have the other unity, which unfolds and makes all the differences bloom as plants, as it were" (SW IV, 456).

85. This appears to draw on the distinction between principle (= ground) and cause that goes back to Giordano Bruno. Cf. Bruno 1998, 36–37 and the passage from Bruno quoted by Jacobi in his *Spinoza Letters*: "*Principle* is the *inner* ground of a thing, the source of its possible existence; *cause* is the *external* ground of a thing, the source of its actual, present existence" (JW IV/2, 6).

86. Vetö (1977, 144–45) also interprets this passage from Würzburg as anticipating the 1809 fundamental distinction.

87. Schelling himself cites the 1806 *Aphorisms* (SW VII, 174, §§162–63). See also the 1804 *Würzburg System* (SW VI, 407–8); the 1806 addition to *On the World Soul* (SW II, 371, 376); and the 1810 *Stuttgart Private Lectures* (SW VII, 453).

88. The images of birth and "parenting" in the last section take on a new dimension in light of Schelling's discussion of love and the relation between the sexes.

89. According to Iber and Buchheim, love requires that each principle give up its independence (Iber 2004, 135; Buchheim 2004, 32). However, I believe this passage clearly shows that the independence is retained.

90. This reflects Schelling's two-tiered ontology of revelation (see Thomas, forthcoming). Being in a higher sense means being *revealed* and thus existing (in the sense defined in section 3). As noted above, the ground of God's existence is the ground of the *existence* of that-which-exists. Interpreted in terms of the present distinction: the ground is necessary for that-which-exists to exist in a higher sense, but it has a being independent of the ground.

91. The phrase "precedes him as existing" (*ihm als Existierenden vorangeht*) is ambiguous. Does this mean the ground (1) precedes the ideal principle (that-which-exists) without qualification, or (2) precedes the ideal principle *insofar as* it is already existing? We have noted that Schelling in his reply to Eschenmayer emphasizes that the ground is the ground of *existence*, not of that-which-exists. This would favor the second interpretation.

92. Correia and Schnieder note that this is also a feature of contemporary theories of grounding. They refer to it as "asymmetry." Correia and Schnieder 2012, 4.

93. KU §65, AA 5, 374. Cf. AA 5, 373. Kant had previously mentioned the "mutual dependence" between the preservation of one part of a tree and the preservation of the others (§64, AA 5, 371).

94. It is noteworthy that Schelling speaks of the ground in this passage not as "that which generates the One," but as "that through which [*wodurch*] the One is generated." This is again evidence of the instrumentality of the ground.

95. In the 1801 *Darstellung* Schelling writes that "all potencies reciprocally presuppose each other" (§94, *Erläuterung*, SW IV, 166). Cf. the passage in the 1806 *Aphorisms*, where Schelling refers to the whole of nature as a "magic circle" (*ein magischer Kreis*), which is there "in one fell swoop" (SW VII, 206).

96. In the *Erlangen Lectures* (1821), Schelling defines system in terms of mutual presupposition: "Every ordered whole of parts [*Glieder*] that mutually condition and reciprocally presuppose [each other] is a system." He adds: "One part lives and dies with the other" (HKA II/10, 673–74).

Chapter 5

1. For instance, Hermanni (1994, 18) claims that carrying out a theodicy is the "leading intention" of the text. Heidegger famously claims that "Schelling's treatise . . . is at the core a metaphysics of evil" (GA 42, 169; Heidegger 1985, 98).

2. It should be noted, however, that Schelling writes at the beginning of the section on the "formal essence of freedom" that "insight into [the formal essence] seems to be bound up with difficulties no smaller than the explanation of the real concept" (SW VII, 382), i.e., freedom as a capacity for good and evil. I suspect one should not always take Schelling's superlatives at face value, since he is fairly liberal in using them. Cf. "the highest point in the investigation" (on the *Ungrund*) (SW VII, 406), "the highest question of this whole investigation" (the question of theodicy) (SW VII, 394), and "the greatest object of the question [of evil]" (on evil's actuality as opposed to its possibility) (SW VII, 373).

3. I therefore disagree with Gardner's claim that "Schelling's aim cannot be to explain freedom and evil, for what he shows is that freedom and evil are necessarily and in themselves *ungrounded*" (Gardner 2017, 153).

4. "Withdrawing from the action by renouncing reason seems more like flight than victory. By the same right someone else could turn his back on freedom in order to thrown himself into the arms of reason and necessity" (SW VII, 338).

5. "But chance is impossible; it contradicts reason as well as the necessary unity of the whole" (SW VII, 383). We will treat this section in more detail in the final chapter.

6. See especially Hermanni 1994 for a comprehensive treatment of the problem of evil in the *Freiheitsschrift*.

7. Schelling moves a little too quickly in his argument here.

8. In other words, the principle of sufficient reason requires that one account not only for why there is something rather than nothing but also for those cases where there is nothing rather than something.

9. Cf. "Evil meanwhile announces itself in nature only through its effect" (SW VII, 377).

10. Cf. SW VII, 379–80, 388, 402, 404.

11. Kant, *Religion within the Limits of Mere Reason*, AA 6, 22–23n. ("Positive" here means having actual quantity and not being a mere absence; it does not mean the opposite of negative, since evil is a negative quantity in this scheme.) Schelling has a similar critique of Spinoza, to whom he attributes the view that evil is merely relative (something with a lesser degree of perfection). Schelling notes that this theory does not provide the basis for an opposition between good and evil (SW VII, 353–54). Expressed mathematically: +4 is less positive and thus evil relative to +6, but +4 does not actively resist +6. For that, one would need a negative quantity (e.g., –4). For Spinoza's discussion of evil and imperfection, see the preface of Part IV of the *Ethics* (Spinoza 1994, 197–200). He considers good and evil to be mere "modes of thinking" that result from comparison—and from the relative situation of the person making the comparison (199).

12. See also the treatment of human freedom in the *Stuttgart Private Lectures* (SW VII, 457ff.).

13. However, Schelling also defines spirit as selfhood (*Selbstheit*) raised to unity with the ideal principle (SW VII, 364).

14. It is curious that Schelling does not say "possibility of evil" but "possibility of good and evil." This seems to suggest that *good* is also not possible without this separability—and thus God would be incapable of good. However, Schelling clearly associates God with the good when treating his relationship to self-revelation as a "moral being" (SW VII, 394ff.). Love and goodness determine the divine decision for revelation, which is conscious and morally free (SW VII, 397). One could perhaps say that the separability of the principles makes good and evil possible *as possibilities*; the good is a "moral necessity" for God. Cf. SW VII, 396–97.

15. For a discussion of the relationship of Schelling's account of evil to Kant, see Hermanni 1994, 129, 132–36.

16. In the *Stuttgart Private Lectures* (1810) Schelling writes: "Evil is not a mere privation of the good, not a mere negation of inner harmony, but positive disharmony" (SW VII, 468).

17. This way of structuring Schelling's theodicy strategy is somewhat different from Hermanni's division into two theodicy "trials." In the first trial, the question is whether God is responsible for the evil in the world. In the second trial, the question is whether God is responsible for the human ability to do evil (1994, 16–18).

18. Schlegel 1808, 97–98, 127.

19. Schlegel 1808, 125–26.

20. In his letter to Windischmann from May 9, 1809, Schelling refers to Schlegel's book, noting that the true system lies somewhere in the middle of the three systems (emanation, dualism, and pantheism) and has components of each "organically interwoven." There is a point where each has its application (Plitt II, 156).

21. As Schelling remarks in a key footnote, "This is the only correct dualism, namely that which at the same time permits a unity" (SW VII, 359n). Schelling returns to the question of dualism vs. pantheism in his discussion of the *Ungrund*, as we will see below. Cf. SW VII, 406, 409–10.

22. For this reason, Heidegger claims that Schelling ends up denying the immanence of things in God (GA 42, 172–73; Heidegger 1985, 100). However, Schelling explicitly affirms that "nothing is outside of God" (SW VII, 359) even after introducing the problems that evil poses for the doctrine of immanence (cf. SW VII, 410).

23. This would also place limits on the existing God's power vis-à-vis the ground. It is Marquard's thesis that all attempts to provide a theodicy do so by restricting God's power in one way or another. In the case of Schelling's theodicy, this restriction is *within* God (the ground of his existence), whereas the Christian approach is to place this restriction *next to* God (human freedom) (1995, 58–59). However, Marquard does not acknowledge that what he calls the Christian approach is integral to Schelling's theodicy as well.

24. In the *Erster Entwurf* (1799). See Rang 1988, 177 and Lauer 2010, 50–52.

25. See Buchheim 2000, 57–58.

26. See SW VII, 373–74, 375–76, 380, 400–401. It is noteworthy that both of the reasons that Schelling provides for the activation of the self-will are teleological: they give the purposes that this activation serves. But Schelling makes clear that the excitation of the self-will does not happen "by the free will of God, who moves in the ground not by virtue of his free will or heart but only by virtue of his properties" (SW VII, 401). This helps to distance God (as a free being) from this precondition of evil, but it raises the question of why the ground acts purposively if it does not have free will. The purpose (self-revelation) would have to be "built into" the ground insofar as it is part of God's nature.

27. See SW VII, 403 for another reference to the "creaturely will" as the "possible principle of evil." Earlier Schelling had designated the self-will "the ground of evil" and referred to its origin in the ground: "The ground of evil must lie . . . in that which is most positive in what nature contains, as is actually the case in our view, since it lies in the revealed centrum or primal will of the first ground" (SW VII, 369).

28. Cf. the "basic law of opposition" in the *Stuttgart Private Lectures* (1810): "No life without opposition" (SW VII, 435).

29. For example, see GA 42, 270, 274–77; Heidegger 1985, 156, 158–60; Habermas 1954, 268ff.; Marx 1984, 78–79.

30. SW VII, 365–66, 370–71. Cf. "Evil is not merely privation of the good but positive disharmony" (SW VII, 468).

31. "For evil is not aroused selfhood in itself but only to the extent that it has completely torn itself away from its opposite, the light or the universal will" (SW VII, 399–400). Cf. "[Self-will] is not itself evil, but only when it becomes dominant [*herrschend*]" (SW VII, 467).

32. "Evil is nothing other than the primal ground of existence to the extent this ground strives toward actuality in created beings" (SW VII, 378).

33. Hermanni 1994, 240–46; Buchheim 2000, 48–50, 55–60. Buchheim emphasizes that universal evil is only the possibility of evil and contrasts it with the actuality of evil (49). Although this is true if one understands moral evil as actual evil, Schelling himself treats universal evil in the section explicitly devoted to the actuality (*Wirklichkeit*) of evil (SW VII, 373ff.), and the struggle between universal evil and good that he describes is an actuality.

34. "[The human being] cannot remain undecided because God must necessarily reveal himself" (SW VII, 374).

35. For an overview and critique of Hegel's approach to evil, see Beiser 2005, 270–75.

36. Cf. "There is a source of sadness in [God] that can, however, never come into actuality, but rather serves only the eternal joy of overcoming" (SW VII, 399).

37. Hermanni 1994, 244–45. There is one other problematic passage for the interpretation of Hermanni and Buchheim. Schelling notes that it is only in opposition to sin that the essence of God before all existence is revealed (SW VII, 391). Hermanni interprets this as referring to the wrath of God. Hermanni 1994, 244n157.

38. This is McGrath's interpretation (2012, 169n11).

39. This phrase is used in the *Exsultet* chant of the Easter Vigil liturgy. It also has a history in the theodicy literature. For example, see Leibniz, *Theodicy*, Part I, §10 (Leibniz 1985, 129).

40. Hermanni cites this passage as evidence that moral evil cannot be a necessary condition of revelation (1994, 243).

41. Schelling began reading the *Theodicy* on January 16, 1809. On January 18 and 19 he notes that he spent the whole day (*toto die*) reading it, finishing it on January 21. Schelling began work on the *Freiheitsschrift* in February (TB 6–7).

42. Cf. Leibniz, *Theodicy*, Part II, §132 (Leibniz 1985, 203).

43. Cf. Schelling's statement that Spinoza erred in that his necessity was "not living and personal" (SW VII, 397).

44. *Theodicy*, Part III, §345 (Leibniz 1985, 332).

45. Schelling evidently does not regard this as jeopardizing God's freedom, as Leibniz does. As we will see in the final chapter, Schelling unites freedom with necessity, and he does not regard a choice between possibilities as necessary for freedom—at least at this stage of his philosophical development. Cf. SW VII, 429.

46. In my view, Schelling commentators are not sufficiently troubled by this passage, which tends to be ignored. Knappik (2019) addresses the over-arching problem, but focuses on the "one possible world" line and not this passage. Buchheim (2009) treats this section of the *Freiheitsschrift* in some detail, arguing that Schelling offers an improvement over Leibniz's theodicy.

47. This is also the interpretation of Buchheim (2000, 48).

48. This is essentially the interpretation of Knappik (2019). Buchheim also suggests that Schelling allows for different possibilities of free actions within the *same* possible world (2009, 372). One might object, however, that one cannot include different possibilities for free actions without thereby producing different possible worlds—at least as Leibniz uses the term "possible world."

49. There is a more adventuresome and speculative possibility for resolving this difficulty. As we will see in Schelling's treatment of the formal concept of freedom, the essence of a human being includes all the actions of that human being, and this essence is determined by a fundamental act of freedom outside of time (SW VII, 383–85). Schelling also says that God yields the ideas (presumably including human essences) to the ground so that they can be raised up out of the ground in the act of creation (SW VII, 404). One could therefore understand the freely constituted human essences as already built into this archetype of the only possible world in the ground.

50. This is a clear echo of Athanasius. Earlier Schelling had also referred to the Incarnation: in opposition to the "spirit of evil," the word (or Word) takes on humanity and selfhood and becomes personal (SW VII, 377). In this context, the spirit of evil seems to be a form of universal evil (the arousal of the self-will) and not moral evil. If that is the case, then the Incarnation is necessary regardless of human freedom—a departure from orthodox Christian teaching.

51. In my view, this is a problem for Knappik's approach in his otherwise excellent article (2019). He concedes that God's action in history is just as necessary as the initial creation; however, he also contends that this action is a reaction to human free actions, which (according to Knappik's reading) are contingent.

52. See the discussion of the formal concept of freedom in the final chapter.

53. Schelling does say that all the consequences of self-revelation were foreseen in God (SW VII, 396) and that God foresaw that evil would follow—at least by way of accompaniment—from self-revelation (SW VII, 402).

54. Unless, of course, human freedom was somehow included in the divine nature. Conceivably, one might understand the essences of human beings (as determined eternally through the intelligible deed of freedom) as somehow in the divine nature—like living ideas in the mind of God. Cf. SW VII, 347 and the discussion in chapter 7 of *esse virtuale* in Meister Eckhart.

55. For instance, Egloff (2016, 6) speaks of the "ontologische Aufwertung" of the irrational in Schelling's *Freiheitsschrift*.

56. Cf. "Ground is the reason for the gaps in reality, what Schelling calls the 'irreducible remainder'" (McGrath 2012, 131).

57. Egloff also notes that the irrational in Schelling is opposed more to the understanding than to reason (2016, 6). See also 198n18 and Lauer 2010, 144.

58. Cf. SW IV, 299; IV, 366–67.

59. Cf. SW VI, 153; VII, 146–47. See also Schelling's account of the relationship between *Verstand* and *Vernunft* in the *Stuttgart Private Lectures* (1810).

There he emphasizes the activity of the understanding and the passivity of reason (SW VII, 471–72). Cf. Schelling's association of human reason with the mystical *primum passivum* in God (SW VII, 415).

60. Although the epistemological significance of the understanding is not emphasized in the *Freiheitsschrift*, Schelling refers to it at the end of the text, relating it to the dialectical nature of philosophy and science in terms that mirror the divine understanding's ordering of nature (SW VII, 413–14, 415).

61. Here one might object to my argument that the irrational does not undermine the system because it is only irrational with respect to the understanding. Schelling himself repeatedly associates system with the divine understanding (cf. SW VII, 336–37, 398, 421). Thus, it seems that anything that is incomprehensible for the understanding falls outside the system. One possible answer: the way that God creates through the understanding is not the way that he originally knows through the understanding. The original divine knowledge involves the immediate viewing of an image, and in this respect resembles an "intuitive understanding." Cf. SW VII, 360–61, 396–97, 398.

62. Schelling makes this explicit in the *Stuttgart Private Lectures* (1810). See SW VII, 425, 435.

63. Buchheim notes: "Der Schöpfungsprozeß ist insgesamt nur 'Scheidung'" (2011a, 160, §327).

64. Cf. Moiso 1995, 199–200.

65. For a different interpretation of this passage, which ties it to the failure of concepts to be adequate to reality, see Wirth 2003, 203–4.

66. Lauer also makes this point (2010, 144).

67. This is the translation of Love and Schmidt. McGrath and Lauer translate it as "irreducible remainder." See McGrath 2012, 131; Lauer 2010, 144.

68. "Beim rechnen sagt man, dasz zahlen gegen oder in einander aufgehen, ohne dasz etwas übrig bleibt. 7 geht 7mal auf in 49" (Grimm and Grimm 1854–1961, vol. 1, col. 656). This dictionary also cites the following passage from book 4, chapter 18 of Goethe's novel *Wilhelm Meisters Lehrjahre* (1795–96), which bears a striking resemblance to the passage in Schelling: "Es waren verständige, geistreiche, lebhafte Menschen, die wohl einsahen, daß die Summe unsrer Existenz, durch Vernunft dividiert, niemals rein aufgehe, sondern daß immer ein wunderlicher Bruch übrigbleibe" (Goethe 1795, 345). In Goethe it is *Vernunft* and not *Verstand* which is doing the dividing.

69. Grimm and Grimm 1854–1961, vol. 1, col. 653. Cf. "Denn gleichwie Gewächs aus der Erde wächst und Same im Garten aufgeht, so lässt Gott der Herr Gerechtigkeit aufgehen" (*Lutherbibel*, Jes. 61,11).

70. Schelling also expresses this idea with the language of light and darkness, connected to childbirth: "The human being is formed in the maternal body, and from the darkness of that which lacks understanding . . . luminous thoughts grow" (SW VII, 350). This language borrows heavily from the theosophist

Friedrich Christoph Oetinger (1702–82), who also notes the non-originality of the understanding (Oetinger 1765, 5, 8). I owe these references to Höfele 2019, 117–18.

71. McGrath has a nuanced view of the question, although he comes close to this position when he writes: "In the maximum reach of the understanding, every order is revealed to be *in fact* contingent, grounded in something 'ruleless,' something out of which order has been brought but which is not itself ordered" (2012, 4). However, McGrath also affirms the importance of order for the ideal side of Schelling's philosophy.

72. Schelling describes the origin of this understanding only a few lines after the passage on the irreducible remainder. Its origin is independent of the ground: "An inner, reflexive representation [*Vorstellung*] is generated in God himself. . . . This representation is at the same time the understanding" (SW VII, 360–61).

73. See the reply to Eschenmayer's objections to the notion that understanding arises from what lacks understanding. Schelling emphasizes the role of the ground as the condition for *revealing* the understanding (SW VIII, 173–74).

74. In his *Timaeus* commentary (1794), Schelling also calls the "preexisting primal matter" *regellos*. It is unruly because it has "not yet partaken in the form of the understanding" (T 27).

75. For a similar account of chaos as an original unity (*Ureinheit*) in which nothing is distinguished, see the discussion in the *Philosophy of Mythology* (SW XII, 596–602, esp. 600–601).

76. In the *Identitätsphilosophie*, the absolute is known through reason, which is a designation for intellectual intuition. The latter is not explicitly present in the *Freiheitsschrift*, but Schelling does characterize reason as an "original wisdom": it is not activity but "indifference" (SW VII, 415).

77. The passage refers to reason, not just the understanding. However, Schelling calls it "unadulterated, pure reason" (*lautere reine Vernunft*), thus emphasizing its "purity." I would therefore interpret this as the one-sided reason of idealism. In Stuttgart, Schelling identifies the understanding with "subjective reason" (SW VII, 455).

78. Schlegel 1808, 141.

79. The latter is Eschenmayer's position. He had claimed that faith is necessary for access to a personal God "beyond the absolute." Schelling engages extensively with Eschenmayer in *Philosophy and Religion* (1804), firmly rejecting his notion of going "beyond the absolute" (cf. SW VI, 50–51). Schelling does not mention him directly in the *Freiheitsschrift*, though he may have him in mind at SW VII, 412. In his published reply to Eschenmayer, Schelling rejects his claim that freedom, virtue, and beauty cannot be thought in a concept (SW VIII, 162–63).

80. For this reason, I do not share Christopher Lauer's view that Schelling moves reason to the periphery in the *Freiheitsschrift*. See Lauer 2010, 135–37.

81. He goes on to affirm Lessing's view that revealed truths should be developed into truths of reason (SW VII, 412).

82. Though Schelling does not directly acknowledge it, this could very well apply to his previous philosophy as well. See Theunissen 1965, 176–78. Although Schelling notes that the interpenetration of realism and idealism was his intention even in his first writings (SW VII, 350), his previous treatments of the ideal part of philosophy lack a dynamic interplay of forces, especially in his account of God.

83. For a treatment of Schelling's "theory of life" in relation to mechanism and vitalism, see Rang 1988, 170–74; Beiser 2002, 538–44.

84. See Rang 2000, 212–17; Beiser 2002, 531–32.

85. See Rang 2000, 216–30.

86. The reciprocity of organic grounding is emphasized by Matthews 2011, especially 161–67.

87. For an excellent discussion of paradoxical language in Meister Eckhart (that also applies to Schelling), see Tobin 1986, 162–63. Cf. the "mystery of love" as an example (SW VII, 408).

88. These characteristics are loosely based on Rudolf Otto's classic work from 1917, *Das Heilige* (2014), and its account of the numinous as *mysterium tremendum*. Mystery is an object of wonder (29) that is "wholly other," insofar as it "falls outside the realm of the accustomed, understood and familiar" (31). It is "irrational" insofar as it withdraws from our conceptual thinking and from "sayability" (75–77). In my view, "mystery" is a neglected topic within philosophy. Marcel's distinction between mystery and problem is sometimes invoked (1965, 100–101). Kant has an account of mystery in the *Religionsschrift*: mystery cannot be universally communicated because it surpasses all of our concepts from a theoretical point of view (AA 6, 137–42).

Chapter 6

1. Love and Schmidt incorrectly translate *bezeichnen* as "describe" rather than "designate."

2. In other contexts, I have already mentioned the difficulty in translating *Wesen*. As we will see below, its meaning with respect to the *Ungrund* is especially problematic. For this reason, I occasionally leave it untranslated.

3. SW VIII, 165; VIII, 81. We will return to these passages below.

4. This is also an instance of the "terminological plurality" in his philosophical development.

5. This recalls the traditional problem of divine naming. See, for example, the work *On the Divine Names* by Pseudo-Dionysius the Areopagite.

6. For the facts about Schelling's acquaintance with Boehme, see Brown 1977, 114–15 and Buchheim 2011b, xl–xlv.

7. For an account of the *Ungrund* in Boehme, see Brown 1977, 54ff.; Bruneder 1958, 101–15.

8. *Von der Gnadenwahl*, I, 3 (Böhme 1955–1960, vol. 6, part XV).

9. Cf. Boehme: "Und können doch nicht sagen, dass das Jah vom Nein abgesondert, und zwei Dinge neben einander sind, sondern sie sind nur Ein Ding, scheiden sich aber selber in zwei Anfänge" (*177 Theosophic Questions*, Question 3). Quoted in Dörendahl 2011, 193.

10. Brown 1977, 14.

11. McGinn 2005, 84–86.

12. McGinn cites four groups of meanings that the Middle High German word *grunt* has: (1) physical ground or earth; (2) bottom or lowest side of a body, surface, or structure; (3) origin, cause, beginning, reason, or proof; (4) the essence, or what is inmost, hidden, and most proper (2005, 87).

13. McGinn 2005, 121.

14. McGinn notes that Eckhart also uses paradoxical phrases like "groundless ground" (*gruntlôs grunt*) (2005, 121).

15. For an overview of how these terms are used in the history of philosophy, see Trappe 2001.

16. There is also a sense in which *Abgrund* simply means "depths" (*Tiefe*). Cf. SW VII, 363.

17. There is another meaning of the prefix *un-* in German, giving the word a negative value: an *Untat* is a crime or misdeed—a *Tat* ("deed") that should not have happened. Ehrhardt interprets the *Ungrund* in Schelling along these lines: it is a ground that should not be. This is because the *Ungrund* is indifference, but there *should be* difference for the sake of life, love, and personal existence (1995, 226, 224n10). However, I do not detect any hint of a negative evaluation in Schelling's discussion, since indifference is a necessary condition for the duality of principles.

18. Grimm and Grimm 1854–1961, vol. 24, col. 1030.

19. "Absolute identity" here does not mean the same thing that it means in the passage in the *Freiheitsschrift* where Schelling emphasizes the distinction between absolute identity and the *Ungrund*. We will return to this point.

20. "Only the absolute or God is that which affirms itself absolutely, and thus is what is affirmed by itself. For, according to its universal idea, *absolute* is only that which is of itself and through itself" (SW VI, 148).

21. Cf. Hennigfeld 2001, 127.

22. According to Heidegger, Schelling does not fully appreciate that the "jointure of being" (*Seynsgefüge*) as the unity of ground and existence "makes a jointure of being as system impossible." Ultimately Schelling "falls back into the rigidified tradition of Western thought without creatively transforming it." He thus attempts to save system and ultimate unity by reformulating the absolute as *Ungrund* (GA 42, 279–80; Heidegger 1985, 161–62). Heidegger only devotes

two paragraphs to the *Ungrund* in his 1936 lectures, referring to it simply as "the absolute."

23. Or what is effectively the last line. What is technically the last line offers the (unfulfilled) promise of a series of future treatises dealing with the ideal part of philosophy (SW VII, 416). The 1834 reprint of the *Freiheitsschrift* strikes this line, possibly at the direction of Schelling himself. See Ehrhardt 1995, 227n24.

24. A little earlier Schelling had identified "original wisdom" as the genuine goal of philosophy. Reason is original wisdom in which "all things are together and yet distinct." He then says that reason is "indifference" (SW VII, 415), thus connecting this description to the *Ungrund*.

25. Schelling refers to this designation in his reply to Eschenmayer (SW VIII, 165).

26. For a discussion of the systematic implications of the *Ungrund*, especially with respect to the question of overcoming dualism, see Sallis 1995, 231.

27. See Thomas 2014, 33–35. Gabriel also makes this point (2020, 137), though I find his identification of the *Ungrund* with the "essence [*Wesen*] of human freedom" in the title to be implausible. In the opening lines (SW VII, 336), Schelling makes clear that this refers to the *concept* of human freedom.

28. This is God in a broad sense, not God regarded absolutely (*absolut betrachtet*). Schelling reserves the latter designation for God insofar as he exists (the ideal principle in God). Cf. SW VII, 358, 359.

29. Other possible translations for *Wesen* include "being" (*Sein*) and "substance" (*Substanz*). Rang (2000, 96–97) points to passages in the *Würzburg System* in which Schelling uses the terms more or less interchangeably. If we identify *Sein* with *Wesen* in the context of the *Ungrund*, I believe that *Sein* has its meaning in contrast with becoming (cf. SW VII, 403). "Substance" can also simply mean "a being" (*Seiendes*), but it has Spinozistic undertones that are certainly present in Schelling.

30. For a more extensive treatment of the relationship of the two principles to the *Ungrund* in light of the mediated account of the copula, see Thomas 2014, 32–35.

31. There is some ambiguity in Schelling's use of the term *Ungrund*. On the one hand, he uses it interchangeably with indifference (cf. SW VII, 406–7). In this sense, it is the same *Wesen* as love, but not yet love. On the other hand, he says "the initial *Ungrund*" (*der anfängliche Ungrund*) is no longer indifference but love (SW VII, 408). This could mean that the term *Ungrund* refers to the *Wesen* that is indifference (at the beginning) and love (at the end). Or, in line with the first sense, it could mean that the same *Wesen* that is the initial *Ungrund* (indifference) is also love. Ehrhardt (1995, 229) emphasizes the adjective "initial" in the phrase "initial *Ungrund*," and interprets this to be a qualification that distinguishes it from what Schelling had earlier designated as *Ungrund*.

32. The phrase "all in all" (πάντα ἐν πᾶσιν) comes from St. Paul (1 Cor. 15:28). Indeed, much of the eschatological language that Schelling uses at SW VII, 405-6 and VII, 408 is drawn from this passage, which treats the end times.

33. This same problem arises in the *Weltalter*: how can God, who is changeless and beyond becoming, *become* that-which-is (*seiend*)? Schelling's answer is that this happens only in relation to another, not in itself (SW VIII, 255-56, 298-99).

34. It goes all the way back to Schelling's letter to Hegel from February 4, 1795. Hegel had asked about the relation of a personal God to the so-called "moral proof" for the existence of God. Schelling responds: "We are reaching *further* than for a personal [divine] being" (Plitt I, 76-77).

35. It may seem strange that Schelling refers to the "concept of the absolute," but in his reply to Eschenmayer (1812) he makes clear that the fact that there is a concept of a thing does not mean that the thing *is* a concept (SW VIII, 163).

36. As Dörendahl notes, the genuine investigation in the treatise begins with the introduction of difference (the fundamental distinction), and only toward the end does the *Ungrund* appear as the principle of unity (2011, 193).

37. This is also the case with the *Stuttgart Private Lectures*, which Schelling gave the following year (1810).

38. Cf. "Philosophy is utterly and completely [*ganz und durchaus*] in the absolute" (SW IV, 392).

39. Of course, philosophical construction for Schelling consists in showing how each of the particular forms of reality really is the absolute. In this sense, philosophy never leaves the absolute. See the fourth essay in the *Further Presentations* (1802), which treats philosophical construction (SW IV, 391ff.).

40. Schelling had long been aware of the objection that his conception of the absolute makes unnecessary any discussion beyond the general treatment of the absolute. In *Further Presentations* (1802), he answers this objection through his distinction between essence and form (SW IV, 392), which we will turn to in the last section of this chapter.

41. Cf. the description of the end of creation in the *Stuttgart Private Lectures*: "The end is in the beginning—only now everything is *explicitly* what it was before *implicitly*" (SW VII, 483-84).

42. The role of the *Ungrund* as the *potenzlos* substrate of the potencies is confirmed by the passage from the reply to Eschenmayer cited above (SW VIII, 165).

43. This is my interpretation of the place of love, although Schelling does not define it in precisely this way. Love is "a general unity that is the same for all [*gegen alles*] and yet grasped by nothing; it is free from all and yet a beneficence [*Wohltun*] acting in all" (SW VII, 408). Its place is above the potencies, uniting them at the end of the process of their unfolding.

44. For this reason, I have reservations about Schwab's thesis that the *Ungrund* is an answer to Hegel's *Phenomenology of Spirit*—at least if this thesis

means that Schelling is developing something essentially new as a response to Hegel. See Schwab 2018, 151–55.

45. Mine, noting the distinction between absolute indifference and identity in the *Freiheitsschrift*, concludes: "From this it becomes clear that he no longer remains at the standpoint of his *Identitätsphilosophie*" (1983, 21). Rang sees the discussion of indifference in the *Freiheitsschrift* as a critique of the idea of "the absolute identity of all opposites" in previous works. The distinction between absolute indifference and absolute identity makes explicit two different conceptions of the absolute that Schelling had previously allowed to stand side by side (Rang 2000, 26; 28n).

46. Schelling also refers to absolute identity as the "spirit of love" (SW VII, 409) and notes that "only God as spirit is the absolute identity of both principles, but only because and to the extent that both are *subordinated* to his personality" (SW VII, 409).

47. As the unity of the two principles, spirit is closely aligned with personality and existence, which Schelling also defines in terms of the unity of the two principles. See especially SW VII, 394–95.

48. See Rang 2000, 12.

49. I believe Schelling is also referring to what he here calls "absolute identity" when he denies that absolute indifference is a "product of opposites" (SW VII, 406). This is precisely what absolute identity is in this context.

50. This could also be translated as "precedes all oppositions." As Rang notes (2000, 11n), the German word *Gegensatz* can mean both "opposition" (Lat. *oppositio*) and "opposite" (Lat. *oppositum*).

51. Cf. SW IV, 237, 239. In *Bruno* Schelling denies that anything is opposed in the absolute, even though he refers to the absolute as the "unity of all opposites" (SW IV, 236) and the "unity of unity and opposition" (SW IV, 239). In their identity in the absolute, the opposites cease to be opposites. For the interpretation of these phrases, see Rang 2000, chapter 1.

52. Spinoza, Letter 50, *Opera* (Spinoza 1925), vol. IV, 240.

53. Brown 1977, 54.

54. See the discussion of the distinction between reason and understanding/reflection in chapter 5.

55. Cf. the section "Reflection as Instrument of Philosophizing" in Hegel's 1802 *Differenzschrift* (HW 2, 25ff.).

56. This is in the tradition of "negative theology" that goes back at least as far as the Neoplatonists.

57. Thus, Schelling also discusses what he calls the "three highest forms under which the absolute is posited" in the passage of the *Würzburg System* (1804) that treats the syllogisms (SW VI, 528).

58. Schelling uses the neither-nor construction in other texts in the *Identitätsphilosophie*—for example, in *Bruno*: "The *Wesen* of the One is neither one

[opposite] nor the other of all [pairs of] opposites" (SW IV, 252). For a discussion of the neither-nor construction, see Rang 2000, 22ff.

59. See Schwab's discussion of the *Entzug* ("withdrawal") of the *Ungrund* (2018, 152–53).

60. Schelling begins the body of this important text with a definition of reason: "I name *reason* absolute reason, or reason to the extent that it is thought as total *indifference* of the subjective and the objective" (§1, SW IV, 114, emphasis added to "indifference").

61. SW IV, 126. In the 1804 *Würzburg System*, absolute identity and indifference are distinguished: "Absolute identity is equality of *essence* [*Wesens*], or it is essential, qualitative unity. Indifference is merely quantitative unity, quantitative equilibrium [*Gleichgewicht*]" (SW VI, 209). However, in other contexts Schelling identifies the two (cf. SW IV, 125).

62. In his essay on negative magnitudes, Kant defines opposition: "Two things are opposed to each other if one thing cancels that which is posited by the other" (AA 2, 171). +4 and +6 are different magnitudes, but they are not opposed, while +4 and –4 are opposed.

63. The dialogue refers to two unities: one opposed to opposition, and one that unites unity with opposition. But these are also framed as (1) a unity that is opposed to *difference*, and (2) a unity that unites unity with difference (SW IV, 236).

64. With respect to absolute identity, neither qualitative nor quantitative difference is possible. See the 1801 *Darstellung*, §§23, 25 (SW IV, 123–25).

65. The word *gegen* can mean "toward" when describing a comportment.

66. As we saw in chapter 4, there is only quantitative difference, or difference in the relative balance of subjectivity and objectivity, which accounts for the difference among the potencies.

67. Cf. "Nothing, we said, is finite in the universe, except to the extent it is in opposition, thus not conceived in itself. . . . Matter itself and every part is its own world, microcosm, in which the macrocosm [*die große Welt*] is perfectly copied and reproduced [*nach- und abgebildet*]" (SW VI, 385).

68. Being without relations to other things is also part of what it means to be a "thing in itself" in both Kant and Schelling. See Rang 2000, 69.

69. There is something curious in this passage. We have seen that the principles are *in* the *Ungrund* as its predicates. But now Schelling says that the *Ungrund* is *in* each principle. So is the *Ungrund* in the principles or are they in it? Both: what is in the absolute shares the nature of the absolute. Thus, insofar as something is in the absolute, the absolute is in it. Cf. Hölderlin's aphorism at the beginning of *Hyperion* (1990, 1): "Non coerceri maximo, contineri tamen a minimo, divinum est." (Not to be confined by the greatest, but to be contained in the smallest—that is divine.)

70. Quoted in Leibniz's *Discourse on Metaphysics*, §32 (Leibniz 1989, 64). In fact, there are profound connections between this "microcosmic" aspect of

Schelling's system and Leibniz's monadology. Indeed, in the 1806 *Aphorisms*, Schelling refers to the particular in the absolute as its own world or *monas* (SW VII, 163). According to Leibniz, every monad "represent[s] the whole universe exactly and in its own way, from a certain point of view . . . as if in a world apart" (Leibniz 1989, 143). "Point of view" here would correspond to quantitative difference in Schelling.

71. Cf. the *Stuttgart Private Lectures*: "Because the same *Wesen* is in each, there is an *essential* unity between them. . . . However, there is also an actual opposition or dualism, in that they cannot cancel one another out. For, because of the fact that A individuates itself in B and in C, both receive the same right to exist" (SW VII, 422).

72. Asmuth, for example, regards this as an unsurmountable problem: "Now Schelling is no longer able to explain how something follows from the *Ungrund*" (2012, 202).

73. Here one can object: why would the *Ungrund* be the beginning if it is part of a circle? A circle has no beginning or end. In the passage on the circle, Schelling notes: "Here there is no first and no last" (SW VII, 358). One response: although everything presupposes everything else, not everything is a presupposition *in the same way*. As "the unconditionally absolute" and the *Wesen* of all that is, the *Ungrund* is prior both conceptually and in terms of dignity.

74. Eschenmayer raises this objection, referring to the "chameleon of the *Ungrund*" (SW VIII, 154). Unfortunately, Schelling does not directly address this point in his reply.

75. This seems to be the interpretation of Werner Marx: "The gap that the 'transition' from the 'nonground' to 'eternal oneness' must overcome cannot be bridged by deducing a chain of grounds or reasons. . . . It rather belongs to the nature of this 'transition' that it must be a 'leap' " (1984, 68).

76. One might see a hint of freedom in the intentions Schelling cites: "It divides itself *so that* there is life and love and personal existence" (SW VII, 408, emphasis added). But it is hard to see how the *Ungrund* can have intentions.

77. For example, *Das erklärt sich leicht* means "That is easily explained." See Durrell 2011, 308.

78. See especially *Ennead* VI.9, "On the Good or the One" (Plotinus 1988, 303, 311).

79. SW VI, 161. Cf. *Darstellung meines Systems* (1801) §15, Zusatz 1 (SW IV, 120).

80. "Absolute identity *is* only under the form of the proposition $A = A$" (§15, SW IV, 120; cf. IV, 117). A footnote refers to "the form $A = A$ or the form of subject-objectivity" (SW IV, 126n).

81. §20, SW IV, 122–23; VI, 31.

82. SW VI, 168. Rang explains this rather bold thesis by noting that affirming or denying is a necessary moment in all knowledge (2000, 41). However, saying

that affirming is a *moment* in knowledge is not the same as saying affirming *is* knowledge, and vice versa. Schelling seems to be making the latter claim.

83. In *Philosophy and Religion* (1804) this identification is explicit: "If one wanted to call [1] pure absoluteness, the absolutely simply essence [*Wesen*] of the same, *God* or *the absolute*; but [2] the form by contrast . . . *absoluteness*, there would not be much to object to" (SW VI, 30; emphasis on "the absolute" added). Cf. SW IV, 374, 379.

84. The form is "inseparable" (*unzertrennlich*) from the essence and one with it (SW VI, 161).

85. As Rang notes (2000, 96–97), Schelling sometimes uses the word *Wesen* in a narrower sense; however, when speaking of the relationship with form, he uses *Wesen* and *Sein* interchangeably.

86. Cf. "The inner of the absolute, or the essence of the same . . ." (SW IV, 374).

87. Because of this "inseparable" (*unzertrennlich*) relationship, Schelling notes that there is "here no transition from essence to form, no 'before' and no 'after'" (SW VI, 161).

88. On the equiprimordiality of the essence and form of the absolute, see Peetz 1995, 112.

89. My presentation is something of an oversimplification. Schelling has several different ways of describing the two sides of the act: (1) the essence in the form, and the form in the essence (SW V, 219); (2) ideality in reality, and reality in ideality (SW V, 281); and (3) the infinite in the finite, and the finite in the infinite (SW IV, 391).

90. Schelling uses *Wirkung* in relation to the act of absolute self-knowledge in his lectures on art. He refers to the "eternal effect(ing) [*Wirkung*] of the absolute act of knowledge" (SW V, 486).

91. Schelling even indicates in the 1801 *Darstellung* that the essence of the absolute is connected to the quantitative difference of the potencies (and thus appearance) through a chain of necessary conditions. We have seen that the essence of absolute identity can only exist under the form $A = A$, or the form of subject-objectivity (§15, SW IV, 120). But the form $A = A$ only exists if there is quantitative difference (§24, SW IV, 124–25). Schelling observes in a footnote that if there were no differentiability (*Unterscheidbarkeit*), the form qua form would be destroyed (SW IV, 126). Thus, if the quantitative difference of the potencies is a necessary condition for the form of subject-objectivity, and this form is a necessary condition for the *Wesen* of absolute identity, we can conclude that the quantitative difference of the potencies is a necessary condition for the *Wesen* of absolute identity. Thus, the *Ungrund* is even tied to quantitative difference and the potencies (which belong to appearance) through a "circle of presupposition."

92. This is another sense of the word *Ungrund*: that which does not reveal itself, or that which does not provide the ground for revelation. This sense is

present in Boehme, but it is also implied in what seem to be contrasts in Schelling between the *Ungrund* and the ground of existence—which is also a ground of revelation, since existence is fundamentally tied to revelation. See Schelling's references to the *Ungrund* as "preceding all ground" (SW VII, 406, 407) and "*before* and *above* all ground" (SW VIII, 172).

Chapter 7

1. I therefore disagree with Gardner (2017, 151–52), who claims that Schelling in the *Freiheitsschrift* "has pushed speculative thought beyond the Principle of Sufficient Reason." He makes this claim with respect to the freedom to do good and evil. On the question of whether evil and the irrational violate the principle, see my discussion in chapter 5.

2. As discussed in chapter 1, Schelling also mentions the opposition between freedom and necessity in the opening pages in the context of relating freedom to "the whole" (SW VII, 338).

3. Schelling here refers to the "formal essence of freedom," though he elsewhere refers to the "formal concept of freedom" (SW VII, 352) and the "concept of formal freedom" (SW VII, 351). I believe that all of these expressions refer to the same thing. The term may come from Fichte, who refers to "formal freedom" in his *System der Sittenlehre* (1798). For a discussion of the relation of Schelling's account to Fichte, see Binkelmann 2015.

4. In the first *Critique*, Kant describes the "intelligible character" of a cause, which is the law of its causality insofar as it is not appearance but in itself. "Now according to its intelligible character this acting subject would not stand under any conditions of time; for time is the condition only of appearances and not of things in themselves" (A 539/B 567).

5. We discussed this passage in the section on divine grounding in chapter 3. See section 2 of this chapter.

6. On this point, see Jacobs 1995, 126–27.

7. That the content concerns the *what* is self-explanatory. The form is sometimes described as the "way of being" (*Art zu sein*), i.e., *how* something is what it is. Cf. SW VI, 161; IV, 121; IV, 391.

8. See Hermanni 1994, 143.

9. Schelling also refers to this as the "equilibrium" (*Gleichgewicht*) and the "indifference" (*Gleichgültigkeit*) of the "power of choice" (*Willkür*) (SW VII, 382–83). In a later discussion he uses the Latin phrase *aequilibrium arbitrii* (SW VII, 392).

10. We should note that the concept of freedom in the third antinomy is not the same as what Schelling characterizes as the "usual concept of freedom."

Kant defines transcendental freedom as "an *absolute spontaneity* of causes whereby they can begin *on their own* a series of appearances" (KrV, A 446/B 474).

11. For a discussion of Reinhold's development of Kant's theory of freedom as background for Schelling, see Gardner 2017, 134–37.

12. For Leibniz's discussion of Buridan's ass, see *Theodicy*, Part I, §49 (Leibniz 1985, 150).

13. Spinoza cites the ignorance of the causes of things as the source of the idea of freedom. See Appendix to Part I of the *Ethics* (Spinoza 1994, 110). Hermanni (1994, 143–44) cites a passage in Leibniz's *Theodicy* (Part I, §50; Leibniz 1985, 150) that refers to the "imperceptible causes" of our decisions.

14. In this sense, Leibniz affirms that all truths are determined, but there are nonetheless contingent truths. Schelling, however, also rejects absolute contingency in the modal sense—at least in the *Freiheitsschrift*—because this requires possibilities that are not actualized. Later, he criticizes what he calls the "formal concept of possibility," according to which everything is possible that is not self-contradictory. This is an "empty possibility" that is "in itself false" and is only valid for the human understanding, not for God (SW VII, 397–98). See chapter 5, section 2.

15. Hermanni (1994, 144) also connects this passage with the principle of sufficient reason.

16. Hermanni (1994, 151) writes that this is "Schelling's version" of the principle of sufficient reason. I would instead say that it is a direct implication of the principle.

17. As discussed in chapter 1, this is an essential feature of reason for Kant and accounts for its "architectonic" character. At the beginning of the *Freiheitsschrift*, Schelling also refers to "reason, which presses for unity" (SW VII, 337).

18. In the *Lectures on the Method of Academic Study* (1803), Schelling says that empirical necessity is a way "to elongate contingency by pushing back necessity *ad infinitum*" (SW V, 291). In the *Further Presentations* (1802), he humorously compares the causal law to the English national debt: one borrows from a second person to pay the first, then from a third person to pay the second, ad infinitum (SW IV, 344). For Schelling's full critique, see SW IV, 341–45.

19. This is also part of the argument for the thesis in Kant's third antinomy (KrV, A 444–46/B 472–74).

20. Neither Kant (in his mature thought) nor Schelling (in the *Freiheitsschrift*) seriously consider a compatibilist conception of freedom. For Schelling, such a conception would presumably make the being (*Wesen*) of the human being something merely "given" and thus destroy all moral responsibility. See sections 3 and 4 below. For a discussion of Kant's rejection of compatibilism, see Ameriks 2000, 19–20, 71–75, 147–48. A strong notion of responsibility is also Kant's reason for rejecting compatibilism and embracing "absolute freedom" (147).

21. I therefore think that Schopenhauer's criticism is unfair when he accuses Schelling of re-presenting Kant's ideas without giving him credit (ASW III, 608).

22. Sometimes Kant calls this "transcendental freedom" to distinguish it from "practical freedom." The latter requires self-determination through the moral law. Transcendental freedom is necessary but not sufficient for practical freedom. See KrV, A 533–34/B 561–62; A 801–2/B 829–30.

23. After characterizing the standpoint of idealism, Schelling also uses the word "intelligible" in his own account. The "life before this life" does not precede this life temporally, because the intelligible is outside of time (SW VII, 387). The deed whereby the *Wesen* of the human being is determined is an "intelligible deed" (SW VII, 389).

24. Koßler (1995, 196ff.) notes that this transferal of freedom to the whole of one's intelligible character—and away from individual actions—is anticipated by Jakob Friedrich Fries in his 1807 treatise *Neue oder anthropologische Kritik der Vernunft*.

25. Kant is far from claiming (theoretically) that things in themselves are free. He only intends to establish "that nature at least does *not conflict* with the causality from freedom" (A 558/B 586). Ameriks (2000, 342) notes the limitations of Kant's account, since he lacks "a nonpractical evidence base for the absolute freedom that he puts so much weight upon." Nonetheless, Ameriks argues that this is a superior position to that of Reinhold and Fichte, who insist on absolute freedom but "undercut" the theoretical framework for making sense of it. In my view, Schelling escapes this criticism, because he retains key aspects of Kant's framework—even if he fills in that framework in a way that is much more dogmatic than Kant would allow.

26. Though rhetorically powerful, it expresses ideas already articulated in some of Schelling's earliest writings on freedom and self-positing, drawing on Fichte (cf. SW I, 400). For an interpretation of this passage, see Höfele (2019, 111–13), who reads it in the context of Schelling's evolving philosophy of will. Höfele also notes the continuity with Schelling's earlier writings but sees a shift in emphasis in the language of will, which builds on the language first developed in the 1806 appendix to *On the World Soul* (SW II, 362).

27. Snow (1996, 169–72) also connects this passage to Schelling's account of the intelligible deed and provides an analysis of each of the predicates.

28. Obviously "being" must have two senses here. In the sense that is denied, it is purely objective and therefore opposed to (subjective) knowledge. By contrast, *genuine* being—or being in the "proper" (*eigentlich*) sense—is prior to the opposition between being and knowledge.

29. This distinction between being (*Sein*) and appearance is also articulated in the *Freiheitsschrift* in terms of the distinction between being (*Sein*) and becoming (*Werden*) (cf. SW VII, 346). He observes that compulsion is felt only

in becoming, not in being (SW VII, 386). Moreover, God is a life, not merely a being (*ein Sein*), and being actualizes itself and becomes sensible in becoming (SW VII, 403). That passage is part of a movement to rehabilitate becoming and appearance in the *Freiheitsschrift*: they are not simply shadows of reality.

30. In this respect it resembles the individual notion of a thing in Leibniz. See the *Discourse on Metaphysics*, §13.

31. "Being governed by laws" (*Gesetzmäßigkeit*) is closely associated with necessity, both for Kant and for Schelling. In fact, in the *System of Transcendental Idealism* (1800), Schelling sometimes speaks of uniting freedom and *Gesetzmäßigkeit* rather than freedom and necessity. See SW III, 600; cf. I, 330–31.

32. Cf. "Every substance has a perfect spontaneity . . . [and] everything that happens to it is a consequence of its idea or of its being, and nothing determines it, except God alone" (Leibniz, *Discourse on Metaphysics*, §32; Leibniz 1989, 64).

33. *Ethics*, Part I, Def. 7 (Spinoza 1994, 86). Cf. "God acts solely from the *laws of his own nature* alone, and is compelled by no one" (Part I, Proposition 17; Spinoza 1994, 97, emphasis added). Schelling cites these passages from Spinoza in a footnote when discussing the identity of freedom and necessity in the 1795 *Philosophical Letters on Dogmatism and Criticism* (SW I, 331n).

34. Hermanni 1994, 146. For the connection with Spinoza's definition, see also Jacobs 1995, 128.

35. See the discussion of derived absoluteness in chapter 3.

36. One could also say that each monad is uncreated, insofar as it is eternally present as an idea in the mind of God. Nevertheless, even if the intelligible essence is not determined *by* anything else, it is still simply given and the human being plays no active role in its determination.

37. There is a tendency among Schelling scholars, going back to Theunissen, to closely identify—or even equate—the intelligible deed with original sin: it is "supposed to be identical with the Fall" (Theunissen 1965, 185n15). One should not forget, however, that morally good actions are also determined in this deed.

38. Cf. "An undetermined ground is also a non-determining ground—and, to that extent, no ground" (SW V, 144).

39. By "reflexive" I mean that it acts upon itself—that is, its action is *self-directed*. My use of the term does not imply reflection or consciousness, as it sometimes does in German.

40. For Fichte, the I is "self-reverting acting" (*in sich zurückkehrendes Handeln*) (FW I, 462).

41. He does use the word "choice" in the passage immediately before this section, which serves as a transition: despite the general necessity of sin, evil always remains the "choice" of the human being (SW VII, 382). See also SW VII, 374. In light of the evidence presented below, I believe that Schelling here is speaking loosely. Cf. Gerlach 2019, 246–47.

42. He later defines "religiosity" as "the highest decidedness for what is right, without any choice" (SW VII, 392). He also rejects the notion that divine freedom involves choice (SW VII, 397–98).

43. Schelling does say that the human being is an "undecided being" in the "original creation" (SW VII, 385), and he associates this with a mythological state of innocence (cf. SW VII, 374, 379, 382). On the other hand, he clearly excludes the possibility that the intelligible essence determines itself out of a state of being purely undetermined, because this would lead back to conceiving freedom as arbitrariness (SW VII, 384; cf. 392). Kosch (2014, 150) also notes the apparent inconsistency. To reconcile these two positions, I would point out that *Unentschiedenheit* often refers to an initial state of forces where they are still unseparated and indistinct (cf. SW VIII, 278; WA I, 95–96). The ground has the role of enlivening them and drawing them out of this state of "undecidedness" (SW VII, 374; 379). I would therefore place the undecidedness and the eternal decision on different levels: the undecidedness is at the level of the temporal interplay of forces; the decision is outside of time. By contrast, Gerlach (2019, 249) views the undecidedness as a "structural element" of the eternal decision, which is always already decided.

44. I interpret "character" to refer to the intelligible *Wesen* of the *Freiheitsschrift*. This is also Gerlach's view (2019, 236), though he also identifies a second sense of character that admits of degrees. The passages in the *Weltalter* that treat the eternal deed of freedom also refer to character (WA I, 93ff.; WA II, 177–78, 183–84; SW VIII, 304). For Kant's original use of the phrase "intelligible character," see KrV, A 538ff./B 566ff.; A 556/B 584. See also Koßler 1995, 195ff.

45. Schelling acknowledges that the decision seems to exclude the possibility of conversion, because it is made once and for all. His solution is to include conversion within the original act (SW VII, 389). This seems unsatisfying—why decide to do evil and repent "at the same time"? We will return to this point in the conclusion.

46. Schelling speaks of different lives or "a double life" in several writings in the years preceding 1809: a temporal life in appearance, and an eternal life in the absolute (SW IV, 230; VI, 41; VI, 218–19; VI, 536; VII, 162–64; VII, 190). The life in the absolute is the "idea" (SW VI, 187), which is identified with the thing in itself and its *Wesen* (SW VII, 162; IV, 387).

47. Cf. "It is a constant, never ceasing deed and can for that reason never *again* be brought before consciousness" (WA II, 183, emphasis added). The same passage refers to the deed "sinking into the night of unconsciousness."

48. GA 42, 266; Heidegger 1985, 153–54.

49. Archiv der Berlin-Brandenburgischen Akademie der Wissenschaften, Archiv-Sign.: NL Schelling, 86, S. 20.

50. In one of the passages cited above, the In-itself is identified as "what is eternal, resting on itself, will, freedom" (SW VII, 347). Something that is in itself does not *have* freedom but *is* freedom.

51. Cf. "When applied to the I, *self-positing* and *being* are completely the same" (FW I, 98).

52. Schelling replies as follows to the question of why this particular individual is destined to act in an evil manner and not another: "The question presupposes that the human being is not initially act and deed and that he as a spiritual being has a being which is prior to, and independent of, his will, which, as has been shown, is impossible" (SW VII, 388). Kant confronts a similar question in the *Critique of Pure Reason* (A 556/B 584).

53. Schindler is therefore incorrect when he writes that Schelling "comes in the *Freedom Essay* to identify freedom with ability or power *rather than* a kind of actuality or perfection" (2012, 232).

54. This echoes a line from Jacobi's influential Appendix VII to the second edition of his *Spinoza Letters*. See JW IV/2, 152; Jacobi 1994, 375.

55. I thank Kevin Brennan for pointing out the connection to Eckhart several years ago. I am also grateful to Ian Moore for directing me toward helpful sources on this aspect of Eckhart's thought.

56. *Predigt* 52 (Eckhart 1993, 552; Eckhart 2006, 440). Cf. similar statements in *Predigt* 2 (Eckhart 1993, 24).

57. See Largier 1993, 760–62 and Tobin 1986, 162–63. For a discussion of Eckhart's distinction between *esse virtuale* and *esse formale*, see Tobin 1986, 59–62.

58. *Predigt* 52 (Eckhart 1993, 554; Eckhart 2006, 440).

59. It is not clear how well Schelling knew Meister Eckhart. It is true that in the *Weltalter* he refers to "an older German author" who calls the will that wills nothing "poor" (WA I, 15). However, Schelling may have in mind another author in the German mystical tradition. See Höfele 2019, 158–59.

60. Structurally, this is similar to the Agrippan trilemma, used by ancient skeptics: "Any response you give to the why-question will either terminate arbitrarily, or lead to an infinite regress, or move in a circle" (Franks 2005, 18). Franks reads the German Idealists as responding to this trilemma by turning to absolute grounding (387).

61. This is essentially the classical argument against an infinite regress, which reaches at least as far back as Aristotle and the argument for an unmoved mover. See Aristotle, *Physics*, book 8, chapter 5; Aquinas, *Summa Theologiae* I, q. 2, a. 3.

62. A variation on this solution is to narrow the scope of the principle to a subset of what exists (e.g., contingent beings). Cf. the early-Kant: "It is only the existence of contingent things which requires the support of a determining ground, and . . . the unique and absolutely necessary Being is exempt from this law" (AA 1, 396; Kant 1992).

63. See the discussion of the relation between affirming and grounding in chapters 2 and 3.

64. Cf. Fichte's line: "I am absolutely, because I am" (FW I, 98). This also recalls the line from the mystic Angelus Silesius: "The rose is without why; it

blooms because it blooms." Heidegger discusses this verse from Silesius in his lecture course on the principle of ground (Heidegger 1957, 68ff.; Heidegger 1991, 35ff.).

65. In the *Ages of the World*, Schelling refers to a "groundless freedom that is necessary through itself" (WA I, 93).

66. The same ambivalence can be seen in Schelling's earlier writings. A system, he writes, is a whole that "bears itself" (*sich selbst trägt*). But then he adds that transcendental freedom or willing, the principle of the system, is by its nature "the most groundless" (SW I, 400).

67. For an account of the history of the concept, see Summerell 2002.

68. Plotinus 1988, 277.

69. See Summerell 2002, 497ff., 506ff. He cites the objection of Caterus to the passage in Descartes's *Meditations* where Descartes claims that if one were "from oneself" one would give oneself all the perfections (AT VII, 49–50). Caterus insists that the phrases "cause of himself" and "from himself" should be interpreted negatively (AT VII, 95).

70. *Summa Theologiae*, I, q. 2, a. 3, resp. (Thomas Aquinas 2006, 23).

71. One might interpret this as "temporally prior," which would align with the temporality of causal relations in Kant. However, for Aquinas, God is capable of efficient causality and God cannot be temporally prior because he is eternal.

72. Outside of the lectures on the history of philosophy and the late lectures on revelation, it is mentioned in the 1812 polemic against Jacobi (SW VIII, 61–62; cf. SW VIII, 81). In early works, however, he does say that the I posits itself "through absolute causality" (SW I, 96, 234).

73. The closest Schelling comes to referring to the absolute as *causa sui* is the 1804 *Würzburg System*: "The cause of a thing is that which affirms the thing; the thing as effect is what is affirmed. The two are not-one in what is not absolute, but in the absolute they are absolutely one" (SW VI, 148). This seems to suggest that the absolute is cause of itself, because it affirms itself. This is Rang's interpretation (2000, 42–43). However, later in the work, Schelling clarifies: "By 'cause' I understand here something that affirms [but] that is different from what is affirmed by it" (SW VI, 177). Causality requires non-identity between cause and effect, thus excluding the possibility of a *causa sui*. Notably, Leibniz also avoids the phrase. God is not his own cause but his own *reason* (cf. Leibniz 1989, 210).

74. *Ethics*, Part I, Def. 1 (Spinoza 1994, 85).

75. Descartes, *Response to the Fourth Set of Objections*, AT VII, 243. See Summerell 2002, 507.

76. In *Further Presentations* (1802), he says that the ideas "are themselves gods, for each for itself is absolute, and yet each is grasped in the absolute form" (SW IV, 405). Elsewhere he equates ideas and things in themselves. See SW VI, 185.

77. But Schelling does use the language of "self-positing" and "self-affirming," which seems to indicate that the intelligible *Wesen* is also the source of its own being. As discussed in chapter 3, whatever is affirmed by God is *itself* self-

affirming. Thus, the ideas are affirmed by God (and thus dependent), but at the same time self-affirming. (How to conceive the two together is not completely clear: their self-affirming has to be conceived as embedded within God's self-affirming.)

78. I therefore disagree with Theunissen (1965, 187), who claims that the intelligible deed rules out the createdness of human beings, and thus Schelling abandons his intention to account for the *derived* absoluteness of human freedom.

79. Indeed, Schelling identifies this as the core of Leibniz's theodicy: the ultimate source of evil is the eternal truths in the mind of God, independent of his will (SW VII, 367-68). Because God does not determine his own essence, he cannot be responsible for those eternal truths.

80. Presumably this account applies to God as well, since it is not meant to account for what is uniquely human about freedom. Schelling, however, does not state this explicitly.

81. Elsewhere I argue that this is a crucial difference with Schopenhauer's very similar account of transcendental freedom. Though Schopenhauer also locates ultimate freedom in the eternal *Wesen* of the human being, this *Wesen* is groundless, not self-grounding, because the principle of ground only applies to appearances. See Thomas 2022.

82. Strawson 1994, 5.

83. Strawson 1994, 6. Strawson, however, requires that one consciously choose to be the way one is. For Schelling, it is not a choice, but a pre-conscious deed, though it might involve a more original form of consciousness (see above).

84. O'Connor (2013, 7-8) also connects Schelling and Strawson, though he does not discuss the concept of *causa sui*.

Conclusion

1. For example, see GA 42, 279; Heidegger 1985, 161; Hermanni 1994, 247-61; Peetz 1995, 211-25; Hennigfeld 2001, 142.

2. Technically, Schelling says this about the concept of freedom, but the place of the concept would presumably reflect freedom's place in reality.

3. *The Vocation of Man* (1800), FW II, 256.

4. "All true, i.e., absolute freedom is an absolute necessity. No further ground can be provided for an act of absolute freedom; it is so because it is so—i.e., it simply *is* and [thus it is], to that extent, necessary" (SW VII, 429).

5. To my knowledge, Schelling commentators have not treated this problem as I have framed it, though Bowman (2020) explores a similar problem—how the temporal order of nature is grounded in the eternal deed. Hermanni (1994, 254-61) notes that the eternal deed, like Fichte's *Tathandlung*, is supposed to be a principle of explanation for the world of experience. He argues that this cannot be reconciled with the deed's role as the source of moral responsibility.

6. Cf. SW VII, 154. This is true for both Kant and Schelling. See Rang 2000, 69.

7. *Ethics*, Preface to Part III (Spinoza 1994, 152).

8. A similar difficulty is present in Kant's account of transcendental freedom, as Schelling recognized in his early writings. See SW I, 397.

9. For a slightly different interpretation of the problem, see Bracken 1972, 65–66, 121–22. Bracken also sees a tension between freedom and natural causality, but he does not formulate the problem in terms of coordination. Instead, he interprets the pre-human development of nature as the "ground" for the intelligible deed (65), and he seems to interpret "ground" deterministically, which would leave no room for freedom. In my interpretation, the intelligible deed is radically independent of the (temporal) development of nature, thus making coordination the problem.

10. Cf. "The activity by which the objective world is produced is originally identical with that which expresses itself in willing" (SW III, 348). It is curious that Schelling never develops this thought in the *Freiheitsschrift*, even though he returns to the relationship between freedom and necessity in the section on the formal concept of freedom.

11. See the second section of chapter 5.

12. Most of the references to "providence" (*Fürsehung* or *Vorsehung*) have to do with affirmations of foreknowledge (SW VII, 378; 396; 402). The only reference to a providential order (SW VII, 387) alludes to the historical problem without taking a stance.

13. Theunissen 1965, 180–81, 187.

14. In earlier works he had identified the ideas with things in themselves (SW VI, 183) and associated them with the process of begetting (SW VI, 35).

15. In the section on divine freedom, Schelling concedes that there are infinite possibilities in the ground, though only one possible world that accords with God's nature (SW VII, 398).

16. It is true that Schelling is very critical of Leibniz's conception of a divine choice between possible worlds (SW VII, 397–98). What he rejects is the notion that more than one world is possible when God's nature is considered. But one can affirm that only one world is possible, and this world is determined through the described selection.

17. "Even if all beings in the world were only thoughts in the divine mind, they would have to be living precisely for this reason" (SW VII, 347).

18. The relation between the two levels is the subject of Habermas's dissertation (1954). See also Beach 1994, 164–69.

19. For example, the "original undecidedness" of the human being is discussed in the context of formal freedom, which suggests that it is on the level of the In-itself (SW VII, 382, 385). However, Schelling also connects it to the

temptation toward evil through the arousal of the ground, which takes place in the development of nature (SW VII, 374, 379).

20. See the last section of chapter 6. It is true, of course, that certain features of appearance are determined by what is in itself—for instance, individual human actions, which are determined in the eternal deed.

21. He formulates his answer in terms of the acceptance of the grace needed for conversion, which is the precondition of returning to the good in Christian theology. But I believe his point can be generalized as I have formulated it.

22. This is Hermanni's objection (1994, 154–55). See also Peetz 1995, 216.

23. See the discussion in chapter 4. The word is also used at SW VII, 367n and 391.

24. I have used Emerson's own translation, quoted in his essay "Fate" from 1860 (1981, 352).

25. Schopenhauer attributes this saying to Malebranche (ASW I, 548), though it is not a verbatim quotation. Malebranche regards the compatibility of freedom and providence as a mystery in book 3, part 1, chapter 2 of *The Search after Truth* (Malebranche 1997, 205).

26. Van Inwagen 2000.

Bibliography

Schelling's Texts

Sämmtliche Werke. Division I: 10 vols. (= I–X); Division II: 4 vols. (= XI–XIV). Edited by Karl Friedrich August Schelling. Stuttgart: Cotta, 1856–61.

Historisch-kritische Ausgabe. I. Werke; II. Nachlaß; III. Briefe. Edited by the Schelling-Kommission der Bayerischen Akademie der Wissenschaften. Stuttgart-Bad Cannstatt: Frommann-Holzboog, 1976–.

Philosophische Untersuchungen über das Wesen der menschlichen Freiheit und die damit zusammenhängenden Gegenstände. Edited by Thomas Buchheim. 2nd ed. Hamburg: Meiner, 2011.

Philosophical Investigations into the Essence of Human Freedom. Translated by Jeff Love and Johannes Schmidt. Albany: State University of New York Press, 2006.

Die Weltalter: Fragmente, in the original versions of 1811 and 1813. Edited by Manfred Schröter. Munich: Beck, 1946.

Aus Schellings Leben: In Briefen. Edited by Gustav L. Plitt. 3 vols. Leipzig: Hirzel, 1869–70.

Timaeus (1794). Edited by Hartmut Buchner. Stuttgart-Bad Cannstatt: Frommann-Holzboog, 1994.

Philosophische Entwürfe und Tagebücher 1809–1813: Philosophie der Freiheit und der Weltalter. Edited by Lothar Knatz, Hans Jörg Sandkühler, and Martin Schraven. Hamburg: Meiner, 1994.

Grundlegung der positiven Philosophie: Münchener Vorlesung WS 1832/33. Edited by Horst Fuhrmans. Turin: Bottega d'Erasmo, 1972.

Other Primary Texts

Aristotle. 1924. *Aristotle's Metaphysics: A Revised Text with Introduction and Commentary.* Edited by W. D. Ross. Princeton: Princeton University Press.

———. 1983. *The Complete Works of Aristotle: The Revised Oxford Translation*. Edited by Jonathan Barnes. 2 vols. Bollingen Series. Princeton: Princeton University Press.

Böhme, Jakob. 1955–1960. *Sämtliche Schriften*. Reprint of the edition of 1730 in 11 volumes. Edited by Will-Erich Peukert. Stuttgart: Frommann-Holzboog.

Bruno, Giordano. 1998. *Cause, Principle, and Unity*. Translated and edited by Richard Blackwell and Robert de Lucca. Cambridge: Cambridge University Press.

Descartes, René. 1964–76. *Oeuvres de Descartes*. Edited by Charles Adam and Paul Tannery. Rev. ed. 11 vols. Paris: Vrin/C.N.R.S.

———. 1984–91. *The Philosophical Writings of Descartes*. Translated by John Cottingham, Robert Stoothoff, and Dugald Murdoch. 3 vols. Cambridge: Cambridge University Press.

———. 1996. *Meditations on First Philosophy*. Translated by John Cottingham. Cambridge: Cambridge University Press.

Eckhart, Meister. 1993. *Werke I*. Edited with commentary by Niklaus Largier. Frankfurt: Deutscher Klassiker.

———. 2006. "Sermon 52." In *The Essential Writings of Christian Mysticism*, edited by Bernard McGinn, 438–43. New York: Modern Library.

Emerson, Ralph Waldo. 1981. "Fate." In *The Portable Emerson*, edited by Carl Bode and Malcolm Cowley, 346–74. New York: Penguin.

Fichte, Johann Gottlieb. 1845–46. *Sämmtliche Werke*. Edited by Immanuel Hermann Fichte. 8 vols. Berlin: Veit.

———. 1988. *Fichte: Early Philosophical Writings*. Translated by Daniel Breazeale. Ithaca: Cornell University Press.

Goethe, Johann Wolfgang von. 1795. *Wilhelm Meisters Lehrjahre*. Vol. 2. Frankfurt.

Grimm, Jacob, and Wilhelm Grimm. 1854–1961. *Deutsches Wörterbuch*. 32 vols. Leipzig: Hirzel.

Hegel, Georg Wilhelm Friedrich. 1969–71. *Werke in zwanzig Bänden*. Edited by Eva Moldenhauer and Karl Marcus Michel. Frankfurt: Suhrkamp.

Hölderlin, Friedrich. 1990. *"Hyperion" and Selected Poems*. Edited by Eric L. Santner. New York: Continuum.

Jacobi, Friedrich Heinrich. 1811. *Von den göttlichen Dingen und ihrer Offenbarung*. Leipzig: Fleischer.

———. 1812–25. *Werke*. Edited by Friedrich Roth and Friedrich Köppen. Leipzig: Fleischer.

———. 1994. *Main Philosophical Writings and the Novel "Allwill."* Translated by George di Giovanni. Montreal: McGill-Queen's University Press.

———. 2000. *Über die Lehre des Spinoza in Briefen an den Herrn Moses Mendelssohn*. Edited by Marion Lauschke. Hamburg: Meiner.

Kant, Immanuel. 1900–. *Gesammelte Schriften*. Edited by the Preußische Akademie der Wissenschaften. Berlin: De Gruyter.

———. 1987. *The Critique of Judgment*. Translated by Werner S. Pluhar. Indianapolis: Hackett.

———. 1992. *Theoretical Philosophy, 1755–1770*. Translated by David Walford and Ralf Meerbote. Cambridge: Cambridge University Press.
———. 1996. *The Critique of Pure Reason*. Translated by Werner S. Pluhar. Indianapolis: Hackett.
———. 2002. *The Critique of Practical Reason*. Translated by Werner S. Pluhar. Indianapolis: Hackett.
———. 2009. *Religion within the Bounds of Bare Reason*. Translated by Werner S. Pluhar. Indianapolis: Hackett.
Kierkegaard, Søren. 1992. *Concluding Unscientific Postscript to "Philosophical Fragments."* Translated by Howard V. Hong and Edna H. Hong. Princeton: Princeton University Press.
Krause, Karl Christian Friedrich. 1828. *Vorlesungen über das System der Philosophie*. Göttingen: Dieterich.
Krug, Wilhelm Traugott. 1801. *Briefe über den neuesten Idealismus*. Leipzig.
Leibniz, Gottfried Wilhelm. 1875–90. *Die philosophischen Schriften*. Edited by C. I. Gerhardt. Berlin: Weidmann.
———. 1903. *Opuscules et fragments inédits de Leibniz*. Edited by Louis Couturat. Paris: Alcan.
———. 1985. *Theodicy*. Translated by E. M. Huggard. La Salle, IL: Open Court.
———. 1989. *Philosophical Essays*. Translated by Roger Ariew and Daniel Garber. Indianapolis: Hackett.
———. 1999. *Philosophische Schriften*, 4. Band, Teil A. Berlin: Akademie Verlag.
Malebranche, Nicolas. 1997. *The Search after Truth*. Translated and edited by Thomas M. Lennon and Paul J. Olscamp. Cambridge: Cambridge University Press.
Marcel, Gabriel. 1965. *Being and Having: An Existentialist Diary*. Translated by Katharine Farrer. New York: Harper & Row.
Nietzsche, Friedrich. 1996. *Beyond Good and Evil*. Translated by Walter Kaufmann. New York: Random House.
Oetinger, Friedrich Christoph. 1765. *Der Irrdischen und himmlischen Philosophie, Zweyter Theil*. Frankfurt and Leipzig.
Otto, Rudolf. 2014. *Das Heilige: Über das Irrationale in der Idee des Göttlichen und sein Verhältnis zum Rationalen*. Munich: Beck.
Plato. 2001. *Timaeus*. Translated by Peter Kalkavage. Newburyport, MA: Focus.
Plotinus. 1988. *Ennead VI.6–9*. Translated by A. H. Armstrong. Loeb Classical Library. Cambridge, MA: Harvard University Press.
Ramus, Petrus. 1555. *La Dialectique de Pierre de la Ramée*. Paris: André Wechel.
Schlegel, Friedrich. 1808. *Ueber die Sprache und Weisheit der Indier: Ein Beitrag zur Begründung der Alterthumskunde*. Heidelberg: Mohr und Zimmer.
Schopenhauer, Arthur. 1960–65. *Sämtliche Werke*. Edited by Wolfgang Frhr. von Löhneysen. 5 vols. Stuttgart: Suhrkamp.
Spinoza, Baruch. 1925. *Spinoza Opera*. Edited by Carl Gebhardt. 4 vols. Heidelberg: Winters.

———. 1994. *A Spinoza Reader: The Ethics and Other Works*. Translated by Edwin Curley. Princeton, NJ: Princeton University Press.

Thomas Aquinas. 2006. *The Treatise on the Divine Nature: Summa Theologiae I, 1–13*. Translated by Brian J. Shanley. Indianapolis: Hackett.

Secondary Literature

Adams, Robert Merrihew. 1994. *Leibniz: Determinist, Theist, Idealist*. New York: Oxford University Press.

Ameriks, Karl. 2000. *Kant and the Fate of Autonomy: Problems in the Appropriation of the Critical Philosophy*. Cambridge: Cambridge University Press.

Antognazza, Maria Rosa. 2007. *Leibniz on the Trinity and the Incarnation: Reason and Revelation in the Seventeenth Century*. Translated by Gerald Parks. New Haven: Yale University Press.

Asmuth, Christoph. 2012. "Grund—Tiefe—Ungrund: Überlegungen zur Begründungsproblematik im Anschluss an Schellings *Freiheitsschrift*." In *Schellings Philosophie der Freiheit*, edited by Diogo Ferrer and Teresa Pedro, 191–206. Würzburg: Ergon.

Beach, Edward Allen. 1994. *The Potencies of God(s): Schelling's Philosophy of Mythology*. Albany: State University of New York Press.

Beiser, Frederick C. 1987. *The Fate of Reason: German Philosophy from Kant to Fichte*. Cambridge, MA: Harvard University Press.

———. 2002. *German Idealism: The Struggle against Subjectivism, 1781–1801*. Cambridge, MA: Harvard University Press.

———. 2005. *Hegel*. New York: Routledge.

Berger, Benjamin, and Daniel Whistler. 2020. *The Schelling-Eschenmayer Controversy, 1801: Nature and Identity*. Edinburgh: Edinburgh University Press.

Binkelmann, Christoph. 2015. "Derivierte Absolutheit: Die Bedeutung des transzendentalen Idealismus Fichtes für Schellings *Freiheitsschrift*." *Schelling-Studien* 3: 115–31.

Bowman, Brady. 2020. "Schelling on Eternal Choice and the Temporal Order of Nature." In *Schelling's Philosophy: Freedom, Nature, and Systematicity*, edited by G. Anthony Bruno, 115–33. Oxford: Oxford University Press.

Bracken, Joseph. 1972. *Freiheit und Kausalität bei Schelling*. Freiburg: Alber.

Brouwer, Christian. 2011. *Schellings Freiheitsschrift: Studien zu ihrer Interpretation und ihrer Bedeutung für die theologische Diskussion*. Tübingen: Mohr Siebeck.

Brown, Robert F. 1977. *The Later Philosophy of Schelling: The Influence of Boehme on the Works of 1809–1815*. Lewisburg, PA: Bucknell University Press.

Bruneder, Gertrud. 1958. "Das Wesen der menschlichen Freiheit bei Schelling und sein Ideen-geschichtlicher Zusammenhang mit Jakob Böhmes Lehre vom Ungrund." *Archiv für Philosophie* 8: 101–15.

Bruno, G. Anthony. 2020. "The Facticity of Time: Conceiving Schelling's Idealism of Ages." In *Schelling's Philosophy: Freedom, Nature, and Systematicity*, edited by G. Anthony Bruno, 185-206. Oxford: Oxford University Press.

Buchheim, Thomas. 1996. "Das Prinzip des Grundes und Schellings Weg zur *Freiheitsschrift.*" In *Schellings Weg zur Freiheitsschrift: Legende und Wirklichkeit*, edited by H. M. Baumgartner and W. G. Jacobs, 223-39. Stuttgart-Bad Cannstatt: Frommann-Holzboog.

———. 1999. "'Metaphysische Notwendigkeit des Bösen': Über eine Zweideutigkeit in Heideggers Auslegung der Freiheitsschrift." In *Zeit und Freiheit: Schelling—Schopenhauer—Kierkegaard—Heidegger: Akten der Fachtagung der Internationalen Schelling-Gesellschaft*, edited by István Fehér and Wilhelm Jacobs, 183-91. Budapest: Éthos Könyvek.

———. 2000. "Schelling und die metaphysische Zelebration des Bösen." *Philosophisches Jahrbuch* 107: 47-60.

———. 2004. "Grundlinien von Schellings Personbegriff." In *"Alle Persönlichkeit ruht auf einem dunkeln Grunde": Schellings Philosophie der Personalität*, edited by Thomas Buchheim and Friedrich Hermanni. Berlin: Akademie Verlag.

———. 2006. "'. . . eine sehr reele Unterscheidung': Zur Differenz der Freiheitsschrift." In *Kritische und absolute Transzendenz: Religionsphilosophie und philosophische Theologie bei Kant und Schelling*, edited by Christian Danz and Rudolf Langthaler, 182-99. Freiburg: Alber.

———. 2009. "Freispruch durch Geschichte: Schellings verbesserte Theodizee in Auseinandersetzung mit Leibniz in der Freiheitsschrift." *Neue Zeitschrift für systematische Theologie und Religionsphilosophie* 51: 365-82.

———. 2011a. "Anmerkungen des Herausgebers." In *Philosophische Untersuchungen über das Wesen der menschlichen Freiheit und die damit zusammenhängenden Gegenstände*, by Friedrich Wilhelm Joseph Schelling, 89-188. Edited by Thomas Buchheim. 2nd ed. Hamburg: Meiner.

———. 2011b. "Einleitung." In *Philosophische Untersuchungen über das Wesen der menschlichen Freiheit und die damit zusammenhängenden Gegenstände*, by Friedrich Wilhelm Joseph Schelling, ix-lv. Edited by Thomas Buchheim. 2nd ed. Hamburg: Meiner.

Cooper, John W. 2006. *Panentheism—The Other God of the Philosophers: From Plato to the Present*. Grand Rapids, MI: Baker Academic.

Correia, Fabrice, and Benjamin Schnieder. 2012. "Grounding: An Opinionated Introduction." In *Metaphysical Grounding: Understanding the Structure of Reality*, edited by Fabrice Correia and Benjamin Schnieder, 1-36. Cambridge: Cambridge University Press.

Danz, Christian. 2018. "Natur und Geist: Schellings Systemkonzeption zwischen 1801 und 1809." In *Systembegriffe um 1800-1809: Systeme in Bewegung*, edited by Violetta L. Waibel, Christian Danz, and Jürgen Stolzenberg, 97-116. Hamburg: Meiner.

Dörendahl, Roswitha. 2011. *Abgrund der Freiheit: Schellings Freiheitsphilosophie als Kritik des neuzeitlichen Autonomie-Projektes*. Würzburg: Ergon.

Durrell, Martin. 2011. *Hammer's German Grammar and Usage*. 5th ed. London: Hodder.

Egloff, Lisa. 2016. *Das Böse als Vollzug menschlicher Freiheit: Die Neuausrichtung idealistischer Systemphilosophie in Schellings Freiheitsschrift*. Berlin: De Gruyter.

Ehrhardt, Walter E. 1995. "Das Ende der Offenbarung." In *F. W. J. Schelling: Über das Wesen der menschlichen Freiheit*, edited by Otfried Höffe and Annemarie Pieper, 221–34. Berlin: Akademie Verlag.

Eidam, Heinz. 2000. *Dasein und Bestimmung: Kants Grund-Problem*. Berlin: De Gruyter.

Förster, Eckart. 2012. *The Twenty-Five Years of Philosophy: A Systematic Reconstruction*. Translated by Brady Bowman. Cambridge, MA: Harvard University Press.

Frank, Manfred. 2014. "Identity of Identity and Non-Identity: Schelling's Path to the Absolute System of Identity." In *Interpreting Schelling: Critical Essays*, edited by Lara Ostaric, 120–44. Cambridge: Cambridge University Press.

———. 2018. *Reduplikative Identität: Der Schlüssel zu Schellings reifer Philosophie*. Stuttgart-Bad Cannstatt: Frommann-Holzboog.

Franks, Paul. 2005. *All or Nothing: Systematicity, Transcendental Arguments, and Skepticism in German Idealism*. Cambridge, MA: Harvard University Press.

Franz, Michael. 1996. *Schellings Tübinger Platon-Studien*. Göttingen: Vandenhoeck & Ruprecht.

Freydberg, Bernard. 2008. *Schelling's Dialogical Freedom Essay: Provocative Philosophy Then and Now*. Albany: State University of New York Press.

Gabriel, Markus. 2015. "Schelling." In *The Oxford Handbook of German Philosophy in the Nineteenth Century*, edited by Michael N. Forster and Kristin Gjesdal, 88–107. Oxford: Oxford University Press.

———. 2020. "Schelling on the Compatibility of Freedom and Systematicity." In *Schelling's Philosophy: Freedom, Nature, and Systematicity*, edited by G. Anthony Bruno, 137–53. Oxford: Oxford University Press.

García, Marcela. 2015. "Schelling's Theory of Judgment and the Interpretation of the Copula." *Schelling-Studien* 3: 25–49.

Gardner, Sebastian. 2017. "The Metaphysics of Human Freedom: From Kant's Transcendental Idealism to Schelling's *Freiheitsschrift*." *British Journal for the History of Philosophy* 25: 133–56.

Gerlach, Stefan. 2019. *Handlung bei Schelling: Zur Fundamentaltheorie von Praxis, Zeit und Religion im mittleren und späten Werk*. Frankfurt: Klostermann.

Habermas, Jürgen. 1954. *Das Absolute und die Geschichte: Von der Zwiespältigkeit in Schellings Denken*. Bonn: PhD diss., Rheinische Friedrich-Wilhelms-Universität.

Heidegger, Martin. 1949. *Vom Wesen des Grundes*. Frankfurt: Klostermann.

———. 1957. *Der Satz vom Grund*. Stuttgart: Klett-Cotta.
———. 1975–. *Gesamtausgabe*. Frankfurt: Klostermann.
———. 1984. *The Metaphysical Foundations of Logic*. Translated by Michael Heim. Bloomington: Indiana University Press.
———. 1985. *Schelling's Treatise on the Essence of Human Freedom*. Translated by Joan Stambaugh. Athens: Ohio University Press.
———. 1991. *The Principle of Reason*. Translated by Reginald Lilly. Bloomington: Indiana University Press.
———. 1995. *Schellings Abhandlung über das Wesen der menschlichen Freiheit*. 2nd ed. Edited by Hildegaard Feick. Tübingen: Niemeyer.
———. 2006. *Sein und Zeit*. 19th ed. Tübingen: Niemeyer.
———. 2010. *Being and Time*. Translated by Joan Stambaugh. Revised by Dennis J. Schmidt. Albany: State University of New York Press.
Hennigfeld, Jochem. 2001. *F. W. J. Schellings "Philosophische Untersuchungen über das Wesen der menschlichen Freiheit und die damit zusammenhängenden Gegenstände."* Darmstadt: Wissenschaftliche Buchgesellschaft.
Hermanni, Friedrich. 1994. *Die letzte Entlastung: Vollendung und Scheitern des abendländischen Theodizeeprojektes in Schellings Philosophie*. Vienna: Passagen.
Höfele, Philipp. 2019. *Wollen und Lassen: Zur Ausdifferenzierung, Kritik und Rezeption des Willensparadigmas in der Philosophie Schellings*. Freiburg: Alber.
Hogrebe, Wolfram. 1989. *Prädikation und Genesis: Metaphysik als Fundamentalheuristik im Ausgang von Schellings "Die Weltalter."* Frankfurt: Suhrkamp.
Iber, Christian. 2004. "Personalität in Schellings *Freiheitsschrift*." In *"Alle Persönlichkeit ruht auf einem dunkeln Grunde": Schellings Philosophie der Personalität*, edited by Thomas Buchheim and Friedrich Hermanni. Berlin: Akademie Verlag.
Jacobs, Wilhelm G. 1995. "Die Entscheidung zum Bösen oder Guten." In *F. W. J. Schelling: Über das Wesen der menschlichen Freiheit*, edited by Otfried Höffe and Annemarie Pieper, 125–48. Berlin: Akademie Verlag.
Jantzen, Jörg. 1995. "Die Möglichkeit des Guten und des Bösen." In *F. W. J. Schelling: Über das Wesen der menschlichen Freiheit*, edited by Otfried Höffe and Annemarie Pieper, 61–90. Berlin: Akademie Verlag.
Kahl-Furthmann, Gertrud. 1976. "Der Satz vom zureichenden Grunde von Leibniz bis Kant." *Zeitschrift für philosophische Forschung* 30: 107–22.
Knappik, Franz. 2019. "What Is Wrong with Blind Necessity? Schelling's Critique of Spinoza's Necessitarianism in the *Freiheitsschrift*." *Journal of the History of Philosophy* 57: 129–57.
Kosch, Michelle. 2006. *Freedom and Reason in Kant, Schelling, and Kierkegaard*. Oxford: Oxford University Press.
———. 2014. "Idealism and Freedom in Schelling's *Freiheitsschrift*." In *Interpreting Schelling: Critical Essays*, edited by Lara Ostaric, 145–59. Cambridge: Cambridge University Press.

Koßler, Matthias. 1995. "Empirischer und intelligibler Charakter: Von Kant über Fries und Schelling zu Schopenhauer." *Schopenhauer-Jahrbuch* 76: 195–201.
Krell, David Farrell. 2005. *The Tragic Absolute: German Idealism and the Languishing of God*. Bloomington: Indiana University Press.
Krings, Hermann. 1995. "Von der Freiheit Gottes." In *F. W. J. Schelling: Über das Wesen der menschlichen Freiheit*, edited by Otfried Höffe and Annemarie Pieper, 173–87. Berlin: Akademie Verlag.
Largier, Niklaus. 1993. "Kommentar." In *Meister Eckhart: Werke I*, edited with commentary by Niklaus Largier, 713–1106. Frankfurt: Deutscher Klassiker.
Lauer, Christopher. 2010. *The Suspension of Reason in Hegel and Schelling*. London: Continuum.
Marquard, Odo. 1995. "Grund und Existenz in Gott." In *F. W. J. Schelling: Über das Wesen der menschlichen Freiheit*, edited by Otfried Höffe and Annemarie Pieper, 55–59. Berlin: Akademie Verlag.
Marquet, Jean-François. 1973. *Liberté et existence: Étude sur la formation de la philosophie de Schelling*. Paris: Gallimard.
Marx, Werner. 1984. *The Philosophy of F. W. J. Schelling: History, System, and Freedom*. Translated by Thomas Nenon. Bloomington: Indiana University Press.
Matthews, Bruce. 2011. *Schelling's Organic Form of Philosophy: Life as the Schema of Freedom*. Albany: State University of New York Press.
McGinn, Bernard. 2005. *The Harvest of Mysticism in Medieval Germany*. New York: Herder and Herder.
McGrath, S. J. 2012. *The Dark Ground of Spirit: Schelling and the Unconscious*. Hove, East Sussex: Routledge.
Mercer, Christia. 2001. *Leibniz's Metaphysics: Its Origin and Development*. Cambridge: Cambridge University Press.
Mine, Hideki. 1983. *Ungrund und Wissenschaft: Das Problem der Freiheit in der Spätphilosophie Schellings*. Frankfurt: Lang.
Moiso, Francesco. 1995. "Gott als Person." In *F. W. J. Schelling: Über das Wesen der menschlichen Freiheit*, edited by Otfried Höffe and Annemarie Pieper, 189–220. Berlin: Akademie Verlag.
O'Connor, Brian. 2013. "Self-determination and Responsibility in Schelling's *Freiheitsschrift*." *Studies in Social and Political Thought* 21: 3–18.
Ohashi, Ryôsuke. 1995. "Der Ungrund und das System." In *F. W. J. Schelling: Über das Wesen der menschlichen Freiheit*, edited by Otfried Höffe and Annemarie Pieper, 235–52. Berlin: Akademie Verlag.
O'Regan, Cyril. 2011. "The Trinity in Kant, Hegel, and Schelling." In *The Oxford Handbook of the Trinity*, edited by Gilles Emery and Matthew Levering, 254–66. Oxford: Oxford University Press.
Parkinson, G. H. R. 1965. *Logic and Reality in Leibniz's Metaphysics*. Oxford: Clarendon Press.
Peetz, Siegbert. 1995. *Die Freiheit im Wissen: Eine Untersuchung zu Schellings Konzept der Rationalität*. Frankfurt: Klostermann.

———. 2006. "Kraft der Freiheit: Überlegungen zu Schellings Konzept der Willensfreiheit." In *Die Ethik Arthur Schopenhauers im Ausgang vom Deutschen Idealismus (Fichte/Schelling)*, edited by Lore Hühn, 505–21. Würzburg: Ergon.
Pinkard, Terry. 2002. *German Philosophy 1760–1860: The Legacy of Idealism*. Cambridge: Cambridge University Press.
Rang, Bernhard. 1988. "Schellings Theorie des Lebens." *Zeitschrift für philosophische Forschung* 42, no. 2: 169–97.
———. 2000. *Identität und Indifferenz: Eine Untersuchung zu Schellings Identitätsphilosophie*. Frankfurt: Klostermann.
Rescher, Nicholas. 2003. "Leibniz and the Concept of System." In *On Leibniz*, 106–16. Pittsburgh: University of Pittsburgh Press.
Sallis, John. 1995. *Delimitations*. 2nd ed. Bloomington: Indiana University Press.
———. 1999. *Chorology*. Bloomington: Indiana University Press.
———. 2005. *The Gathering of Reason*. 2nd ed. Albany: State University of New York Press.
Sandkaulen, Birgit. 2000. *Grund und Ursache: Die Vernunftkritik Jacobis*. Munich: Fink.
Schindler, D. C. 2012. *The Perfection of Freedom: Schiller, Schelling, and Hegel between the Ancients and the Moderns*. Eugene, OR: Cascade Books.
Schwab, Philipp. 2018. "Von der Negativität zum Ungrund: Hegels *Phänomenologie des Geistes* und Schellings *Freiheitsschrift*." In *Systembegriffe um 1800–1809: Systeme in Bewegung*, edited by Violetta L. Waibel, Christian Danz, and Jürgen Stolzenberg, 131–55. Hamburg: Meiner.
Schwenzfeuer, Sebastian. 2012. *Natur und Subjekt: Die Grundlegung der schellingschen Naturphilosophie*. Freiburg: Alber.
Snow, Dale. 1996. *Schelling and the End of Idealism*. Albany: State University of New York Press.
Steigerwald, Joan. 2015. "Ground and Grounding: The Nature of Things in Schelling's Philosophy." *Symposium* 19: 176–97.
Strawson, Galen. 1994. "The Impossibility of Moral Responsibility." *Philosophical Studies* 75: 5–24.
Sturma, Dieter. 1995. "Präreflexive Freiheit und menschliche Selbstbestimmung." In *F. W. J. Schelling: Über das Wesen der menschlichen Freiheit*, edited by Otfried Höffe and Annemarie Pieper, 149–72. Berlin: Akademie Verlag.
Summerell, Orrin F. 2002. "Self-Causality from Plotinus to Eckhart and from Descartes to Kant." *Quaestio: Annuario di storia della metafisica* 2: 493–518.
Theunissen, Michael. 1965. "Schellings anthropologischer Ansatz." *Archiv für Geschichte der Philosophie* 47: 174–89.
Thomas, Mark J. 2014. "The Mediation of the Copula as a Fundamental Structure in Schelling's Philosophy." *Schelling-Studien* 2: 21–40.
———. 2022. "Freedom and Self-Grounding: A Fundamental Difference between Schelling and Schopenhauer." In *Freedom and Creation in Schelling*, edited

by Henning Tegtmeyer and Dennis Vanden Auweele, 289–311. Stuttgart-Bad Cannstatt: Frommann-Holzboog.

———. Forthcoming. "A True Proteus: Non-Being in Schelling's *Ages of the World*." In *Zeit—Geschichte—Erzählung: F. W. J. Schellings "Weltalter,"* edited by Lore Hühn, Philipp Höfele, and Philipp Schwab. Baden-Baden: Alber.

Tilliette, Xavier. 2004. *Schelling: Biographie*. Translated by Susanne Schaper. Stuttgart: Klett-Cotta.

Tobin, Frank L. 1986. *Meister Eckhart: Thought and Language*. Philadelphia: University of Pennsylvania Press.

Trappe, Tobias. 2001. "Ungrund, Urgrund." In *Historisches Wörterbuch der Philosophie*, vol. 11, 168–72, edited by Joachim Ritter, Karlfried Gründer, and Gottfried Gabriel. Basel: Schwabe.

Van Inwagen, Peter. 2000. "Free Will Remains a Mystery." *Philosophical Perspectives* 14:1–19.

Vetö, Miklos. 1977. *Le fondement selon Schelling*. Paris: L'Harmattan.

Von Balthasar, Hans Urs. 1947. *Prometheus: Studien zur Geschichte des deutschen Idealismus*. Heidelberg: Kerle.

Whistler, Daniel. 2021. "The Schlegelian Context of Schelling's Account of Freedom." In *Schellings Freiheitsschrift—Methode, System, Kritik*, edited by Thomas Buchheim, Thomas Frisch, and Norma C. Wachsmann, 71–90. Tübingen: Mohr Siebeck.

Wippel, John F., ed. 2011. *The Ultimate Why Question: Why Is There Anything at All Rather Than Nothing Whatsoever?* Washington, DC: Catholic University of America Press.

Wirth, Jason M. 2003. *The Conspiracy of Life: Meditations on Schelling and His Time*. Albany: State University of New York Press.

Index

absolute, 7, 77, 172, 225–26
  defined, 68, 100, 310n73
  self-affirmation of, 79, 83–84
  self-knowledge of, 69, 104, 212–15, 275n63
  Ungrund as, 4, 189, 191, 194–96, 197–203
  See also derived absoluteness
absolute identity, 7, 77, 87, 93, 121, 123–24, 250, 254
  potencies and, 125, 131
  principle of identity and, 48, 69, 73, 81–86
  Ungrund and, 186, 196, 197–99, 203, 207, 297n19, 300n45
  See also principle of identity
abyss (*Abgrund*), 1, 185, 238, 297n16
  See also groundlessness
actions, 153, 224–25, 228–31, 253, 257, 313n20
actualization (*Verwirklichung*), 128, 130, 136–37, 188, 193, 270n81
  See also existence
Adams, Robert Merrihew, 274n52
affirmation (*Affirmation, Bejahung*), 67–69, 83–86, 302n82
  See also self-affirmation
all-from-one model, 31, 36, 164, 252, 254
  defined, 7, 209
  Schelling's rejection of, 7–8, 88, 179, 195, 209–11, 249–51
Ameriks, Karl, 305n20, 306n25
Antognazza, Maria Rosa, 272n22, 272n25, 272n29
appearance (*Erscheinung*)
  as actuality, 106, 257, 274n56
  rehabilitation of, 106, 256–57, 307n29
  vs. things in themselves, 104, 106, 223, 225–28, 243
Aquinas. *See* Thomas Aquinas
architectonic, 22, 305n17
Aristotle, 89, 309n61
  predication, 62–63
  science, 29
  senses of cause, 6
  senses of priority, 59–62, 273n40
aseity (*a se*), 100, 129, 240–41, 286n55
Asmuth, Christoph, 302n72
Athanasius, 293n50
Augustine, 149–50

Baader, Franz von, 184
Balthasar, Hans Urs von, 13
Beach, Edward Allen, 312n18
begetting (*Zeugung*), 6, 95, 98–103, 107, 142, 280n57
  and derived absoluteness, 98–100, 241, 245–46, 247, 255

beginning point, 186, 188, 194–97, 209
  multiplication of, 7–8, 214, 250,
    251–52
being (*Sein*)
  vs. becoming, 99, 103, 188, 193–94,
    306n29
  designation for real principle, 117,
    283n23
  vs. life, 188, 307n29
  primordial being (*Ursein*), 68, 105–
    106, 228, 239, 256–57, 306n26
  senses of, 140, 213, 288n90,
    298n29, 306n28
Beiser, Frederick C., 267n43, 267n45,
  278n22, 292n35, 296nn83–84
Berger, Benjamin, 284n37, 285n47
Binkelmann, Christoph, 304n3
birth/giving birth, 102, 137–38,
  287n82, 288n88, 294n70
body, 56, 61–62, 141, 142–43, 160
  as image for the real, 118, 138, 141,
    176, 178, 221, 259
Boehme, Jacob
  language of ground, 132, 258
  Schelling's relation to, 15–16, 184,
    263nn36–37
  Ungrund in, 4, 15, 184, 200, 303n92
Bowman, Brady, 310n5
Bracken, Joseph, 262n22, 312n9
Brennan, Kevin, 309n55
Brouwer, Christian, 272n24
Brown, John, 155
Brown, Robert F., 184, 263n35,
  286n66, 296n6, 297n7, 300n53
Bruneder, Gertrud, 263n35, 297n7
Bruno, G. Anthony, 279n39
Bruno, Giordano, 279n42, 288n85
Buchheim, Thomas, 262n20, 269n79,
  273n35, 273n46, 280n49, 281n62,
  288n89, 294n63, 296n6
  fundamental distinction, 282n2,
    282n5, 283n16

problem of evil, 159–60, 292n33,
  292nn46–47, 293n48
Buridan's ass, 224

caput mortuum, 169
Caterus, Johannes, 310n69
causa sui, 10, 101, 230, 232, 237–44,
  310nn72–73
  impossibility of, 240, 243, 265n21
  See also self-grounding
cause and causality
  affirmation and, 68, 310n73
  vs. condition, 60–61, 133
  critique of, 226, 240, 305n18
  determinism and, 106, 222–23,
    225–27, 229
  vs. ground, 94–95, 118, 133,
    134–35, 279n42, 287n81, 288n85
  ideal principle as, 137–38, 246,
    286n65
  mechanistic, 103, 141, 172, 174,
    177
center point of philosophy, 2, 31–32,
  101, 218, 250, 311n2
chance (*Zufall*), 10, 31, 147, 166, 210,
  224–25
  See also contingency
chaos, 171–72, 295n75
character (intelligible), 304n4, 306n24,
  308n44
choice (*Wahl*), 3, 157, 163, 233–34,
  292n45, 307n41, 308n42
circular grounding, 8, 40, 142–43,
  214, 233, 250, 257, 289n95
  See also reciprocal grounding
common sense, 72, 233–37, 243–44,
  257–59
compatibilism, rejection of, 10, 36,
  268n58, 305n20
concealment. *See* hiddenness
concepts (*Begriffe*), 27, 63, 175,
  274n57, 280n51, 299n35

Index | 327

limitations of, 201–202, 294n65, 296n88
condition of the possibility (conditio sine qua non), 6, 60–62, 102, 179
vs. determining ground, 61, 96–98, 148, 156–57
God as, 96–98, 106–107, 241
ground of existence as, 12, 133–34, 137, 138–39, 156–58, 246
as primary sense of ground, 6–7, 133, 144, 217, 245, 249–50, 257
in substance-predicate relation, 60, 61, 63, 70
and systematic grounding relations, 139–44
Ungrund as, 186, 203, 207–11, 213–15, 246, 303n91
connection (*Zusammenhang*)
feature of system, 23–24, 143, 225
and principle of ground, 28–31, 143–44, 225, 253
consciousness/unconsciousness, 169, 188, 210, 224, 233–35, 308n47, 311n83
construction, philosophical, 299n39
containment
of actions in intelligible essence, 229
of predicates in subject, 61, 62–64
of things in God, 76, 96, 101–103, 107, 271n12
See also copula; immanence; pantheism
contingency (*Zufälligkeit*), 10
rejection of, 31, 147, 224–26
relative vs. absolute, 173–75, 239, 251–52
contradiction (*Widerspruch*), 264n3
contradiction, principle of, 48, 49, 271n6
conversion, 153, 257, 308n45, 313n21
Cooper, John W., 271n14

coordination, problem of, 252–56
copula
absolute copula, 82–83
antecedens-consequens account, 58–62, 71
defined, 49, 53
ground-consequence account, 66–69, 71
grounding and, 56, 60–62, 66–69, 70
implicitum-explicitum account, 62–66, 71–72
law of identity and, 53, 70, 72–73
mediated account, 54–58, 70–71, 113, 192–93, 196
nature of God and, 55, 73
ontological implications of, 49, 56, 63, 113
Correia, Fabrice, 288n92
creation
divine freedom and, 14–15, 87–88, 161–66, 210, 278n26
ex nihilo, 267n53
intelligible deed and, 241–42
necessity of, 161–66
pantheism and, 95
potencies and, 66, 131
process of, 130–31, 167–69, 256
as revelation, 103, 112, 130
Crusius, Christian August, 6, 49

Danz, Christian, 264n4, 278n23
decision (*Entscheidung*), 233–34
demonstration, 29, 34, 41
dependence/independence, 279n46
combining, 96–97, 100, 139–40, 241–42, 249
grounding and, 94–95
independence in absolute, 206–208
mutual dependence of parts, 28, 143–44
objects of knowledge and, 104

dependence/independence *(continued)*
  parts and whole, 102, 140
  within pantheism, 37, 247
derived absoluteness, 8, 180, 249, 251, 260, 311n78
  begetting and, 98–101, 246, 255
Descartes, René, 38, 135, 175–76, 240, 310n69
determining ground *(Bestimmungsgrund)*, 6, 10, 30–31, 217
  of being vs. essence, 68–69, 99, 241
  vs. condition, 61, 96–98, 148, 156–57
  freedom and, 218, 223–24
  in subject-predicate nexus, 63–64, 70
determinism
  empirical, 225–27, 229, 253
  principle of ground and, 33–34, 218
  as problem for system of freedom, 4, 35–36, 143–44, 247–48
  required for systematic unity, 42, 225
  Schelling's stance on, 10, 36, 217–18, 251–52, 259
difference
  absence of, 204–205, 206
  identity and, 52, 53, 76, 78, 93
  vs. opposition, 205, 301nn62–63
  quantitative (difference of form), 84–85, 121, 131, 301n66, 303n91
Di Giovanni, George, 268n62
disease, 102, 155
disjunction, 197, 202, 205–206
distinction of ground/what exists, 3–4, 10–12, 110–44
  general characterization, 111–19
  mistaken interpretations of, 11–12, 13, 126–27
  potencies and, 119–26, 127, 135–36
  relation to *Ungrund*, 185–86, 189–92, 202, 205–209, 273n39

divine foreknowledge, 163, 165, 270n81, 293n53, 312n12
divine freedom, 14–15, 87–88, 155, 161–66, 210, 291n26
  relation to human freedom, 220, 254–55, 311n80
divine understanding
  as ideal (creative) principle, 119, 131, 137, 162, 166–73, 246, 286n65, 295n72
  system in, 23, 26–27, 43–45, 270n81, 294n61
  as the Word, 272n24
division *(Scheidung)*, 131, 166–71, 294n63
Dörendahl, Roswitha, 297n9, 299n36
dualism, 189–90, 256–57
  internal, 109–10, 114, 209, 250, 282n10
  problem of evil and, 146, 154–55
duality *(Dualität)*, 186, 207–209
dynamic explanation, 177–79

Eckhart, Meister, 1, 185, 237, 296n87, 309n59
Egloff, Lisa, 293n55, 293n57
Ehrhardt, Walter E., 297n17, 298n23, 298n31
Eidam, Heinz, 262n15
Emerson, Ralph Waldo, 258, 313n24
Epicurus, swerve in, 31, 224
equiprimordiality *(Gleichursprünglichkeit)*
  defined, 8
  of essence/form, 213–14
  of parts of system, 143
  of principles of identity and ground, 48
  role in treatise, 101, 250–51, 262n23
Eschenmayer, Carl August von, 111, 125, 194, 295n73, 295n79, 302n74
essence. See *Wesen*

Index | 329

eternal deed. *See* intelligible deed
eternity, 34–35, 231, 235
   the eternal (*das Ewige*), 82, 85–86, 276n10
   and things in themselves, 105, 219–20, 228
Euclid, 29, 34
evil
   analogy with disease, 102, 155
   effectiveness of, 150–51, 157, 221–22
   ground of, 145–46, 148–57
   as inversion, 135, 136, 151, 152–53
   outside God, 106, 154–55
   radical evil, 232
   relation to good, 71–72, 149–51, 156–61, 207, 275n64
   revelation and, 156, 157–61
   senses of, 158–61
   universal evil, 158–61, 218, 221
evil, problem of, 3, 5, 42, 109–10, 145–46, 148–57, 247
excitation (*Erregung*), 155–57, 158–61, 291n26
existence (*Existenz*)
   distinguished from that-which-exists, 11, 126–27, 133, 138
   meaning of, 11, 128–32, 283n23, 300n47
   as revelation, 11, 115, 129–32, 133, 134, 136–37, 257
Existierende, das (that-which-exists)
   activity of, 129–31
   designation for ideal principle, 12, 116–19
   distinguished from existence, 11, 126–27, 133, 138
   original vs. derivative, 131
   as understanding, 119, 131, 137, 162, 167–173
   See also distinction of ground/what exists
explanation, 145–46, 176–77

Fall, the, 106, 161, 277n21, 307n37
fatalism, 32, 33, 34, 224
   See also determinism
feeling (*Gefühl*), 151, 180–81, 235
   of freedom, 42, 180, 281n70
felix culpa, 161
Fichte, Johann Gottlieb, 114, 256, 311n5
   freedom, 221, 251, 304n3, 306n25
   fundamental principles, 49, 99, 272n28
   Schelling's criticism of, 21–22, 90
   (self-)positing, 67, 83, 100, 232–33, 236, 309n64
   system and science, 29–30, 38, 40, 135, 266n28, 266n35
finite, the
   relation to infinite, 7, 34–35, 81, 86–87, 210–11
   origin of, 86–87
forces (*Kräfte*), 114, 168, 308n43
   life as interplay of, 174, 177–79
form
   vs. essence, 84–85, 201, 210–15, 304n7
   in nature, 168, 171
   as source of difference, 85
formal concept. *See under* freedom
Förster, Eckart, 267n48
foundation
   ground of existence as, 133, 134–36, 143, 160, 178, 246
   of system, 25, 38–41, 115, 135
Frank, Manfred, 272nn26–27
Franks, Paul, 262n17, 309n60
Franz, Michael, 284n31
freedom
   contextualization of, 2–3, 42, 249
   divinization of, 8, 101, 241, 251

freedom *(continued)*
  formal concept of, 31, 59, 109–10, 148–49, 157, 159, 217–22, 248, 304n3
  necessity and, 20, 31–32, 163–64, 218, 222–30, 235–36, 239, 254, 264n3, 267n41
  real concept of, 5, 110, 145, 148–49, 150, 219–22, 236
  See also divine freedom
Freydberg, Bernard, 262n23, 270n80, 270n4
Fries, Jakob Friedrich, 306n24

Gabriel, Markus, 3, 261n8, 298n27
García, Marcela, 272n18
Gardner, Sebastian, 263n26, 289n3, 304n1, 305n11
geometry, 29, 34, 41, 95, 162
  See also necessity: geometrical necessity
Georgii, Eberhard Friedrich von, 111, 129
Gerlach, Stefan, 307n41, 308nn44–45
God
  considered absolutely, 113, 154, 282n7
  development of, 65, 131, 196
  as life, not system, 43–45, 179
  perspective of, 90, 92, 189
  place within system, 41, 112, 251
  relation to things, 51–52, 66–69, 75–76, 85–87, 91–107, 246
  senses of, 113–14, 154, 196, 298n28
  See also absolute; creation; divine foreknowledge; divine freedom; divine understanding; evil, problem of; immanence; pantheism; personality; revelation; Trinity
Goethe, Johann Wolfgang von, 267n48, 294n68

goodness, 290n14, 307n37
  as motivation for creation, 161–64
  relation to evil, 71–72, 149–51, 156–61, 275n64
gravity, 59, 120, 123–24, 137–38, 140, 178, 284n32, 288n84
ground, principle of. *See* principle of ground
ground, problem of, 1–5, 110, 249, 261n11
  solution to, 245–48
groundlessness (*Grundlosigkeit*), 4, 30, 146, 166, 185–86
  vs. self-grounding, 238–39, 242, 252, 310nn65–66
ground of existence
  designation for real principle, 12, 116–19
  evil's possibility and, 151, 154–57
  grounding character of, 132–39, 246
  as longing (*Sehnsucht*), 132, 137, 258, 286n67, 287n83
  nature as, 117, 123–24, 176, 178–79
  See also distinction of ground/what exists

Habermas, Jürgen, 106, 157, 312n18
Hegel, Georg Wilhelm Friedrich, 262n19, 299n34, 300n55
  criticism of Schelling, 2, 77, 85, 212, 261n5, 299n44
  evil and theodicy, 159–60
  identity and difference, 276n2
  panentheism, 52
  speculative sentence, 273n46
Heidegger, Martin, 235, 281n70, 310n64
  equiprimordiality, 8, 250
  evil in Schelling, 3, 157, 289n1, 291n22
  failure of system, 43, 269n78, 270n83, 297n22, 311n1

meaning of ground, 262n14, 286n67
principle of ground, 64, 270n1, 270n4, 278n30
Schelling's distinction, 11, 126, 282n3, 286n63
significance of treatise, 2, 261n5
system, 29, 264n11, 268n59, 268n69, 280n59
Ungrund, 187, 297n22
Hennigfeld, Jochem, 263n34, 269n79, 270n4, 280n57, 297n21, 311n1
Hermanni, Friedrich, 114, 115, 230, 285n50, 286n63, 304n8, 311n1, 311n5, 313n22
principle of ground, 266n38, 305nn15–16
problem of evil, 3, 159–60, 289n1, 289n6, 290n15, 290n17, 292n37, 292n40
hiddenness, 11, 56, 65, 130, 163, 212, 287n78
of forms within nature, 168–69, 171–72
Hindenburg, Carl Friedrich, 125
history, 109, 151, 159–60, 165, 250, 251, 254–55, 256–57
Höfele, Philipp, 263n32, 276n2, 295n70, 306n26, 309n59
Hogrebe, Wolfram, 3, 271n18, 272n31
Hölderlin, Friedrich, 301n69

Iber, Christian, 288n89
idealism
criticized as one-sided, 45, 110, 136, 148, 176, 178–79
freedom in, 14, 109–10, 148, 219–21, 226–31
relation to realism, 117–18, 138, 176, 221, 284n27
ideal part of philosophy, 117–18, 221, 265n15, 284n26, 298n23

ideal principle. See *Existierende, das*
ideas (divine), 101–102, 215, 251, 280n61, 308n46, 310nn76–77, 312n14
creation and, 256, 293n49
Identitätsphilosophie
all-from-one model, 7, 88, 250
appearances in, 104, 106, 223, 225, 250, 256
causality in, 226, 240, 305n18
difference in, 121, 131, 206
essence-form relation, 84–85, 211–15
infinite-finite relation, 35, 81, 87
meaning of identity, 77, 83
potencies, 120–25, 284n37
principle of identity, 48, 81–86
reason in, 27, 167, 223, 264n10, 295n76
relation to *Freiheitsschrift*, 14, 79, 92, 264n4
identity
difference and, 52, 53, 76, 78, 93
divine identity, 139–40
kinds of, 77–79
as sameness (*Einerleiheit*), 51, 52, 73, 77–78
of subject and predicate, 53
of whole and parts, 52
See also absolute identity; unity
identity, principle of. See principle of identity
imagination, 13, 104
immanence (within God), 63
freedom and, 105–106, 271n12
grounding within, 93–95, 107
pantheism as, 34–35, 51–52, 75–76, 81
See also containment; pantheism
Incarnation, 161, 165, 293n50
indecision (*Unentschiedenheit*), 156, 233, 308n43, 312n19

independence. *See* dependence/
    independence
indifference
    as equilibrium of potencies, 121,
        131, 204, 301n61
    senses of, 203–204
    Ungrund as, 192–97, 197–202,
        203–209, 298n31, 300n45
individuality, 27, 37, 51, 218, 221,
    268n62, 287n73
indivisible remainder. *See* irreducible
    remainder
infinite, the
    identity with finite, 81, 86–87
    infinite progression from God,
        84–86, 91
    transition to finite, rejection of,
        35, 86–87, 210–11, 269n72,
        277n19
In-itself, the, 104–106, 220, 223,
    227–28, 238–39, 253, 256–57
intellectual intuition, 90, 104–105,
    167, 202, 295n76
intelligible deed, 59, 232–37, 241–43,
    250–51, 253, 255–56, 257,
    306n23
intelligible essence (*Wesen*), 96–97,
    99, 220, 226–37, 253, 256
interdependence, 40, 111, 288n93
    See also reciprocal grounding
intuitive understanding, 265n16,
    294n61
    See also intellectual intuition
irrational, the, 10, 14, 146–48,
    166–75, 176, 224
irreducible remainder (*der nie
    aufgehende Rest*), 10, 147,
    169–71, 180

Jacobi, Friedrich Heinrich, 24, 32–38,
    177, 194, 210, 309n54
    ground/cause distinction, 6, 94–95

principle of ground, 9, 33–35
reading of Spinoza, 21, 29, 33–38,
    52, 86, 94–95
system of freedom impossible, 4–5,
    35–38, 50, 175
See also Pantheism Controversy
Jacobs, Wilhelm G., 304n6, 307n34
Jantzen, Jörg, 282n4

Kahl-Furthmann, Gertrud, 271n7
Kant, Immanuel, 4, 6, 90, 98, 238,
    280n50, 296n88, 301n62
    affirmation, 67
    appearances vs. things in
        themselves, 104, 106, 219–20,
        223, 227, 256, 304n4
    construction of matter, 178
    evil, 150–51, 152, 232
    freedom, 219–21, 225–27, 231–32,
        243–44, 306n22, 306n25, 309n52,
        312n8
        third antinomy, 222–23, 304n10,
            305n19
    nature of reason, 22, 25, 305n17
    organic nature, 39, 40, 103, 141–42,
        174, 177
    principle of ground, 91, 266n23,
        278n34, 309n62
    rejection of compatibilism, 10, 36,
        305n20
    system, 21, 22, 38, 39, 40
Kierkegaard, Søren, 27
Knappik, Franz, 292n46, 293n48,
    293n51
knowledge
    of absolute, 196, 201–203
    as affirmation, 69, 275n62
    and dialectic, 294n60
    divine vs. human, 90, 103–105
    freedom and, 233–34
    self-knowledge of absolute, 69, 104,
        212–15, 275n63

Kosch, Michelle, 3, 283n20, 308n43
Koßler, Matthias, 306n24, 308n44
Krause, Karl Christian Friedrich, 51–52
Krell, David Farrell, 287n77, 287n82
Krings, Hermann, 283n13
Krug, Wilhelm Traugott, 7

language
  about the absolute, 201–203
  of mysticism in Schelling, 15–16, 180–81, 184–85, 258
  ordinary language, 72, 180, 258
  terminological plurality, 115, 276n6, 296n4
Largier, Niklaus, 309n57
Lauer, Christopher, 291n24, 293n57, 294nn66–67, 295n80
lawfulness (*Gesetzmäßigkeit*), 307n31
law of ground. *See* principle of ground
law of identity. *See* principle of identity
Leibniz, Gottfried Wilhelm, 310n73
  copula, 55–56, 272n29
  freedom, 230, 231–32, 305nn12–13, 307n32
  individual notion, 280n48, 307n30
  monadology, 265n18, 301n70
  necessity and possibility, 162–65, 305n14
  predication, 53, 58, 62–63
  preestablished harmony, 254, 256
  principle of ground, 8, 34, 47, 48–49, 64, 89, 91–93, 231
  rationalism of, 7, 175–76
  system, 21, 269n74
  theodicy, 292n39, 311n79, 312n16
  Trinity, 55, 98, 100
Lessing, Gotthold Ephraim, 24, 32, 33, 34, 39, 296n81
libertarianism, 10, 144

life, 102–103
  before this life, 59, 234, 237, 252–53, 258, 306n23, 308n46
  vs. being, 188, 307n29
  existence and, 128
  God as life, not system, 43–45, 179
  grounding and, 96, 176–81
  opposition needed for, 78, 155–56, 172, 177–78, 199
light, 59, 120, 123–24, 137–38, 140, 151, 178, 284n32
living rationalism, 10, 175–81, 259
longing (*Sehnsucht*), 132, 137, 258, 286n67, 287n83
love, 257, 299n43
  existence and, 128, 158
  motivation for creation, 163, 251
  mystery of, 139–40, 207–208, 258
  Ungrund and, 187–89, 192–97, 298n31
  will of, 152–53, 156, 158

magnetic line, 121–22, 204
Malebranche, Nicolas, 313n25
manifestation. *See* revelation
Marcel, Gabriel, 296n88
Marquard, Odo, 291n23
Marquet, Jean-François, 271n4, 275n1, 276n8
Marx, Werner, 263n37, 291n29, 302n75
Matthews, Bruce, 296n86
McGinn, Bernard, 185, 261nn1–2, 297nn12–14
McGrath, S. J., 263n35, 292n38, 293n56, 294n67, 295n71
mechanism, 103, 141, 172, 174, 177
Mendelssohn, Moses, 32, 33
Mercer, Christia, 278n35
microcosm, 24–25, 102, 140, 179, 206, 265n18, 268n67, 301n67, 301n70
Mine, Hideki, 300n45

334 | Index

Moiso, Francesco, 294n64
monism, 109–10, 189–90, 262n17
Moore, Ian Alexander, 309n55
mutual grounding. *See* reciprocal grounding
mystery, 13, 92, 258–60, 296n88
   freedom and, 10, 237
   united with reason, 2, 16, 180–81
   See also love: mystery of
mysticism, 1, 206–207, 237, 263n36, 294n59, 309n59
   and Schelling's language, 15–16, 180–81, 184–85, 258
   See also Boehme; Eckhart; Silesius

nature, 24, 117–18, 123–24, 214, 250, 251
   causality in, 225–26, 253–55, 312n9
   formation of, 167–71
   as ground of existence, 117, 123–24, 176, 178–79, 286n72, 287n75
   irrational elements in, 147, 166, 173–74
Naturphilosophie, 24, 112, 117–18, 203
   theory of life in, 103, 155, 177–78
necessity
   absolute necessity, 10, 162–64, 173–74, 252
   of creation, 87–88, 161–66
   empirical necessity, 225–27, 229, 305n18
   freedom and, 20, 31–32, 163–64, 218, 222–30, 235–36, 239, 254, 264n3, 267n41
   geometrical necessity, 162, 173–74, 177
   inner necessity, 229–31, 248
   moral necessity, 161–63, 173
   system and, 31
negative philosophy, 8, 12, 176, 279n38
negative theology, 258, 300n56

Neoplatonism, 149–50, 240, 300n56
Nietzsche, Friedrich, 243
non-being (*Nichtseiendes*), 173, 280n51
non-ground. *See Ungrund*

O'Connor, Brian, 311n84
Oetinger, Friedrich Christoph, 15, 258, 295n70
Ohashi, Ryôsuke, 269n76
ontology of revelation, 257, 286n59, 288n90
opposition (*Gegensatz*), 300n50, 301n62
   of freedom and necessity, 20, 31–32, 101, 218, 222–30, 264n3, 267n41
   to God, 76, 78
   of good and evil, 150–51, 157–58, 160–61
   necessary for life, 78, 155–56, 172, 177–78, 199
   revelation through, 157, 160–61
   Ungrund and, 189, 197, 199–201, 205–207
   unity and, 78, 276n2
O'Regan, Cyril, 272n24
organic grounding, 102–103, 141–44, 176–80
organisms
   as model for system, 39–41, 43, 102, 141–42, 178, 248
   as systems, 24, 26
Otto, Rudolf, 296n88

panentheism, 51–52
pantheism
   definitions of, 50–51
   essential to system, 50, 51
   evil and, 110, 149, 154–55
   meaning of copula and, 53, 57, 65, 69–70

as problem for freedom, 4–5, 32, 50, 247
in Spinoza, 34–35
true sense of, 75–76, 271n11
See also immanence
Pantheism Controversy, 4–5, 21, 24, 29, 32–34, 51
Parkinson, G. H. R., 271n6, 278n35
Parmenides, 23
particular vs. universal, 152–53, 156
part-whole relation, 22–24, 28, 37, 40–41, 102, 140, 206
in pantheism, 52, 247
Paul, Saint, 299n32
Peetz, Siegbert, 262n23, 287n81, 303n88, 311n1, 313n22
perfection, 71
personality (divine)
as dynamic unity, 128–29, 162, 174, 178, 210, 300nn46–47
personal God, 175, 194–96, 257, 299n34
Pinkard, Terry, 281n68
Plato, 89, 92
Platonic matter, 118, 267n53, 295n74
Timaeus, 39, 118–19, 136, 178, 268n68
Plotinus, 211, 239–40
positing (*Setzen*), 67, 98, 274n59, 274n61
See also self-positing
positive philosophy, 8, 90
possibilities (alternative), 15, 163, 165, 312nn15–16
potencies (*Potenzen*)
general account, 120–22, 124–25
grounding and, 125–26, 136, 143, 276n4, 284n36
ground/what exists as, 119–20, 122–26, 127, 198
lacking potency (*potenzlos*), 196, 198–99, 299n42

priority among, 60, 135, 143, 273n38
simultaneity of, 269n73
unfolding of, 65–66, 125, 131, 193–97, 299n43
predication, 3, 62–63
Ungrund and, 192, 197, 199–203, 205–207
See also copula
preestablished harmony, 166, 232, 254–56
primordial being. *See under* being
principle
first principle(s), 29, 30–31, 48, 73, 195, 214, 250, 283n15
ground and what exists as, 114–15
principle of contradiction, 48, 49, 271n6
principle of ground (*Satz vom Grund*), 1, 8–10
as implicit, 8–9, 47, 80, 82, 270n1, 276n8
in Jacobi's Spinoza-reading, 33–38
problem of evil and, 145–46
relation to principle of identity, 4, 9, 48–49, 79–82
relation to system, 20, 28–32, 253
Schelling's versions of, 80, 110, 144, 217, 245–46
traditional version of, 80, 209, 217–18, 223–25, 231, 238, 246
transformation of, 88–95
principle of identity, 76, 229
and copula, 53, 70–73
as highest principle, 48, 73, 270n3
relation to principle of ground, 4, 9, 48–49, 79–82
principle of sufficient reason. *See* principle of ground
priority, meaning of, 58–62, 140–41
privation, evil as, 149–51
problem of evil. *See* evil, problem of

problem of ground. *See* ground, problem of
Proclus, 266n33
providence, 166, 254–56, 312n12, 313n25
Pseudo-Dionysius the Areopagite, 296n5

Ramus, Petrus, 273n34
randomness. *See* chance; contingency
Rang, Bernhard, 263n31, 272n31, 301n68, 310n73, 312n6
  absolute identity, 300n45, 300n48, 300nn50–51, 301n58
  knowledge as affirmation, 275n62, 302n82
  life, theory of, 291n24, 296nn83–85
  Sein, meaning of, 280n53, 298n29, 303n85
rationalism
  defined, 9, 176
  Schelling's relationship to, 9–10, 146–48, 175–77, 249–50
  See also living rationalism
Raue, Johann, 272n29
real concept. *See under* freedom
realism-idealism relation, 117–18, 138, 176, 221, 284n27
real principle. *See* ground of existence
reason (*Vernunft*)
  demand for systematic unity, 21–23, 31, 42, 154–55, 190, 225, 264n10
  identity associated with, 53, 77, 78
  nature of, 181, 236, 259, 266n29, 294n59, 298n24, 301n60
  renunciation of, 42–43, 175
  vs. understanding, 78, 166–67, 201–203, 223, 259, 293n59
reciprocal grounding, 39, 41, 61, 139–44, 179, 213–14, 246, 248
reflection (*Reflexion*), 52, 72, 167, 201–203, 223, 225, 233

Reinhold, Carl Leonhard, 30, 223, 306n25
religiosity, 308n42
Rescher, Nicholas, 264n5
responsibility, moral, 10, 231–33, 234–35, 242–44, 251
revelation
  creation as, 103, 112, 130, 164–65, 251, 256–57
  evil and, 156, 157–166
  existence and, 11, 115, 129–32, 133, 134, 136–37
  logic of the copula and, 64–65
  opposition and, 157, 160–61
  Ungrund and, 187–89, 193–97, 212, 215, 303n92
Romanticism, 32

Sallis, John, 119, 262n13, 264n8, 281n66, 284n28, 287n77, 287n82, 298n26
Sandkaulen, Birgit, 279n41
Schindler, D. C., 269n75, 277n20, 309n53
Schlegel, Friedrich, 21, 50, 154–55, 175, 267n42, 271n9, 290n20
Schnieder, Benjamin, 288n92
Schopenhauer, Arthur, 9, 28, 243, 311n81, 313n25
  criticism of Schelling, 2, 184, 306n21
Schwab, Philipp, 261n5, 299n44, 301n59
Schwenzfeuer, Sebastian, 284n35, 285n50
science (*Wissenschaft*), 22, 23, 28–30, 266n35
self-affirmation, 67–69, 79, 83–86, 94, 186, 239
  and derived absoluteness, 99–100, 310n77
  See also affirmation

Index | 337

self-grounding, 10, 186, 228
   freedom as, 218, 232–33, 237–44, 248, 252
   God as, 230, 276n5
   system as, 25–26, 28, 265n19, 310n66
   See also *causa sui*; self-affirmation; self-positing
self-positing, 67, 83, 228, 280n55, 283n14, 306n26
   and intelligible deed, 100, 232–33, 236–37, 239, 310n77
   See also positing
self-will. *See under* will
sexual difference, 139–40
Silesius, Angelus, 309n64
sin, 151, 232, 292n37, 307n37, 307n41
Snow, Dale, 278n22, 280n56, 306n27
soul, 56, 185, 141, 142–43, 273n33
   as image for the ideal, 118, 138, 221, 259
Spinoza, 200, 275n62, 277n14
   causa sui, 230, 232, 240, 242
   criticism of, 163, 176, 177, 284n25
   evil, 290n11
   freedom, 36, 230, 253, 268n57, 305n13, 307n33
   God's relation to things, 37, 52–53, 66–67, 81
   Jacobi's reading of, 32–38, 94–95
   necessity/determinism, 36, 163
   substance, 36–37, 268n60, 298n29
   system of reason in, 21, 24, 29
   See also Pantheism Controversy
Spinozist Controversy. *See* Pantheism Controversy
spirit, 142–43, 153, 157, 285n42, 290n13
   as unity of two principles, 151, 174, 198–99, 300nn46–47
Steigerwald, Joan, 287n83
Stoics, logic of, 58

Strawson, Galen, 10, 242–43, 258–59, 311nn83–84
Sturma, Dieter, 7
subject (of predication). *See* copula
substance
   and predicates, 60, 62–63, 192
   in Spinoza, 36–37, 268n60, 298n29
sufficient reason, 6–7, 31, 91, 93, 217, 225, 231, 251–52
sufficient reason, principle of. *See* principle of ground
Summerell, Orrin F., 310n67, 310n69, 310n75
system
   essential features of, 20–26
   etymology of, 22–23
   metaphors for, 38–41, 135, 289nn95–96
   principle of ground and, 20, 28–32
   real vs. ideal, 26–27, 34, 44–45
   science and, 22, 23, 28–30
   systematic form, 19, 263n1
system of freedom
   alleged failure of, 15, 42–45, 248, 263n34
   meaning of, 2–3, 4
   problem of, 4–5, 19–20, 35–38, 101, 175
   solution to problem, 135, 143–44, 181, 247–48, 259

tautology, 61, 271n16
temptation, 156, 313n19
Teresa of Ávila, 206–207
theodicy, 3, 146, 155–56, 158, 159–60, 161–66, 291n23
   See also evil, problem of
theogony, 2, 101–102, 281n62
theosophists, 263n36
   See also Boehme; Oetinger
Theunissen, Michael, 3, 255, 261n10, 280n59, 296n82, 307n37, 311n78

things in themselves, 104–106, 219–20, 223, 227–28, 243, 301n68
  as ideas, 215, 310n76
Thomas, Mark J., 272n19, 282n6, 286n59, 288n90, 298n27, 298n30, 311n81
Thomas Aquinas, 240, 268n55, 309n61, 310nn70–71
Tilliette, Xavier, 283n19
Timaeus. See under Plato
time, 130, 233, 243, 253, 257, 286n61
  independence from, 219–20, 226–28, 231
  See also eternity
Tobin, Frank L., 296n87, 309n57
totality
  absolute vs. relative, 24–25, 206, 265n17
  feature of system, 24–25
  God as, 52, 85, 113, 154, 195
Trappe, Tobias, 297n15
Trinity, 55, 98, 272n24

unconditional, 25–26, 226, 238–39
  See also absolute
undecidedness (*Unentschiedenheit*), 156, 233, 308n43, 312n19
understanding (*Verstand*)
  ideal (creative) principle as, 119, 131, 137, 162, 166–73, 246, 286n65, 295n72
  original vs. creaturely, 167, 171
  vs. reason, 52, 78, 166–67, 201–203, 259, 293n59
  universal will as, 151
  See also divine understanding
Ungrund, 4, 183–215, 253
  copula and, 65, 192–93
  as essence of absolute, 210–15
  as ground, 183, 185–86, 203, 207–11, 215, 246
  indifference and, 192–97, 197–202, 203–209, 298n31, 300n45
  love and, 187–89, 192–97, 207–208, 298n31
  process of revelation and, 187–89, 193–97, 212, 215, 303n92
  relation to ground/what exists, 185–86, 189–92, 202, 205–209, 273n39
unity
  essential unity, 302n71
  feature of system, 22–24, 31, 42, 154–55, 190, 225
  of ground/what exists, 128–29, 139–40, 198–99
  identity as, 77–78
  love as, 193, 197, 299n43
  as progressive/creative, 78, 84–86, 89, 93–95
  spirit as, 151–52, 153, 174, 198–99, 300n46
  Ungrund and, 190, 195, 209
universal vs. particular, 152–53, 156
universal will. *See under* will
unruly, the (*das Regellose*), 147, 168–69, 171–72

Van Inwagen, Peter, 10, 259
Vetö, Miklos, 12, 285n51, 288n86
vitalism, 177
Von Balthasar, Hans Urs, 13

Wesen (being/essence)
  ambiguity of term, 57, 112, 279n47, 282n5, 298n29
  copula as, 57–58, 113, 192, 282n6
  essence of absolute, 84, 201, 206, 210–15, 303n91
  intelligible essence, 96–97, 99, 220, 226–37, 253, 256
  relation to ground/what exists, 112–13, 191–92, 206
  Ungrund as, 113, 183, 188–89, 190–97, 202, 209, 211–12, 261n8
Whistler, Daniel, 267n42, 284n37, 285n47

whole (*das Ganze*). *See* part-whole relation; totality
will (*Wille*), 236–37
　ground/what exists as, 114, 283n14
　self-will (*Eigenwille*), 114, 135, 151–53, 155–61, 168, 291n26
　universal will, 114, 151–53, 156, 168
　will of love, 152–53, 156, 158

willing (*Wollen*), 236–37
　as primordial being (*Ursein*), 14, 68, 105–106, 228, 237, 239, 306n26
Wippel, John F., 279n38
Wirth, Jason M., 294n65
wisdom, original, 298n24
Wolff, Christian, 6, 49
wonder, 92, 180–81, 237, 258, 279n40, 296n88